Politics for Profit

Businesspeople run for and win elected office around the world, with roughly one-third of members of parliament and numerous heads of state coming directly from the private sector. Yet we know little about why these politicians choose to leave the private sector and what they actually do while in government. In *Politics for Profit*, David Szakonyi brings to bear sweeping quantitative and qualitative evidence from Putin-era Russia to shed light on why businesspeople contest elections and what the consequences are for their firms and for society when they win. The book develops an original theory of businessperson candidacy as a type of corporate political activity undertaken in response to both economic competition and weak political parties. Szakonyi's evidence then shows that businesspeople help their firms reap huge gains in revenue and profitability while prioritizing investments in public infrastructure over human capital. The book concludes by evaluating policies for combating political corruption.

David Szakonyi is Assistant Professor of Political Science at George Washington University and Research Fellow at the Higher School of Economics in Moscow, Russia. His research focuses on political economy, autocracy, and corruption. His dissertation received the APSA Gabriel A. Almond Award for the Best Dissertation in Comparative Politics and the Robert C. Tucker/Stephen F. Cohen Dissertation Prize.

Cambridge Studies in Comparative Politics

Other Books in the Series

Christopher Adolph, *Bankers, Bureaucrats, and Central Bank Politics: The Myth of Neutrality*

Michael Albertus, *Autocracy and Redistribution: The Politics of Land Reform*

Santiago Anria, *When Movements Become Parties: The Bolivian MAS in Comparative Perspective*

Ben W. Ansell, *From the Ballot to the Blackboard: The Redistributive Political Economy of Education*

Ben W. Ansell and David J. Samuels, *Inequality and Democratization: An Elite-Competition Approach*

Adam Michael Auerbach, *Demanding Development: The Politics of Public Goods Provision in India's Urban Slums*

Ana Arjona, *Rebelocracy: Social Order in the Colombian Civil War*

Leonardo R. Arriola, *Multi-Ethnic Coalitions in Africa: Business Financing of Opposition Election Campaigns*

David Austen-Smith, Jeffry A. Frieden, Miriam A. Golden, Karl Ove Moene, and Adam Przeworski, eds., *Selected Works of Michael Wallerstein: The Political Economy of Inequality, Unions, and Social Democracy*

S. Erdem Aytaç and Susan C. Stokes, *Why Bother? Rethinking Participation in Elections and Protests*

Andy Baker, *The Market and the Masses in Latin America: Policy Reform and Consumption in Liberalizing Economies*

Continued after the Index

Politics for Profit

Business, Elections, and Policymaking in Russia

DAVID SZAKONYI
George Washington University, Washington DC

CAMBRIDGE
UNIVERSITY PRESS

CAMBRIDGE
UNIVERSITY PRESS

University Printing House, Cambridge CB2 8BS, United Kingdom

One Liberty Plaza, 20th Floor, New York, NY 10006, USA

477 Williamstown Road, Port Melbourne, VIC 3207, Australia

314–321, 3rd Floor, Plot 3, Splendor Forum, Jasola District Centre, New Delhi – 110025, India

79 Anson Road, #06–04/06, Singapore 079906

Cambridge University Press is part of the University of Cambridge.

It furthers the University's mission by disseminating knowledge in the pursuit of education, learning, and research at the highest international levels of excellence.

www.cambridge.org
Information on this title: www.cambridge.org/9781108491631
DOI: 10.1017/9781108869089

First published 2020

Printed in the United Kingdom by TJ International Ltd. Padstow Cornwall

A catalogue record for this publication is available from the British Library.

ISBN 978-1-108-49163-1 Hardback
ISBN 978-1-108-79874-7 Paperback

For

Mary Catherine

Contents

Figures

Tables

Acknowledgments

I am eternally grateful to a wide and entertaining group of mentors, colleagues, and friends, without whom this book would never have found its way to print. First and foremost, my gratitude goes to Tim Frye, whose unending support, encouragement, and constructive criticism can never fully be appreciated. The best decision I ever made in graduate school was taken before I even got there: coming to Columbia to work with Tim. While there, I was fortunate to overlap with Yotam Margalit, who pushed me hard to express my ideas more directly and accept the challenges of identification head on. I now ask of my own graduate students many of the same tough questions he leveled at me early on. A very special thanks also goes to John Reuter, who guided me into the intricacies and opportunities of Russian politics and was a vital sounding board during all stages of the project. Perhaps more importantly, my long coauthorship with John has helped me to write more clearly and persuasively. I hope those lessons are evident here.

The book also greatly benefited from invaluable feedback from many people who either read parts of manuscript or heard me out as I struggled to connect theory and empirics. Scott Gehlbach has been a champion of the project from the very beginning; his encouragement and guidance helped me recognize there was still more to say on businesspeople in office. Stan Markus provided incisive comments for the main theoretical chapters and helped me think more broadly about the role of property rights in the larger story. The list may be long, but the book is also indebted to help from Quintin Beazer, Michael Best, Noah Buckley-Farlee, Bo Cowgill, Olle Folke, Shigeo Hirano, Hande Inanc, Phil Keefer,

Yegor Lazarev, Jeffrey Lenowitz, Eddy Malesky, Israel Marques, Suresh Naidu, Will Pyle, Johannes Urpelainen, and Camille-Strauss Kahn. Early versions of chapters improved from comments received at the 2014 and 2017 American Political Science Association Conferences, the 2014 and 2015 Annual ISCID conferences, the 2015 Academy of Management Annual Conference, and the 2014, 2015, and 2017 ASEEES Conferences. I also thank seminar participants at Columbia, Florida State, Duke, MIT, George Washington, University of Washington, UCSD, Colorado, Harvard, New Economic School, and the Coase Institute.

Funding and institutional support from a variety of sources made possible the data collection and fieldwork in Russia. I want to especially thank Andrei Yakovlev for giving me an academic home in Moscow for the many years it took to complete the project. Andrei and Tim's leadership of the International Center for the Study of Institutional and Development (ICSID) at the Higher School of Economics in Moscow, Russia, has set the standard for productive collaborations between foreign and Russian scholars. I would not have been able to build the datasets without ICSID as well as help and friendship from my wonderful colleagues there, including Alexei Baranov, Nina Ershova, Guzel Garifullina, Olga Masyutina, Eugenia Nazrullaeva, and Michael Rochlitz. This book was prepared within the framework of the HSE University Basic Research Program and funded by the Russian Academic Excellence Project "5–100." In Perm, the joyful academics at the Center for Comparative History and Political Studies went out of their way to help me arrange interviews. While in Russia, I relied on financial support from the Mellon Interdisciplinary Graduate Fellowship, the Social Science Research Council, the Center for International Business Education and Research at Columbia, and the Harriman Institute. This book was supported by the National Science Foundation Graduate Research Fellowship under Grant No. DGE-11-44155. Bill McAllister closely read many drafts and facilitated such a warm community at Columbia University's Interdisciplinary Center for Innovative Theory and Empirics.

I could not have asked for a better place to begin my professional academic career than George Washington University. The political science department's much deserved reputation for collegiality and thoughtfulness made for the perfect home to work through the many issues that cropped up writing the manuscript. I am immensely fortunate to have such supportive colleagues right down my hall: Mike Miller, Celeste Arrington, Adam Dean, Evgeny Finkel, Eric Kramon, and Yon Lupu. Our innumerable coffees, lunches, and beers helped me better understand the publishing process and generally how to navigate junior professordom.

The journey from dissertation to book is never easy, but without the intellectual sanctuary of the Harvard Academy, mine might never have happened at all. My years there gave me both the freedom and community to sink back into the project, pulling out weeds and pouring fertilizer over some slower to germinate chapters. I cannot thank Bruce Jackan and Kathleen Hoover enough for running such a tight, supportive ship. My informal writing partners, Mariano Sanchez-Talanquier and Rachel Sweet, workshopped several of the chapters and never pulled their punches. Next round of coffee and sweets in the museum cafe is on me.

I would particularly like to thank Tim Colton and Tom Remington. My monthly lunches with each helped me nail down some lingering framing questions and draw out a longer history of businesspeople in Russian politics. Tim also graciously and patiently chaired my book conference, the single most helpful step in the long writing process. Scott Gehlbach, Tom Remington, Ben Ross Schneider, Yuhua Wang, and Vineeta Yadav all gave the entire manuscript a close, critical read and identified many areas for improvement. In particular, Ben marked up the entire manuscript by hand, the perfect resource for tackling the many loose ends in that draft. The full-day conversation, funded and organized by the Academy, was the capstone of an unforgettable and productive year in Cambridge.

I am very grateful to several publishers for permission to reprint substantial portions of text from my published journal articles. Much of empirical analysis from "Businesspeople in Elected Office: Identifying Private Benefits from Firm-Level Returns," *American Political Science Review* 112 (2): 322–338 (2019), appears in Chapter 5. In addition, the theory and empirical analysis of Chapter 6 largely draw on "Private Sector Policymaking: Business Background and Politicians' Behavior in Office," *Journal of Politics* Forthcoming (2020). I use these materials with permission from Cambridge University Press and the Southern Political Science Association. Both individual chapters benefitted immensely from the comments of the two journal editors and several anonymous reviewers, as did the manuscript as a whole.

Finally, my sincerest gratitude goes out to two loved ones. Although the writing process dredged up both good and bad memories of her own PhD experience, my mother Diane instilled the confidence in me to push forward. Her steadfastness and intelligence will always be an inspiration. This book is dedicated to Mary Catherine Wellons, who has lovingly endured a decade of fieldwork, uncertainty, and arcane battles with data collection. One of her most unheralded skills is knowing when to take work home, and more importantly, when to not. Writing this book has ultimately been one of the happiest and most fulfilling periods of my life, and I owe everything to her for supporting me every step of the way. MC – thank you.

Introduction

"You can't get by here without help from the government."

Aleksandr Shpeter
Director, Tomsk Housing Construction Company
Deputy, Tomsk Region Legislative Duma

In 2008, the worldwide financial crisis dealt a severe blow to the construction industry in Tomsk, a charming academic center in Russia dubbed the "Siberian Athens" for the numerous universities that call the city home.[1] A crisis of liquidity forced banks to stop lending altogether to the industry, freezing almost two-thirds of construction projects dead in their tracks. Demand for apartments dropped by nearly 80 percent and dozens of firms teetered on the brink of bankruptcy. One construction manager become so desperate he started spreading false rumors to customers that his competitors had already closed up their shops. Out of the half million total residents in Tomsk, some 30,000 construction workers risked losing their jobs.[2]

Government officials scrambled to stem the bleeding. Frozen projects meant lost revenue from corporate taxes and land privatizations, money that was urgently needed to patch up safety nets and prevent an even further drop in unemployment. Strategic plans were drawn up to offer financial assistance for borrowers to buy apartments and for

[1] Epigraph quoted from published interview: Solomon Vygon, "Aleksandr Shpeter: Svetyashhiesya Okna Novogo Doma, Bal'zam Na Dushu." *Argumenty i Fakty*. October 18–24, 2006.

[2] For more information on the crisis in Tomsk, see Svinin (2008); Sergeev (2009); Ivonina (2009); Petrov (2008).

developers to complete unfinished projects. Even longstanding traditions of appealing to the federal center were upended. Russian presidents famously meet in person one-on-one with governors in front of the TV cameras, positioned across from one another as if they were locked in a fierce chess match. But for the first time in the country's history, Tomsk governor Victor Kress held a videoconference with then Russian President Medvedev to discuss financial assistance for his region's construction sector.

Observers later marveled at how a single company commanded the lion's share of the government's attention. All but unknown to the public just two years before, the Tomsk Housing Construction Company (TDSK) was officially designated a "system-forming enterprise," which made it eligible for loan guarantees and direct subsidies. The company also received a number of large, federally guaranteed state contracts, including forty-six alone from the regional government to resettle residents living in dilapidated housing and two more from the Ministry of Defense to construct apartments for officers.[3] This preferential treatment flew in the face of widespread criticism over how TDSK managed its finances and had sent a state investment fund into bankruptcy after defaulting on a 500 million ruble ($19 million) loan.[4] In one of its suburban development projects, it even refused to supply electricity to the street lamps, leaving the whole neighborhood in the dark. TDSK's rescue came at the expense of four other local, large construction companies which "simply disappeared from the market."[5] By 2013, TDSK was firmly the dominant player in the Tomsk construction industry, with a 42 percent market share and over 5,000 employees.[6]

Why did TDSK emerge triumphant while similar companies failed to catch the eye of government officials? Not lost on many at the time was the fact that TDSK's director and plurality owner, Aleksandr Shpeter, was also a longtime deputy of the Tomsk Regional Duma, the region's legislature. In that capacity, he served as the chairman of the Committee on Construction and Transport, as well as on the Committee on Economic Policy. A local businessperson held a uniquely powerful legislative position precisely at the time his firm was navigating a tough financial period. This book asks how and why businesspeople like Shpeter acquired such power in the first place.

[3] Litvinova (2009).
[4] Drokova and Rudnyev (2008).
[5] Tomsk Vice-Mayor Evgeniy Parshuto quoted in Mikhailov (2012), p. 300.
[6] Mikhailov (2013).

BUSINESSPEOPLE IN ELECTED OFFICE WORLDWIDE

Businesspeople running for and winning elected office are a staple of modern politics. Titans of various industries have headed national governments in Ukraine (chocolate), Chile (airlines, finance, television), and Finland (telecoms). Across eighteen Latin American countries, no fewer than 118 of 278 political parties during 1975–2009 had at least one primary leader come from the business community.[7] The mayor of New York City for most of the 2000s, Michael Bloomberg, commanded a billion-dollar empire in financial data services before taking office, while Richard Riordan ran Los Angeles for much of the 1990s after a successful career in venture capital. And we would be remiss not to mention Donald Trump, who succeeded where Carly Fiorina and Mitt Romney had failed before in convincing US voters that business experience was a strong qualification to hold the country's highest office.

Businesspeople are particularly well represented in legislative branches around the world. Approximately 20 percent of members of the most recent convocations of the US House of Representatives have come directly from the private sector, a percentage that has remained remarkably steady over the last 100 years.[8] Moonlighting politicians, i.e. those who earn outside income from the private sector, make up a significant share of parliamentarians in Italy, Germany, the United Kingdom, and Canada.[9] Table I.1 presents a wider snapshot of national legislatures from beyond the OECD, demonstrating that on average, one-quarter of deputies have some kind of business background.

This interest in holding office among the capitalist class is not just a recent trend. Turn-of-the-century politics in the United States were in large part dominated by businessperson legislators. In their book on inequality in the United States, Jacob Hacker and Paul Pierson write:

> Our generation is not the first in which the optimistic prediction that democracy will naturally temper excesses of income and wealth has failed to ring true. In the early twentieth century, similar problems – and laments – were widespread. Financial and industrial titans commanded vast economic power that they used not just to despoil the environment, suppress attempts to organize, and head off consumer protections, but also to buy off politicians who might stand in their way. The problem was particularly acute in the U.S. Senate whose members

7 Barndt (2014).

8 Carnes (2012).

9 Gagliarducci, Nannicini, and Naticchioni (2010); Pan et al. (2014); Fedele and Naticchioni (2016).

TABLE I.1 *Businesspeople dominate national legislatures*

Country	Pct. (%)	Year	Type	Source
Bangladesh	59	2008	Members	Chowdhury (2009)
Benin	31	2011	Members	Koter (2017)
Chile	19	2001	Members	Carnes and Lupu (2015)
China	17	2008	Members	Truex (2014)
Cyprus	21	2011	Members	Katsourides (2012)
Kyrgyzstan	27	2005	Candidates	Sjöberg (2011)
Mexico	18	2000	Members	Carnes and Lupu (2015)
Thailand	17	2005	Candidates	Croissant and Pojar Jr (2005)
Uganda	16	2011	Members	Josefsson (2014)
Ukraine	30	2007	Members	Semenova (2012)

were still appointed by state governments. The legendary journalist William Allen White portrayed the institution as a "millionaires' club", where a member, "represented something more than a state, more than even a region. He represented principalities and powers in business. One Senator ... represents the Union Pacific Railway System; another the New York Central; still another the insurance interests of New York and New Jersey" (Hacker and Pierson, 2011, p. 79).

Nearly half of the members of the British Parliament in the late nineteenth century served as company directors.[10] Members of the House of Lords still openly mix business and politics, with Richard Allan, Lord Allan of Hallam, working as Facebook's European policy director since 2009.[11] Over the last 100 years, Argentine businesspeople with diversified empires have used elected office to pursue preferential economic policies.[12] Mexican firm directors helped write several of the important financial laws in the late 1800s and early 1900s.[13]

The fact that so many businesspeople run for office is rather puzzling. True, many economic elites enter politics for personal reasons, such as the pursuit of fame and power. But the many drawbacks of holding public office suggest that other factors are at play. Electoral campaigns require massive amounts of time and money. Governing can be burdensome, from the hours spent dealing with constituent demands to the increased media scrutiny. These responsibilities force businesspeople to divert their

[10] Braggion and Moore (2013).
[11] Scheck and Forelle (2014).
[12] Paniagua (2017).
[13] Musacchio and Read (2007).

attention away from the area where they especially excel: making money in the private sector. Why do businesspeople set aside their often extraordinarily successful careers for the uncertainty and vicissitudes of public office? And what should citizens expect from governments to which a good number of elected officials arrive straight from the business world?

This book provides answers to both questions. The first part puts forth a novel explanation for the puzzle of why businesspeople run for office. I argue that we need to approach businessperson candidacy first and foremost as a type of non-market strategy. In other words, many businesspeople seek positions in government primarily to unlock political benefits and make money for their own firms. Clearly, firms have other more conventional avenues at their disposal to achieve political influence. For example, they can make contributions to political campaigns or lobby government officials. However, in weakly institutionalized societies, relying on these strategies gives rise to a thorny commitment problem: politicians regularly shirk the promises they make to special interests, particularly firms. The central argument of this book is that businessperson candidacy helps solve this commitment program. Sending members of a firm's management team directly into government removes the need for political intermediaries and offers proximate access to policymaking. By leveraging vertical integration within the firm and keeping government relations in-house, businessperson candidacy allows firms to go around untrustworthy politicians. Businesspeople absorb the high costs of candidacy and governing when traditional corporate political activities become unreliable and ineffective.

The second part of the book then examines how electing active businesspeople to public office changes the way governments are run. Analyzing business participation at multiple levels of political office, I show that businesspeople effectively co-opt political institutions to benefit both their own firms and the wider business community. The effects are large and troubling: businessperson politicians not only remarkably improve their firms' performance on the back of government contracts, but also reshape government budgets, procurement mechanisms, and tax policy to prioritize firm growth, rather than investments in citizens and human capital. To demonstrate these effects, I draw on an array of quantitative and qualitative evidence on businessperson politicians in Putin-era Russia, a country where they make up over one-third of regional legislators, mayors, and municipal deputies. I conclude the work by offering new proposals for strengthening institutions and preventing businessperson politicians from corrupting the representation of the public interest.

BUSINESSPERSON CANDIDACY AS NON-MARKET STRATEGY

Achieving success in the business world requires more than just efficiently delivering products and services or organizing production and supply chains. Firms are embedded in complex business environments, where many actors can influence their ability to build competitive advantage.[14] Through their regulatory power, governments can dramatically influence, both positively and negatively, the cost of doing business. Protests and popular boycotts can damage firms' reputations. Cooperation with charities can bring substantial good will.

Non-market strategy collectively refers to the steps firms take to manage relationships with these stakeholders.[15] Example non-market strategies include efforts to coordinate private activists,[16] practice corporate social responsibility,[17] or engage policymakers (such as through lobbying or campaign contributions).[18] This book examines how firms decide upon specific *corporate political activities*, a subset of actions under the umbrella of non-market strategy where firms engage with government officials to gain competitive advantages.

Securing access to policymakers can have striking effects on firm financial and operating performance, but not all firms view political action as a worthwhile investment. Some firms can credibly threaten to exit markets, depriving governments of tax revenue and investment. This structural power can confer immense political influence and frees firms from having

[14] See Baron (1995*a*). In this book, I treat firms as unified actors, led by sophisticated managers who decide on strategies that best allow them to navigate their non-market environment. Recent work on non-market strategy in the United States has begun to dig deeper into how the internal management and ownership structure of a firm affects its ability to influence policymaking (Kim, 2008; Hansen and Mitchell, 2000). For most of the developing world, and particularly Russia, the development of corporate governance lags and the organization of government relations is far from sophisticated.

[15] This definition draws heavily on work such as Baron (2009) and Minor (2016). On the other hand, *market strategy* encompasses actions taken to create value within the firm's production chain or with other economic actors through contracts and agreements.

[16] Walker (2014).

[17] Barnett (2007).

[18] Baron (1995*b*).

to expend resources directly on political activities.[19] But firms across a variety of settings do invest considerable sums into politics, a clear indication that their structural power cannot alone deliver necessary political dividends. In some cases, failing to actively invest in political relationships can doom revenue generation, particularly for firms reliant on the government for subsidies and contracts.[20] Other firms face financial difficulties and see government assistance and bailouts as the only ways forward to rescue their declining fortunes.[21] For firms working in highly regulated industries, minimizing red tape can be an effective way to lower costs and increase profitability.[22] In states with weak rule of law, worries over expropriation and property rights violations drive political engagement.[23] Firms invest resources in political action because they expect to either promote their economic interests further, or at a minimum protect their domain from perceived threats.[24]

Corporate political activities seek to unlock these benefits by influencing policy through direct and indirect channels. To date, much of the literature has focused on firms' use of *indirect* strategies, such as lobbying and making campaign contributions, particularly because of the vast sums spent on each in the United States.[25] Firms contribute information, money, and/or votes to politicians in exchange for access and influence.[26] Politicians then become intermediaries and advocate on a firm's behalf. Yet indirect strategies provide no guarantee that the exchange of policy will take place. Offering larger contributions should increase the likelihood that deals struck with politicians will hold, but uncertainty about the enforcement of these agreements can reduce their attractiveness.

19 Lindblom (1977).
20 Grier, Munger, and Roberts (1994); Pittman (1977).
21 Damania (2002); Kim (2008); Hillman (1982).
22 Hart (2001); Grier, Munger, and Roberts (1994).
23 Frye (2006); Markus (2012); Markus and Charnysh (2017); Earle and Gehlbach (2015).
24 Walker and Rea (2014).
25 See Coen, Grant, and Wilson (2012) and Lux, Crook, and Woehr (2011). This domination is largely due to an overemphasis on the United States over the last 30 years. The vast and consistent growth of business participation in politics in the United States beginning in the 1970s also coincided with strict campaign finance laws and related regulations enforcing transparency about both business lobbying and campaign contributions (Lawton, McGuire, and Rajwani, 2013). The unmatched access to data from a vibrant pluralist country has dramatically sapped attention away from corporate political activity in other developing and developed countries.
26 Hillman and Hitt (1999).

By removing the need to use political intermediaries, businessperson candidacy for political office emerges as a distinct type of *direct* non-market strategy.[27] I define a businessperson candidate as any individual who runs for elected office while simultaneously serving as director, deputy director, or on the board of directors at the time of his or her electoral campaign.[28] Direct strategies such as businessperson candidacy closely bind politicians and firms and provide a stronger guarantee that an individual firm's interests will be represented. Firms do not need to persuade politicians to represent them. Instead, the politician is part of the firm's management team and strongly incentivized to pursue its interests. Running candidates for political office thus serves as an alternative mechanism for building insider political capital and is potentially available to all firms in places where elections are held. Firms develop political ties not through bribe-making or backdoor dealings, but out in the open by appealing to voters. Businessperson candidacy in that respect democratizes how political connections are made.[29]

Sending a director into elected office offers tremendous political influence for firms. In Thailand, businessperson politicians are intimately involved in drafting and changing legislation to suit their firms' interests, such as altering regulations, passing protectionist policies, and driving through new state contracts designed for their enterprise.[30] Evidence from China suggests that entrepreneurs who are members of formal political institutions enjoy preferential access to loans from banks.[31] In Russia, businessperson legislators can gain unfettered access to the executive branch by virtue of their political status and weight in opening doors to bureaucrats. Much of their political ammunition derives from the "deputy request," a powerful instrument available to Russian legislators

[27] Developing political connections more generally also qualifies as a direct strategy. In Chapter 1, I examine the difference between a firm director running for office and a firm bringing on board a current politician.

[28] In most post-Soviet countries, the title of firm director is equivalent to the Western titles of Corporate Executive Officer (CEO) or Director General.

[29] The claim that businessperson candidacy is a type of non-market strategy does not negate that some CEOs run for office for personal reasons, including sheer political ambition. Many businesspeople do step back from their companies upon taking office and completely shift gears into professional political life. Given the tremendous opportunities to secure firm advantages (as well as weak institutions in place worldwide to prevent conflicts of interest), it is reasonable to expect that many firm directors approach public service with a self-interested motivation to help their companies.

[30] Bunkanwanicha and Wiwattanakantang (2009).

[31] Li et al. (2008).

to compel bureaucrats to open inspections, conduct audits, and make life miserable for their rivals.

But these benefits come at a significant cost in terms of time, money, and potentially reputation. Firms must pay for their candidate's electoral campaign or chalk up the money to pay for a spot on the party list.[32] These investments disappear if the businessperson candidate loses the election. Campaigns can be vicious and intrusive, exposing candidates to increased attention from the media and blowback from consumers and business partners who may disagree with their political positions. Upon winning election, businessperson politicians also acquire a whole new set of political duties (and constituents) to add to their normal commitments to firm management. They must find a way to juggle these competing responsibilities between the public and private sectors, and often find themselves with considerably less time to spend on that which they presumably hold most dear: running their businesses.

PUZZLE AND THEORETICAL FRAMEWORK

This presents an intriguing puzzle. Why do some businesspeople run for political office, when other less expensive political avenues are available? Which firms decide to shoulder the huge demands of campaigns and governing for the chance to achieve direct political representation? In Chapter 1, I lay out an argument that businesspeople run for elected office when they cannot trust that the politicians they lobby will represent their interests. At heart is a micro-level commitment problem that plagues *indirect* strategies such as lobbying or making campaign contributions: firm directors have no guarantee that the money they give to a politician will be returned in-kind with policy. Indirect strategies raise the risk of politician shirking, leading to political market failure and inadequate representation of firm interests. Using a variety of examples of politicians reneging on promises and even extorting local businesspeople, I make the case that lobbying and campaign contributions are far from smooth and predictable channels to build political influence.

Even more painful is the fact that conventional solutions to this commitment problem have little bite to constrain politicians from shirking. Firms cannot specify written quid pro quo contracts with politicians

[32] Engvall (2014); Mereu (2003).

where policy influence is traded for contributions such as money, information, and/or votes. Developing the trust required to enforce informal agreements requires repeated interactions over time between stable actors,[33] something that often is absent in settings where politicians regularly change parties and care little about long-term reputations. Business associations also offer little relief: mandated to reach consensus amongst their members, their interest in punishing shirking politicians on behalf of individual firms often falls short.

Argument

The central argument in this book is that businessperson candidacy helps solve the commitment problem better than other institutional- and reputation-based mechanisms. Drawing on the literature on vertical integration,[34] I contend that directly occupying a seat allows a firm to achieve political representation in-house ("making" rather than "buying" representation through a professional politician). Delegating the CEO to work simultaneously as the firm's chief political agent reduces monitoring and agency costs, and becomes an effective avenue for firms to secure their desired policies. When professional politicians fail to properly represent constituents and interest groups, their hold on elected office is vulnerable to direct challenges from these spurned actors. Broken campaign promises can lead to upheaval among the type of individuals that contest elections and often attract outsider candidates who might not otherwise have run.

This theoretical framework implies that greater concerns about politician shirking will drive businesspeople to run for office themselves. Firms opt into businessperson candidacy when politicians are deemed untrustworthy stewards of their interests. I argue first that shirking occurs when the degree of economic competition is high, giving politicians multiple suitors to choose from and reducing the efficacy of indirect strategies. Politicians can accept competing offers from rival firms, and then allocate excludable benefits (such as licenses, contracts, and guarantees). This inevitably leads to some firms being spurned, and in response drives them to seek more direct political access.

Winning access to exclusive policymaking clubs like legislatures enables a firm to ensure that policy its interests will be pursued and

33 Großer, Reuben, and Tymula (2013).
34 Coase (1937); Williamson (1981).

its competitors' attempts to carve out similar access can be stymied. A rival holding a legislative seat means that indirect strategies become less effective. Firms therefore copy each other's routes into politics, just as they mimic product strategies and entry into new markets.[35] Competition generates a type of "arms race" between firms, whereby more and more elaborate, involved political investments (culminating in elected office) are needed to ensure consistent access to policymaking. Businessperson candidacy emerges as a strategy of the strong to protect their advantages against their rivals.

Next, I argue institutionalized parties care about long-term reputations and cultivate ties with donors by demonstrating fidelity in carrying out campaign promises. Greater party discipline curbs shirking by member politicians and facilitates quid pro quo transactions with firms that provide contributions. Businesspeople will therefore run for office in greater numbers where parties are weak. When parties cannot constrain their members from defecting and have a weak hold on access to ballots and resources, businesspeople see opportunities to take office themselves. All firms would be better off if none of their directors personally ran for public office: they could save on the costs of the campaign and delegate politics to the politicians. The absence of strong political parties prevents firms from aggregating their interests and cooperating to check the reneging impulses of designated political representatives.

Both acute competition and weak parties are examples of demand-side factors. They drive businesspeople to seek office because lobbying and campaign contributions get swallowed up by shirking politicians. I further claim that supply-side factors also influence the decision of businesspeople to run. Only large firms (endowed with substantial financial assets or workforces) have the resources to afford the steep costs of businessperson candidacy. Campaign costs also depend on the income of the constituency to be courted. Most expenses, such as paying activists and printing campaign materials, need to be paid locally: higher wages and input prices drive up the price of running a campaign. Firms located in wealthier jurisdictions will be less likely to run candidates, since these expenses needed to attract voter support outweigh the benefits of having a director in office.

[35] Lawton, McGuire, and Rajwani (2013); John et al. (2015); Massini, Lewin, and Greve (2005); Xia, Tan, and Tan (2008).

This explanation of businessperson candidacy differs from other theoretical approaches which emphasize the importance of electoral institutions in shaping the incentives for firm directors to run.[36] I argue that the pivotal voter is not central to the decision-making calculus of businesspeople. Concern over politicians reneging on agreements, and not voters punishing corruption, drives firms to consider alternative methods for achieving policy influence. Empirically I find that greater transparency and electoral accountability are not significantly correlated with the probability of a firm adopting the strategy of businessperson candidacy. Firms are more concerned that their rivals will beat them into political office and undermine other strategies used to secure influence.

Finally, coordinating political activity could help firms save on the costs of the campaign and delegate politics to chosen representatives that advocate for their collective issues. Yet firms rarely unite around any issues or around specific political strategies.[37] Opportunities to engage in collective action, such as through business associations, fall flat in the face of weak leadership and intense interfirm rivalries. Firms have to rely on their own individual efforts to acquire particularistic benefits from the government.

Testing the Argument

In Chapter 3, I put these hypotheses to the test using a variety of quantitative and qualitative data. First I draw on an original dataset on regional elections in Putin-era Russia. I collected data on 41,471 candidates to 83 regional legislatures from 2004 to 2011, including demographics such as birthdate, gender, and place of employment. Next, using a computer algorithm to mine a database of firm registrations, I identified all firms these candidates served as director or on the board of directors at the time of their electoral campaign. Together with independently collected firm-level and sector-level variables, this one-of-kind dataset allows for an analysis of the myriad factors affecting the decision to run for office.[38] In addition to the observational data, I analyze new evidence from questions placed on a recent survey of 654 firms that ask businesspeople about their participation in regional elections.

36 Gehlbach, Sonin, and Zhuravskaya (2010).

37 Hiscox (2004); Gimpel, Lee, and Parrott (2014); Hillman, Keim, and Schuler (2004).

38 For a detailed description of the firm-level data used throughout this book, please consult Part A of the Appendix.

The quantitative analysis uncovers significant empirical support for my main arguments. Fierce economic competition is a strong driver of interest among firms in running candidates for office. This effect is magnified for the largest firms in each region who are much more likely to put forward candidates to protect their position in sectors marked by many rivals. Firms expend considerable resources to protect their market advantages, especially when other rivals can contest their political access. More institutionalized political parties, however, help mitigate the commitment problem and reassure firms that politicians will act as more dependable representatives. When parties are more developed and concerned about their long-term reputations, firm managers can be confident that allocating resources to lobbying and the parties' electoral campaigns (indirectly) will be just as effective at achieving their political goals. Given the alternatives, businessperson candidacy is not worth its substantial cost. To reiterate this last point, I show a variety of evidence connecting the cost of elections and firms' ability to pay as decisive factors motivating businessperson candidacy.

Finally, I turn to roughly seventy semi-structured interviews with a range of more influential actors in three Russian regions: Tomsk, Ryazan, and Perm. In selecting regions, I prioritized finding variation along several dimensions of theoretical interest for explaining businessperson candidacy. First, collectively the three regions vary significantly in terms of economic structure: Perm has a rich manufacturing base with many firms working in natural resources, Ryazan focuses primarily on agricultural production, while Tomsk falls somewhere in between. These differences in market conditions and competition between different types of firms provide insight in how rivalries affect demand for political office among firms. Additional leverage is gained from variation in political openness. Perm has historically been one of the most open and democratic regions in Russia, with opposition parties waging fierce challenges to the ruling party United Russia's dominance. On the other hand, United Russia has enjoyed a smoother ride to the top in both Tomsk and Ryazan. Although the data from the interviews are not used to explicitly test my theories, this variation across economic and political structures increases my confidence that the quantitative findings are not specific to one specific type of region.

Throughout 2013 and 2014, I spoke with businessperson candidates (winning and losing), deputies without direct business interests, journalists, academics, and civil society representatives from the three regions. These wide-ranging conversations provide additional support for the reasons businesspeople to run for office. Again politician shirking takes center stage. Interviewees spoke candidly about legislators regularly defecting from informal agreements and selling out interest groups. Fears over shirking were most pronounced for firms caught up in fierce rivalries: getting locked out of parliament meant conceding crucial political ground and losing out on key opportunities to tap into government largesse. But where political parties had made substantial inroads in carving out a long-term presence in the region, many of these concerns were alleviated. In these instances, strong parties helped adjudicate disputes between firms behind closed doors and reassure competing interests that all actors making financial contributions would get their voice heard. Putting up directors themselves for office became superfluous.

Deciding How to Run

Deciding to run for office is only the first in a series of tough decisions on the road to direct representation. In Chapter 4, I develop three theoretical extensions to demonstrate how businesspeople navigate the array of electoral rules, political parties, and time-related opportunity costs to give themselves the best chance at winning elected office. Each political choice carries its own set of costs and benefits, from the personal and financial expenditures to get on the ballot to variation in the degree of political influence one can achieve while in office. But interestingly, how businesspeople make these decisions often comes down to the specific resources and political needs of the firms they direct. Studying variation across several firm characteristics, such as assets, ownership, and corporate governance structures, is crucial to understanding why businesspeople gravitate towards certain electoral systems and political parties, as well as send certain representatives of their firm to run for office. Accordingly, this chapter takes advantage of the rich firm-level dataset presented in analyzed in Chapter 3 to illustrate how these choices are made.

First, I address the issue of ballot choice. Russia's mixed-member electoral rules compel candidates to make a choice: run in a single member district and represent a clear geographic constituency, or bid for a place on a party list and try one's hand through the proportional representation system.[39] Given the incredible resources required for

[39] Some candidates run on both tickets, which I analyze separately in Chapter 4.

successful candidacy, I argue businesspeople want to maximize the return on their investment by carving out as much localized autonomy as possible and retaining the ability to pursue their own firms' self-interest. Winning office in specific geographic districts offers politicians more independence and liberates them from party strictures.[40] In general, businesspeople prefer seats from single-member districts, rather than those proffered through party lists. Other firm traits predict how businesspeople choose between ballots. Larger firms can independently bankroll their own electoral campaigns in single-member districts. And firms with stronger ties to their communities can convert their resources more easily into political capital, particularly the personal vote, and "go-it-alone" without having to rely on party lists.

Next up is the decision about whether to line up with a political party, and if so, which one. Political parties can help affiliated businesspeople win contentious races and then provide a leg-up in influencing policymaking and accessing government officials. But clearly all parties are not created equal: the rise of the United Russia ruling party has created a clear hierarchy of power and resources. Businesspeople have to decide which, if any, parties provide the most bang for their buck.

To show how this decision is made, I argue that first we have to understand how parties operate at the regional level in Russia. In many respects, the allocation of candidates to parties is most analogous to an auction. Before each election, parties announce (privately, of course) the availability and price of spots on their party lists, with prospective candidates then bidding for a designated rank, and thus the probability of winning a seat. Prices paid depend on normal forces of supply and demand: the more candidates interested and the more political influence offered by a given party, the higher the prices demanded.

This again means that firm and market characteristics are essential for predicting party affiliation among businessperson candidates. Firms with more financial resources and operating in more regulated sectors have both the means and the interest in running as members of the ruling party. Access to bureaucratic officials is worth the high cost of entry. Moreover, rival firms rarely find shelter under the umbrella of a single political party. I develop a new measure, the *Effective Number of Parties per Sector*, and show that competing economic interests join competing political parties. The lack of coordination within sector lends additional

40 Thames (2005); Tavits (2009).

evidence to the claim that regional parliaments function as sites of economic competition between firms. Competitors in a single market see greater dividends from strengthening rival parties than trying to address their differences within a single grouping. Electoral competitiveness can depend as much on economic market dynamics than on personal and ideological rivalry.

Finally, firms have a variety of qualified employees they can send into elected office to represent their interests. A complicated trade-off emerges: designating a CEO to run can impose substantial opportunity costs on firm management, while delegating to another member of the management team may lead to inadequate political representation. I conclude the chapter by showing how the commitment problem examined in Chapter 1 rears its head again with regard to delegating political authority. Where political parties are stronger, firms can feel more confident that even a lower-ranked employee can ride the party's coattails to a legislative seat and then effectively get the firm's voice heard within the political faction.

BUSINESSPERSON RENT-SEEKING AND POLICYMAKING

The second part of the book looks at what happens when businesspeople take the reins of government. Businessperson politicians are beholden to two different constituencies when taking office: their firms' shareholders (who presumably help fund the campaign) and their voters (who put them in office). However, we have little evidence about the micro-level (firm) or macro-level (polity) consequences of electing businesspeople to higher office. Individual leaders have been shown to produce dramatic effects on policymaking and economic outcomes.[41] Businessperson politicians who engage in self-enrichment diverge from the preferences of the voters that elected them. Institutions then need to be redesigned to ensure that the type of leaders selecting into political office acts in the public interest.[42]

Firm-Level Benefits from Businessperson Candidacy

I begin by investigating how firms perform when they have a director hold political office. Chapter 5 uses a regression discontinuity design

41 Jones and Olken (2005).
42 Besley (2005); Braendle (2016).

(RDD) that identifies the causal effect of political connections on firm-level outcomes. Using the main dataset on firms connected to regional candidates in Russia, I exploit close elections where the determination of the winner and runner-up is near randomly assigned.[43] This identification strategy moves beyond matching and cross-sectional comparisons to estimate how developing a political connection can improve a firm's bottom line.[44] The results indicate that firms derive significant benefits from having their director win political office. Firms connected to winning candidates increase revenue by roughly 60 percent and profit margin by 15 percent over a single term in office.

Several underlying mechanisms are consistent with these findings. On one hand, bank lenders might look more favorably upon firms whose directors hold elected office, viewing their political success as a sign of creditworthiness.[45] Alternately, bureaucrats may be more inclined to offer favorable treatment to firms with directors who are also serving in government. Teasing out which mechanism is driving the results helps inform policymakers about the best set of reforms to curb rent-seeking, such as by working to equalize access to finance or punishing bureaucrats who offer preferential treatment to connected firms. Exploiting data on ways legislative power could lead to firm benefits, I find that serving in office increases a firm's probability of accessing state procurement by approximately 40 percent, but has no effect on its financial leverage. The results indicate the main benefits from businessperson candidacy come from opportunities to influence the bureaucracy rather than alleviating credit constraints.

The book also presents new evidence about how structural and institutional factors impact the value of non-market strategy.[46] First, winning office leads to larger returns in wealthier regions and those endowed with natural resources. Richer governments mean bigger profits for those firms who can get their directors inside. But stronger democratic institutions do not constrain businessperson politicians from using their office to help their firms. Instead, where the ruling party faces greater opposition, firms with directors in office enjoy better access to government and better performance. Why doesn't competition between parties lead to stronger

[43] Lee (2008); Eggers et al. (2014).
[44] Acemoglu et al. (2013); Fisman (2001); Hillman and Hitt (1999).
[45] Houston et al. (2014).
[46] Treisman (2007); Faccio (2006); Li, Poppo, and Zhou (2008); Fisman (2001); Siegel (2007).

monitoring and less rent-seeking? I argue that more politically competitive legislatures are better able to exert influence on policymaking, regulatory actions, and budget processes, and thus attract more interest from businesspeople looking for real access. These bodies become the key fora through which economic demands are negotiated, private favors exchanged, and ultimately money made. The results also show that joining an opposition party does not doom a firm director's ability to help his or her firm. Political institutions, such as legislatures, help ruling parties distribute rents not just to their supporters, but also potential opponents.

Competition between rival *firms* that have secured political representation, however, reduces of the value of winning office. Multiple foxes in the henhouse means each one gorges less. When winning firms encounter other potential rent-seekers who have won political office, they find it more difficult to carve out private benefits. If at least three firms from a single sector win direct representation, none reap any financial gains over the term. Firm returns also diminish when more businesspeople overall enter parliament, regardless the sector they operate in. I argue that parliamentary deliberations most resemble a marketplace, with firm-specific profits dropping as new players enter. Economic rivals perform an important oversight function by helping check one another's political advantages and curb illicit rent-seeking. Those who stand to lose the most from others gaining connections are often the best positioned to monitor their peers.

Businesspeople as Policymakers

Next the book asks: do businesspeople govern differently? Beyond working to help their individual firms, businessperson politicians craft policies that affect the constituents who elected them into office. Building off a close examination of the traits and skillsets businesspeople bring with them into elected office, Chapter 6 develops and tests two sets of hypotheses about the specific policy choices businesspeople make in government. First, I argue that given their background bringing goods and services to market, businesspeople have different preferences for government action and increased interest in solving issues important to the wider business community. Working from this set of preferences, politicians coming from the private sector prioritize economic growth over other political objectives and generally advocate for pro-business policies.

But businesspeople are often talented managers with deep experience running efficient enterprises and boosting firm productivity. Many of these skills may find ready application in government administration. Thus, we might also expect businesspeople to apply their private sector know-how and to try to improve the way government works. They could increase the quality and lower the cost of public service delivery, for example, by eliminating wasteful spending, balancing budgets, and making government dollars go further.

The question then arises: do businesspeople shape government to run *for* business (i.e. by adopting pro-business policies) or *like* a business (i.e. by increasing government efficiency)? To distinguish between the two potential channels, I adopt a two-part research design. First, using another RDD, I compare municipalities where businessperson mayoral candidates barely won office and those where they barely lost. The dataset includes over 68,169 candidates from 2008 to 2016, nearly a quarter of whom worked in the private sector before running for office. To measure pro-business and pro-efficiency outcomes, I collect data on the budgets for 25,240 municipalities and over 1 million procurement contracts. Next, at the regional level, I draw on the main legislator dataset described earlier to calculate the percentage of businessperson politicians that served in eighty parliaments over the same period. Leveraging panel data with region and year fixed effects, I analyze variation in regional budget expenditures and tax policies for the years these politicians spend in office.

Businesspeople, whether working either as city mayors or regional legislators, do more to run government *for* business, rather than *like* a business. Both at the municipal and regional levels, businessperson politicians allocate significantly more money to so-called "economic infrastructure," i.e. the construction of roads, railroads, and ports. These expenditures reduce the obstacles to doing business for local enterprises, providing immediate benefits to firm performance. And at the regional level, the more businesspeople take office, the lower the revenue generated from corporate taxes, suggesting business are catching tax breaks. Businesspeople in elected office do not cough up similar money to pay for investing in "social infrastructure," such as health care and education. The results do not show either that electing more businesspeople into office leads to lower unemployment or more private investment. Politicians coming from the private sector use their time in government to help the business community, without prioritizing policies that have a stronger and more lasting impact on economic growth.

Next, this pro-business approach to government does not translate into improved government performance, as captured using a variety of metrics. First, I find no evidence that businessperson mayors run more balanced budgets: indeed, at the regional level, more businessperson legislators are associated with greater deficits and a larger volume of bond issuances. Government does not become smaller or more fiscally sound when businesspeople take charge. Second, drawing on a burgeoning literature in economics, I create new indicators of efficiency in public procurement, which accounts for an average of 13 percent of domestic GDP in countries worldwide. Given the many pitfalls and corruption risks inherent to allocating state contracts, a consensus is growing internationally that holding transparent, open auctions is the best way to fairly select competent suppliers and lower the prices government pay for key inputs. However, Russian municipalities run by local businesspeople often deviate from these best practices. Where businessperson mayors take office, construction contracts (such as for roads and public housing) are much more likely to be allocated using negotiated mechanisms, and not competitive auctions. The construction sector in Russia is often viewed as a huge black hole for rent-seeking,[47] and my findings suggest that businesspeople in elected office do little to close off these opportunities.

All together, Chapters 5 and 6 find that businessperson politicians in Russia exert unparalleled influence on the political institutions they populate, and pass policies that put their own self-interest over that of the public's. According to multiple representative surveys, voters in Russia care less about the government repairing roads than they do about it providing affordable housing, quality education, and working to prevent alcohol and drug abuse. On the other hand, improving economic infrastructure is a top priority for companies, as evidenced by both firm surveys and international evaluations of Russia's business environment.

In all, firms who send directors into office face a win-win situation: they derive immense specific benefits for themselves, such as achieving access to state procurement, while simultaneously being able to reallocate public money to ease their costs of doing business. And for the most part, businessperson politicians face few obstacles navigating institutional frameworks and co-opting the state. Political competition, partisan alignment between levels, and separation of powers play little role in preventing businesspeople from imposing their preferences on policymaking.

[47] Orttung and Zhemukhov (2014).

In all, this book shows that electing businesspeople to public office results in economic and political outcomes highly skewed towards the interests of economic elites, and consequently, lower quality representation for the average voter.

THE CASE OF RUSSIA

Post-Soviet Russia is in many respects an ideal case to study businessperson candidacy. To read only journalistic accounts of life under Putin would be to errantly believe that all politics was decided in the Kremlin. A wealth of new scholarship written in the neo-institutionalist vein of authoritarianism studies has pushed back against the notion that the so-called "power vertical" neatly explains Russian politics.[48] Candidates and political parties invest massive resources to contest elections, resulting in not only fierce political competition, but also varying degrees of control exerted by the ruling party over both national and subnational politics.[49] In Moscow, policymaking can generate heated battles between different ministries, agencies, and political groups.[50] Though the country has flirted with more personalist concentrations of power, Russia's regime type hews closely to the "competitive authoritarian" label: the political field is clearly tilted towards the ruling party United Russia, but free political expression has yet to be extinguished and opposition forces pose significant challenges through democratic institutions. In that regard, Russia shares many political characteristics with the dozens of other hybrid political regimes.

Russia is also a federal state, with important decision making delegated to its eighty-five subnational units and thousands of municipalities. Lower-level governments collectively provide for a substantial portion of public services, with regional and municipal spending accounting for roughly 9 percent and 6 percent of Russia's GDP, respectively. Where this money is spent, whether on education, health care, or infrastructure to name the most important line-items,[51] gets decided at the ground level. Interest groups, and particularly firms, make huge investments

[48] Reuter and Remington (2009); Reuter and Robertson (2015); Sharafutdinova (2010); Saikkonen (2015).

[49] Reuter (2017).

[50] Noble (2017).

[51] See the Appendix for a detailed breakdown of subnational spending.

in the political arena to influence how subnational governments allocate budgets, regulate industries, and provide public goods. Taking a more macro-level perspective, Russia in many ways is a typical middle-income country,[52] experiencing the same challenges pertaining to decentralization, strengthening the rule of law, and fighting corruption witnessed in other BRICS members (Brazil, India, South Africa), or countries in Latin America (Mexico, Venezuela) and Southeast Asia (Malaysia, Indonesia, and the Philippines).

The plethora of subnational units in Russia also exhibit incredible variation in democratic development, resource wealth, and economic production.[53] Partly as a legacy of Soviet development plans, Russia's industrial and agricultural bases are spread out throughout its vast territory. As a result, there are regions in Russia with per capita GDP levels rivaling those of OECD members, with neighboring areas mired deep in poverty and underinvestment. Some regions have seen the United Russia ruling party fight tooth and nail to achieve majorities in regional legislatures, while others more resemble the several authoritarian states of Central Asia. Elections command substantial attention from both elites and voters, with large financial contributions being funneled from firms to candidates.[54] Achieving legislative influence is seen as key to securing long-term business interests, with 30 percent of firms in a firm survey of 2011 responding that they prefer working with legislative officials if they choose to lobby at the regional level.[55]

Regional politics in Russia can be messy, unpredictable, and ultimately a huge boon for scholars of comparative politics. The variety of political and economic settings offers a rich natural laboratory to examine how structural and institutional characteristics affect the incentives and consequences of businesspeople running for office. Moreover, it improves our ability to generalize findings to other settings where conflicts of interest have also been found between politicians and bureaucrats,[56] while allowing us to hold constant macroeconomic factors that might imperil a cross-national study. In the conclusion, I explore how my main arguments about businessperson candidacy and time in office apply to other countries beyond the post-Soviet space.

[52] Shleifer and Treisman (2014).
[53] Bruno, Bytchkova, and Estrin (2013); Pyle (2009); Beazer (2014).
[54] Mironov and Zhuravskaya (2016).
[55] Reuter and Turovsky (2014).
[56] Acemoglu et al. (2013).

Finally, since the fall of the Soviet Union, private businesspeople have actively participated in elections at levels comparable to the variety of developing and developed countries mentioned above. Chapter 2 lays out the rich history of Russian businesspeople showing interest in holding political office during the post-Soviet transition. For example, during the 1990s, businesspeople were behind the creation of several political parties, including the Party of Economic Freedom created by the president of the Russian Commodities and Raw Materials Exchange Konstantin Borovoi in 1992, Civic Union founded by industrialist and trade association head Arkady Volsky, and the Russian Socialist Party created by the president of JSC Ferein, Vladimir Bryntsalov, in 1994.[57] By 2003, roughly 20 percent of all parliamentary candidates at the national level were officially linked to large or medium-size businesses, most with high spots on the lists.[58] That year, banker Boris Fyodorov, who also served as a deputy prime minister and ran for regional office, remarked that there was "not a single large company in Russia that is not involved in politics."[59] Other observers agreed, remarking that "becoming a deputy is the most widespread form of participation in 'high-level politics' by representatives of business."[60]

At the regional level, this book finds that approximately 40 percent of legislators served as a director of a firm at the time of their campaigns. Businesspeople do not just seek places in legislative bodies; they are well-represented in the executive branch. Gehlbach, Sonin, and Zhuravskaya (2010) document that from 1991 to 2005, over half of gubernatorial elections had at least one businessperson run for office. Chapter 6 finds 23 percent of mayoral candidates came directly from the private sector. These candidates represented parties from across the political spectrum, from the ruling United Russia party to even the Communist Party, which faced internal tensions for filling its ranks with millionaires alongside factory workers.[61] Although running for office is quite popular among members of the business community, it is not the only way to influence politics. Firms regularly lobby and contribute financially to politicians in attempts to curry political favor, making Russia a great place to examine the trade-offs between these strategies.

[57] *Kommersant* (2011).
[58] Mereu (2003).
[59] Myers (2003).
[60] Sedlak (2007).
[61] Myers (2003).

As the figures about national legislatures worldwide indicate in Table I.1, this level of business participation in government is in the middle of the pack, with the necessary caveat that similar studies in other countries are still in their infancy. Russia is neither relatively rich nor poor in its number of businessperson politicians, positioning the country as an optimal setting for digging deep into the variation driving differential participation. Indeed, Russia compares quite closely with other countries transitioning from communism where businesspeople regularly enter politics, such as Ukraine[62] and China,[63] as well as emerging markets such as Thailand, Argentina, and Brazil, with both high levels of businessperson candidacy and starkly different political trajectories.[64]

From a logistical standpoint, Russia also offers several empirical advantages for such a study. First, regional and municipal politicians in Russia do not face restrictions on working in the private sector while in office ("moonlighting"), a potential complication for a study of firm-level incentives to enter politics. There was no law at the regional or municipal levels during the period under study which banned businesspeople from running for office.[65] Similarly, deputies at the two subnational levels in Russia do not receive parliamentary immunity, another possible motivation for businesspeople to seek office. However, serving in government does raise the costs of a prosecution since charges can be construed as politically motivated. But without full parliamentary immunity, businesspeople are still vulnerable.[66]

Finally, the Russian government also stands apart in making available comprehensive data on both candidates and firms that allow me to identify and track businessperson candidates over time. The Russian

[62] Markus and Charnysh (2017).

[63] Truex (2014).

[64] Bunkanwanicha and Wiwattanakantang (2009); Freytes (2015).

[65] A recent study on the restrictions to the entry of public servants into legislatures suggested that the legal environment in Russia is very similar to the rest of the world; very few countries have passed laws to prevent businesspeople from running for office (Braendle and Stutzer, 2013). At the national level in Russia (the State Duma), deputies are banned from engaging in business while in office *and* deputies are granted immunity. Among other reasons, these two laws motivate the book's focus on subnational variation.

[66] For example, deputy status does not always provide complete protection. In early 2013, construction tycoon and member of the Irkutsk City Duma Mikhail Pakhomov was found murdered inside a rusted metal barrel filled with concrete. Even Deputy Pakhmonov's affiliation with the ruling United Russia was insufficient to save him being "tortured and killed over an outstanding $80 million loan" (Roth 2013).

Central Election Commission consolidates data on all candidates to subnational office, including information on their previous place of work. In addition, federal regulations in Russia require firms to submit full registration, management and annual financial data to state statistical agencies. These firm-level data provides coverage of the universe of firms for the entire time period of the study. This remarkable degree of data availability provides a unique opportunity to study political connections on a scale unavailable to researchers using surveys or data from publicly traded companies.[67]

CONTRIBUTIONS TO THE LITERATURE

This book fills an important gap in our understanding of the ways economic interests are represented and aggregated in policymaking. To date, we know considerably more about the influence of business "on the state," than we do of business working "within the state." For all the attention paid to activities such as lobbying and campaign contributions, the issue of businesspeople directly occupying elected office has mostly eluded scholars. Of the few studies that do address the entrance of businesspeople into elected politics, none have investigated the issue systematically, from the many decisions involved in running for office to what the average voter should expect from electing an individual with a private sector background.

The theoretical frameworks and analyses developed in this book help to remedy this. In doing so, the results provide an empirical basis for the claim that quid pro quo transactions between politicians and interest groups often break down due to a lack of enforcement mechanisms.[68] Politician shirking deflates the effectiveness of many indirect strategies (such as making campaign contributions and lobbying) and may help explain the unrealistic expectations many interest groups have about achieving a positive return on their political investments.[69] Interest

[67] In Part A of the Appendix, I assess the validity of these expansive datasets. Drawing on exemplary work by Russian investigative journalists and academics, I conclude that although the data are not without their faults, they offer a reliable, and ultimately the best, window into company ownership and performance since 2000.

[68] Großer, Reuben, and Tymula (2013); Snyder Jr (1992).

[69] Gordon, Hafer, and Landa (2007).

groups approach the trade-offs involved with choosing between multiple strategies within the "political investment portfolio,"[70] not just by analyzing the resources and availability of each route into politics, but also the probability that a politician follows through on his or her end of the bargain. This book shows how commitment problems inherent to interest group politics can lead to greater interest in more direct strategies, particularly businessperson candidacy.

Once in office, businesspeople take advantage of their direct access to policymaking to reshape political institutions to fit their own narrow interests. This book shows that concerns about businessperson politicians carrying conflict of interests are far from unfounded: their elected authority offers opportunities to enact discretionary policies that direct public monies and rents to private firms. Even though individual rent-seeking may decline when many businesspeople take office, collectively these officials still push for outcomes of shared interest to the business community. This variant of rent-seeking behavior can cause serious distortions for economic growth, perhaps more than politicians simply using public office to increase their personal wealth.[71] Recent work has questioned whether direct strategies of achieving political access pay off for the bottom line.[72] By expanding the scope of the analysis beyond ultra-wealthy oligarchs, this book presents causally identified evidence that businessperson candidacy is a lucrative and effective non-market strategy. Businesspeople in office are able to reengineer budgets and deficit spending to fit their own priorities, rather than cater to constituents.

Elections are supposed to prevent this very scenario from happening. When politicians fear being voted out of office, they may more closely conform their decisions to the policy preferences of voters. Yet recent work has argued that understanding the degree to which politicians represent the views of their constituents also requires paying attention to their "personal roots of representation."[73] That is, politicians' behavior often depends on their personality, family history, work experience, and self-interest. The results shown here build on this existing literature to show how leaders' actions depends on not just on their education, race, gender, or social class,[74] but importantly their occupational background

70 Schneider (2012).
71 Querubin and Snyder Jr (2011); Fisman, Schulz, and Vig (2012); Eggers and Hainmueller (2009).
72 Markus and Charnysh (2017).
73 Burden (2007).
74 Besley, Montalvo, and Reynal-Querol (2011); Hopkins and McCabe (2012); Chattopadhyay and Duflo (2004); Carnes (2012).

in the private sector. In contrast to a wealth of work drawing on correlational analysis and matching methods,[75] the book uses a series of causal identification strategies to demonstrate that a career in the private sector can produce dramatic effects on politician behavior and ultimately political outcomes. By electing businesspeople to office, voters increase the probability of policies designed to benefit the business community, without making government run more efficiently.

The politically connected firms that reap these rewards earn their place not based on their market success or productivity, but on the ability of their directors to win popular elections. As such, elections directly determine economic winners and losers. Scholars and policymakers alike often lament the pernicious effects of "state capture,"[76] whereby firms exert undue influence over government. Rather than only analyzing consequences, this book illustrates how powerful firms actually orchestrate the takeover of executive and legislative branches, resulting in an oligarchic form of rule where business representation can squeeze out other groups in society. The cohesive preferences and outcomes achieved by businesspeople are even more impressive considering the heterogeneous set of industries and financial interests they represent. In line with work on the United States,[77] this book finds that different types of governing institutions do little to affect how businessperson mayors and legislators affect policy.

In that regard, the findings speak to current debates about economic underpinnings of political regimes, especially where democracy has not completely taken root.[78] Neo-institutional explanations of the durability of nondemocratic regimes have grown in popularity as of late in comparative politics.[79] Much work has focused on how and why some authoritarian governments sanction nominally democratic institutions such as legislatures and political parties in order to extend their hold on power.[80]

However, the actual individuals and their economic interests who populate these political institutions often are sidelined from analysis. Indeed as Samuel Huntington wrote, "the main threat to an authoritarian regime is the diversification of the elite resulting from the rise of new groups controlling autonomous sources of economy power, that is from the

[75] Witko and Friedman (2008); Dreher et al. (2009); Carnes (2013, 2018).
[76] Hellman, Jones, and Kaufmann (2003); Hertel-Fernandez (2019).
[77] Tausanovitch and Warshaw (2014); de Benedictis-Kessner and Warshaw (2016).
[78] Haber (2006); Pepinsky (2009).
[79] Gandhi (2008); Magaloni (2006); Svolik (2012); Gehlbach and Keefer (2012).
[80] Brancati (2014).

development of an independently wealthy business and industrial middle class."[81] Indeed, the most significant challenges to modern authoritarian regimes come precisely from economic elites that use their sizable resources to defect.[82]

Understanding why some regimes persist and others break down requires looking at how well integrated powerful economic elites are into government processes. This book shifts the focus back exactly to why these individuals actually join and legitimate "black box" institutions such as legislatures in the first place: their motivations, payoffs, and governing capabilities. One clear reason is the financial benefits. I provide causal evidence that institutions such as elections and legislatures govern rent distribution among elites from across the political spectrum.[83] These transfers enable ruling parties to both retain the loyalty of their members as well as co-opt other groups within society.[84] Moreover, other institutions such as electoral rules shape how businesspeople approach candidacy and achieve political autonomy within legislatures to push for their narrow aims. By utilizing the natural experiment of close elections, I show that institutions are not epiphenomenal to larger societal dynamics,[85] but instead can have independent effects on the behavior of elites and interest groups.

Given the risk of businesspeople co-opting legislatures, policymakers may want to regulate the entry of individuals such as businesspeople who have clear conflicts of interests affecting their decision making. The overarching goal behind such efforts is to shape political selection and attract "good types" of candidates to office, without imposing excessive barriers to entry. Businesspeople do have much to offer for governance. They possess valuable expertise about economic issues and can make important contributions to improving the way government works. Which policies best balance this trade-off between attracting qualified, skilled businesspeople to enter government, but also curbing their ability to misuse their office for their own self-interest?

The book's conclusion ends with an extended discussion of the mechanisms and feasibility behind several different options. First, governments need to erect strict limitations on what activities businesspeople engage

[81] Huntington (1970, p. 20).
[82] Arriola (2012); Junisbai (2012).
[83] Blaydes (2011); Gandhi and Lust-Okar (2009).
[84] Reuter and Turovsky (2014); Reuter and Robertson (2015).
[85] Pepinsky (2014).

in while serving in office. Incompatibility rules limit the degree conflicts of interest (and time) can corrupt policymaking. At a minimum, no government officials should be allowed to simultaneously hold positions in the private and public sectors, and must recuse themselves from any government roles that regulate their former businesses. In the same vein, cross-national evidence suggests that requiring officials to fully divest from their businesses is impractical and leads to a shrinking pool of businesspeople willing to serve in government. Although selling stakes in firms that present obvious conflicts of interest must still be made mandatory, forcing candidates from the private sector to part with all of their investments would significantly disincentivize their participation. Instead, the operative principles must be full transparency and vetting. Effectively monitoring and preventing conflicts of interest demands that businessperson disclose complete information about their personal assets and firm performance while serving in government.

1

A Theory of Businessperson Candidacy

Many strategies are available for firms to build political influence. They can make contributions to political campaigns, lobby elected officials to get their voices heard, or in weak institutional settings, even buy laws directly from politicians. Why then would a businessperson run for political office, when so many less expensive (and potentially just as influential) avenues are available? This chapter develops an original theory to address this puzzle. I begin by outlining the various strategies firms employ in the political arena, drawing a distinction between *indirect* strategies (where politicians act as intermediaries in representing firms) and *direct* strategies (where politicians are employees of the firm). I then introduce and explore how businessperson candidacy, an often overlooked example of the *direct* strategy variety, functions in practice. Having a firm director run for office produces an unparalleled set of political benefits but with significant financial and time-related costs.

Firms face tough decisions about which of these strategies to choose. Although cheaper and more accessible, indirect strategies such as lobbying and campaign contributions provide no guarantee that the politician targeted will not renege on the bargain and cease representing a firm's interests. Standard solutions to solving this type of credible commitment problem in market settings, such as contracts, repeated interactions, or reputation, often fail to gain traction in the political arena. Even empowering the median voter – by strengthening democracy and electoral accountability – fails to ensure that politicians will stick to the promises they make, whether they be to interest groups or constituents as a whole.

Running for elected office helps solve this commitment problem. By removing the need for political intermediaries, businessperson candidacy best aligns the incentives between active politicians and firm management. Sending a director to work in government exemplifies an in-house solution to achieving political access that mitigates agency loss, a way to vertically integrate corporate political activity. When businesspeople fear that an elected politician will shirk on their promises to special interests, directly occupying a legislative seat becomes a more viable legal avenue to achieve political influence.

This logic holds that we should see a greater incidence of businessperson candidacy when the risk of politician shirking increases. This chapter then derives testable hypotheses to identify the conditions under which firms face the greatest level of uncertainty about the trustworthiness of their politicians. First, I argue that greater economic competition increases the likelihood that rival firms will make competing offers and undermine the effectiveness of indirect strategies. Businesspeople run for office in response to perceived threats from other large competitors that can persuade politicians to defect from other agreements. The drive to place directors in elected office at times resembles an arms race: firms fear their rivals gaining clearcut advantages through their own direct representation and match their entry into elections. Businessperson candidacy becomes a best response to other firms using the same strategy.

Second, strong political parties discipline shirking by legislators and ensure that exchanges between interest groups and politicians are enforced. When parties are weak, businessperson candidacy gains appeal as an effective means to circumvent unreliable, unconstrained politicians. Finally, businesspeople must also pay sizable costs in order to win electoral campaigns. Firms with larger financial assets and workforces can afford paying the cost of running for office, as can those located in poorer regions where the expenditures required to build voter support and win elections are lower. Although ego motivations and personal characteristics certainly drive some powerful businesspeople to seek office, the overarching concern in running for office stems from a need to protect firm political interests. Holding elected office only becomes an attractive corporate political strategy when more conventional avenues lose their efficacy and provide little payoff for a firm's bottom line.

1.1 INDIRECT STRATEGIES: POLITICAL ACCESS THROUGH INTERMEDIARIES

Two types of strategies have historically dominated academic studies on corporate political activity: making campaign contributions and lobbying officials.[1] That focus is not unwarranted. The sums of money devoted to both are simply enormous. Lobbying expenditures in the United States regularly exceed $2 billion every year,[2] while interest group activity in Europe[3] and China[4] does not lag too far behind. In countries that allow private financing of elections, total campaign contributions can reach into the billions.[5] Firms considering the decision to engage in politics often begin by considering these two approaches.[6]

Both are examples of what I term *indirect* corporate political strategies. Firms contribute money, information, and votes to politicians in exchange for access and influence.[7] The politician then becomes an intermediary and advocates on the firm's (or interest group's) behalf to secure desired policies. The key point, discussed in full in the next section, is that indirect strategies involve firms delegating representation to a third party. Within the standard principal–agent framework, firms act as principals who commission politicians to work on their behalf as agents.

1 Coen, Grant, and Wilson (2012).

2 Drutman (2015*b*).

3 Recent estimates on lobbying the European parliament suggest that €1 billion is now being spent on over 30,000 lobbyists. (Traynor 2014).

4 Thousands of trade associations now vie for political influence at all levels of the Chinese government (Kennedy, 2009).

5 It is not just the United States that is experiencing huge amounts of money flowing into elections. Countries in the developing world such as Kenya, India, and Indonesia have seen a stupendous increase in campaign expenditures, largely financed through corporate donations (Quraishi and Van Der Staak 2015, Latif Dahir 2017).

6 Markus and Charnysh (2017) describe a somewhat wider array of strategies available to the politically interested ultra-rich: for example, bankrolling political parties and acquiring media outlets. Since the median firm director in most countries cannot afford these expenditures, this chapter narrows the discussion of indirect strategies to those more economically feasible.

7 See Hillman and Hitt (1999). A fine line exists between indirect strategies and outright bribery. For example, Harstad and Svensson (2011) view the two as substitutable, contingent on the level of development and enforcement in a country. Though legal in most countries, indirect strategies are often strictly regulated. Firms are restricted with regards to the type and amount of contributions that can be made (Norris and Van Es, 2016), and must report their contacts with politicians to try and allay concerns that interest groups and politicians are engaged in corruption.

1.1.1 Campaign Contributions

The first indirect strategy involves firms providing donations to candidates' campaign war chests. Winning and holding elected office often depends on one's ability to raise resources from private companies.[8] This may be especially true in countries with less programmatic competition between political blocs, where large amounts of cash are needed to directly buy off voters. Campaign contributions can take multiple forms. Financial donations help campaigns buy advertising, pay staff, and distribute materials. Firms can also mobilize their employees to vote in favor of candidates and parties.[9]

Firms often expect a return on their political investment once their targeted politician wins elected office. Donating to campaigns is thought to benefit firms in several ways. The most cynical of readings holds that companies can directly exchange contributions for policy through a quid pro quo. Politicians offer legislation, regulations, or state-backed financial instruments in exchange for resources they can use to get (re)elected.[10] Although early work pushed back against the idea that money can buy policy,[11] increasingly sophisticated research designs suggest that the appeal of entering a quid pro quo relationship often motivates firms to donate to campaigns. Evidence from Brazil and Russia demonstrates that contributing firms enjoy greater access to state contracts and preferential finance.[12] Investors also appear to reward contributing firms by inflating their stock price in anticipation of future political benefits.[13]

Although Russian law allows both individuals and firms to donate within limits as long as contributions are reported, Barsukova and Zvyagintsev (2006) document massive sums of illicit money funneled to candidates from firms looking to make a "political investment" in policy. Another view holds that firms donate money to ensure consistent access to politicians. They may not receive any concrete benefits but can hedge against the possibility of unfavorable policies and defend their domain against threats from rivals or even the government.[14] But either way, firms do not make contributions altruistically: justifying this

[8] Snyder Jr (1990); Grier, Munger, and Roberts (1994).
[9] Frye, Reuter, and Szakonyi (2014, 2019); Hertel-Fernandez (2017).
[10] McMenamin (2012).
[11] Ansolabehere, Snyder Jr, and Ueda (2004).
[12] Boas, Hidalgo, and Richardson (2014); Mironov and Zhuravskaya (2016); Claessens, Feijen, and Laeven (2008).
[13] Cooper, Gulen, and Ovtchinnikov (2010).
[14] Baysinger (1984).

type of expenditures to shareholders requires a reasonable expectation of receiving something in return.

1.1.2 Lobbying

After elections have been decided, firms mostly move onto the second type of *indirect* strategy: lobbying. At least in the United States, the resources spent on lobbying governments generally dwarf those spent through campaign contributions.[15] Drutman (2015*a*) reports an 85 percent increase in money spent on US lobbyists during the 2000s, reaching over $2 billion by 2010. Firms account for three-quarters of that spending, exceeding the money they donated to campaigns by a factor of twelve.

Why is lobbying often more appealing for so many firms? First, whereas contributions help lawmakers fund their campaigns, lobbying provides a resource perhaps more essential and influential during the actual policymaking process: information. Lobbyists perform important research functions for legislators, helping them understand and evaluate the political and economic consequences of proposed legislation.[16] Lobbying also takes place behind closed doors, and even with some countries requiring documentation of contacts with politicians, the public rarely finds out about the content of those meetings. Perhaps most importantly, lobbying comes with less uncertainty: firms can be sure that the politician they are investing in has real political clout, as opposed to supporting a candidate who has yet to take office.

Lobbying can take a variety of forms. Larger companies look to develop in-house capacity, taking on government relations experts to work full-time to promote their interests. Companies with fewer resources outsource lobbying to professional teams.[17] Finally, some firms band together into trade associations that pool their resources and present a unified voice on behalf of an industry or the greater business community.[18] Very few countries impose limits on the amount of resources that can be spent on generating the policy-relevant information that most lobbyists provide. This can lead to extraordinary sums being pumped into the policymaking process.

[15] Milyo, Primo, and Groseclose (2000).
[16] Hall and Deardorff (2006); Nownes (2013).
[17] Drutman (2015*a*).
[18] Coen, Grant, and Wilson (2012).

Firms absorb the costs of lobbying because it helps their bottom line.[19] US firms have had notable success achieving policy aims by lobbying the government individually.[20] Benefits include lower taxes, bailouts, favorable energy regulations, and preferential labor policies.[21] Lobbying through associations also helps companies learn about rivals who participate in the same organizations.

Russian firms similarly look to lobbying as an effective strategy to build influence. Even without official legislation to sanction and regulate lobbying, firms openly engage politicians over the drafting of travel regulations, car sales, and fertilizer taxes in the State Duma, Russia's national parliament.[22] A recent investigative piece by Meduza, an independent media outlet, describes "armies of fixers" descending on Duma deputies and ministry officials to push for their corporate financiers' interests.[23] Powerful firms, such as those working in agriculture and natural resources, have won substantial individual concessions in recent years on the back of government relations strategies. Many firms also lobby at lower levels of government, noting in surveys that such activism can yield important policy dividends.[24] For example, roughly 17 percent of firms from eight cities across Russia answered that they "sometimes" or "always" were able to influence legislation at the regional level.[25] Indirect strategies hold general appeal among Russian firms, even if the precise regulations governing them are somewhat underdeveloped.

In these contexts, firms can cultivate an array of clientelistic relationships, whereby lawmakers come to depend on special interests for information, expertise, and sometimes even financial assistance to govern effectively. Japan's dalliance with the "iron triangle" of political parties, bureaucrats, and large corporations exemplifies this type of mutually supportive, interlocking relationship.[26] The friendly policy climate that emerges can prove to be a much larger, more sustained boon for firm interests than one-off transactions about specific needs.

This somewhat ideal type of business–government relations presupposes the existence of numerous factors conducive to cooperation

[19] Hill et al. (2013).
[20] Gordon and Hafer (2007).
[21] Richter, Samphantharak, and Timmons (2009); Blau, Brough, and Thomas (2013); Kang (2015); Facchini, Mayda, and Mishra (2011).
[22] Denisov (2010).
[23] Bekbulatova (2018).
[24] Reuter and Turovsky (2014); Marques, Govorun, and Pyle (2014).
[25] Frye (2002).
[26] Johnson (1982); Colignon and Usui (2001).

between such disparate actors. For one, policymakers must be willing to extend a "helping hand" to business actors, rather than a "grabbing hand."[27] In countries such as Russia, this assumption should not be taken lightly, as business has much to fear from a newly resurgent, predatory set of government officials, bent on rent-seeking more than promoting economic growth.[28] There is no shortage of surveys and anecdotes demonstrating the difficulties Russian businesses face in negotiating with state actors on equal terms.[29] Building such mutually beneficial ties requires leverage, something in short supply among firms not deeply embedded in official networks. Below, I discuss in much greater detail why firms are just as often taken advantage by policymakers as helped by them.

Finally, though many firms employ professional lobbyists to build political inroads, many directors express an often healthy degree of skepticism about the difference between lobbying and bribery. A survey of 153 experts in Tula Oblast in 2008 uncovered that the majority viewed lobbying public officials as a type of corruption and thus often very negatively.[30] Pushing one's personal financial interests through intermediaries behind the scenes, no matter whether money was exchanged, acquires a shadowy overtone and can carry both reputation and legal risks.

1.2 DIRECT STRATEGIES

Firms also can opt to forgo the use of political intermediaries. In contrast to lobbying and making contributions, *direct* political strategies cut out the middleman by blurring, and in many instances erasing, the line between the politician and the firm. The goal behind direct strategies is to better align incentives between the two actors. When politicians become employees of the firm (or at a minimum financially invested), they benefit monetarily when the firm's performance excels.

1.2.1 Bringing Politicians On Board

Direct strategies generally come in several forms. First, current politicians may be invited to become employees or shareholders of the firm.

[27] Frye and Shleifer (1997).
[28] Rochlitz (2014); Yakovlev, Sobolev, and Kazun (2014); Kazun (2015).
[29] Frye, Yakovlev, and Yasin (2009).
[30] Murashhenkov (2009).

They might be appointed onto the board of directors, be offered ownership stakes, or brought on as informal consultants or advisors. Political connections constructed this way are widespread across a number of different contexts. Using a sample of forty-seven countries, Faccio (2006) estimates that approximately 3 percent of firms have some kind of connection to politicians. The hiring of current politicians is not limited to places with weak legal environments, as scholars have identified strong political ties among firms in Spain, Australia, and the United States.[31]

A growing body of literature shows that firms benefit immensely from taking on board active politicians. First, connected firms command superior information about the policymaking process, allowing them to better shape their engagement and anticipate future political action that could affect their activities.[32] Perhaps more importantly, connected firms acquire powerful actors on the inside to act as their de facto lobbyists. Below I go into greater detail about the many levers politicians can pull to help firms. But on the whole, this type of relationship-building seems to generate a row of positive returns for firms, from improved access to state contracts, a lower cost of capital, and overall better operating returns.[33]

But offering current politicians a seat at the firm's table can also backfire. Political connections can undermine a firm's competitiveness, investment behavior, and ability to innovate.[34] Politicians may not have the human capital or experience necessary to make the best decisions for firm interests. Ties are being built where none existed before, necessitating a steep learning curve on both sides and, possibly, costly negotiations. Since buying off politicians with firm management roles is illegal, politicians may require substantial contributions from firms to take the risk, and may threaten to withhold their influence if firms do not pay up. Given their superior bargaining position, they can more easily extract resources and engage in rent-seeking.[35] Developing ties with current politicians is by no means a silver-bullet political strategy. Firms have much to lose by bringing unknown outsiders into the fold.

[31] Pérez, Sánchez, and Martín (2015); Gray, Harymawan, and Nowland (2016); Faccio, Masulis, and McConnell (2006).

[32] Hillman (2005).

[33] Goldman, Rocholl, and So (2013); Khwaja and Mian (2005); Boubakri et al. (2012); Amore and Bennedsen (2013); Li, Poppo, and Zhou (2008).

[34] Desai and Olofsgard (2008).

[35] Faccio, Masulis, and McConnell (2006).

Political connections can also be formed by hiring former politicians. Many countries around the world have rich traditions of powerful officials easily landing lucrative post-public employment in the private sector upon leaving their government work.[36] In Japan, the word *amakudari*, or "descent from heaven," describes the time-honored practice of civil servants finding their way to jobs in large corporations, or for smaller players, the many upstream suppliers within the production chain.[37] Their knowledge of the policymaking process and contacts with current regulators are incredibly beneficial for companies seeking political access. Other noted variants of the practice include the *pantouflage* system in France (literally translated as "shuffling wearing indoor slippers"), which customarily works through school and university connections,[38] and "parachute appointments" (*nak-ha-san-in-sa*) in South Korea, the highly politicized positioning of politicians and bureaucrats into corporations.[39]

These "revolving door" mechanisms, whereby ex-civil servants join both private and public companies, still rely on intermediaries, albeit fewer in number, to get policies done. As well-connected and capable as these formal officials may be, they still have to work through currently serving politicians to achieve any real policy aims. And again, companies that provide such golden parachutes, such as Japanese banks offering soft landings for officials from the Ministry of Finance and Bank of Japan, were saddled with more non-performing loans.[40] The assignment of former bureaucrats to private companies is also managed top-down by government officials hoping to save troubled firms; evidence suggests the arrival of such political connections may do little to right the ship and correct bad firm performance.[41] In Russia, Rastorguyev (2014) finds that officials are much more likely to be placed in state-owned enterprises, such as those operating in the natural resources and defense sectors, than they are in the private sector. Private firms have to rely on other avenues to build political capital.

[36] Makkai and Braithwaite (1992); Gormley Jr (1979); Palmer and Schneer (2016).
[37] Calder (1989); Mizoguchi and Van Quyen (2012).
[38] Savage (1974).
[39] Lee and Rhyu (2008).
[40] Horiuchi and Shimizu (2001).
[41] Yu and Main (2012).

1.2.2 Becoming Bureaucrats

Besides bringing outside politicians on board, firms may take a spin at the "reverse revolving door" and send their own employees to become bureaucrats within the executive branch.[42] Winning appointments helps builds direct representation within the bureaucracy, allowing the company to get firsthand input in how regulations are drafted and implemented. Over the last decade, activist shareholders such as the AFL-CIO have worked hard to expose the practice of big banks, such as Goldman Sachs, Citi, and Morgan Stanley, lavishing multimillion dollar bonuses on employees who enter government service.[43] US tax law may have even incentivized the practice by allowing employees to hold onto their vested stock options after leaving their firms if they choose to enter government service. Defense contractors such as Northrop Grumman have been found to engage in similar incentive schemes.[44] Company insiders take up new work at any number of government positions, from bankers becoming industry regulators in the United States[45] or taking top policymaking positions in Latin America and Southeast Asia.[46]

Placing employees inside the bureaucracy is no easy task. Arguments that businesspeople merit civil service appointments can often fall on deaf ears, especially under left-leaning governments or in settings where political control over the bureaucracy overrules bringing in certain private sector expertise or management skills. Many countries also employ complex meritocratic recruitment systems that narrow the range of positions open to private sector employees who have not passed required examinations and put in their time in government.

In the case of Russia, private companies have been thwarted as of late in their attempts to stock bureaucracies with their own representatives. One of the main centralizing reforms instituted during President Putin's first two terms in office involved the cancellation of gubernatorial elections. Beginning in 2004, the top-level regional executives, or governors, were instead appointed by Moscow. In one fell swoop, the federal center acquired immense authority to dictate who got what positions, often opting for non-ideological candidates who toed the party line rather than

42 Li and Liang (2015); Ferguson and Voth (2008).
43 Dayen (2015).
44 Fang (2013).
45 Brezis and Cariolle (2019).
46 Bowornwathana (2004); Phongpaichit and Baker (2004); Schneider (2010).

promote special interests. Barsukova (2011) writes that the new appointments were intended to demonstrate "who's the boss" to leading financial groups in the regions. Many of these groups lost their roles as puppeteers over the executive branch and many doors into key regulatory agencies were simply slammed shut.[47] Businesspeople were forced to look to other avenues to maintain their political influence, including financing campaigns to regional and municipal legislatures.[48]

Data from the Russian regions support this story about business tending to stay away from the bureaucracy. Buckley and Reuter (2019) collect data on all 2,790 vice-governors serving in Russia's regions between 2001 and 2012, including their occupational and educational background. Vice governors are powerful bureaucrats directly appointed by the governor, with responsibilities for key policy portfolios such as construction, housing, economic planning, healthcare, and education. Given their power to sign executive orders and oversee policy implementation, one might expect them to be prime targets of business lobbying, and where opportunities arise, for these roles to be actually filled by representatives of leading companies. A simple exercise to code their previous place of work before taking office uncovers that only 238 (or 8.5 percent) of these bureaucrats had come directly from the private sector.[49] The vast majority had worked at lower level administrative bodies, such as mayor's offices and specific departments. As influential as these positions may be, securing them may be more difficult than expected.

1.2.3 Businessperson Candidacy

The final *direct* strategy, businessperson candidacy, is this book's main object of study. Businessperson candidacy denotes the practice of firms sending their own high-level employees (directors, trusted managers, or members of the board of directors) to contest elections and win positions within political institutions.[50] Over the last two decades alone, active

47 Grashhenkov and Mejer (2016).

48 Medvedev (2010); Barsukova (2006).

49 I coded whether they had worked as a director or deputy director, or on the board of directors (either as chairperson or as a regular member) of a private or state-owned enterprise in their last place of work, according to official biographies or other public sources.

50 At times, the decision to develop the political connection lies with the government, and not the firm. Beginning in the late 1990s, the Chinese government has embarked on a comprehensive strategy of inviting entrepreneurs to join the Chinese Communist Party; the connected firms then prosper from newfound political ties (Han, 2007; Dickson,

businesspeople have run for top executive roles at the national level in countless places, winning elections in Ukraine, Finland, Argentina, Italy, Thailand, and the United States.

This book focuses much of its attention on businesspeople who vie for positions in the legislative branch. Businesspeople abound in legislative institutions. Chaisty (2013) documents that nearly half of deputies in the Russian State Duma worked previously in the private sector; formally these leaders are supposed to step back from their business empires upon taking office, but few do in reality. In China, a full 20 percent of the 11th National People's Congress (2008–2012) are chairmen or CEOs of various companies.[51] At lower levels, surveys of entrepreneurs found that 17 percent of respondents were members of People's Congresses and 35 percent were members of the Chinese People's Political Consultative Conference, a body similar to a regional advisory legislative house.[52]

Winning a spot in a legislature also offers several advantages over developing connections within the bureaucracy. Legislators draft key economic policies, whereas bureaucrats interpret and implement them.[53] Appointments to executive branch positions also can be fewer in number (compared to seats in a legislature) and often hinge more on one's ability to govern rather than win over voters. Assuming responsibility for an entire administration also places much greater governing demands on businessperson politicians. Businesspeople take on full-time roles as policymakers, while many countries permit legislators to earn outside income and combine their legislative duties with other types of employment. Many high-level appointed positions may not be attractive for firm interests, especially if executives take on responsibility for foreign policy or areas less interesting to the business community.[54]

2007). We might expect that in more authoritarian regimes, the decision (and opportunity) to pursue public office comes down from top rather than from the bottom up. But many competitive authoritarian regimes encourage self-motivated competition among elites for legislative office (Blaydes, 2011). A key precondition for businessperson candidacy then is somewhat free access to the ballot, and accordingly a reasonable chance at winning elections. In the Conclusion, I go into greater depth about the types of political regimes where we would expect businessperson candidacy to hold greater appeal.

51 Truex (2014).

52 Li, Meng, and Zhang (2006). See also Hou (2019) for work on this topic.

53 Naoi and Krauss (2009); Macher and Mayo (2015).

54 The level of government also may matter. In Chapter 6, I show evidence from municipalities in Russia that many of the same dynamics surrounding businesspeople in legislative office hold for those seeking to become mayor. See that chapter for more detailed discussion of the differences between businesspeople serving in the two branches.

How Businessperson Candidacy Helps Firms

The decision to send firm representatives into a legislature differs markedly from the other direct and indirect strategies discussed above. Anecdotal evidence from Russia paints an illuminating picture of just how powerful a seat in a legislature can be. First, when businesspeople personally occupy political positions, they enjoy unmatched ability to shape policy decisions. Businessperson deputies can draft laws to benefit their businesses and push through favorable sectoral regulations and legislation.[55] Budget allocations, public investment decisions and economic development programs require approval of regional legislatures in Russia, who also enjoy the right to set several key tax rates, establish firm-specific loan guarantees and privatize state assets.[56] Laws that serve narrow firm interests can easily be justified on the grounds that they "possess important social-economic significance for one's district."[57] Deputy status also helps protect against legislation that "could raise their taxes, tie them in red tape, or threaten their property rights."[58] Of particular interest is access to state contracts which provide a much more guaranteed source of revenue with an enforceable source of revenue.[59] Business leaders often run for office "attracted by opportunities to gather information about upcoming government decisions," with electoral success becoming a matter of "life or death" for local oligarchs.[60] Legislative seats start to resemble a political "insurance policy" taken to ensure a business kingdom remains solvent in the face of raids and threats.[61]

Much of a legislative's direct policymaking influence in Russia revolves around committee life. The majority of a bill's life is spent under careful discussion in commissions and committees that deputies are required to attend.[62] Throughout this work, committee chairpeople play the most prominent role, holding the power to call and lead meetings, distribute information and materials, provide patronage through jobs and mandates, and invite experts and interest groups to testify, among other activities. Given their high status, these positions are one of the main

[55] Mereu (2003).
[56] Medvedev (2010).
[57] Chistyakova (2005).
[58] Bush (2003).
[59] Sakaeva (2014).
[60] Medvedev (2010, 8).
[61] Interview with Petr Panov, political scientist, Perm. October 3, 2013.
[62] Molokaeva (2014).

avenues for securing spoils and perks.[63] If an interest group wants to exert influence on a specific political issue, then getting a seat at the committee table, or at a minimum the attention of its members, is paramount.

Perhaps unsurprisingly, businessperson deputies in Russia gravitate to committees that oversee and regulate policy areas of interest to their firms. Using data on committee chairpeople and vice-speakers from Reuter and Robertson (2015), I find that 43 percent of the deputies holding these positions were businesspeople.[64] These numbers rise when certain policy areas come into focus. Businessperson deputies chair 49 percent of budget committees, 56 percent of committees overseeing industrial policy, 63 percent of committees overseeing economic development, and 65 percent of committees overseeing agriculture. Compare those figures to health care committees, where only 10 percent of chairpeople come from the private sector. Businesspeople make their legislative presence felt most by controlling the levers of how laws are passed.

Deputy Requests

The most powerful weapon in an average legislator's arsenal is perhaps not one's vote on the floor, but the use of the deputy request ("*deputatskiy zapros*"). In both regional legislatures and the State Duma, deputies have the right to secretly forward appeals to officials that demand inspections, information, audits, and even sanctions for both public and private sector entities. For opposition deputies whose vote on legislation may not count for much under ruling party dominance, deputy requests bestow incredible legal authority regardless of party membership. Such requests are not uncommon in legislatures worldwide, having been studied, for example, in Ukraine and Belgium.[65]

For businesspeople politicians, deputy requests provide a multitude of opportunities to promote their firms' interests. By providing official cover to communicate with bureaucrats, a deputy request can "inform officials about certain 'shady' activities of rival firms"[66] and trigger regulatory

[63] Reuter and Robertson (2015).

[64] Here again I code a businessperson as a director or deputy director, or on the board of directors (either as chairperson or as a regular member) of a private or state-owned enterprise. For more information on methodology, see Chapter 2 and the Appendix.

[65] Herron and Boyko (2015); Baumgartner et al. (2009).

[66] Dmitriev (2009).

inspections. This type of pressure can make life miserable for a competitor, ranging from increased compliance costs to losing one's business outright to rapacious bureaucrats who smell blood in the water. According to one official in the Russian Ministry of Internal Affairs, "not one large-scale corporate conflict that saw the participation of law enforcement officials went through without the use of a deputy request... if there's no real reason to intervene in a conflict, then a request that obligates officials to respond to its contents offers such an opportunity."[67]

In addition, a deputy "can request any information about any topic from any government agency as long as it falls within the competence of that body."[68] This can provide advantages in winning state contracts as well as numerous advantages in timing investments according to policy changes.[69] In fact, several major scandals in Russian politics since 2000 have in part been initiated by deputy requests. In 2004, State Deputy Vladimir Yudin sent a request to the Prosecutor General's office to verify the privatization of OAO Apatit. Soon after, the head of Menatep Group Platon Lebedev was arrested, marking the beginning of the famous Yukos affair that brought down Mikhail Khodorkovsky.[70] At the regional level, a complaint filed by a Saint Petersburg regional deputy in 2017 led to fire safety violations being found at the European University of Saint Petersburg (EUSP) and later contributed to the removal of the university's license to operate.

Deputy requests are big business in Russia. Sitting legislators regularly sell them to outsiders of all kinds, with bidding starting in the tens of thousands of dollars for regular appeals to the hundreds of thousands for phone calls placed personally to state officials or to key agencies, such as the Prosecutor General's office.[71] Deputies serving on prime committees can earn even more, sometime taking a 5–10 percent cut of the profit when firms stand to benefit directly from a request.[72]

At the federal level, deputy requests number can number in the hundreds per year per agency. Head of the Investigative Committee Alexander Bastrykin is on record several times complaining about the extra workload imposed by State Duma deputies, who abused his agency

[67] Vinogradov (2009).
[68] Kokoshkina (2018).
[69] Barova (2014).
[70] Vinogradov (2009).
[71] Barova (2014).
[72] Yekaterinaburg Online (2005).

with over 400 requests alone in the first half of 2009.[73] Officials face legal sanctions for not responding within specific time frames outlined by law, sometimes as short as seven days. Law enforcement officials cannot just look the other way, for fear of drawing attention to their neglect of ostensibly legitimate requests from elected officials. Whereas predatory agents can often undermine the ability of firms to collectively defend their interests through associations,[74] deputy requests skirt this issue by flipping the balance of power in favor of the businessperson politician. Bureaucrats become directly subordinate to deputies. As an extra sweetener, Russian law ensures that the vast majority of these requests remain classified from the general public.

Deputies openly attest to the importance of legislative seats opening doors to engage with powerful elites, in and out of government.[75] In an interview, a current businessperson deputy from Tomsk cited the importance of deputy requests in facilitating these interactions; he made valuable connections by mandating in-person meetings.[76] Regional deputies in Saint Petersburg painted a similar picture: "a deputy mandate is an admission ticket into practically any office, since deputies must be received."[77] Civil servants treat an elected deputy as one of their own, understanding that these lawmakers can invariably appeal to higher-up officials if bureaucratic obstacles are put in their way. Legislators also enjoy expanded social and networking opportunities to expand market foothold and secure new customers.[78] Put succinctly, Roland Nash, chief strategist at a leading investment firm in Moscow, remarked that businessperson candidacy is "the most powerful form of lobbying."[79]

Financial and Opportunity Costs of Running for Office

The potentially huge benefits of winning a deputy seat do not come without costs. In fact, running for office may also be the costliest of all political strategies available to firms. Becoming a politician requires

73 Dmitriev (2009).
74 Markus (2012).
75 Chazan (2000).
76 Interview with Vasiliy Semkin, businessman and deputy of Tomsk Regional Duma, Tomsk, Russia. June 11, 2014.
77 Sakaeva (2014, p. 155).
78 Chernokoz (2013).
79 Mereu (2003).

a massive amount of time and money. In many developing countries, businesspeople often must finance electoral campaigns entirely on their own, without party support.[80] Even in developed democracies, candidates must self-finance. A survey of candidates to national parliaments in eighteen countries found that 46 percent of all campaign expenditures were paid for using personal funds.[81] Connected firms often have to foot the bill.

Running for office in Russia is expensive. One estimate put the cost of winning a seat in a single-member district in the Omsk Regional Duma at $80,000–150,000 in 2002, before much of the real costs of campaigning (paying for advisors and buying television advertising time) began to skyrocket.[82] Securing a place on a party list can be even pricier. Political parties can charge at least $8–10 million for a spot on a federal Duma list and 5–7 million rubles ($160,00–$200,000) for a spot on a regional legislature list.[83] Mironov and Zhuravskaya (2016) examine shadow transfers around gubernatorial elections and find that firms transferred on average a total of $2.5 million to gubernatorial campaigns. The median firm in the data analyzed in the Chapter 2 earned roughly $250,000 in revenue per year during the same period; one electoral campaign would eat into much of that sum, to say nothing about profits.

Elections also carry considerable uncertainty, with spending more money providing no guarantee of victory in competitive races.[84] Politics can be contentious and vicious. Losing at the polls can hurt firms' reputations, especially if associated candidates took divisive or controversial stances in order to get elected. Finally, running for office is a very visible strategy that can attract unwanted negative attention, particularly if voters suspect that firms are attempting to capture the state for their own ends.[85]

The expenses do not end once the election is over. Once in office, a businessperson deputy must allocate time to political responsibilities,

80 Blaydes (2011); Lust (2009).
81 CCS (2015).
82 Barsukova and Zvyagintsev (2006).
83 Interview with Valeriy Otsipov, deputy of Tomsk Regional Duma, Tomsk, Russia. June 9, 2014.
84 Interview with Galina Nemsteva, deputy of Tomsk Regional Duma, Tomsk, Russia. June 10, 2014; Interview with Vasiliy Semkin, businessman and deputy of Tomsk Regional Duma, Tomsk, Russia. June 11, 2014.
85 Hansen and Mitchell (2000).

rather than focusing solely on managing firm operations.[86] During reelection campaigns, voters will evaluate politicians not according to firm performance (like shareholders would), but on their ability to deliver public goods and direct political attention to their constituencies. One deputy in Tomsk admitted that "being a deputy and a businessman at the same time is not easy"; the number of constituent requests for help, especially financial assistance, was a significant burden on his ability to run his firm.[87]. Political expert Ilya Zemin remarked that from the point of view of a deputy, "people come to your office hours with requests for help, and you can help them only by reaching into your own pocket. This can quickly become irritating."[88]

Firms may also need to make contributions mandated by the government in exchange for the elbow room to influence lawmaking. Winning a legislative seat puts a businessperson on the regional political radar, potentially opening him or her up to pressure from influential political elites. Businessperson politicians may enjoy added protection against some legal inquiries, but a seat in the legislature can actually make a firm more vulnerable to pressure from above to sponsor charity events, fund health care and education facilities, and provide discounted prices on goods and services for needy populations. And once connected firms start tapping into rent streams made possible by legislative access, state officials acquire powerful leverage through *kompromat*, or resources that can be used to blackmail. They can then bind the hands, and autonomy, of businessperson politicians, drawing them closer into the orbit of the regime and limiting their ability to strike independent business decisions. This diversion of time and resources from pure economic activities can easily surpass financial expenditures on lobbying or campaign contributions, making businessperson candidacy an especially resource-intensive strategy.

Direct strategies closely bind politicians to firms. Firms receive unfiltered access to policymaking and face markedly fewer obstacles to influencing government officials. These advantages carry their own set of significant costs, which affect the return on political investment. In Russia, if a firm director spends five million rubles on an electoral campaign, then he or she will want ten million rubles in return by the end of

[86] Geys and Mause (2013).
[87] Interview with Vasiliy Semkin, businessman and deputy of Tomsk Regional Duma, Tomsk, Russia. June 11, 2014.
[88] Dunaev (2015).

their term.[89] In the next section, I examine how firms manage the trade-off between the benefits of unhindered access to policymaking and the significant costs required to win and hold elected office.

1.3 HOW FIRMS CHOOSE BETWEEN INDIRECT AND DIRECT STRATEGIES

Firms in most countries, and Russia in particular, have their choice of strategy to pursue their political goals. As profit-maximizers, they gravitate towards those strategies that provide the best return on their investment.[90] Corporate political activity is plagued by uncertainty given the complexities and ambiguities inherent to the policymaking process.[91] As we will discuss in more detail below, many corporate political strategies run into insurmountable obstacles: lobbied politicians will fail to follow through on promises, politically connected board members hold firms hostage and impose extra burdens, and businesspeople lose elections. Firms look to minimize that uncertainty by adopting the most efficacious set of strategies. None of the strategies outlined above are mutually exclusive. Schneider (2012) has written of this menu of options through the framework of a "political investment portfolio." Businesses rationally select political strategies from an array of options, sometimes incorporating multiple approaches in case the preferred course of action fails to meet its objectives. Adopting multiple tactics can cement comprehensive access to the political arena as well as cover a wider variety of policymakers.[92]

However, each approach incurs a potentially expensive set of fixed and variable costs. The median firm will struggle to find the resources to simultaneously fund candidates, employ lobbyists, purchase deputy requests, and fund its own candidates to office. Resource constraints shape what firms can and cannot do in the political arena. Situating these trade-offs under scarcity improves our understanding of the comparative advantages (and drawbacks) of each type of corporate political

[89] Interview with Vasiliy Semkin, businessman and deputy of Tomsk Regional Duma, Tomsk, Russia. June 11, 2014; Interview with Vitalii Kovin, leader of Perm Golos organization, Perm, Russia. October 7, 2013.

[90] Porter (1980).

[91] Heinz (1993).

[92] Schuler, Rehbein, and Cramer (2002); Hadani (2007).

strategy.[93] To be more specific, the remainder of this chapter investigates the circumstances under which businesspeople decide that running for a spot in government eclipses other more conventional routes that could provide political influence, such as lobbying or making campaign contributions.

Part of this choice revolves around the specific political objectives a firm holds. For example, strategies vary in the level of access offered to policymakers. Campaign contributions are usually concentrated during the run-up to elections,[94] with firms making donations in expectation they will receive desirable policies over an entire term in office. The two direct strategies, developing political connections and running for office, similarly offer firms a more permanent foothold in politics, allowing them to periodically exert influence over the long-run. In contrast, lobbying happens on a more issue-specific basis. Firms decide when to engage politically and when to step back, without having made any lasting commitment to a single politician. Smaller firms may simply not be able to attract politicians to join their management or afford to run a candidate for office themselves. Below I explore how firm-specific characteristics shape which avenue they take.

But there also is room for more general theorizing about the tradeoffs between indirect and direct strategies. The key difference between the two is the use of the politician as an intermediary. Under the indirect approach, firms act as principals who engage politicians to work as agents on their behalf. Politicians accept contributions and promise to work towards a mutually agreed upon goal.

This relationship can be altogether precarious. Lobbying and making campaign contributions generate concerns that politicians fail to carry out their side of the deal. A firm may fear that a politician will simply take their donations and give back no political benefits in return. Interactions between firms and politicians suffer from this classic commitment problem plaguing similar principal-agent situations.[95] Morton and Cameron (1992, p. 89) argue that promises made by politicians are not binding: "the winning candidate may renege on her agreement to supply services following the election." Firms run a real risk of losing their investment completely. I argue that one of the key factors driving firms to adopt

93 Spiller and Liao (2006).
94 Krasno, Green, and Cowden (1994).
95 Miller (2005); Issacharoff and Ortiz (1999); Stephenson and Jackson (2010).

more direct strategies, and thus put forward directors for political office, is this "political market failure."[96]

1.3.1 Why do Politicians Shirk?

Why might politicians not follow through on their promises made to firms? The main reason involves intentional shirking. Politicians may choose not to represent firms, even after accepting contributions. Much of this is due to simple greed and criminal behavior. The litany of examples from the popular Russian press almost make one feel a dose of pity for businesspeople, who so often get taken advantage of during their efforts to bribe officials. A local restorer in Volgograd paid both a municipal deputy and FSB official for protection against raiding and for help winning a state tender; the two men stole his money and gave nothing in return.[97] The local entrepreneur association commented that this pattern of extortion and raiding by state officials was very common. In Tambov, a legislator took five million euros from a tobacco company, promising to help them out with resolving a large tax bill. The firm went to the police after it became clear the politicians never planned to execute his part of the deal.[98] A Kirov deputy tricked local businesspeople and citizens out of 500 million rubles ($17 million), and then secured international passports for his wife, son, father, and mother before disappearing completely.[99] Regular citizens also get burned by politicians: a deputy in Sverlodskaya Oblast promised a local felon he could get him a reduced sentence and spare him from prison time (his sentence ironically was also for engaging in extortion). After receiving 1.5 million rubles ($50,000), he simply stashed the cash away without taking any action.[100]

Oftentimes the deputies harass businesspeople to pay up for their services, particularly deputy requests. If businesspeople don't comply, these same requests can be used against them to create even bigger problems. A Krasnoyarsk deputy compelled a local businessman to pay the salaries

[96] See Hall and Deardorff (2006); McCarty and Rothenberg (1996); Snyder Jr (1992). Not all work treats the exchange as prone to failure. Some work argues that lobbying expenditures occur as part of a "spot-market transaction" for policy, similar to a retail market exchange, with implicitly binding contractual obligations in place (Gehlbach, Sonin, and Zhuravskaya, 2010). Politicians accept the highest bids for policy under a menu auction, and businessperson can rest assured that their money is well-spent.

[97] Tarakanova (2008).

[98] Sergeyev (2017).

[99] Novoselov and Lepina (2005).

[100] Pasmi.Ru (2017).

of three of his staff members on a charity project designed to improve his image in the run-up to regional legislative elections.[101] When the businessman refused to pay what would amount to 430 thousand rubles ($14,000), the politicians threatened to use deputy requests to trigger constant regulatory inspections and destroy the company. One of Russia's most famous female businesswomen, the "Queen of Chocolate" Irina Eldarkhanova, commented that "she was extorted out of several tens of thousands of dollars to cancel a court's decision" using deputy requests.[102] In Saint Petersburg, Regional Deputy Vyacheslav Notyag was arrested in 2016 for blackmailing a local firm director for cash in exchange for *not* using deputy requests to create problems for a local construction project.[103]

Greed can also drive politicians to exaggerate their influence within legislative bodies. Granted, some politicians lobbied to represent a firm's interests may sincerely run into obstacles securing the promised policy. Politicians may be new to the legislative process and not completely understand the difficulty of implementing what they have offered a firm.[104] These politicians faithfully, but ineffectively, perform their end of the deal.

However, a closer look at interactions between businesses and politicians in Russia uncovers an abundance of overselling, and ultimately many disappointed firms. In Smolensk, a deputy extorted a construction firm director out of 8 million rubles ($250,000); he didn't have the authority to grant the licenses promised in the deal. Similar machinations occurred in Tula, where a local deputy took $80,000 from a commercial firm in exchange for organizing the privatization of a state-owned enterprise.[105] Having been tipped off about the case, the local prosecutor commented that the deputy had no means to influence the process of privatization deals. Ruling party deputies, who presumably have the right connections, even get caught up in exaggerations. A United Russia deputy of the Bryansk regional legislature got four years in prison for taking 12 million rubles ($400,000) from five different citizens over the course of 2013–15: he took 7 million rubles from two entrepreneurs to organize a joint business project on newly acquired land, 2.8 million

[101] Takiye Delo (2018).
[102] Savkin (2009).
[103] Kokoshkina (2018).
[104] Lobbyists have been known to engage the wrong policymaker in pursuit of their clients' goals (Hillman, Keim, and Schuler, 2004).
[105] RIA Novosti (2005).

rubles from another entrepreneur for a discount in purchasing tractors and trucks, 1 million rubles from another resident to get him a job in the regional legislature, and 1.3 million rubles from another entrepreneur to whom he promised help getting a municipal contract.[106] In the end, he was not in any position to fulfill any of his promises. Extortion can sometimes even bring opposing political parties to work together. Two deputies representing different parties in the Vladivostok city council took 5 million rubles ($170,000) to help a businessperson get a contract signed by the city mayor. Neither had the authority to actually follow through.

The political goals firm pursue also suffer from a problem of ambiguity: defining successful policy interventions is not nearly as simple as the pursuit of a product market strategy.[107] Firms may be led to believe they are purchasing some concrete outcome, but wind up mired in the complexities and unpredictabilities of the policymaking world. Moreover, politicians (working as de facto lobbyists) have selfish incentives to obfuscate how much they have accomplished.[108] The more contributions they can attract, the better their chances of retaining their position in the short term.

Some shirking can also occur for political reasons. Privately a legislator might assure a firm that he or she is committed to pursuing some policy, but when push comes to shove, the firm's request generates conflicts with that legislator's larger political objectives. Politicians have their own preferences that can diverge from their clients and donors.[109] They may say and do things to get elected, knowing full well that they will not follow through later. Demands of special interests regularly conflict with those of politicians' constituents and party leader, both of whom hold sway over how long such officials can remain in office.[110] Firms already struggle to ensure their paid lobbyists faithfully represent their interests.[111] The risk of politicians, who face so many additional pressures, doing the same is even greater. This leads to an asymmetry in preferences between the principal and agent, increasing the rate of shirking.

106 Bryansk Today (2018).
107 Godwin, Godwin, and Ainsworth (2007); Lowery and Marchetti (2012).
108 Drutman (2015*a*).
109 Kersh (2000).
110 Stratmann (1998); Gilens and Page (2014); Hojnacki et al. (2015).
111 Ainsworth and Sened (1993); Lowery and Marchetti (2012).

In Russia, this often involves parties betraying the donors that got them into office once elections are won. Party leaders simply decide to go in a different political direction, and internal conflicts wind up leaving some sponsors in the dust. Take the case of the Communist Party in Ulyanovsk. Local businessman Mikhail Dolgov was a primary financier of the party's electoral success in the 2013 elections; he paid for the public relations efforts and electoral campaign in exchange for a seat in parliament.[112] Dolgov ultimately lost the game of musical chairs afterwards, being left without a mandate by the party he sponsored. In Perm, United Russia backed away from its promises to a prominent sponsor of the party's campaign, choosing a village schoolteacher instead to represent the region in Moscow.[113] The businessperson's shady practices were viewed as a liability for the party.

In Primorsky Krai, United Russia nearly fractured over the removal of several prominent financiers from so-called "*proxodyashiye mesta*," or spots on the closed party list that basically guaranteed candidates a seat in the legislature. The donors' anger spilled out into the public view, as they felt betrayed by party leaders.[114] As a member of the State Duma, Vyecheslav Volodin made himself few friends back in his native region of Saratov as well in 2007 by refusing to honor the results of primaries that gave victory to many businessperson sponsors of United Russia.[115] He preferred teachers, doctors, and high-level party officials, overruling the donors who had thrown their hefty financial support behind the party.

In other instances, a bargain may break down because politicians accept a higher outside offer from a firm's rival. Politicians are beholden to multiple constituents and receive competing offers from many interest groups.[116] If contributions are made under secret all-pay auctions, a firm cannot be sure that its campaign contributions or lobbying expenditures will not be matched or exceeded by a rival group.[117] A local businessperson from Saint Petersburg remarked that "a deputy, even one you finance, will never selflessly fight for your interests ... A deputy can get higher bribes from others or be intimidated at the end of the day."[118]

112 Udal'tsov (2015).
113 Interview with Aleksei Sokolov, journalist, Tomsk, Russia. June 11, 2014.
114 Chernyshev (2007).
115 Bocharova (2007).
116 Rosenthal (2001).
117 Naoi and Krauss (2009); Hall and Deardorff (2006).
118 As quoted on, Sakaeva (2016), p. 3.

Though larger contributions are theoretically presumed to increase the probability that a politician will implement the "bought" policy,[119] firms may be unaware of what their competitors are offering. By its very nature, lobbying happens behind closed doors, and few countries have strict legal regulations to publicize expenditures. Firms have little knowledge about a politician's true intended action and could be sinking money into a black hole.

My interviews in three Russian regions suggest that the trustworthiness of politicians is a pressing concern. Businesspeople often raised the issue of politicians betraying their promises to special interests, and explicitly linked their decision to run for office to deficiencies in representation. A local businessperson in Perm commented how lobbying was simply a waste of money, since lobbyists are not taken seriously, or respected, by politicians.[120] The deputy chairperson of that same parliament noted how paying money to one deputy would not get anything done; deputies rarely responded to their donors.[121] In Rostov region, firm directors took a greater interest in running for office in the mid-2000s as a result of deputies' "short memory": deputies were quickly and conveniently forgetting who had supported them and, unlike an employee, could not be simply fired from their position.[122] An opposition party leader in Perm commented that financial groups didn't trust outsiders or lobbyists to get anything done politically; they had to send their own representatives into power for the wheels to move.[123] The situation was similar in Tomsk where a director of a construction firm and elected deputy of the Tomsk Regional Duma remarked that businesses didn't trust politicians; promises can be suddenly broken and then the entire political investment would be lost.[124] Elected politicians are viewed as easily malleable, ready to renege on a deal if a better one comes along.

Broader analysis of business–government relations in Russia and beyond leads to similar conclusions. In a survey of 654 Russian firms across twelve regions in 2017, I posed the following hypothetical

119 Grossman and Helpman (1994).
120 Interview with Anton Tomachev, local businessperson, Perm, October 8, 2013.
121 Interview with Igor Papkov, Deputy Chairperson, Perm Regional Duma. Perm. October 8, 2013.
122 Smirnov (2010).
123 Interview with Olga Kolokolova, Yabloko Party Leader, Perm, October 6, 2013.
124 Interview with Valeriy Otsipov, deputy of Tomsk Regional Duma, Tomsk, Russia. June 9, 2014.

question to firm directors: "During election campaigns, politicians often make promises to specific firms and individuals. If a politician promises to help a firm (e.g. with regulations or licenses), how likely do you think that they will fulfill their promise?"[125] Directors were then given a five-point scale to choose from, with 1 denoting "very unlikely" and 5 denoting "very likely." The mean response was 2.7, with only one-quarter of firms (25 percent) answering that politicians would be "likely" or "very likely" to fulfill their promises. Voters in Western Europe give their politicians similarly low marks for keeping their campaign promises.[126] Work on Kyrgyzstan further similar evidence that firms cannot always buy preferential treatment; they need to secure direct positions within government to influence how policies are made.[127]

These examples of greed-fueled shirking are only what we know from deputies getting busted by law enforcement or personal interviews with people intimately aware of these breakdowns of corrupt dealings. It is not hard to suspect that the vast majority of politicians who renege on their end of the deal never get caught: firms have few incentives to get the law involved if they will also become implicated in facilitating a bribery scheme. Hence many politicians in Russia believe they can get away with these machinations. A legislative mandate is big business and a ticket to wealth: deputy requests can be sold at incredible prices, firms can be extorted for cash (often with little required in return), access to insider political information can open up new business opportunities to invest in, etc. Deputy status also places an individual above most companies. In all, politician shirking is a very real problem for firms looking to get involved politically.

1.3.2 The Drawbacks of Conventional Solutions

Commitment problems such as shirking are far from intractable. A variety of devices exist to potentially help principals restrain opportunism among agents. First, firms might turn to formal institutions to protect themselves against shirking.[128] One solution would be to design contracts to lock politicians into their promises. After

[125] Additional methodology about how the survey was conducted can be found in the next chapter.
[126] Naurin (2011).
[127] Engvall (2014).
[128] North (1991).

all, firms regularly sign contracts with their other suppliers of key inputs, such as raw materials or consulting services. Some interest groups have enjoyed success convincing politicians to commit to such pledges. Naoi and Krauss (2009) describes politicians in Japan making public promises and signing policy agreements to get support from agricultural lobbies. Thousands of elected officials in the United States have famously signed Grover Norquist's pledge not to raise taxes, receiving endorsements and political support in return.[129]

But contracting over political goods raises a series of thorny issues. First, politics is inherently messy and does not lend itself well to ex ante determinations about possible outcomes. Lowery and Marchetti (2012) note that given the ambiguities bound up in the policymaking process, contracts to regulate interactions between interest groups and lobbyists will necessarily be incomplete and hard to structure. These open-ended agreements are subject to constant renegotiation and reinterpretation. Given the asymmetric informational advantages politicians have within the policymaking process,[130] firms will struggle to untangle what has and what hasn't been accomplished. Monitoring contract fulfillments can send the total cost of using an indirect strategy skyrocketing.

Next, in the vast majority of countries, the practice of buying votes and laws is illegal. That said, evidence from several countries suggests that politicians do write out price lists that document the cost of each legislative policy or service.[131] In Nigeria, powerful donors sponsor candidates, but demand contracts in writing about their future loyalty.[132] But contracts that facilitate such an exchange leave a long paper trail that if uncovered, can destroy politicians' careers or even put them in jail. President Fujimori's government in Peru was toppled shortly after videotapes emerged of politicians accepting cash in return for policy and other favors.[133] A former Minister of Justice in Croatia was engulfed in a major scandal for allegedly reneging on a written contract to reward a large campaign donor with a seat in parliament. When the contract leaked, a corruption scandal and criminal investigation ensued.[134] Because of

[129] Tomz and Van Houweling (2012).
[130] Kersh (2000).
[131] Slinko, Yakovlev, and Zhuravskaya (2005); Ledeneva (2011).
[132] Albin-Lackey (2007).
[133] McMillan and Zoido (2004).
[134] Smilov and Toplak (2008).

these risks, when quid pro quo exchanges are arranged, they are usually signed off on informally. This lends scope for politicians to ex post reinterpret or renegotiate the original agreement to the detriment of the firm. Introducing performance or outcome-based compensation beforehand upends the idea of campaign contributions,[135] which need to be exchanged prior to elections for them to benefit a candidate.

Even if actors carefully write out agreements, contracting over policy outcomes quickly runs into the problem of enforcement. When problems arise with material suppliers, firms can turn to arbitration courts to help settle claims. But in most developed countries, contract and tort systems, which generally serve as the backbone of legal liability, do not regulate political representation.[136] And in Russia, politicians generally have the law enforcement system on their side and can use administrative resources to place pressure on businesses who complain about their treatment.[137] Punishing shirking must be done outside of the legal system.

The most obvious way to punish a politician is to orchestrate their exit from politics during the next election campaign. Firms can switch their endorsements or fund alternate candidates. A recent expose of lobbying in Russia suggests that some interest groups in Russia consider this approach. Political risk consultants offer help identifying troublesome policymakers in parliament. In the words of one such expert, "the simplest option is to ensure that these people fail to get re-elected. You make deals, you set obstacles, and you field your own troublemakers."[138] But hiring such services can prove more expensive than the original lobbying expenditures, and firms still have little guarantee that the new faces in parliament will stick to their promises.[139] Legislators can encroach on a firm's domain without warning and inflict enough damage that funding another candidate years down the line will do little to unwind.

Under conditions of inconsistent third-party enforcement, verbal and supralegal contracts require reputational mechanisms to become self-enforcing. If the exchange takes place as a one-shot game, neither side

[135] Susman and Martin (2006).
[136] Issacharoff and Ortiz (1999).
[137] Interview with Sergei Schpagin, professor, Tomsk State University, Tomsk, Russia. June 9, 2014.
[138] Bekbulatova (2018).
[139] Below I argue that the only way around this problem is to make the firm director herself become the alternate candidate.

develops the necessary trust or capabilities to punish the other for reneging.[140] Building the degree of trust necessary can take time and requires a long-term investment on the part of interest groups.[141]

But many countries suffer from high levels of instability. Both the politicians that pursue office and the economic winners and losers can change within a single electoral cycle. Firms may be more concerned with securing present-day outcomes than making future threats. If a politician believes that a supportive firm will simply not exist by the next election, there are few if any reasons to stick to the bargain. Similarly, politicians need to win immediate reelection, which undermines the notion of a "campaign contribution contract."[142] Interviews suggest that politicians generally do not struggle to raise money from businesspeople, especially given their elevated political influence. They regularly pressure business for campaign contributions, whether in terms of money or votes.[143] For example, firms in Saint Petersburg regularly complain of politicians harassing them to donate money for their campaign in order to enjoy even basic political benefits.[144] According to Sergei Schpagin, "politicians have many responsibilities to many constituencies. They are not responsible to any one businessman."[145] One has to be a huge businessperson in order to control a politician effectively.

Working through parties to punish politicians might be a better option. Political parties oversee candidate selection, coordinate money to campaigns, and can make independent expenditures to their members running for office. If a politician regularly spurns relationships with influential firms, parties have the leverage to hold them accountable. Shirking politicians do damage to the party brand and jeopardize its future financing. Strong parties can reassure contributors that they can freely donate money in exchange for political promises that later won't be reneged upon. Developing strong and public brands solidifies this transaction, for parties can punish deviating politicians who jeopardize the image of the party as a credible political partner. Likewise, candidates

140 Großer, Reuben, and Tymula (2013).
141 Baron (1989); Snyder Jr (1992).
142 McCarty and Rothenberg (1996).
143 Frye, Reuter, and Szakonyi (2014).
144 Ragozina (2007).
145 Interview with Sergei Schpagin, professor, Tomsk State University, Tomsk, Russia. June 9, 2014.

who benefit from party support will be wary of risking it by fraying ties with influential businesspeople who are critical to funding electoral campaigns. As such, political parties may help alleviate the commitment problem between politicians and firms.[146]

Strong parties are not a given in all political contexts. Party brands take years to develop, and party system institutionalization varies markedly across countries,[147] whether due to historical legacies, or the strength of partisan ties.[148] When parties have weak control over their members or exhibit short time horizons, businesspeople have fewer guarantees that the politicians they court can be deterred from taking their money and running. In the next section, I exploit variation in party strength to show how the severity of the commitment problem drives businesspeople to seek political office.

In extreme cases, punishment of shirking can take the form of physical harm. In the Russia of the 1990s, when rule of law was considerably weakened, violence emerged as an effective means of resolving conflicts between firms.[149] Private non-legal enforcement helped fill in where reputation-based business culture and legal institutions were slow to develop. Although violence is both costly and illegal, often just the threat of using it can be enough to enforce commercial agreements.[150] One observer in Ryazan Region noted that during that period, violence helped enforce contracts between businesses and politicians.[151] But as law enforcement improved over the subsequent decade, this option for holding politicians accountable become no longer viable. Businesses could not afford the risk of targeting individual politicians with violence.

In short, politicians may have little to fear from acting against their donors' interests.[152] Because official agreements to keep politicians in check are illegal, businesspeople must rely on personal connections to make sure that their campaign contributions actually lead to desired policy outcomes. The importance of informality comes through

146 Stephenson (2003).
147 Mainwaring and Torcal (2006); Kuenzi and Lambright (2001).
148 Hicken and Martínez Kuhonta (2011); Dalton and Weldon (2007).
149 Gans-Morse (2012); Pistor (1996).
150 Fafchamps (1996).
151 Interview with Aleksander Semenov, professor of the Ryazan' branch of the Moscow State Art and Cultural University, November 18, 2013.
152 Issacharoff and Ortiz (1999).

in conversations with businesspeople in Russia. Firms acknowledged they were basically on their own in terms of interacting with politicians.[153] Politicians felt unconstrained from betraying their promises, and available means to punish them fell flat.

1.4 BUSINESSPERSON CANDIDACY SOLVES THE COMMITMENT PROBLEM

The limited ability of institutional- and reputation-based mechanisms to constrain politicians drives businesspeople to run for office themselves. When businesspeople become politicians, they can act completely in the interests of their firms and not be concerned about the problems of delegating to and monitoring intermediaries. Once elected office is won, firms must still negotiate with other policymakers to get their interests heard, but their concerns about the potential defection of lobbied policymakers are lessened. Holding office frees them from their reliance on the whims of opportunistic politicians.[154]

This approach to mitigating the commitment problem draws on the economic theory of vertical integration. Firms have choices about whether to make an input or buy it from an autonomous seller.[155] The latter imposes transactions costs, one of which involves making sure the contractor delivers the goods as requested. Achieving political access incurs the same trade-off: firms have to decide whether to contract with a lobbyist or politician to advocate on their behalf, or use internal resources to produce the same policy.

I argue that having a businessperson hold elected office allows a firm to essentially benefit from a politician working as an in-house lobbyist. The firm builds out its political capacity from within its ranks, rather than transacting with a potentially unreliable supplier of policy. This alleviates some of the organizational challenges of delegating and monitoring within the firm,[156] since the director and the politician become one. Firms no longer need to expend extra effort to develop monitoring capabilities, or write enforceable contracts, or develop elaborate reward and punishment schemes, all to constrain their businessperson politician. Whether

153 Interview with Elena Zyryanova, deputy Perm Regional Duma, Perm, Russia, October 8, 2013.
154 Tev (2016).
155 Coase (1937); Williamson (1981).
156 Stephenson and Jackson (2010); Lowery and Marchetti (2012).

the politician stays on the firm's payroll or retains an ownership stake, his or her incentive to represent the firm's best interest in politics remains intact. This hierarchical solution streamlines the firm's political strategy, placing the central emphasis on making sure the businessperson politician is adequately compensated not to betray the firm's interests while in office. Choosing a higher-level executive who is financially invested in the firm gives the firm a powerful, motivated political agent.

If businessperson candidacy is being used to overcome contracting problems, we should see more businesspeople running for office when fears of politician shirking are the greatest. Because running for office is so costly, substantial uncertainty must exist about the ability of elected politicians to carry out promises in order for businesspeople to elect the direct approach. The more unreliable intermediaries are perceived to be, the more likely firms should look towards an in-house solution.

1.4.1 Economic Competition and Political Rivalry

First, politicians are more likely to shirk when they have multiple suitors for a single policy.[157] For firms investing in political access, that competition is likely to come from their rivals in the economic arena. Many important political benefits, such as state contracts, construction permits, subsidies, and loan guarantees, accrue to individual firms. Exporting firms require permission to move their specific goods abroad, while manufacturers need licenses to carry out production. Firms facing a threat of expropriation from their rivals or law enforcement bodies look to political connections to protect their own assets, rather than cooperate with others working in their industry.[158]

Most concerning is the possibility that the director of a rival firm wins a seat. Firms fear this outcome. We saw above that businesspeople gravitate towards committee chairpersonships that match their policy area of interest. Seeing a rival rise to such a powerful position can dramatically impair a firm's ability to see its interests adequately represented in the legislature. Chairpeople control the types of bills brought under discussion and are privy to information about the content and flow of the legislative process that is invaluable to investment planning.

[157] Tomz and Van Houweling (2012).

[158] This is not to argue that firms do not work sometimes towards sector-wide benefits. In the final section of this chapter, I discuss the role trade associations play in advocating for these types of policies, and their effects on businessperson candidacy.

Rival businessperson politicians can make much more attractive offers to their colleagues, using their own personal relationships in the chamber or exchanging votes on other legislation. Logrolling legislation induces politician shirking on their promises to interest groups. This type of vote-trading can be common in legislatures with strong representation of business interests, who view the institution as a forum to both network and secure economic advantages.[159] Smaller size groups can facilitate logrolling.[160] The risk of remaining on the outside of lawmaking debates drives firms to expend considerable resources to try their hand at winning a legislative seat themselves. Even though their probability of winning office decreases when large rivals compete for the same seats, the potential costs of not having a direct line to lawmaking processes (while one's rivals do) become unbearable.

Indirect strategies do not work as well when rival firm directors take office. Russian firms are quite circumspect about the ability of lobbyists to get behind closed doors and prevent politicians from defecting. In the words of political scientist Sergei Zyryanov, "business groups are not ready to rely on the services of professional lobbyists, who are hard to find anyway. Because of a lack of trust or the complete absence of capable lobbyists with the equivalent political weight of a deputy, firms prefer to lobby their interests themselves" and thus run for elected office.[161] Firms need at least a seat at the committee table to even begin getting their interests heard.

Seeing a rival win office also opens up vulnerabilities to the dreaded deputy request being deployed against them as a weapon. Preventing this can be difficult; Deputies can charge outsiders exorbitantly high prices precisely because these requests are so effective at stirring up trouble for competitor firms. Purchasing deputy requests from other elected politicians becomes prohibitively expensive. Access to the right legislator for the job comes at a steep price, or can even become impossible if a deputy is in another firm's pocket. Bureaucratic agencies pay attention to deputy committee assignments for signals about how seriously they should take each request. It makes much more financial sense to run and win office on one's own and issue seemingly an unlimited number of requests to paralyze one's rivals, then continue to buy each piecemeal on the black market.

[159] Spector (2008).
[160] Wittman (1989).
[161] Proshu Slova! (2004).

Firms therefore follow one another into politics, just as they copy designs, production approaches, and entry into new markets.[162] Directors study their competitors' behavior, grouping them into reference groups and studying their profitability.[163] Research suggests that firms then adopt the strategies that have offered their competitors the greatest success.[164] High levels of uncertainty, a trait common to the public policy arena, elicit particularly high levels of mimicry among firms.[165] Large organizations are also especially prone to experiment with mimicry, as they have the flexibility to adopt broader, more varied strategies to achieve their economic aims. Using survey data on US lobbying, Drutman (2015*a*) finds that one of leading reasons that firms create Washington offices and get engaged politically is because other companies in their industry are also politically active.

The end result is that firms most concerned about their rivals putting forth candidates should run their own candidates as a counter-strategy. We should expect that the economic structure of an industry affects the likelihood of businessperson candidacy being adopted. Firms with several large rivals that can bear the costs of running for office should be more likely to run for office. Directors fear political benefits accruing to these other large players.

Hypothesis 1. *Economic competition, particularly from large rivals, drives firm directors to run for elected office.*

Businessperson candidacy emerges as a powerful tactic to dominate rivalries, allowing firms the possibility of one-upping their competitors. Schuler, Rehbein, and Cramer (2002) find that intra-industry competition among large firms can resemble an arms race, with firms adopting more intense corporate political activity to prevent their rivals from surging ahead and pursuing particularistic benefits. Turovskii (2004) alternately applies the analogy of a chain reaction to business maneuvering in multiple regions in Russia, including Primorskiye Krai, Sverlodksaya Oblast, and Dagestan. One of the leading producers of potash fertilizers in Perm Oblast, Uralkaliy, thrust itself into regional politics, sending top managers to run for political office at multiple levels. In response to

162 Lieberman and Asaba (2006).
163 Massini, Lewin, and Greve (2005); Xia, Tan, and Tan (2008).
164 DiMaggio and Powell (1983); Mezias (1990).
165 Greve (1998); Haveman (1993).

these new businesspeople entering politics, the value of a deputy seat skyrocketed, and rival firms, most notably Silvinit, adopted the same strategy. Firms realized they would be left completely behind if they didn't match their competitors. This argument thus pushes back against the Olsonian approach to collective action,[166] which holds that collective action should be more likely to occur in concentrated sectors with a small number of large firms. Businessperson candidacy becomes a type of political equilibrium, where the costs of defecting are higher than the benefits.

1.4.2 The Constraining Effects of Strong Political Parties

Second, the structure of political institutions shapes the probability of politician shirking, and thus how firms construct their corporate political strategies.[167] Firms struggle by themselves to punish politicians who defect from agreements, but political parties can step in and play a stronger role. Parties control perks and privileges during the term as well as can facilitate lucrative post-public employment opportunities after politicians exit office. Worries over maintaining outside financial support and staying in power motivate parties to protect their public image as trustworthy stewards of both constituent and special interests. Where politicians are worried about being cut off by parties, their commitment to satisfying donors increases. Simply put, parties both have the means to combat politician shirking through disciplinary measures, and the incentives to maintain reputation.[168]

Institutionalized party systems emerge when elites maintain party allegiances over time and individuals develop durable party identifications.[169] But clearly many party systems are very volatile. New entrants, or so-called "flash parties," can emerge quickly through the efforts of ambitious elites, who see them as useful but temporary vehicles to gain power.[170] Concerns over maintaining consistent brands and reputations also vary. Parties can easily become just a facade for the personal vote centered on the politician.

[166] Olson (1965); Ozer and Lee (2009).
[167] Henisz (2000).
[168] DeBacker (2012); Wittman (1989).
[169] Rose and Mishler (2010).
[170] Kopevcek (2016); Barndt (2014); Arter (2016).

Parties can also fade from the scene if resources dry up or their ideology loses resonance with voters.[171] When parties disband or elites constantly switch parties, voters and interest groups cannot hold politicians accountable. In places such as Russia, intense volatility led to what Rose (2000) calls a "floating system of parties" throughout the 1999s and early 2000s. The array of parties fluctuated constantly, and few made long-term investments in building relationships with constituents. Although the party system in Russia had stabilized by the late 2000s, firm directors already had extensive experience with politicians floating from party to party, donor to donor, with little disciplinary action being taken.

Weakly institutionalized parties not only fail to constrain politicians, they also open up opportunities for businesspeople to independently access ballots. Strong parties are often characterized by significant organizational resources, professional leadership, programmatic capacity, and attachments from voters.[172] Where party brands resonate with voters, unattached candidates face an uphill battle making their case with voters. Party leaders often decide whether to allow a candidate to run on their slate. As shown in Chapter 4, businesspeople would love to pry loose from the party's grip. Firm-related assets, such as recognition in the community or financial resources, allow directors to run their own campaigns and rely less on party organizations.[173]

Therefore, we should expect a correlation between the strength of political parties and the incidence of businessperson candidacy. Political party strength can vary even within a single country, affecting economic and environmental outcomes, as well as how firms interact with the state.[174] If businesspeople believe that parties cannot hold their affiliated candidates accountable, then the need to directly occupy elected office increases.

Hypothesis 2. *Businessperson candidacy will be more common where political parties are weaker and less institutionalized.*

Contributing to a party also greatly simplifies the transactional process by allowing a firm to more transparently register its contributions and

[171] Lupu (2016).
[172] Gibson et al. (1983).
[173] Hale (2005); Smyth (2005).
[174] Gibson et al. (1985); Wilson (2008); Bizzarro et al. (2018); Enikolopov and Zhuravskaya (2007); Fredriksson and Wollscheid (2014); Gehlbach and Keefer (2011).

thus political support. Even though parties often represent encompassing interests and may not see the value in representing specific firm interests on a regularly basis, this arrangement is often preferable to contracting with individual deputies. Firms in Russia remarked that unlike the 1990s where bribes could be directed at single officials and deputies to get things done, the development of more complicated, overlapping corruption systems have forced firms to make payments to multiple politicians to achieve the same effect.[175] This lack of coordination leads to excess rent extraction.[176] Parties help centralize these payments to the benefit of firm interests.

In Russia, deficiencies in party development are also associated with the rise of personalist leadership. Without formal institutions such as legislatures and political parties to constrain them, personalist leaders are less accountable and may be more likely to renege on their promises.[177] They engage in elite reshuffles more often, and rely on other resources, such as charisma, patronage networks, and repressive apparatuses, to keep their governments together.[178] Recent work has shown that these institutions are needed to engender trust that politicians will keep their promises and enforce agreements.[179] Some personalist regimes do use political parties to govern, but fewer resources are invested and policy-making must run through the leader, rather than party structures. In such personalist regimes, we should expect that firms will be more uncertain about whether the government official they lobby will follow through on their promises.

Hypothesis 3. *Businessperson candidacy will be more frequent in more personalist regimes.*

1.4.3 Campaign Costs and Candidate Entry

Running for office is an expensive endeavor. Firm directors must spend potentially enormous amounts of time and money to win elections, not counting the subsequent opportunity costs of devoting effort to policymaking and not solely focusing on their businesses. Businesspeople candidacy is perhaps the most expensive corporate political strategy.

[175] Sakaeva (2015).
[176] Treisman (2000); Shleifer and Vishny (1993); Olken (2007).
[177] Weeks (2014).
[178] Kroeger (2018); Ezrow and Frantz (2011).
[179] Reuter and Szakonyi (2019).

Any analysis of why some firms put forth candidates and others do not must take into account their ability to afford the high costs of campaigning.

In general, campaign costs are a significant barrier to entry for any type of candidate. Citizen-candidate models predict that regulations that increase the costs of entry, such as registration fees or signature requirements, can have a dramatic effect on the number of candidates willing to run for office.[180] Similarly, recent work has claimed that the increases in campaign spending over time in the United States have reduced the size of the overall candidate pool available to run for political office.[181] As the burden of fundraising increases, even professional politicians become less interested in staying in government. High costs require companies to spend capital on campaigns and not on investment projects or other expansionary activities. If campaign demands become too great, then no amount of political influence achieved by winning a seat can compensate a company for the opportunity costs of diverting such a large share of its assets to the political realm. Therefore, we should see fewer businessperson candidates in places where more resources are required to win seats in a legislature.

Hypothesis 4. *More businesspeople will run for office in places where campaign costs are low.*

Lower campaign costs also increase the probability that many firms from a single sector will run for office. The probability then increases that a firm's direct competitor will capture legislative institutions, and deflate the value of indirect strategies. When running for office is inexpensive, we should see more convergence among firms around the same corporate political strategy. Firms must follow the trend and put up their director in elections to keep abreast with their rivals. A self-fulfilling prophecy then occurs: businesspeople expect their rivals to contest seats and put forth their own candidates in order not to be left out. On the other hand, high campaign costs limit the number of firms can afford to run. Indirect strategies become more attractive as firms look to other avenues to build political access. We saw above that running for office can be prohibitively expensive for the median firm in a Russian region, reaching nearly 100 percent of annual revenue. Clearly not all firms can afford this strategy,

180 Braendle (2016).
181 Hall (2015).

and those that do still see their balance sheets hit hard by these extra expenditures on political activity.

1.4.4 An Ability to Pay

Because running for office is so costly, firm size will play a key role in predicting which directors become candidates. Only firms with excess capital not allocated to investment projects can afford to dedicate the time and resources to running a campaign. In addition, larger firms have more employees at their disposal to mobilize and persuade to support a firm director who runs for office.[182] This advantage in orchestrating voter mobilization can reduce the costs of courting voters in a constituency by creating brokers from workplace supervisors to turn out the voter in favor of the firm's candidate. Firm size has been found to be an important determinant of numerous types of corporate political strategy for similar reasons.[183] Part of this relationship between size and candidacy may also be due to demand-size effects. Larger firms may require more substantial policy interventions as their operations grow larger and acquire political implications. Not only can these companies afford to run, but their continued expansion may require getting direct involvement in lawmaking.

Hypothesis 5. *The larger a firm is, the more likely its director will run for office.*

Upon taking office, a businessperson politician then faces significant opportunity costs of governing. Every minute spent working with constituents or sitting in a committee meeting is one not spent in the C-suite. Although the financial returns to businessperson candidacy may be significant, not all firms can afford to allow their talented upper-level management to spend so much time away from the firm's everyday activities. How reliant a company is on specific individuals can turn on a number of factors, including the sector in which it operates and its corporate governance structure. To quote prominent Russian businessperson Ilya Borzenov about his reasons for entering the Sverdlodsk regional legislature:

[182] Hart (2001); Frye, Reuter, and Szakonyi (2014, 2019).
[183] Hillman, Keim, and Schuler (2004); Chong and Gradstein (2009).

I went into politics, because suddenly I had the time and the opportunity to consider another part of my life. Maybe this sounds a little far-fetched, but without understanding how this country is run, its impossible to develop your business. I would have never left my company. Simply today my role in the company is the strategic development of our business. And my free time I can spend on politics.[184]

Some CEOs operate more like "managers," becoming intricately involved with production and employee relations; others exhibit behavior more akin to "leaders," dealing with other executives both inside and outside of their firm.[185] CEOs working in sectors where routine production tasks are paramount may have less latitude to hold down a political position and keep their companies afloat. Founder CEOs may be more critical to daily business operations than outsider firm directors who take their positions within a corporate system that was already functioning before their arrival. I explore the effect of different types of corporate governance structures on businessperson candidacy in Chapter 4.

In all, we should see more businessperson candidacy in places when commitment problems with politicians loom largest. But in some cases, the severity of the commitment problem is not the primary factor determining when businesspeople run. For example, some countries explicitly ban politicians from having connections to their previous employers or earning outside income while in office.[186] Even though businesspeople in these places may not trust politicians to carry out their bidding, their ability to use political office themselves to advance their firm's interest is limited.

Moreover, in industrialized democracies, the cost of running for office is often prohibitively high for a single firm to foot the bill. For example in the United States, the resources needed to mount a national-level electoral campaign have jumped in the past several decades.[187] We might expect then that as the cost of running for office increases, businesspeople should be less likely to seek office. Professional politicians face similar obstacles in raising funds to run campaigns, but do not suffer the same set of opportunity costs as businesspeople in dedicating themselves basically full-time to persuading donors to give money. In an interview,

184 Borisova (2004).
185 Bandiera et al. (2017).
186 See the Conclusion for a more in-depth exploration of cross-national variation in how countries regulate conflicts of interest.
187 Hall (2015).

a Perm businessperson agreed, remarking that as the Russian economy developed, fewer businesspeople would seek political office.[188] In the conclusion, I draw out further the scope conditions for the demand and supply side arguments about the factors driving the entrance of businesspeople into politics around the world.

1.5 ALTERNATIVE EXPLANATIONS FOR BUSINESSPERSON CANDIDACY

1.5.1 Quality of Democracy

The argument that businesspeople run for office to mitigate a commitment problem may overlook the importance of other political institutions. Work has shown that institutions such as the strength of legislatures and extent of democratization can affect the value of political connections. Institutions change how corporate political strategies are deployed, and when underdeveloped, can result in more corrupt and cronyist behavior on the part of firms.[189] Just as different institutional structures dictate where firms direct their campaign contributions and lobbying efforts, the strength of the rule of law and quality of democratic representation may also affect how firms approach the decision to run candidates for office.

Gehlbach, Sonin, and Zhuravskaya (2010) apply this line of argumentation specifically to the issue of businessperson candidacy. The authors argue that when democratic institutions enable voters to hold politicians collectively accountable for their time in office, there is less leeway for businesspeople to secure policies that conflict with the preferences of the pivotal voter. Free and fair elections enable voters to remove politicians that break promises to deliver public goods. If businessperson candidates cannot deviate from promises made to voters, the costs of running for office exceed the firm-level returns they can achieve in office. Other work on developed democracies argues similarly that voters and the media can hold politicians accountable for their promises they make during campaigns.[190] Interest groups can tie the hands of politicians by getting them to sign public pledges, and then mobilizing voters to punish defectors.

[188] Interview with Anton Tomachev, local businessperson, Perm, October 8, 2013.
[189] Macher and Mayo (2015); Lawton, McGuire, and Rajwani (2013).
[190] Tomz and Van Houweling (2012).

In sum, greater democratization compels firms to choose indirect political strategies rather than running for office themselves.

Although strengthening citizen accountability may help reduce corruption,[191] I argue that democratic institutions do not fully explain the variation in businessperson candidacy across different contexts. First, the claim that voters are able to punish politician malfeasance requires that voters can identify the actions of businessperson politicians to divert resources from public goods provision. Under standard accounts of retrospective voting, citizens need information about the policy decisions and performance of elected officials in order to make evaluations. However, growing evidence exists that voters make mistakes not only about attribution, but about the nature of the actual policies in question.[192]

The difficulties of identifying politician behavior that is not in the public interest may be especially present with regard to policies affecting business. Elected politicians are aware of the fallout when voters can pinpoint decisions made in favor of special interests, whether in return for campaign contributions or because the politician himself is an employee of a firm. Such tension creates an incentive to obfuscate. Politicians acting on behalf of businesses will pursue opportunities to gift policy far from public scrutiny.[193] The demands of hiding preferential treatment may be one reason why evidence of the effectiveness of corporate political strategies is so mixed. Simple analyses of voting records and readily observable political behavior may not uncover behind-the-scenes cooperation between firms and politicians. Because politicians are aware of the potential electoral risks of advocating special interests in public office, they rationally maneuver to prevent voters from learning about this behavior.

Even if a voter expects that any candidate from a business background will defend their firm's interests partly at the overall public's expense, this fact alone may not dissuade the voter from lending his or her support. Voters may perceive desirable qualities in businessperson candidates (such as management experience) that outweigh any potential worries about their representation of private firm interests. A proven track record in business may be convincing evidence for

[191] Ferraz and Finan (2008).
[192] Healy and Malhotra (2013).
[193] Gordon, Hafer, and Landa (2007).

voters of a politician's ability to better negotiate for the needs of constituents.[194]

Interviews in Russia suggest that businesspeople (and politicians more generally) are not especially concerned about potential blowback from voters for pushing their interests while in office. Several currently serving deputies dismissed the willingness and ability of voters to think broadly about how politicians were performing and evaluate them on their commitment to the public interest.[195] To them, elections were won and lost during the campaign, when benefits were offered to voters in the months prior to the vote loomed large. This anecdotal evidence aligns with wider studies on accountability that argue that voters in democracies adopt a very myopic or even irrational view of the performance of politicians.[196] Recent events weigh much more heavily than the actions taken over the full term, potentially leaving politicians many tools to mask their own performance and sway voters (engaging in vote buying and political business cycles are two notable examples). Politicians of all types may not be particularly constrained by freer elections from promoting the objectives of special interest groups.

In addition, businesspeople may not be as interested in running for reelection as professional politicians, who have staked their careers on continuously occupying political office. Though some businesspeople may prize their legacy in office, running for office is a still a nonmarket strategy designed at improving firm performance. Winning an election gives a firm multiple years in power to achieve their political aims; a single term in office may be more than enough time. This seems to be the case in Russia, as businesspeople run for reelection at rate roughly six percentage points lower than politicians with other types of backgrounds.[197] Even if voters catch on to their corrupt dealings, with the exception of rare cases, they cannot simply recall politicians within a term for not providing sufficient public goods. The threat of voter punishment during a reelection campaign may not loom as large.

In the empirical analysis, I include commonly accepted measures of democracy as a control variable to account for this theoretical explanation. The key mechanisms to test run through accountability: can

194 For more on how businesspeople play up their management experience, see Chapter 6.

195 Interview with Galina Nemsteva, deputy of Tomsk Regional Duma, Tomsk, Russia. June 10, 2014; Interview with Vasiliy Semkin, businessman and deputy of Tomsk Regional Duma, Tomsk, Russia. June 11, 2014.

196 Bartels (2008); Healy and Malhotra (2009).

197 See the explanation of the data in Chapter 2.

voters hold politicians accountable for the promises they make during elections, and vote them out of office? Do civil society organizations provide an adequate check on egregious abuses of political power, such as rent-seeking? Do politicians fear an active, independent media that will shed light on their corrupt actions in office? If stronger democratization indeed deters entry from businessperson candidates as previously argued, then we should expect negative relationships from variables capturing these dimensions and the number of businesspeople running for office.

This theoretical pathway for democracy is separate from political party strength, which I argue is negatively correlated with interest among firm directors in running for office. In this reading, it is not the level of public accountability, but the centralizing forces and reputational concerns inherent to strong political parties that constrain politicians from acting opportunistically and breaking promises. Political parties are investing more in preserving brands and retaining financial support within society, and thus provide more sustainable avenues through which business can buy policy needs. Hence it is parties' worries over losing donors, and not voters, that prompt strong parties to reign in deputies that abuse their power in office.

1.5.2 Collective Action by Trade Associations, Alliances, and Business-Led Political Parties

Corporate political strategy, no matter the avenue taken, is costly for firms. These expenses, taken together with the complexities of passing policies, often drive firms to cooperate in their appeals to policymakers. Trade associations are key actors in promoting business's political interests, whether by lobbying officials, developing public relations strategies, or funding campaigns.[198] Associations may be organized along sectoral lines to achieve broader aims, as similarities in the nature of production lines and markets demand coordinated policy interventions. The collective weight of member firms increases their bargaining power in the political arena and raises the likelihood of successes in achieving legislation. Firms could credibly threaten to exit markets and collectively punish politicians who defect on promises.

Trade associations could also help solve the coordination problem that arises from businessperson candidacy. All firms would be better off if

[198] Doner and Schneider (2000); Duvanova (2013).

none personally ran for public office. That way, each could delegate its policy aims to its elected politician, and let their representatives negotiate out differences within the halls of the legislature. However, when some businesspeople opt to run for office, others mimic their strategy in order to keep up. I argued above that once one firm achieves direct representation, the expected benefits of lobbying decline. By facilitating dialogue and enforcing agreements, trade associations could enable firms to coordinate not to run candidates in elections, and instead organize lobbying activity collectively. Where business associations are stronger, we might expect firms to forgo the direct strategy of running their own candidates. In the empirical analysis, I test whether firms view membership in trade associations as a superior strategy to running candidates in elections, finding that these avenues for collective action do little to solve persistent shirking problems.

Markus (2012) describes another form of collective action potentially available to firms: the construction of "stakeholder alliances" that incentivize different actors within society such as foreign investors, community organizations, and labor unions to place pressure on governments on behalf of firms. As a defensive strategy, "stakeholder alliances" can allow companies to increase the costs for officials in engaging in expropriation and predation. But for developing relationships with elected relationships, alliances began to show limitations. Although societal actors may excel at drumming up negative publicity about corporate raiding, their ability to compel politicians to hold fast to informal agreements with special interests is much weaker. Community groups and labor unions may also be less interested in advocating firms' political interests, such as subsides, tax relief, or regulatory support. Therefore, while these alliances may prove effective in certain domains, they are unlikely to offer a true substitute for direct political strategies. In Chapter 3, I use survey data to test this proposition.

Beyond associations and alliances, some countries around the world have seen the rise of political parties, or at a minimum legislative fractions, that collectively represent the interests of business. In Brazil, the open-list proportional representation facilitates the formation of groups of legislators from the agricultural sector banding together into the "Bancada Ruralista."[199] This cross-regional faction helped secure targeted transfers, for example, to soy producers. Across Latin America, so-called "corporation-based parties" have sprung up, repurposing "financial

[199] Freytes (2015).

institutions, marketing divisions, retail networks, logistical chains, and legal firms" to help them politically.[200] Though current research positions these new parties as stewards of middle-class concerns, it is certainly within the realm of possibility that party leaders advocate for firm interests upon winning power.

A few caveats are in order. First, the majority of corporation-based parties, at least in Latin America, do not bring together disparate business groups with competing financial interests. According to Barndt (2014, p. 16),

> This is partly because the collective action dilemmas entailed in a particular business sponsoring a party are much less daunting than those entailed in broad-based party building by the business class. When a single conglomerate builds a party, it does not have to negotiate the organization or goals of that party with other businesses. Sponsorship by one conglomerate thus represents a particularly effective form of business party building in Latin America today.

The Russian business community faces similar challenges. Financial-industrial groups have historically sponsored their own political groupings and fielded their own candidates, bringing to bear their incredible economic resources to push for narrow company interests.[201] Cooperation across rivals is lacking, and political parties have not taken up the banner to solve the coordination problems. To quote the political scientist Petr Panov, "United Russia is not united."[202] Deputies protect their own firm's interests, but never those of another sector. In Chapter 4, I explore in much greater detail how businesses choose party affiliations, and the sectoral splintering across party lines that develops.

Even the agricultural sector in Russia has had little success coalescing behind one or another political party. Perhaps the most appealing political vehicle for agricultural groups is the Agrarian Party, founded in 1993 and advocating a leftwing ideological approach to reforming Russia. During the 1990s, much of the lobbying of the agricultural sector in the State Duma ran through this party. However, with the rise of United Russia and changes to electoral rules, the party began quickly shedding support in the early 2000s. From 2004 to 2008, only 2 percent of candidates to regional legislatures ran with an Agrarian Party affiliation. In 2008, the party's inability to win seats at either the regional or federal level led it to merge with United Russia, later dropping much

200 Barndt (2014, p. 6).
201 Hale (2005).
202 Interview with Petr Panov, political scientist, Perm. October 3, 2013.

of its socialist platform and putting forth fewer and fewer candidates under its banner. As described in Chapter 4, agricultural interests rarely fit neatly within specific groups. Deputies representing various dairy sector interests in Orlov sectors ran as independents or under United Russia. Two leading forestry firms in Primorskye Kray, Primorskiylesprom and Terneyles, supported their own candidates for regional office rather than consolidating and working together. Economic rivalry again trumps cooperation.

1.5.3 Personal Characteristics of Office-Seekers

Individuals of all backgrounds choose to run for office for a number of reasons. Though businesspeople may be thinking about their firm's bottom line when considering candidacy, we cannot overlook the potential importance of personal factors in affecting their political ambitions.[203] Schlesinger (1966) described an individual's decision-making process of whether to run for office through the lens of rational choice. Personal characteristics clearly matter: candidates weigh the resources needed, the cost to their families, self-perceived qualifications, and attachment to various issues and ideology.[204] The perceived likelihood of victory can also affect the decision-making calculus, as determined by the availability of open seats, existing political competition, and the level of legislative professionalism.[205]

Businesspeople are not immune to the general attractions of running for office. Successful businesspeople may be especially prone to self-aggrandizement and risk-seeking behavior. The achievement of wealth and status in the economic arena may lead individuals both to desire political authority and believe that their business experience gives them unique qualifications. Egos exert a powerful pull: the taste of financial success and profits can go straight to the head of a self-made businessperson, who sees himself as an outsider and a needed correction to politics as usual. Citing a growing personal commitment to larger societal problems, candidacy is also seen as a logical next step after achieving success (and growing bored) at one's firm.[206] Politicians may also reap considerable individual financial benefits, both while in office and afterwards; the lure

203 Roberts (2018).
204 Maestas et al. (2006); Fox and Lawless (2011).
205 Schlesinger (1966); Stone and Maisel (2003).
206 Interview with Andrei Starkov, businessman and regional deputy, Perm, Russia. June 10, 2014.

of additional personal earnings can loom large for an individual accustomed to prosperity.[207] We also cannot discount those candidates who run office to do good in their communities. Across a number of contexts, businessperson candidates emphasize their financial success and management prowess as potentially useful in fighting for constituent interests and building political coalitions. Other businesspeople view political office as a means to providing input on budget affairs or ensuring that the budget system works properly.[208] In Chapter 6, I put to the test the arguments that some politicians apply their private sector experience to improve constituents' livelihoods.

Such personal ambitions do matter for determining which individuals seek office.[209] However, my interviews with both candidates and observers in Russia indicate that economic, firm-based motivations are much more important. As we will see, nearly 40 percent of all candidates come straight from the private sector. As strong as ego-motivations may be, that frequency suggests other financial incentives are at stake. In fact, the presence of motivations coming from individual personalities and psychological comportments would bias against finding relationships between businessperson candidacy and specific firm characteristics, economic conditions, and the strength of political institutions. Moreover, as I investigate further in Chapter 5, we might not expect firms to benefit so handsomely from having a director in office if that individual was only there to stroke her or her own ego. Businessperson politicians on the whole spend their time in office working on behalf of their firms.

1.6 DISCUSSION AND CONCLUDING REMARKS

The theory developed above builds on a number of theoretical works that argue economic competition has a powerful impact on corporate strategy. Firms encounter their rivals in the political arena, just as they do in economic markets. Politics, in this reading, resembles as a zero-sum game: individual firms benefit from targeted policies, while others lose.[210] The political gains achieved by one firm incentivize its rivals to adopt similar strategies. Economic competition breeds political competition in the pursuit of profits that only policies can unlock. As competition intensifies,

207 Eggers and Hainmueller (2009); Gagliarducci, Nannicini, and Naticchioni (2010).
208 Tagadryan (2007*a*).
209 Maestas et al. (2006); Fox and Lawless (2011).
210 Bonardi, Hillman, and Keim (2005).

the demand for access increases, especially to political institutions such as legislatures that offer a fixed amount of goods (seats). When firms cannot coordinate their political efforts beforehand, we should see a greater number adopt individualistic strategies, culminating in businessperson candidacy.

The arguments in this chapter also make the case that businessperson candidacy emerges when normal politics breaks down. Businesspeople are often not natural politicians: the opportunity costs of running for office are much higher, given the collective duties they assume responsibility for in the public and private sectors. But when indirect political strategies become ineffective or untrustworthy, winning a seat in a legislature becomes an imperative. Thus, professional politicians who fail to champion powerful interest groups within society risk being supplanted by representatives of these groups themselves, in this case firm directors. In the end, lawmaking bodies become forums for direct negotiations between these interests rather than among political delegates who represent a variety of societal factions.

2

Identifying Businesspeople Who Run for Office

Before testing these hypotheses about the conditions promoting businessperson candidacy, we first require compelling measurement of the phenomenon. This chapter defines who qualifies as a businessperson running for office in Russia. It then presents a brief history of the practice in post-Soviet Russia, illustrating the depth of interest among firms in attaining this type of direct representation at all levels of government. But for several reasons, I defend the various advantages of focusing on regional legislatures as the most attractive empirical setting for studying why certain firms put forward directors during elections and others do not.

Identifying connections between candidates and firms can become a murky affair. This chapter dives into the specific measurement techniques used to overcome the challenges of identifying where candidates were working at the time of elections. My approach deploys a new algorithm and a series of matching methods (with a more detailed explanation saved for the Appendix), which uncovers roughly 17,000 businessperson candidates for regional office from 2004 to 2011. The resultant dataset generates a number of intriguing observational findings about who runs for office and why in Russia. Candidates with a business background differ significantly from counterparts coming from other professions. Similarly, specific types of firms appear to gravitate towards the strategy of businessperson candidacy at higher rates. These differences help lay the groundwork for the empirical analysis throughout the rest of the book.

2.1 DEFINING BUSINESSPERSON CANDIDACY

The focus in this book is on individuals with private sector experience who then take elected positions in government. Experience in the private sector, however, varies among candidates. An expansive definition of businessperson candidacy might include any individuals who held ownership stakes in private companies at the time of their campaign. In countries with developed corporate governance structures, firm shareholders play an active role in determining the direction of management, particularly by voting in elections to the board of directors.

In post-Soviet Russia, that ideal role for shareholders diverges from reality. Ownership is largely concentrated directly in the hands of management.[1] Evidence from an original firm survey confirms this: over 70 percent of managers also command large ownership stakes in their firms.[2] An interview with a Perm businessman revealed that it was rare to find a firm where the firm director and primary owner were not the same person; all directors own some share of their companies.[3] Furthermore, it is not even clear who holds ownership stakes in many Russian firms. Individuals often go to great lengths to hide their company holdings,[4] making the identification of end beneficiaries a near-impossible task for the majority of companies.

Throughout the book, I therefore define a businessperson candidate as any individual running for office who held one of the following formal leadership positions in a firm at the time of the campaign: director, deputy director, member of the board of directors, or an individual entrepreneur. These are all individuals active in day-to-day firm management. Although only one-quarter of all corporations in Russia retain a supervisory board of some kind,[5] where present these boards include directors that play an active role in representing the firm with outside actors.[6] I also do not apply any requirements that businesspeople must represent firms of a certain type of ownership or legal structure. Firms can be privately owned, state-owned, or some combination of the two but must be officially registered as commercial entities. Below I go into greater detail about how directors of state-owned enterprises in particular approach electoral politics.

1 Enikolopov and Stepanov (2013).
2 Based on a survey of 654 firms was conducted from June to October 2017 in 12 Russian regions. More detail on methodology can be found in Chapter 3.
3 Interview with Anton Tomachev, businessman, Perm, Russia, October 8, 2014.
4 Chernykh (2008).
5 Iwasaki (2017).
6 Libman, Dolgopyatova, and Yakovlev (2014).

2.1.1 A Brief History of Businesspeople in Russian Politics

Russia's chaotic, far-reaching transition from communism to capitalism offered fertile ground for the entrance of businesspeople into politics. The collapse of the USSR in 1991 brought unprecedented instability to the newly independent Russian Federation, imposing an exhaustive docket on the country's new leaders to both democratize the state and build a market economy. Painful reforms were needed to stave off inflation, redistribute state property, and resurrect falling output. Representative bodies arising from the ashes of Soviet institutions had to construct a new legal and regulatory order that guaranteed basic rights and freedoms, while laying the conditions for economic growth. The executive branch of the once-mighty Soviet state now found itself splintered across competing ministries and agencies, all fighting for relevance in the newly democratized political arena.

Political entrepreneurs of all shapes and sizes rushed to participate in the new institutions through the freer and fairer elections of the 1990s. In many respects, businesspeople stood to benefit most from the delegitimization of the Soviet regime and the clamoring for democracy. Fed up with the corruption, ideological vacuity, and incompetence of much of the Soviet elite, many Russians demanded a change in its leadership. As newcomers to the political game and primary agents of the capitalist transition, businesspeople offered a fresh break with the past. They easily cultivated strong, personalized images owing to their financial success and charisma. The name recognition from making highly visible profitable investments, providing jobs, and donating to social causes translated well into political popularity. For those voters looking for political distance from the Soviet *nomenklatura*, businessperson politicians were an obvious choice.[7] As self-made men and women, businesspeople were also oftentimes the only individuals with sufficient financial resources to afford electoral campaigns. As Russia turned to elections to select its leaders, businesspeople stepped up en masse.

Whatever altruistic slogans firm directors used to persuade voters they were the right people for public office, we cannot forget the incredible economic benefits these elites stood to gain from entering politics during the transition years of the 1990s. Holding federal, regional, and even municipal office meant not just earning a front seat for the political games afoot but the chance to write the rules of the games themselves. Regulations needed to be drafted, factories privatized, tax exemptions allocated,

[7] Turovsky (2007).

natural resources licenses procured. Everywhere there was money to be made, and the most direct route often ran straight through government access.

The first stop for many leading businesspeople during this period was the State Duma. Although certain industries achieved limited success influencing the rollout of policy during the Soviet period, "the introduction of more competitive elections for representative institutions gave business organisations new points of entry into the political system."[8] Businesspeople demonstrated both unbridled ambition and naivete in mobilizing their media assets, financial resources, and reputation in the fight of competitive elections.[9] Many of the first political parties found their political and financial footing thanks to help from leading businesspeople, particularly the Party of Economic Freedom, created in 1992 by Konstantin Borovoi, the president of the Russian Commodities and Raw Materials Exchange, and the Russian Socialist Party created by Vladimir Bryntsalov, the president of JSC Ferein, Vladimir Bryntsalov in 1994.[10] During the 1993 Duma elections, leading industrialists backed the creation of Civic Union, a party advocating stronger government intervention in propping up economic productions and providing price supports to assist the ailing manufacturing base.

But firms also sidestepped traditional political parties and funded their own independent candidates through financial-industrial groups,[11] which often operated as lobbying appendages of their corporate sponsors. Industries varied in their level of self-organization: agricultural firms maintained cohesive bonds, while more resource-intensive sectors saw rivalries spill out into the open on parliamentary floors. Chaisty (2013) calculates that roughly 25 to 30 percent of all newcomers to the State Duma directly represented economic interests, though not all were successful at achieving their policy aims. Nonetheless, a spot in parliament was a vantage point to gather detailed, exclusive information on policy machinations and sit on (and even chair) powerful committees that debated regulations. To quote Vladimir Pribylovsky, a Russian political scientist, "getting a Duma seat means to become a bureaucrat and to stop paying bureaucrats when you want something done."[12]

[8] Chaisty (2013, p. 719).
[9] Kryshtanovskaya and White (2005).
[10] *Kommersant* (2011).
[11] Hale (2005).
[12] Mereu (2003).

Powerful businesspeople also gravitated towards regional politics, especially as Yeltsin's calls for decentralization helped concentrate important governing functions in the hands of local elites. During the 1990s, regional governments helped determine who got access to critical inputs, such as water and raw materials, and special economic zones with generous tax breaks. Businesspeople rushed into politics to influence how these decisions were made. Examples of prominent Russian managers taking over governorships abounded, from Norilsk Nickel CEO Aleksandr Khlopinin becoming head of Krasnoyarsk Krai to billionaire Roman Abramovich taking over the reins of Chukotka, a region in Russia's Far East.[13] This trend continued into the 2000s with nearly 20 percent of regional governorships held by top executives and/or owners of large corporations.[14] Alongside governors, representatives of the industrial and financial elite grew to dominate many regional legislatures. By the late 1990s, over half of regional legislatures in Perm, Smolensk, Penza, Tambov, and Tomsk (among others) were controlled by businessperson politicians, who had crowded out politicians from other socioeconomic backgrounds.[15]

Besides the limited positions available and greater media scrutiny, it also worth noting that under successive Putin administrations in the 2000s, Russian governors lost some of their ability to act as pure conduits for business interests.[16] Governors face strong incentives to minimize political rivals and mobilize the populace in support of the ruling party,[17] which can limit their ability to allocate benefits to narrow financial interests. Other work has argued that the removal of gubernatorial elections has significantly diminished the ability of financial-industrial groups to hold sway over regional politics.[18] This has led to increased attention by businesspeople on regional legislative bodies, the focus of this book.

Why Focus on Regional Legislatures?

According to federal law, businesspeople can run for elected office at the federal, regional, and municipal levels of government in Russia. Although businesspeople have populated numerous political institutions up and down the Russian government, the main individuals studied in this

13 Gehlbach, Sonin, and Zhuravskaya (2010).
14 Chebankova (2010).
15 Kryshtanovskaya and White (2005).
16 Turovskii (2008).
17 Reuter and Robertson (2012).
18 Chebankova (2010).

book are regional legislators. Before diving into why regional legislatures present such a unique analytical opportunity, some background is due on how federalism in Russia works. As a federal state, Russia is made up of eighty-five constituent territories; I follow the norm in the academic literature by referring to them as "regions."[19] These first-level administrative units include oblasts, republics, krais, autonomous okrugs, and federal cities.[20] Republics have slightly higher administrative standing than oblasts, krais, and cities, while autonomous okrugs have slightly lower administrative standing. All in all, the subjects have nearly equal rights within the federation, though they do vary considerably in terms of population (from tens of thousands of people in the smallest autonomous okrugs to millions in Moscow and St. Petersburg) and territorial size.

Russia's federal structure accords regions with budgetary and policy-making responsibilities that hold great appeal for the business community. In the 1990s, these functions swelled in scope, as President Yeltsin attempted to keep the federation together by delegating numerous powers to the regional level. Putin's ascent to the presidency in 2000 marked a return to centralization, both in terms of scaling back many of the governing mandates assigned to regions as well as abolishing direct elections to select their heads (colloquially known as governors).[21]

However, even after this wave of reforms under Putin, regional governments are still critical public service providers. Regional spending accounts for roughly 9 percent of Russia's GDP. To quote a 2016 report, Russian regional governments "represented 95 percent of general government expenditure for housing and utilities, 80 percent for education and cultural activities, and around 85 percent for health," among other areas.[22] This spending flows to a number of different services, including protecting the environment and nature reserves, providing fire protection, building and maintaining roads, and rehabilitating dilapidated housing. These governments also manage a whole host of important policy areas

[19] The total number of regions has changed over time. It was eighty-seven at the beginning of the sample in 2004, and then decreased to eighty-three by 2011 due to several consolidations and merges. It later increased again to eighty-five with the annexation of Crimea and the federal city of Sevastopol in 2014.

[20] The second-level administrative unit is the *municipalnoye obrazovaniye*, or municipality, which is roughly similar to a county. This chapter largely focuses on region-level politics, while Chapter 6 examines business–government relations in more detail at the municipal level.

[21] Ross and Campbell (2008).

[22] Di Bella, Dynnikova, and Grigoli (2017).

of direct interest to the business community. Procurement contracts originating in regional budgetary funds provide incredible opportunities for firms to sell their goods and services to the state. To pay for these expenditures, regional governments retain ample revenue autonomy. Although centralizing reforms stripped them of some of their revenue-generating abilities, regional legislatures still can set land and transportation tax rates, as well as reduce profit taxes by 4 percent, a nontrivial amount even when compared to their previous ability to create tax havens.[23]

Beyond spending and taxation, regional governments also have multiple levers to stimulate investment and economic growth. Regional politicians' ability to stay in office often depends as much on providing quality public services to their constituents as improving the business climate. Regional governments approach economic affairs often in idiosyncratic ways, but the fact remains that their policies hold immediate consequences for how business is conducted. Without natural resources to fuel growth, Novgorod region in the 1990s turned to comprehensive economic development strategies designed to streamline bureaucratic procedures and attract investors.[24] Kaluga has famously courted foreign investment by promising firms direct, transparent access to government officials and constructing industrial parks complete with attractive infrastructure and simplified regulations. Yakovlev et al. (2017) describe how the developmental model currently in place in Tatarstan prioritizes local production and has effectively implemented target industrial policy to stimulate sectors such as agriculture. Regional governments have huge subsidies and attractive loan guarantees at their disposal.

These assets and responsibilities give businesspeople all the more reason to access the regional legislature, where much of the policymaking action takes place. Organized interest groups view these legislatures as key sites of contestation over policy and spoils, where laws with long-term impacts on regional concerns are drafted.[25] Legislative committees convene on issue areas such as agriculture, health care, and education, drafting bills that affect subsidies, state guarantees, and state procurement. Multiple firm surveys confirm that firms prioritize working with legislators as one of the more effective strategies to get involved politically.[26] The high level of business interest in these important lawmaking

[23] Turovskii (2008).
[24] Zimin (2010).
[25] Reuter and Turovsky (2014); Remington (2008).
[26] Marques, Govorun, and Pyle (2014); Reuter and Turovsky (2014).

bodies make them an attractive venue for testing hypotheses about which types of firms pursue direct representation.

But narrowing the focus to regional legislators also comes with several other empirical advantages. First, regional legislators in Russia are not required to leave their businesses behind when taking office. This is not the case for deputies serving in Russia's federal parliament, the State Duma. Since 1994, federal law has explicitly forbidden elected national politicians and governors from receiving outside salaries in the private sector, representing their business interests while in office, or remaining engaged in firm management.[27] As we saw above, hundreds of deputies and governors have flouted these restrictions, but the fact remains that businesspeople can face harsh sanctions when the tide turns and authorities decide to apply the law. Perhaps the most well-known case involved Gennady Gudkov, an opposition leader from the Just Russia party, who was stripped of his seat in the State Duma in 2012 on suspicion of retaining ties to his businesses. But members of other parties, such as the Communist Party and United Russia, have also lost their seats.[28] Analyzing regional legislators helps deflect concerns that such bans are affecting whether businesspeople pursue higher office as an explicit firm strategy.

Next, the firms that put forth their directors to run for regional office are much larger and more often registered in official state firm databases. That makes it considerably easier to match candidates with specific companies, to test hypotheses about the types of firms that adopt this strategy, and to analyze the advantages (or costs) that accrue to connected firms. Identifying such politician - firm links would present significant difficulties farther down the administrative ladder, such as those for mayors or municipal deputies. The vast majority of municipalities are located in rural areas, and the businesspeople that tend to run for office there often represent small, unregistered firms. Collecting even basic information on these tiny enterprises, such as their industry or financial performance, is not possible. State agencies do not have the capacity to enforce reporting requirements for such small enterprises, and most individual proprietorships can keep their books completely private. Again in this regard,

[27] Exceptions are made for research and educational activities not specifically tied to business. See Federal Law of 8 May 1998 N 3-FZ "On the Status of the Member of the Federation Council and the Status of the Deputy of the State Duma of the Russian Federation," Article 6, Clause 2.

[28] See, for example, the case of State Duma Deputy and member of United Russia Alexei Knyshov, who was stripped of his mandate in late 2014 for pursuing state contracts while in office. ITAR-TASS (2012).

regional legislatures occupy the ideal space for analysis between the federal and municipal levels.

2.1.2 Regional Legislative Elections

To examine the factors driving businessperson candidacy, I focus the analysis in this book on elections to regional legislatures. The main dataset covers participants in 159 such elections in 83 regions in Russia from 2004 to 2011. Regional legislatures vary considerably in total size, from 11 seats in the 2009 convocation of the legislature in Nenetskii Autonomous Okrug to 120 seats in the Republic of Bashkortostan in 2008. Elections are staggered in Russia according to an exogenously preset electoral calendar. Legislative elections were held for roughly 10 percent of regions every six months (on unified spring and fall dates) from 2004 to 2011. The irregularity of this calendar dates back to the 1990s, when regional governments set elections as they pleased. Several scholars have exploited the exogeneity this irregular timing introduces in order to study different facets of political and economic development in Russia.[29] For the purposes of this study, analyzing elections occurring in each year across regions allows me to better control for economic shocks, such as the 2008 financial crisis, as well as disentangle regional dynamics from national ones.[30]

This period begins immediately after the passing of a national law in December 2003 that restructured regional political competition by requiring that each region allot at least half of legislative seats to candidates from proportional representation lists.[31] This resulted in the majority of subnational legislatures using a mixed electoral system as well as providing a significant impetus for political party consolidation across the entire country. Each legislature determined the exact ratio of deputies elected either from single member plurality districts (SMDP) or party lists through a proportional representation system (PR).[32]

The dataset includes information on all 41,479 candidates collected from the Central Election Commission of the Russian Federation (CEC). Candidate data comes primarily from the Center in Support of

[29] Szakonyi (2020); Beazer (2014).

[30] Two of the elections (2007 and 2011) were held concurrently with national elections to the State Duma.

[31] Federal Law No. 67-FZ of June 12, 2002. "On the basic guarantees of citizens' electoral rights and the right to vote in referenda." See also Golosov (2011).

[32] Eleven regions used party lists exclusively to select their representatives (Lyubarev, 2011).

Democracy and Human Rights Helix, with missing data gathered directly from the main CEC website. Approximately 41 percent of all legislative seats from 2004 to 2011 were chosen using SMDP rules, with the remainder going to candidates from the party lists. The dataset includes candidates running within both electoral systems. In Chapter 4, I dig further into businesspeople's decision to opt for the SMDP or the PR route during elections, and to preview, find strong correlations between firm characteristics, such as size and sector, and specific ballot choices.

Russian regional legislative elections are as competitive, if not more so, as national-level elections. That said, United Russia still dominated the political scene. Of the 159 convocations in the sample, the ruling party United Russia (UR) on average won 62 percent of the total number of seats in each legislature. Compare that to results on the national level, where UR won 70 percent of seats in the 2007 national parliamentary elections for the State Duma. Overall, UR fared well in just about every region. In 127 of them, or roughly 80 percent, it won at least half of the seats, enough to pass simple legislation without conferring with other parties. In no region did UR fail to earn the most seats, but in that remaining 20 percent it had to govern with systemic opposition parties, such as the Communist Party of the Russian Federation and the Liberal Democratic Party of Russia.[33] Fights between individual candidates also sometimes boiled over. In districts that held plurality elections, the average margin of victory was just over 30 percent, but roughly 23 percent of the total sample, or 634 elections, was decided by less than 10 percentage points.

This tilted playing field affected the political environment in which businesspeople chose to run for office. The competitive authoritarian regime that developed during the 2000s in Russia closed off many opportunities for alternative political forces. Opposition parties faced overt pressure and financing difficulties, while the state applied administrative resources to secure advantages for the ruling party. This might lead to concerns that regional legislatures were not the most attractive venue for the direct lobbying of business interests. Given the monopolization of power in a small ruling elite, other connections might have proven more valuable, such as developing ties to officials in the executive branch

33 Both parties are considered "systemic" due to the feigned resistance they have offered to the governments led by Putin (and Dmitri Medvedev) and his United Russia ruling party. This contrasts with "non-systemic" parties such as Yabloko and the Union of Right Forces which declared their fervent opposition to the ruling party.

or signaling loyalty by funding public projects. However, roughly five candidates stood for each open seat in the 159 regional elections.[34] Thousands of these were active businesspeople. Many candidates spent their own personal funds on the chance to tap into the privileges and power of regional legislative office. Even with the ruling party's electoral dominance, legislatures continue to be fora for economic elites to bargain out their differences and access the immense resources of the state.

Moreover, as I investigate further in Chapter 4, for a variety of reasons the ruling party did not enjoy universal support from the business community. Many leading businesspeople opted to run both as candidates in systemic opposition parties (such as the Communists) and as independents. And many of these nonconformists won election and took office, in turn securing real financial benefits for their firms (as shown empirically in Chapter 5). Therefore, while we cannot neglect the fact that regime type influenced the avenues available to firms seeking political access, the fact remains that businessperson candidacy was still a viable method for protecting and expanding firm interests, just as it can be in other open and closed polities.

2.1.3 Connecting Candidates with Firms

After collecting biographical data on all candidacies to regional legislatures, the next step is to identify which candidates worked for a firm as director, deputy director, or on the board of directors at the time they began their campaigns.[35] Identifying candidates' business affiliation is done by drawing on the Unified State Register of Individual Entrepreneurs (EGRIP) database and related databases in the Professional Market and Company Analysis System (SPARK). SPARK combines data from EGRIP (which mainly contains information on officially registered individual entrepreneurs running microenterprises)[36]

[34] This figure combines the number of candidates running on PR lists and in SMDP districts. On average, there were 2.6 registered candidates in each electoral district through the plurality system.

[35] Candidates for office can work for multiple firms. The datasets include all connections.

[36] To be registered, individual entrepreneurs must run enterprises under a certain size threshold, but then benefit from tax breaks and other simplified regulations. They are closest in definition to a "sole proprietorship." Because these entrepreneurs do not submit financial information to authorities on an annual basis, they are excluded from the firm-level analysis in this chapter. Chapter 6 analyzes the behavior of these entrepreneurs in office, as well as providing a more in-depth definition of what constitutes an entrepreneur in Russia.

with official registration data for nearly three million firms in Russia (e.g. directors, deputy directors, board chairs, board members). In all, the SPARK dataset contains basic demographic information (age, registration date, etc.) and unique tax identification numbers on almost 12 million businesspeople of various types in Russia, aggregating information on all their related firms and organizations.

I use a Python algorithm to match each candidate to his or her entry in EGRIP and, subsequently, every legal entity that they have been affiliated with. The Appendix contains additional information on the specifics of the algorithm and the SPARK database. Candidates across the databases are matched using their first name, last name, middle name, and region.[37] Manual matching was used where entries in EGRIP did not exist, but information on previous occupations (i.e. the firms they managed) was available through their official candidate registration with the CEC.[38]

Some candidates noted on their registration that they were involved in business at the time of their campaigns, but a corresponding entry could be not found for them in EGRIP or for the firms they listed. Many of them were self-described businesspeople who had not officially registered their firms with authorities. I code these individuals as businessperson candidates, but cannot conduct firm-level analysis because of their absence in the data. The results presented below should thus be read with that caveat in mind: the analysis centers on firms (and their directors) large enough to comply with official registration requirements. In Chapter 6, I use the full candidate-level data with any experience in the private sector (i.e. including both firm directors and individual entrepreneurs) to analyze differences in policymaking between businessperson and non-businessperson candidates.

This approach to identifying business connections only includes candidates running in elections up to December 2011. In late 2012, the SPARK system updated its information management tools and added several technological obstacles to prevent researchers from querying its databases using programming scripts. Therefore, the analysis is limited to

[37] Unfortunately, the SPARK database does not provide information on family or social ties to measure whether a firm was represented by a relative or friend of its registered management.

[38] This extra manual check also allowed me to identify firm– politicians links in the rare event where one or both of the two sides had misspelled entries in their respective databases. In a handful of cases, verification internet searching and other sources in the public domain allowed me to match the candidate to his or her EGRIP entry in a way the algorithm could not because of the misspelling.

businessperson candidacy during the period of 2004–2011, for which we have firm connections based on the SPARK database. For the most recent period (2012–2016), I code businessperson candidacy using candidates' self-reported official registration data about their occupation at the time of the campaign and an indicator if they appeared in the entrepreneur database (which can identify them as a businessperson but lacks information on specific firm connections). I analyze this extended dataset in the Appendix, finding that the main results of this chapter are robust to adopting this alternate coding approach.

2.1.4 Descriptive Statistics: Candidate Level

Using this measurement strategy, I first find that 41.2 percent of all candidates, or 17,105 individuals, were actively working in the top management of a firm or as individual entrepreneurs at the time of their candidacy for regional office. Businessperson candidacies occurred at significant rates across all of Russia's 83 regions studied in the sample. Figure 2.1 maps the percentage of businesspeople as a share of all candidates for regional office across the country. I collapse the data to the region level, since all regions had multiple legislative terms during period.

Several interesting patterns emerge. First, high rates of businessperson candidacy are distributed evenly across geographic areas of Russia, rather than being concentrated for example, in the agricultural belt in southern

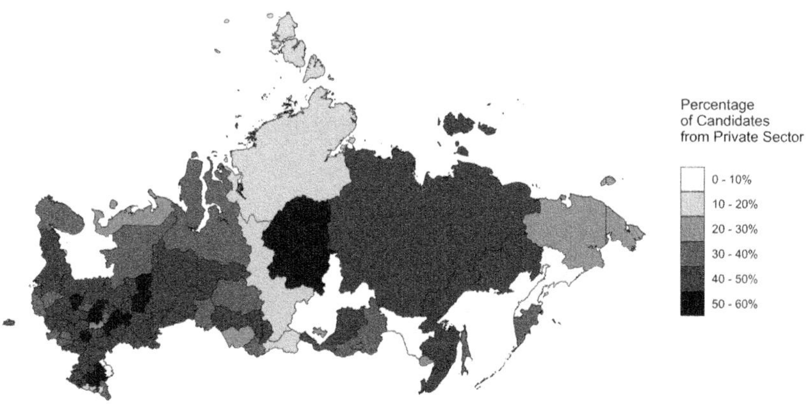

FIGURE 2.1: Businessperson candidates across regions
This figure plots the percentage of candidates that had a business background in each region. For regions with multiple elections in the sample, I take the average over the period.

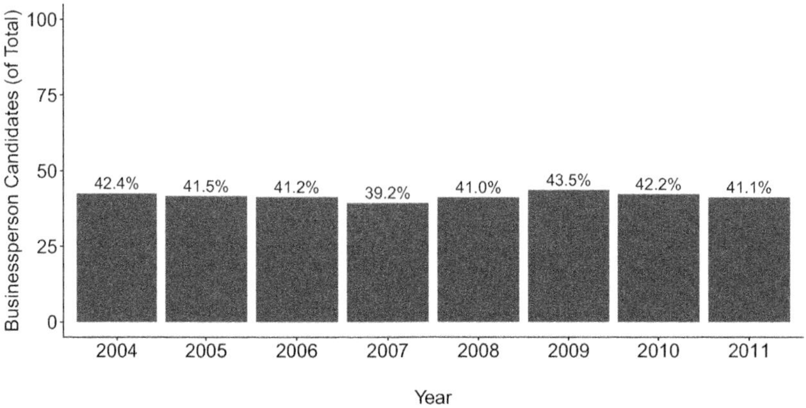

FIGURE 2.2: Businessperson candidates over time
This figure plots the percentage of candidates that had a business background in each year (averaged across all regions that held an election that year).

Russia where economic reforms were adopted at slower rates in the 1990s (Berkowitz and DeJong, 1999) or only in areas far from the federal center of Moscow. Firm directors run for office in a variety of economic landscapes across Russia. Second, the vast majority of all regions (78 percent) saw over a third of candidates for regional legislative office come from the private sector. It is not the case that a small number of regions are driving the average rate across the country, as this type of candidacy is more or less evenly spread out. Businesspeople are by far the largest demographic group running for office at the regional level, followed by leaders from local education, health care, and scientific institutions.

The rate of businessperson candidacy also remains remarkably consistent over time. Figure 2.2 plots the percentage of businesspeople (as a share of all candidates) each year from 2004 to 2011. The result is nearly a flat line, even amidst the economic fluctuations Russia experienced during these years. Starting in 2008, Russia suffered a dramatic fallout from the worldwide financial crisis, as both economic growth and private investment spiraled downward. These events did not appear to shake the business community's interest in holding elected office, which remained remarkably stable.

How do businessperson candidates compare to candidates running for office with different backgrounds? Even though businesspeople represent a substantial proportion of all candidacies, there are still large numbers of doctors, lawyers, educators, and administrators running in the same

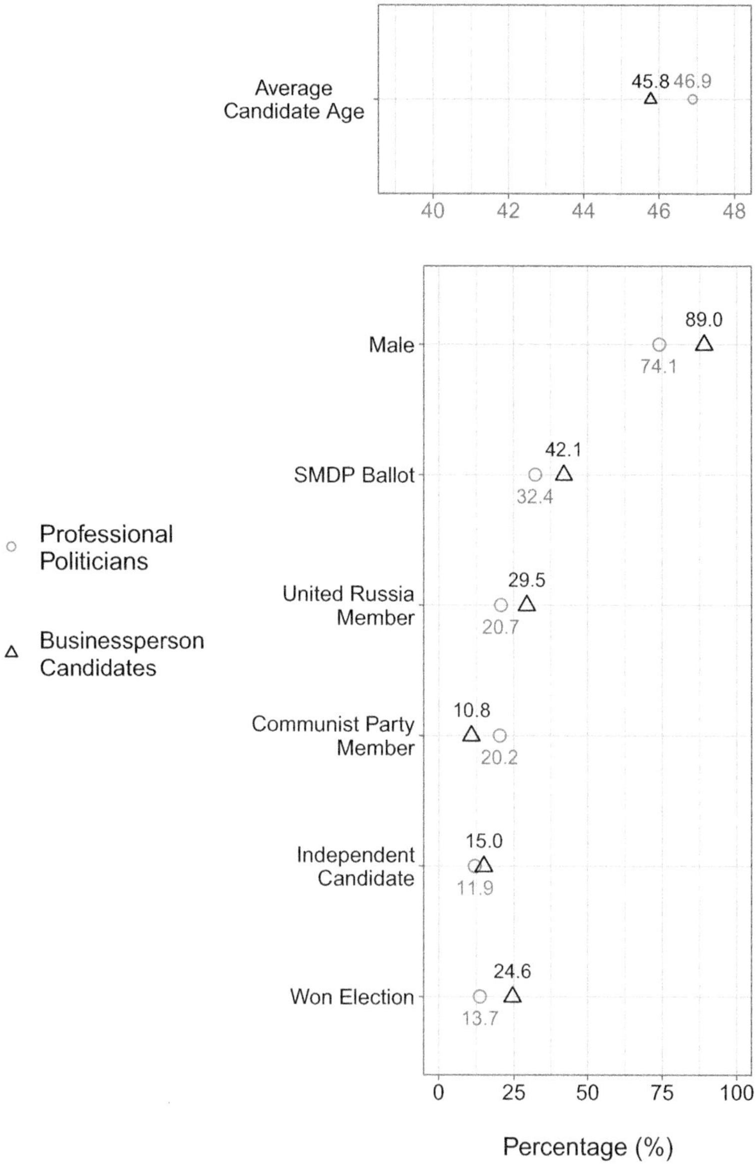

FIGURE 2.3: Businessperson versus professional candidates

This figure plots the differences in demographic characteristics of businessperson candidates versus professional politicians (a residual category for all politicians not coming from the private sector). The top panel compares the average candidate age between the two groups. The bottom panel plots the percentage of candidates that fell into each category. For example, 89 percent of businessperson candidates were male, compared to 74.1 percent of professional politicians.

elections. The focus in this book is just on individuals coming from the private sector, so for ease of exposition, I collapse information on these other demographic groups into the umbrella term "professional" politicians (even if they have not made their careers solely in politics). Figure 2.3 presents simple comparisons between the two groups of politicians using candidate demographics, partisan membership, and electoral performance.

The top panel compares the average candidate age between the two groups. Businessperson candidates are roughly 1.2 years younger (at 45.8 years old) on average than their "professional politician" counterparts (at 46.9 years old). The business community in Russia during the 2000s was still rather young, as the transition to capitalism begun in the early 1990s was still in full swing. The private sector offered a faster route to financial success and public prominence than other slower-moving sectors, such as education or government administration.[39]

The bottom panel plots the percentage of candidates that fell into each category. For example, 89 percent of businessperson candidates were male, compared to 74.1 percent of professional politicians. Men in Russia generally display higher levels of risk tolerance and gravitate more towards entrepreneurial activities in search of higher wages.[40] This leaves a stark gender imbalance across occupations, with more men filling key roles in private sector management while women are represented more heavily in education, health care, and various roles in state-owned enterprises.[41] These gendered differences in employment preferences are then reflected in statistics on who runs for political office.

Next, we see that businesspeople represent certain political factions more than others. First, 29.5 percent of candidates from the private sector are affiliated with the ruling party United Russia, compared with 20.7 percent of other types of candidates. During the 2000s, United Russia ascended into its current role as the ruling party in Russia, by constructing a dominant coalition of elites and, by the end of the decade, achieving a majority of seats in regional legislatures throughout Russia. Much of the party's surge capitalized on the personal popularity of its leader Vladimir Putin. By the end of the 2010s, United Russia deputies

[39] Gerber (2001) finds a curvilinear relationship between age and entry into self-employment and entrepreneurship using household surveys in Russia. The peak of curve occurs at the age of 27, with the effect of age on entrepreneurial activity becoming negative.

[40] Karhunen and Ledyaeva (2010).

[41] Gerber and Mayorova (2006); Semykina and Linz (2007).

not only controlled lawmaking in regional legislatures, but also regional and local administrations.[42] That trajectory of success, as well as the spoils that followed from electoral dominance, made the party an attractive home for companies looking to expand their economic footprint. Alignment with the party of power indeed may generate greater profits, as some recent work has suggested.[43] In Chapter 4, I take a closer look at the theoretical motivations behind the party affiliation of businessperson candidates, connecting factors, such as resource abundance and firm regulatory needs, with the choice of which party they join.

Businesspeople subsequently ran as members of the Communist Party at roughly half the rate of professional politicians. This should come as little surprise. Although the Communist Party drastically moderated its diatribes against capitalism during the Putin era, it still derives a significant base of support from pensioners and agricultural workers who may not always look fondly upon the business community. For example, the elderly still are more likely to profess an affinity for the tenets propagated under the Soviet Union and may still harbor anger towards the capitalist class of newly independent Russia. That said, a non-negligible 10.8 percent of all businessperson candidates still ran with a Communist Party affiliation. Parties across the political spectrum are still highly dependent on external contributions and financial support, and even given the obvious ideological contradictions, a number of regional branches of Communist Party have made hearty entreaties to local businesspeople.

Finally, businessperson candidates are much more successful at winning office than other types of candidates. The unadjusted statistics indicate that 24.6 percent of businesspeople take seats in regional legislatures, compared to a rate of 13.7 percent among "professional politicians." This difference holds even controlling for the type of ballot structure that candidates run on. Given their resource advantages, businesspeople can make larger financial donations and secure higher spots on party lists. As I describe in further detail in the next chapter, parties rely on these financial contributions to such a large extent that they explicitly entertain bids from wealthy elites in exchange for access to regional legislatures. Larger donations result in a higher probability of winning a seat.

42 Reuter (2017).
43 Yakovlev and Zhuravskaya (2009); Maury and Liljeblom (2009).

In plurality races, businesspeople enjoy not only resource advantages for use in campaigning (both in terms of money to buy ads and employees to mobilize politically), but also name recognition among the larger public. This is especially the case for firms that provide significant employment to their local community and are actively engaged in the delivery of vital social services, such as health and child care for their workers. Businesspeople not only contest elections in high numbers, they are also very adept at securing seats in legislatures. Chapters 5 and 6 show in more detail what happens to policymaking when such a large proportion of lawmakers are drawn from the business community.

2.1.5 Descriptive Statistics: Firm Level

Not all firms send members of their management teams to run for political office. Exploring that variation requires detailed data on the different types of firms connected to political candidates. Using the Python algorithm described above generated a dataset of 9,475 firms linked to candidates at the time of their campaign. I should note this number is much lower than the roughly 17,000 candidates that were linked to some degree with the private sector (either through the algorithm or their self-reported previous occupation). First, I must limit the sample to only those firms that were registered in the same region as a given legislative election *and* that submitted financial information (balance sheets) for the year of the election. This was done to enforce consistency across observations. Second, many candidates are registered as individual entrepreneurs. Official firm databases in Russia do not require these entrepreneurs to submit annual financial information or even basic data on the sector or size of their enterprises. For these reasons, the analysis focuses only on official registered companies where a member of the management team ran for political office.

Table 2.1 compares these "Candidate Firms" (i.e. firms that had a director run for office) with all 933,750 firms active in the same regions during the same election years.[44] In other words, these latter "Non-Candidate" firms were in a position to potentially run a

[44] This universe of firms is collected from the Orbis service (a service of Bureau Van Dijk). A competitor to SPARK, Orbis aggregates all balance sheet information for registered Russian firms. The underlying data are identical. For a firm to be considered "active" at the time of the campaign, it must have filed its financial information with authorities for that calendar year.

TABLE 2.1 *Comparing candidate and non-candidate firms*

	Candidate Firms	Non-Candidate Firms
(1) Number of Unique Firms	9,475	937,750
(2) Importer (%)	24.41	8.63
(3) Exporter (%)	17.33	5.43
(4) Number of Subsidiaries	1.19	0.17
(5) Municipal State-Owned Enterprise (%)	3.29	1.73
(6) Regional / Federal State-Owned Enterprise (%)	2.43	0.7
(7) Firm Age (years)	10.86	5.37
(8) Total Assets (ths. $)	847,244	82,288.17
(9) No. Employees	259.13	43.85

This table gives aggregate statistics for firms whose director ran for elected office ("Candidate Firms") and those that did not engage in businessperson candidacy ("Non-Candidate Firms"). Each row gives the mean of the variable for each group. The data for both groups comes from Orbis, a service of Bureau Van Dijk.

candidate for office at the same time, but opted not to. Looking at differences in means, firms that have directors run for office are roughly 9–10x larger in size (as measured by both the size of their assets and number of employees). Running for office is an expensive undertaking and it is unsurprising that only firms with substantial financial and labor resources can afford to adopt this strategy. "Candidate Firms" have many more subsidiaries, indicating their geographic reach within a region and need for political representation beyond the municipality where their headquarters is located. They are also much more connected to global markets, engaging in importing and exporting activities at a rate of roughly three times that of "Non-Candidate Firms."

I then plot the percentage of "Candidate" versus "Non-Candidate" firms according to their industry in Figure 2.4. Stark differences emerge. First and foremost, firms engaged in basic retail and wholesale trade adopt the strategy of businessperson candidacy at much lower rates. Firms engaged in manufacturing, mining, and agriculture are all more heavily represented among candidate firms than non-candidate firms. This could be evidence that firms in sectors characterized by more asset specificity are more interested in sending representatives into elected office. I discuss these patterns further in the next chapter.

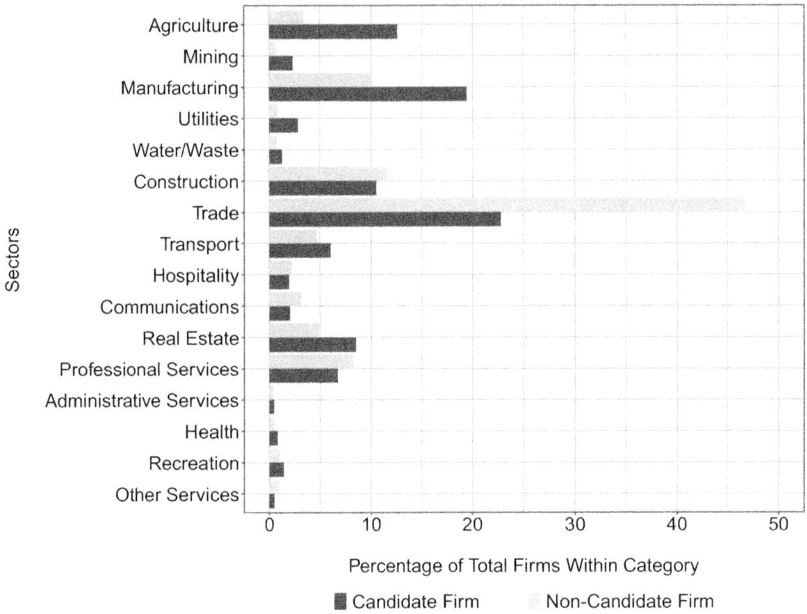

FIGURE 2.4: Sectoral distribution of candidate firms

This figure plots the percentage of firms that fall into each sector, based on whether they put forth a candidate or not. For example, roughly 46 percent of all Non-Candidate Firms (firms without a candidate for office) worked in trade, compared to 23 percent of Candidate Firms (firms that had a candidate for office).

The Case of State-Owned Enterprises

The descriptive evidence in Table 2.1 suggests that businessperson candidates more often represent state-owned enterprises, with the differences being substantively large. This may come as a surprise, since business person candidacy might theoretically be irrelevant for directors of such firms. After all, SOEs should have their own channels to communicate with relevant government officials and resolve various challenges to their productive activities. Many of these very same officials sit on SOE boards and assume responsibility for managing how and when dividends are transferred to state budgets and other overtly political decision-making that justifies (in their own eyes) why the state should be allowed to retain ownership of commercially-oriented firms. Why then would an SOE director then run for political office herself?

The answer lies in the fact that SOEs are still commercial entities competing in open markets. State ownership confers many advantages, but SOEs still need to work the same political channels to generate revenue and remain competitive. They vie for procurement tenders on open electronic systems, secure export licenses from ministries, and require the same licenses and permits to register and market their goods. Sector-wide regulations rarely, if ever, exclude SOEs from their dictates. Many cannot even rely on soft budget constraint or unconditional bailouts:[45] if a regional government considers a SOE to be too ridden with loss, privatization is always on the table. Finally, there are often multiple SOEs competing within a single industry. Governments cannot offer equal treatment to all of these enterprises; by creating scarcity in meting out preferential treatment, officials can better ensure that SOEs are run efficiently. Not all the lessons of Soviet-style management are lost on current government officials. SOEs have adapted to the competitive marketplace, with state ownership providing a leg-up but not necessarily an escalator to economic success.

As a result, SOE directors may view elected office as a key asset not only for promoting the interests of their enterprise, but also keeping their often lucrative jobs. Deputy status offers an insurance policy against privatization and increases the probability that SOEs will thrive. This type of competition for political benefits by the already well connected is by no means unique to Russia. Subnational governments, by definition having easier access to officialdom, also use various lobbying techniques to extract privileged treatment from higher level governments. For example, US cities regularly lobby the federal government to secure earmarks and grants,[46] while Russian regions elaborately court the authorities in Moscow to increase their intergovernmental transfers from the center.[47] In China, state-owned enterprises join leading business associations to improve the quality and frequency of their contacts with officialdom.[48] Therefore, we might expect interesting dynamics to emerge among SOEs and their interest in regional office and I include all such firms in the analysis.

2.2 DISCUSSION AND CONCLUDING REMARKS

Businesspeople running for elected office have been a common occurrence in post-Soviet Russia. Politicians with a clear foot in the private

[45] Kornai (1986).
[46] Goldstein and You (2017).
[47] Sharafutdinova and Turovsky (2017).
[48] Deng and Kennedy (2010).

sector occupy important positions up and down the Russian government, from municipal council members to State Duma deputies. Yet even given this high degree of interest, not all firms have allocated the resources to send their director into politics. Descriptive statistics suggest significant and interesting variation in rates of candidacy across different types of firms, sectors, and regions. The next four chapters exploit this rich dataset on connections between firms and politicians to first illuminate the conditions under which businessperson candidacy becomes more common, but also key questions about how businesspeople approach campaigning and then govern while in office.

3

Economic Competition, Weak Parties, and Businessperson Candidacy

Chapter 1 argued that uncertainty over access to political decision making drives the decision among firms to run for office. Businesspeople face a difficult commitment problem: politicians regularly defect from the agreements they strike with special interests, and traditional market-based and institutional solutions offer little relief. Moreover, when rival firms win legislative office, indirect strategies become toothless. Running for and winning elected office, on the other hand, enables firms to go around these unreliable intermediaries and achieve direct policy influence. This theoretical framework then predicts that we should see the highest levels of businessperson candidacy when the risks of politician shirking loom largest.

This chapter provides a series of empirical tests for the book's main hypotheses. I begin with the observational data at the firm level, using multilevel and fixed effects models to investigate how businessperson candidacy depends on factors such as economic competition, weak party institutionalization, and varying barriers to political entry. Next, I aggregate the firm-level data to the region level to further probe the result that political party weakness drives the interest among firms in running for office. As an out-of-sample test, I then bring to bear evidence from an original firm survey conducted in 2017 to examine how the decision to run for office is shaped by economic competition from large rivals and opportunities for collective action. Finally, I draw on primary sources and qualitative data from over 70 interviews with regional political actors to fill out the primary narratives driving businessperson candidacy. In all, this chapter finds broad support for the main hypotheses: fears of politician shirking, defined along several dimensions, significantly influence whether firms run representatives in campaigns for elected office.

3.1 DETERMINANTS OF BUSINESSPERSON CANDIDACY: FIRM REGISTRATION DATA

What explains why some businesspeople run for political office, while others do not? The comparisons in the previous chapter suggest that at least at the firm level, size and sector matter to a great deal. But such descriptive statistics only reflect differences in means; given potential correlations between the indicators, conclusions should be drawn rather lightly. In this section, I outline and implement an empirical strategy that uses the official firm registration and financial data from SPARK to test both the region-level and firm-level hypotheses derived in Chapter 1.

3.1.1 Variable Measurement

Hypothesis 1 holds that firms run candidates for office when they face fierce competition in their sector, particularly from large rivals. To test this claim, I calculate a standard Herfindahl-Hirschmann Index (HHI) for each sector in each region in each year. Because in the Russian context firm directors run for office at the regional level, this measure should precisely capture differences in competition across both years and regions.[1] Although firms do compete over inputs (such as electricity subsidies or construction permits that grant access to land), identifying these very industry-specific concerns across industries, regions, and years would be a heroic undertaking. For the purposes of studying businessperson candidacy, the distribution of market share within industry (as measured by revenue) best captures the type of competition that drives entry into political office.

For each region-year when a legislative election was held, I calculated every firm's market share, where markets are defined according to two-digit industry codes of the All-Russian Classification of Kinds of Economic Activity (or OKVED).[2] I then summed the squares of the

[1] This approach mirrors the empirical work by the US Department of Justice and the Federal Reserve to measure competition within markets (Rhoades, 1993). For example, Petersen and Rajan (1995) use a Herfindahl index to identify the effect of credit market competition on how firms establish relationships with creditors. In many respects, the HHI is the industry standard.

[2] OKVED is the internationally recognized industry classification used by the Russian State Statistics service during this period.

market shares for each firm in their industry. Since I am interested in competition, for ease of interpretation I calculated a so-called "Inverse HHI," where the HHI is inverted by subtracting it from one. This allows us to accord higher values of this index with greater competition within a given industry. This approach is common in the literature.[3]

$$Inverse\ HHI = 1 - \sum_{i=1}^{n}(MarketShare_i)^2 \tag{3.1}$$

The Inverse HHI takes values of 0 to 1, with those industries with values closer to 1 approaching "perfect" competition. In Figure 3.1, I plot the distribution of competition measures across sectors in Russia. Each point/line is an average of all the 159 region-years (regional elections) in the dataset. The points represent the mean level of competition for each

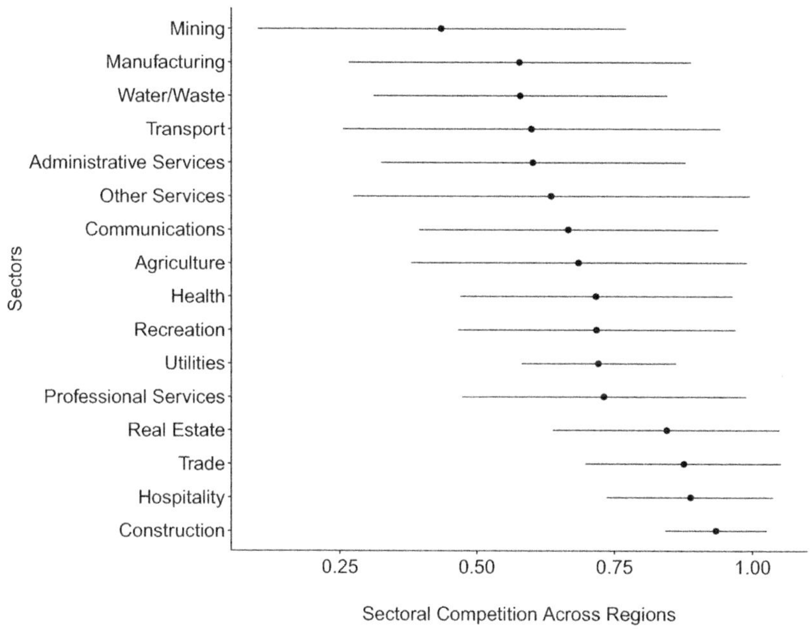

FIGURE 3.1: Sectoral competition in Russia
This figure plots the inverse Herfindahl-Hirschmann Index for each of the above sectors. Greater values of this index indicate greater competition, as in market share is distributed more evenly across the firms of each sector. Sector-level scores are averaged across all region-years in the dataset. The dots indicate this mean while the bars depict one standard deviation above and below the mean.

[3] Nawrocki and Carter (2010); Drucker (2015).

sector, while the bars depict one standard deviation above and below that mean. There is great variation across sectors in Russia. The construction industry in Russia is highly competitive, with the majority of region-years approximating perfect competition (with a score of 1). There are very few dominant players in terms of market share. Similar patterns are shown for trade and hospitality, two sectors with low barriers to entry and less dependence on immobile assets. On the other hand, mining and manufacturing are both marked by weak competition. A few large actors in each dominate the sector. Overall we see significant variation both across sectors and across regions (as evidenced by the large standard deviation bars), indicating that firms in Russia face potentially big and meaningful differences in their competitive environments.

Hypothesis 1 also predicts that large firms will be especially likely to respond to competitive conditions by sending their directors into elected office. Part of this clearly is driven by the resources they have available for funding campaigns. Below I describe several measures to get exactly at this mechanism. However, relative size within an industry also matters. Firms are concerned their rivals will also run for office, thereby triggering an arms race and making businessperson candidacy a mandatory strategy for protecting firms' political interests. To capture this dynamic, I create a binary "Top 5" measure which indicates if a firm's revenue places it within the five largest firms within its regional industry.[4] I interact this indicator with the measure of sectoral competition (the Inverse HHI) to capture how within-industry rivalry compels large firms to seek political office. Legislative office allows them, for instance, to erect high barriers to entry for other firms and preserve their dominant market position.

To test Hypothesis 2 (party institutionalization), I use two independently collected measures of political party strength from the Russian Central Electoral Commission. First, I calculate the total expenditures on rent, communal services, communications, transport, and salaries per region by the four major political parties that had representation in the Russian State Duma over this time period: United Russia, the Communist Party of the Russian Federation, Just Russia (and Rodina), and the Liberal-Democratic Party of Russia.[5] When controlling for regional

4 In the Appendix, I show the results are robust to using other measures of a firm's relative position atop the industry hierarchy.

5 The results are robust to alternate formulations of this variable, including expanding the definition of national parties to include all parties present in the 2003–7 convocation of the Russian State Duma.

wealth, this variable ("National Party Strength – Expenditures") helps capture how well-established each party is in the region using their spending behavior as well as long-term investment in sustaining an active office. The more total money the four parties collectively spend on these line-items, the more strongly their presence is felt on the ground. We should expect then that the firms will be less likely to run for office when parties are stronger, as captured by the money they spend on these line-items.

The data on expenditures comes from annual regional reports that each party is required to submit to the Central Election Commission.[6] Hutcheson (2012) discusses in greater detail the reliability of these party spending data, noting that although scholars believe the figures underestimate total electoral financing, the reports are audited by the Central Election Commission which has the power to deregister parties found to be concealing funds. His conclusion is that the data are simply the best available on party activities.

The second measure builds off the fact that in Russia, candidates to legislative office at all levels of government do not need to be affiliated with a political party to participate in an election. Instead, they can run as independents if they can amass the necessary number of signatures on their own to submit to the electoral commission. Following Gehlbach, Sonin, and Zhuravskaya (2010), I create a proxy for regional variation in party institutionalization by measuring differences in the nominating practices for candidates in single-member districts. I calculate the percentage of non-businessperson candidates that affiliated with one of the four national parties: "National Party Strength – Nominations." I specifically exclude all businessperson candidates. Hypothesis 2 holds that businesspeople are making ex ante deliberations about party strength. By incorporating businessperson political affiliation into the measure, we are potentially confusing the predictor with the outcome, and biasing the results in favor of the hypothesis.[7]

6 For a detailed overview of the information Russian electoral law requires that parties submit, see Appendix 8 from Postanovlenie N 163/1158–5 "About Recommendations for Compiling Reports on Contributions to and Expenses by Political Parties, Regional Branches of Political Parties, and other Registered Structures of Political Parties and About Recommendations for Compiling Financial Reports for Political Parties."

7 In the Appendix, I show the results are also robust to using a measure of party nominations that include current businessperson candidates. Both measures come from the same election year where the businesspeople's decision to run for office is taken. I adopt this approach in order to keep the measures of party institutionalization as temporally adjacent to the decision as possible.

This approach has both advantages and disadvantages over that used in Gehlbach, Sonin, and Zhuravskaya (2010), who derive their measure using the percentage of party-affiliated candidates to the State Duma from each region. Because the State Duma moved to a full proportional electoral system in 2005, measuring variation in national candidate party affiliation after the 2007 national parliamentary elections is impossible. All candidates are affiliated with parties and the number of independents in the State Duma drops to zero. Coding party affiliation for regional legislative candidates overcomes this problem (independents are still present in regional legislatures throughout the period), while also providing a more localized measure of party penetration into regional politics. This however comes at a cost: data on candidate affiliation is missing for the eleven regions that did not use a mixed-member system to elect regional deputies (where part of the seats represented single-member districts).

Hypothesis 3 argues that that businessperson candidacy will be more attractive when personalist regimes undermine formal institutionalization and cause uncertainty for candidates. I follow the convention in the literature and use a dummy indicator for whether a region is an ethnic republic. Hale (2003) demonstrates that the ethnic policies implemented under the USSR helped institutionalize strong identity-based social networks in Russia's ethnic republics. When the Soviet Union collapsed, regional leaders drew upon these networks to develop powerful local machines that helped them consolidate their hold on power, extract concessions from the federal center, and take control over the local bureaucracy. Many ethnic republics are still dominated by personalized political systems,[8] resulting in the weakening of national party institutions and the exacerbation of commitment problems among elites.[9]

I test Hypothesis 4 (the costs of running for office) using a variable that measures the annual gross regional product for each region (e.g. the regional equivalent of GDP). These data are taken from the Russian State Statistics Agency. I argue that variation in the amount of money required to run a campaign depends on the income of the median voter. From buying advertising time on television to printing posters

8 Sharafutidnova (2013).

9 Reuter and Szakonyi (2019).

and flyers for distribution, elections require large expenditures to win.[10] The resources needed to fund these activities correlates with the wealth of the constituency: where wages are higher, the price of basic campaign materials rises. In countries where voter rights are not protected, campaigns must also incur an additional set of expenses through vote-buying. Citizens who sell their vote can place extraordinary demands on parties and candidates, especially where there are multiple suitors for their vote. Corstange (2016) shows that wealthier citizens capitalized on party competition to engage in increased vote-selling at higher prices. Richer localities require more attention and resources to swing over to a candidate or party's side, and thus deter businesspeople from seeking office.[11]

Hypothesis 5 holds that larger firms are more likely to run candidates for office. I measure firm size by logging the total assets of each firm (in rubles) in the year the businessperson ran for election. In addition, I include a binary indicator if a firm is among the "Top 5" largest in its region-specific industry. Although the measure of total assets allows us to estimate the monotonic relationship between size and candidacy, the incredible costs of running for office require that firms be not just above average in size, but potentially huge compared to their rivals. Therefore, I also include this non-parametric indicator alongside the continuous measure of assets.

Chapter 1 also introduced several alternate explanations that also could influence the propensity of businesspeople to run for office. First, greater democratization and associational life could help businesses solve joint commitment and coordination problems by providing mechanisms of accountability. As a control, I include several variables measuring institutional constraints, accountability, and media freedom from the Carnegie Democracy Index, developed by the Moscow Carnegie Center's Regional Monitoring Project.[12] The Democracy Index incorporates

10 An even better proxy for the cost of running would be how much television stations charge candidates to run for political office. Unfortunately, I have been unable to track down any sort of cross-regional data about these costs.

11 Campaign costs are shaped by a number of political or economic factors that do not lend themselves well to measurement, including the probability of winning a seat, the expectations of voters, or the appointment power of the office; the price of lobbying for policy can similarly differ across institutional settings (Palda, 1992; Artés and Viñuela, 2007; Fox and Lawless, 2011).

12 The Carnegie Index is the best and most widely used time-varying assessment of subnational democracy in Russia during this period. Many works use this index or individual

expert evaluations of regional political development along ten dimensions of democratization (each on a 1 to 5 scale).[13]

Using this index, I build two aggregate composites, a minimal and a maximal version that capture different components scored by experts. The "minimal" index simply adds the scores of three of the key dimensions directly capturing institutional constraints: the openness of political life (e.g. transparency), electoral competitiveness, and the strength of civil society. This is a reduced-form proxy for how well interest groups can prevent politicians from defecting on the promises they make, whether public or private. The "maximal" index adds these three dimensions to the scores on media freedom, pluralism, and regional political structure. This provides a more comprehensive look at the state of democracy in each region. I alternate including both measures in the model specifications.[14]

So far, the models include four measures of political institutions at the regional level. Two measure party institutionalization ("Expenditures" and "Nominations"), while two measure accountability ("Maximal" and "Minimal"). Because of how the latter two democracy indexes are constructed, we might expect a high degree of collinearity to emerge between them and the party strength measures. This would undermine our ability to cleanly estimate the effects of all the variables. The Appendix presents a correlation matrix between the four measures. First we see that the two measures of party strength are correlated at 0.66 (significant at the 99 percent level). This improves our confidence that the measures are capturing a key dimension of institutionalization.

Second, we see an even higher level of correlation between the "maximal" and "minimal" definitions of accountability: 97 percent and

components, including Sharafutdinova (2006), Akhmedov and Zhuravskaya (2004), and Freinkman and Plekhanov (2009). Though not without its flaws, validation exercises have confirmed that the index appeals to a standard definition of democracy and reflects a conception of "liberal democracy" (and not broader or more minimalist ones) (Libman and Obydenkova, 2015).

13 The ten dimensions are regional political structure, openness or closedness of political life, electoral integrity, political pluralism, media independence, civil society, corruption, economic liberalization, elites, and local self-government. See Appendix for further explanation of the components.

14 This excludes four components that all measure political developments related, but not central, to conceptions of democracy: corruption, economic liberalization, regional political structure, and elites. The first two are more closely related to the effect of government actions on the economic environment, while the latter concern the way municipalities relate to the regional center and the diversity of elites. The results do not change when these four components are added in.

significant again at the 99 percent level. Both measure the degree to which politicians are accountable to voters and other societal actors. The two groups of measures are not strongly correlated with one another. "National Party Strength – Expenditures" correlates with the two accountability measures at roughly 0.18, while "National Party Strength – Nominations" correlates with them at roughly -0.02. We can be more confident that these four measures are picking up different dimensions about how citizens, parties, and the media engage politically at the regional level.

Markus and Charnysh (2017) among others make the claim that firms' interest in political office may be motivated by threats of expropriation and predation among government officials.[15] Where the rule of law is weak and bureaucrats are unconstrained from harassing firms, businessperson candidacy may become more attractive. Unfortunately, reasonable, time-varying measure of property rights protections at the region level are not available for the period under study. Instead, below I use data from a survey of firms that better taps their individual experiences with bureaucrats, as well as trade associations and community alliances.

Finally, I include several control variables at the firm, sector, and region levels. First, I include dummy variables for whether firms imported or exported during the period (Orbis) and the age of firm in logged years (Orbis). I exclude all firms working in finance, since they are regulated at the federal level, as well as firms listed on national stock exchanges.[16] At the sectoral level, I include a measure of total sector turnover (all firms operating in each region-sector-year). Industries that contribute more to a region's economy may not only have more firms interested in political access, but also enjoy preferences among political parties in terms of allocating spots on party lists.

Given the limited nature of the bulk data from Orbis, I am only able to see if a firm is 100 percent owned by the state (unitary enterprises). Because of this restriction, any SOEs that have both state and private ownership, therefore, enter the sample coded as private firms. I am, however, able to code which type of government asserts control over its

15 See Hou (2019) for a similar argument applied to China.

16 A very small number of publicly traded businesses run candidates at the regional level. Because much of their political activity is focused on Moscow, I did not want to confuse a businessperson candidate with experience in one of these companies with someone necessarily running to help that firm in the region. The main results do not change when these companies are included.

activities: federal, regional, or municipal.[17] SOEs at all three levels are managed off-budget by the ministry to which their commercial activities are mostly closely related, with profits (and losses) held on that ministry's (or agency's) books.[18] I include dummy variables for each type of enterprise in all of the main specifications. In the Appendix, I show models that exclude SOEs from the sample, finding that the main results are robust to solely looking at private firms.

Because of the lack of data on partial state ownership, the number of SOEs that enter the analysis sample is rather small. Of the roughly 1.2 million firm-years, 2,153 are from federal SOES, 6,163 from regional SOEs, and 20,351 from municipal SOEs, totaling roughly 2.4 percent of the sample. Even conditional on firm size, SOE directors do seem to run for office at a slightly higher rate than their private sector counterparts. Among firms with over $1 million in assets, the likelihood that an SOE puts forth a candidate is roughly 80 percent higher than that of a private firm.

At the regional level, I proxy for opportunities for rent-seeking by coding a dummy indicator for the presence of natural resources (oil, gas, and metal) in each region using data from the Russian Federal Agency for Subsoil Use. Unfortunately, data on the percentage of gross regional product derived from the exploitation of natural resources are not available for a number of years in the sample (which would offer a time-varying indicator of how dependent regions are on mineral wealth). I also include measures of the logged total population and the level of urbanization in each locality (both taken from the Russian State Statistics Agency). Finally, I control for the total volume of each sector for each region-year (logged) in order to produce more refined estimates of the effect of industrial concentration that are independent of industry size. Full summary statistics for all the variables used can be found in the Appendix.

3.1.2 Empirical Strategy

All analysis is done at the firm level.[19] The primary outcome variable studied is a binary indicator for whether a firm saw a member of its upper-level management run for regional legislative office in that

[17] In official parlance, these correspond to *Federalyne Gosudarstvennye Unitarnye Predpriyatiya* (FGUPs), *Gosudarstvennye Unitarnye Predpriyatiya Subyekta* (OGUPs), and *Munitsipalnte Unitarnye Predpriyatiya* (MUPs).

[18] Sprenger (2010).

[19] For summary statistics on the dataset used in this analysis, please see the Appendix.

year. In addition, I create an additional outcome variable that follows Gehlbach, Sonin, and Zhuravskaya (2010) in denoting some firms as connected to "serious" candidates. Given the wide variety of personalities running for office in Russia, restricting the analysis to candidates with a realistic chance of winning office allows us to better test the incentives for businesspeople to both run for and actually hold elected office. Some businesspeople may view campaigns as opportunities for free advertising and act differently than their counterparts who are truly interested in serving in office. I create an additional binary indicator that denoted whether a firm was connected to a candidate that either received more than 5 percent of the vote in a plurality race, held one of the top ten "core" spots on the party list, or were among the top three members of a geographic grouping.[20] To address potential concerns that problems arise with using electoral data to assess the seriousness of candidates,[21] I show robustness checks in the Appendix that only use data on candidates on party lists, where rank is assigned before the election.

Studying the full range of determinants of businessperson candidacy requires an empirical approach that takes into account variation at three levels of analysis: region, sector, and firm. Individual firms are nested in two groups: sectors and regions. Several variables capturing the importance of sectoral and institutional context therefore do not vary for each individual firm, while others do not vary over time because of the cross-sectional nature of expert evaluations. For example, fixed effects models at the region level are thus inadvisable. In addition, the hypothesis arguing the importance of oligopolistic competition requires between-sector variation to be properly tested, which precludes the use of fixed effects at this level.

Because we cannot assume that standard errors will be independent across individual firm observations, my primary strategy adopts a multilevel modeling approach. Multilevel modeling provides unbiased standard errors for our firm-level parameter estimates given the clustered

[20] See Lyubarev (2011). Regions vary in their use of methods to allocate seats, and some follow the practice of the Russian State Duma of partitioning the party list into a set of geographic groupings intended to more closely connect representatives with the electorate. Using rank data, I coded where candidates were listed within these groupings, an indicator of prominence as well as likelihood of entering the legislature if the party passed the electoral threshold.

[21] The concern might be that electoral results reflect the campaign and other factors, rather than the actual intention of the businessperson candidacy, thus adding something akin to post-treatment bias.

nature of the data.[22] The lack of substantial variation over time across several of the key predictors (such as natural resource endowments) further necessitates a flexible approach across multiple groups. Therefore, I first estimate firm-level coefficients as fixed, rather than random, across sectors and regions; the firm-level intercept is modeled as a function of random effects at the other levels of analysis. Intercepts are thus allowed to vary at the sector (fifty-four units) and the region (eighty-three units) level. I include year fixed effects as none of the main predictors are time-dependent, and thus might drop out of the analysis. The general form of the equation estimated is:

$$y_{ijkl} = \alpha + \beta' F_i + \gamma' S_j + \lambda' R_k + \phi_j + \zeta_k + \theta_l + \varepsilon \qquad (3.2)$$

where F represents firm-level determinants, S represents sectors-level determinants, R represents region-level determinants, ϕ represents sector-level random effects, ζ represents region-level random effects, and θ represents year-level fixed effects.[23] All errors are clustered at the region level.

As a robustness check, I ran OLS models that include region, sector, and year fixed effects. All time-invariant indicators at the region-level (such as the presence of natural resources) necessarily fall out of this model, but this empirical approach helps capture exogenous shocks that could hit all regions in one year as well as region and sector-specific factors that could influence a firm's decision to act politically. Standard errors here are clustered at the sector level.

3.1.3 Firm-Level Empirical Results

The main results measuring the determinants of businessperson candidacy are shown in Table 3.1. Column 1 shows a multilevel model with region, year, and sector random effects, but no interaction terms. Columns 2 and 3 include an interaction term between the indicator for a "Top 5" firm and regional competition, and then alternate between the two different measures of party institutionalization (based on expenditures and candidate nominations). To hone in on firms with a greater ability to afford this political strategy, Column 4 runs the same multilevel model, but subsets the sample to firms with assets more than $1

[22] Gelman and Hill (2006); Bryk and Raudenbush (1992).

[23] Multilevel Poisson and logistic models failed to converge, most likely due to the difficulty of producing estimates using a large dataset at multiple levels of analysis.

	Firm Had Candidate					Firm Had Serious Candidate	
	(1)	(2)	(3)	(4)	(5)	(6)	(7)
Firm-Level Predictors							
Total Assets (logged)	0.002***	0.002***	0.003***	0.007***	0.002***	0.002***	0.002***
	(0.00005)	(0.00005)	(0.0001)	(0.0001)	(0.0005)	(0.00004)	(0.0004)
Top 5 Firm	0.050***	0.030***	0.026***	0.033***	0.028***	0.026***	0.025***
	(0.001)	(0.002)	(0.002)	(0.003)	(0.005)	(0.002)	(0.004)
Firm Age (logged)	0.003***	0.003***	0.003***	0.006***	0.003***	0.002***	0.003***
	(0.0001)	(0.0001)	(0.0001)	(0.0002)	(0.0004)	(0.0001)	(0.0004)
Importer	0.006***	0.006***	0.007***	0.005***	0.007***	0.006***	0.006***
	(0.0004)	(0.0004)	(0.0005)	(0.001)	(0.001)	(0.0004)	(0.001)
Exporter	0.005***	0.005***	0.006***	0.002***	0.005***	0.004***	0.005***
	(0.0005)	(0.0005)	(0.001)	(0.001)	(0.001)	(0.0004)	(0.001)
Federal SOE	−0.010***	−0.010***	−0.010***	−0.018***	−0.010**	−0.008***	−0.008***
	(0.002)	(0.002)	(0.003)	(0.003)	(0.004)	(0.002)	(0.003)
Regional SOE	0.009***	0.009***	0.009***	0.004**	0.009**	0.006***	0.006*
	(0.001)	(0.001)	(0.002)	(0.002)	(0.004)	(0.001)	(0.003)
Municipal SOE	−0.006***	−0.007***	−0.008***	−0.012***	−0.007***	−0.007***	−0.007***
	(0.001)	(0.001)	(0.001)	(0.001)	(0.002)	(0.001)	(0.002)
Sector-Level Predictors							
Total Sector Revenue	0.004***	0.004***	0.004***	0.004***	0.004***	0.004***	0.004***
(logged)	(0.0002)	(0.0002)	(0.0002)	(0.0003)	(0.0003)	(0.0001)	(0.0003)
Sectoral Competition	0.013***	0.007***	0.007***	0.005**	0.008***	0.007***	0.008***
	(0.001)	(0.001)	(0.001)	(0.002)	(0.003)	(0.001)	(0.002)
Sectoral Competition*		0.027***	0.036***	0.012***	0.031***	0.026***	0.029***
Top 5 Firm		(0.003)	(0.003)	(0.004)	(0.008)	(0.002)	(0.005)

(continued)

TABLE 3.1 *(continued)*

	Firm Had Candidate					Firm Had Serious Candidate	
	(1)	(2)	(3)	(4)	(5)	(6)	(7)
Region-Level Predictors							
Gross Regional Product (logged)	−0.012***	−0.012***	−0.016***	−0.019***	−0.015***	−0.007***	−0.008***
	(0.002)	(0.002)	(0.002)	(0.003)	(0.002)	(0.002)	(0.003)
Total Population (logged)	0.005**	0.005*	0.006**	0.008**	0.041*	−0.00001	−0.004
	(0.002)	(0.002)	(0.003)	(0.004)	(0.023)	(0.002)	(0.027)
Natural Resources	0.001	0.001	0.001	−0.005		0.001	
	(0.004)	(0.004)	(0.004)	(0.006)		(0.003)	
Ethnic Republic	0.009**	0.009**	0.011***	0.019***		0.005	
	(0.004)	(0.004)	(0.004)	(0.007)		(0.003)	
National Party Strength – Expenditures	−0.005***	−0.005***		−0.008***	−0.007**	−0.004***	−0.007***
	(0.001)	(0.001)		(0.002)	(0.003)	(0.001)	(0.003)
National Party Strength – Nominations			−0.005**				
			(0.002)				
Aggregate Accountability (Maximal)	0.001***	0.001***	0.001**	0.002***	0.0004	0.0003**	−0.00002
	(0.0002)	(0.0002)	(0.0002)	(0.0003)	(0.0003)	(0.0001)	(0.0003)
Region, Sector Effects	Random	Random	Random	Random	Fixed	Random	Fixed
Year Effects	Fixed	Fixed	Fixed	Fixed	Fixed	Fixed	Fixed
Observations	940,149	940,149	802,175	480,353	898,735	940,149	898,735

*p<0.1; **p<0.05; ***p<0.01 Columns 1–4 and 6 use multilevel linear probability models estimated using OLS with region, sector, and year random effects; Columns 5 and 7 use OLS models with region, sector, and year fixed effects. The dependent variable in Columns 1–5 is a binary indicator for whether a firm was connected to a businessperson candidate, i.e. had a director run for office in a regional legislative election. Column 4 subsets to firms that had at least $1 million in assets at the time of the campaign. The dependent variable in Columns 6–7 limits the sample to "serious" businessperson candidates who received more than 5 percent of the plurality vote, held one of the top ten "core" spots on the party list, or were among the top three members of a geographic grouping. The number of observations drops in Column 3 due to missingness in the variable National Party Strength – Nominations; some regions use a proportional representation system exclusively.

million.[24] In Column 5, the three sets of random effects are replaced by fixed effects. Finally, in Columns 6 and 7, the outcome variable studied captures only "serious" candidates, estimating multilevel (random) and OLS (fixed) effects models in turn.

The empirical evidence provides concrete support for the hypotheses developed in Chapter 1. First, we see that the degree of sectoral competition is positively correlated with firms' interest in businessperson candidacy as non-market strategy. Across all the model specifications, the greater values of the inverse HHI noted in a sector (indicating more within-sector competition), the more likely member firms will put forward directors in regional legislative elections. A one standard deviation increase in the level of sectoral competition more than doubles the probability that a given firm will run for office.[25] Firm directors enter the political arena partly in response to market forces: their ability to protect their own interests against fierce competition may depend on the direct political access they can achieve.

The results indicate that the uncertainty created by sectoral competition is particularly salient for large firms. First, we see that being one of the five largest firms in one's sector has an extremely large effect on the likelihood of running for office: top five firms run at a rate nearly five times higher than their smaller counterparts.[26] The importance of such market dominance also comes through controlling for total firm assets, which is also positive and statistically significant. Even more interestingly, we see a strong and positive interactive effect on being one of these industry leaders in competitive sectors. Large firms are much more likely to put forward candidates to protect their position in sectors marked by many rivals. Firms fear these rivals will gain decisive advantages in the political arena. Competition increases the attractiveness of businessperson candidacy, especially when a firm's ability to earn revenue comes under threat. This effect also holds when only firms with over $1 million in assets are included in the analysis (Column 5).

The flip side of this argument is that monopolistic firms see much less value in businessperson candidacy. As competition in a sector decreases, the leading firms can rest more assured that other political strategies will bear fruit and their competitive advantages adequately defended

24 I assume a somewhat stable ruble exchange rate during the period of 30 rubles to the dollar.

25 Candidate Firms comprise roughly 1 percent of the entire sample.

26 This result is robust to using different thresholds for non-parametrically defining large firms, such as being within the top 10 or the top 20 largest firms in each sector. See the Appendix for the results on these alternate measures.

without direct representation in the literature. Many firms in highly concentrated sectors still run for office (the coefficient on "Top 5 Firm" is still positive even when competition is basically null). The need to expend such resources lessens when there are fewer rivals for the same exclusive goods.

Stronger political institutions, however, help mitigate the commitment problem with individual politicians. When national parties (i.e. those bound by reputation concerns over time) are more active in a region, businesspeople run for office at a lower rate. Institutionalization, whether measured by the amount of money spent by political parties or the percentage of candidates they can recruit to run under their banner, changes the incentives for businesspeople to run for office. A one standard deviation increase in the amount of money spent by party officials decreases the probability of a firm running for office by roughly 40 percent. These results are robust to both the multilevel and the fixed effects specifications. When parties are more developed and concerned about their long-term reputations, firm managers can be confident that allocating resources to lobbying and the parties' electoral campaigns (indirectly) will be just as effective at achieving their political goals.

Beyond direct measures of party institutionalization, we also see evidence that businessperson candidacies are more likely to occur in ethnic republics. Personalist regimes employ fewer rules and norms to govern spoil distribution and manage elite conflict, raising the risk that unwritten agreements with politicians will not be honored. That heightens the risk on investment through contributions and lobbying, while raising the appeal of directly occupying a seat in the legislature. All four of the multilevel models present consistent and positive point estimates on this indicator for ethnic republic status. Weaker formal institutions, whether indicated by party development or the role of personalism, spur firms to seek direct representation.

Firms also pay attention to the potential costs of running for office. We see consistent evidence from the models in Table 3.1 that businessperson candidacy occurs much more often in poorer regions, as measured by gross regional product. This result comes through after controlling for population, urbanization, the presence of natural resources, and various measure of party strength. Clearly, the wealth of voters is not the only factor affecting the cost of elections. For example, more competitive electoral races generally require more financial resources from candidates. But the overall wealth of a region strongly determines the price of a seat on a party list.

Other firm-level indicators also merit attention. Even controlling for firm size, both importing and exporting firms are more inclined to seek regional office. These companies conduct business beyond their own regional markets and often depend on support from politicians to expand abroad. Exporting behavior is often taken as a sign of firms' competitiveness and the quality of its product. This suggests that more productive firms seek out political connections to expand their economic foothold. But more importantly, regional governments can help secure licensing and export permits, while also facilitating trade expositions and connections with larger, international firms. An overt presence in the legislature helps unlock these goodies. Firms working in larger sectors are also more interested in this strategy, presumably because their importance to the regional economy dictates a more participatory role in governance.

Finally, I find that region-level state-owned enterprises are more likely to see their directors run for office than private firms, while those owned by federal and municipal governments generally stay away from regional legislative contests. This makes sense: each type of state-owned enterprise courts political access with its overseer government. Federal and municipal SOEs presumably see greater value in concentrating their political expenditures at the level of government from which they are owned, rather than vying for a spot in a regional legislature. I do find that excluding all SOEs from the analysis returns the same results on sectoral competition and party institutions, as well as the other main predictors of interest. In this regard, (regionally-owned) SOEs behave in the political sphere more similarly to private firms than perhaps is commonly believed, as their economic success depends on opening doors to bureaucrats.

Several factors previously identified as affecting businessperson candidacy in Russia appear to play less of a role during the period under study. The point estimates on national resource endowments are positive but not statistically significant in any of the specifications. One reason for this divergence from the results in Gehlbach, Sonin, and Zhuravskaya (2010), who also study businesspeople candidates in Russia but in earlier years, is that the federal government asserted more control over the exploitation of oil and gas. The federal transfer system set up to redistribute wealth between the regions may have decreased interest in using regional legislatures to access massive government rents.

Finally, at the firm level, we see a positive relationship between the level of democratization and the incidence of businessperson candidacy. This result is not just specific to the measure of accountability used. In the

Appendix, I show that both the maximal and minimal definitions of accountability both return positively signed point estimates (as in they predict higher rates of businessperson candidacy). Moreover, I find that regions more supportive of the United Russia party in national elections also saw greater businessperson candidacy.[27] Stronger support for UR is often taken as an indicator of less democratic development, as the ruling party has developed stronger inroads and curbed competition. Overall, during this period, we see consistent evidence that democratization may not serve as the best check on businesspeople running for political office. In the next section, I discuss this result further when looking at the regional-level results.

Other characteristics of industries, beyond their economic structure, influence firms' interest in businessperson candidacy. State dependence is generally considered a motivating factor for businesspeople to engage in wider arrays of political activity.[28] Minimizing regulatory burdens can be an effective way to lower costs and increase profitability.[29] Interviews with Russian businesspeople also highlighted that local firms operating in industries that were historically highly dependent on the government for subsidies, regulations, and permits are much more involved politically.[30] In Figure 3.2, I plot the sector-level intercepts and standard errors from the linear multilevel model presented in Column 1 of Table 3.1. Here I use the NACE 2 primary sector code instead of the two-digit OKVED sector code to simplify presentation. Measuring state dependence at the sectoral level is not clearcut, but some scholars propose using approximations of "asset specificity," or how tied certain industries are to fixed, immobile assets, as a indicator of both interest in and vulnerability to government regulation.

We see a strong relationship between the level of asset specificity of a sector and whether member firms are likely to opt for businessperson candidacy. Sectors such as mining and agriculture see much higher rates of businessperson candidacy, though only the effect on mining is precisely estimated. On the other hand, firms working in trade, a typical example of a more gently regulated services sector, are far less likely to run candidates. One exception is construction, which as Figure 3.1 indicates, is

[27] UR results were taken from the national elections closest to but temporally prior to the regional election in each case, either in 2003 or 2007.

[28] Grier, Munger, and Roberts (1994); Pittman (1977).

[29] Hart (2001).

[30] Interview with Anna Bykova, Higher School of Economics, Perm, Russia. October 4, 2013.

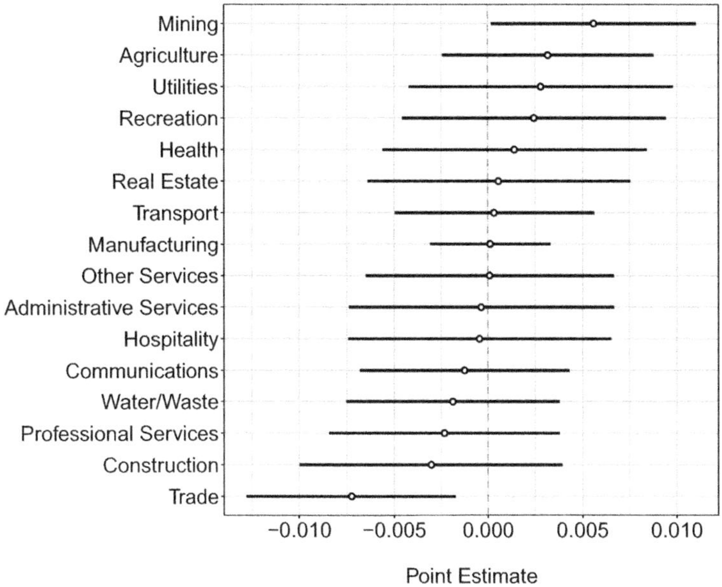

FIGURE 3.2: Candidacy broken down by sector: Random effects
This figure plots the sector-level random effects from the multilevel model used in Table 3.1, Column 1. Dots indicate the point estimate with the lines showing 95 percent confidence intervals.

highly decentralized compared to its peers. Although many large firms must work through government channels to get access to the permits and land they need to build on,[31] not all firms can afford the expensive costs of running for office.

In summary, the firm-level analysis presents consistently strong evidence that both market structure and party institutionalization play a strong part in the calculations of firm directors about whether to run for political office. All of these findings are robust to different model specifications, as well as when only the largest firms working in the region are analyzed. The results hold even when the outcome measure is limited to firms either running in single-member districts or through party lists. Both more oligopolistic competition and weaker party development propel businesspeople into politics, no matter the type of electoral rules in place.[32] But campaign costs also matter: larger firms have the resources

[31] Interview with Lilia Shiraeva, Regional Deputy, Perm, Russia. October 2, 2013.

[32] In Chapter 4, I look at firm preferences over different routes into elected office, finding that businesspeople in general gravitate towards running in plurality race. However,

to shoulder the bill, while firms in wealthier regions are deterred by the expenses required to win elections.

3.1.4 Region-Level Empirical Results

Several of the key predictors used to test the theory of businessperson candidacy are measured at the region, rather than the firm level. To probe the robustness of the results at the firm level, I next collapse the data on businessperson candidacy to the level of the regional election. This approach necessarily shrinks sample size and statistical power, but provides another opportunity to compare how differences in regional political and economic structure affect the incentives for businesspeople to go into politics. Analyzing region- (or state-) level data also mirrors other academic work about why businesspeople run for office.[33] Unfortunately, testing the hypothesis on oligopolistic competition (a sector specific measure) cannot be done using region data.

The unit of analysis is the main regional election, i.e. the election that preceded each parliamentary convocation.[34] I aggregate the firm data to the region level by calculating the percentage of candidates that came from the private sector and who ran for office in each legislative election.[35] I include a measure of legislature size, the logged number of seats, in all models to control for variation across regions in the supply of points of institutional access. The dataset analyzed in this section looks at the period 2004–2011 in order to more closely resemble the analysis of firm registration data. In the Appendix, I demonstrate that extending the dataset to 2016 using an alternate coding scheme returns robust results.

Table 3.2 presents OLS models that include year fixed effects and cluster errors at the region level. The predictors are identical to those used in the firm-level analysis (Table 3.1), save for one exception. First, to control for the number of firms that could potentially put forward directors to run for office, I include a logged measure of all firms operating in the region during the year of the election from the Russian State Statistics Agency.

variation in market structure and party strength also predicts when firms vie for spots on party lists.

33 Gehlbach, Sonin, and Zhuravskaya (2010); Rosenson (2006).

34 For this analysis, I exclude midterm elections.

35 The SMDP and PR candidates are pooled. The results are robust to subsampling between the two types of ballots.

	Businessperson Candidates (%)					
	(1)	(2)	(3)	(4)	(5)	(6)
Total Population (logged)	0.052***	0.084***	0.051***	0.079***	0.055***	0.089***
	(0.019)	(0.020)	(0.018)	(0.019)	(0.021)	(0.022)
Gross Regional Product (logged)	0.002	−0.030*	0.003	−0.028	−0.0004	−0.035*
	(0.018)	(0.017)	(0.017)	(0.017)	(0.020)	(0.019)
Ethnic Republic	−0.019	0.002	−0.018	0.004	−0.026	−0.010
	(0.020)	(0.020)	(0.021)	(0.019)	(0.022)	(0.024)
Aggregate Accountability (minimal)	0.002	0.008**				
	(0.004)	(0.004)				
Aggregate Accountability (maximal)			0.002	0.005**		
			(0.002)	(0.002)		
Press Freedom					−0.004	−0.012
					(0.011)	(0.008)
Natural Resources	0.011	−0.007	0.009	−0.011	0.018	0.007
	(0.016)	(0.015)	(0.017)	(0.016)	(0.014)	(0.018)
Unemployment	−0.581***	−0.496	−0.580***	−0.500	−0.648***	−0.476
	(0.132)	(0.332)	(0.131)	(0.327)	(0.098)	(0.403)
Number of Candidates (logged)	0.015	−0.023	0.015	−0.022	0.013	−0.012
	(0.020)	(0.019)	(0.020)	(0.018)	(0.018)	(0.021)
National Party Strength – Expenditures	−0.041**		−0.040**		−0.043***	
	(0.017)		(0.018)		(0.016)	
National Party Strength – Nominations		−0.102**		−0.092**		−0.130***
		(0.041)		(0.044)		(0.043)
Year Fixed Effects	Yes	Yes	Yes	Yes	Yes	Yes
Observations	150	133	150	133	143	125
R^2	0.533	0.528	0.534	0.533	0.560	0.526

*$p<0.1$; **$p<0.05$; ***$p<0.01$ The outcome variable is the ratio of businesspeople running for office divided by the total number of candidates to each regional legislature. All models use simple OLS with year fixed effects and errors clustered on region. The minimal accountability measure uses four components of the Carnegie Democracy Index, while the maximal adds an additional three.

The results largely align with those derived from the firm level analysis. First, party institutionalization, as measured by both the level of expenditures and the percentage of SMDP candidates affiliated with parties, is strongly and negatively correlated with businessperson candidacy. This provides additional evidence that businesspeople refrain from running when political parties are strong.[36] However, although the effect of gross regional product is negative, it is statistically indistinguishable from zero in these models.

Finally, the region analysis indicates that more democratic regions attract greater numbers of businessperson candidates. The effect is substantive and significant using both measures of accountability from the Carnegie Democracy Index. This aligns with other work done on businesspeople running for legislative office in Russia. Rastorguyev (2012) finds that since 2003, entrepreneurs have been more likely to win office in regional assemblies located in regions with more democratic institutions. Businesspeople may actually be drawn to strong political institutions because they provide more opportunities to influence the rules and regulations that govern the business environment. More autocratic settings, in contrast, may be marked by a more closed policymaking process whereby representative institutions play a lesser role and efforts to gain political influence are better served by lobbying, instead of direct participation.

The difference in time period (1991–2005 versus 2004–2011) and level of governance studied (candidates to regional governorships rather than legislative office) may also help explain the difference between the results presented here and those found in Gehlbach, Sonin, and Zhuravskaya (2010). Given their greater authority and visibility, governors in Russia may face more scrutiny from the press and civil society, and have less leeway to blatantly promote their own financial interests while in office. Regional legislators in Russia attract much less media coverage and may find it easier to work towards private and public interests simultaneously. Therefore, stronger democracy has a weaker effect on the decision of firms to run candidates to legislative office than to the executive branch.

[36] As an additional check, I ran analysis at the candidate level, using the same predictors in a model examining whether a given candidate running for regional office from 2004 to 2011 came from the private sector. This candidate-level approach returns the same results: regions with stronger political parties see fewer businessperson candidates.

3.2 EVIDENCE FROM A FIRM SURVEY

The final quantitative evidence for the hypotheses comes from an original firm survey that asks firm directors and other members of the management team about their experience running for and/or holding elected regional office. The main advantage of tapping into survey data is that firm directors who have considered running for office can speak openly about market conditions, competition from rivals, and the political and associational strategies they use to protect their firms' interests. For example, survey data can be used to test the hypothesis that membership of business associations may help protect businesses against shirking by politicians and thus substitute for candidacy to legislatures. Although the sample is considerably smaller than the universe of registered firms analyzed above, surveys contain much richer information about firm behavior.

The survey I analyze includes 654 Russian firms and was conducted between June and October 2017. The sample consisted of medium-sized (100–249 employees) and large (over 250 employees) firms working in three primary sectors (manufacturing, transport, and construction) in twelve regions.[37] It should be noted that the survey was primarily designed to study firm preferences for vocational education: the investigators kindly allowed me to place several questions related to businessperson candidacy at the end.[38] Therefore, the main research objective was to study firm behavior in regions that were lauded for their best practices in vocational education reform by the Russian Agency for Strategic Initiatives, and not to create a representative sample across all of Russia.[39] The survey is roughly representative of firms within each region, with a slight oversampling of larger firms (over 250 employees) in order to ensure high response rates.

All respondents were asked whether anyone from their firms ran for legislative office in the most recent regional elections. Of the 654 firms, 71 (or 11.1 percent) replied that someone had. Among firms of this size, that

[37] I exclude large holding companies from the analysis as I am interested in within-sector dynamics at the region level.

[38] See Marques (2017) for more details on survey methodology. All interviews were completed in-person with the chief executive, financial, or legal officer of each firm. I thank Thomas Remington and Israel Marques for generously providing space on their questionnaire.

[39] The twelve regions were Samara, Sverdlodsk, Tambov, Ulyanovsk, Perm, Krasnoyarsk, Vladimir, Kursk, Voronezh, Novosibirsk, Chelyabinsk, and Vologda. See the Appendix for descriptive statistics about the sample used.

puts businessperson candidacy as a quite common form of non-market strategy. For the sake of comparison, 23.6 percent of all firms replied they were members of a national business association, while 9.4 percent were members of a regional business association. Over three quarters of all businessperson candidates from this sample of firms aligned with United Russia, with the remainder choosing one of the three systemic opposition parties (Communists, LDPR, or Just Russia). Over two-thirds of these candidates (69 percent) won their elections and took their seats in the regional legislative elections. I also analyze electoral victory as an outcome variable, but this selection should also be taken into account when interpreting results. The likelihood of businessperson candidates winning their elections, as calculated using the firm registration data, was considerably lower (roughly 25 percent).

The empirical strategy for analyzing these data is intended to approximate the specifications run in Section 3.1.3 above that use the official firm registration data. First, I measure the severity of competition from direct rivals with a three-point scale that asks respondents to classify competition from other firms in their region as non-existent, not very strong, or very strong. The median firm in this survey is quite large, meaning that this question captures exactly that type of high-level competition predicted to cause uncertainty and fears among firms about the credibility of their political access. Therefore, in some respects, this measure of competition both complements and surpasses that used above with the observational data. Here we can direct identify which firms are worried about maintaining competitive advantage, and link that with their political strategies.

As control variables to mirror the analysis using the registration data, I measure firm age (logged), the number of employees (logged),[40] a binary variable for whether they had exported any of their product over the last three years,[41] and binary indicators for regional/federal and municipal state ownership. I also include a nine-point scale that asks firms to compare revenue in 2016 to the previous year. This latter measure provides insight into whether faster growing firms are more likely to pursue political office for their directors.[42]

[40] The survey did not ask firms about turnover or assets. Employees are the best benchmark available for size.

[41] The survey does not ask firms about their importing activities.

[42] The nine-point scale ranges from negative growth of 11 percent or greater to a positive value of 11 percent or greater.

The survey also enables additional investigations into how relations with the state and other political institutions affect the decision to run directors in campaigns. First, to test whether the presence of trade associations or community alliances affects interest in candidacy, I code binary indicators for whether a firm is a member of a national and/or regional trade association. I also include two measures of expropriation risk and property rights protection, drawing on work by Markus (2012). On a five-point scale, firm directors were asked to rank the seriousness of (1) corruption and (2) rackets as obstacles to doing business. The former assesses whether motivations to run arose from perceptions of threats coming from public sector actors, while rackets capture how much predatory private actors pose a risk to firm operations. Next, I measure firms' interest in achieving certain benefits from the government through the percentage of their sales that are go directly the state (federal, regional, or municipal). This indicator ranges from 0 to 100. Full summary statistics can be found in the Appendix.[43]

Table 3.3 presents the results from OLS models that look at (a) whether a firm ran a candidate for regional legislative office and (b) whether a firm's candidate won office. I alternate including fixed effects for the sixteen subsectors within manufacturing, construction, and communications represented among the firms. All models cluster errors at the region level.

First, we see again that competition from regional rivals plays a major role in determining whether firm directors run for political office. For every unit shift on the three-point scale, a firm is 3–4 percentage points more likely to engage in businessperson candidacy, a 40 percent increase from the baseline. The survey results confirm what was found using the registration data: the more competition a firm faces, the more likely it is to send a representative to run for elected office. Other indicators of the severity of competition also noted in the survey, such as competition across regional markets or competition on international markets, fail to predict interest in businessperson candidacy. This nonmarket strategy is most often used for firms to keep up with their rivals through copying their business strategies, worried all the while that these competitors can outbid them for exclusive benefits from political leaders.

Next, we also see some evidence that larger firms are more likely to run candidates, though the point estimates on the number of employees

43 Because the sample contains only twelve regions, I do not include covariates at that level.

TABLE 3.3 *Evidence from Russian firm survey*

	Candidate from Firm Ran			Candidate from Firm Won		
	(1)	(2)	(3)	(4)	(5)	(6)
Regional Competition	0.032**	0.035**	0.030**	0.028***	0.028**	0.026**
	(0.014)	(0.015)	(0.013)	(0.010)	(0.012)	(0.012)
Firm Age (log)	0.018	0.004	0.008	0.020	0.008	0.011
	(0.025)	(0.015)	(0.016)	(0.022)	(0.014)	(0.013)
No. Employees (log)	0.040	0.027	0.021	0.032	0.020	0.015
	(0.025)	(0.024)	(0.022)	(0.025)	(0.024)	(0.020)
Regional / Federal SOE		0.365***	0.337***		0.379***	0.359***
		(0.111)	(0.112)		(0.103)	(0.102)
Municipal SOE		−0.003	−0.0003		−0.003	0.009
		(0.062)	(0.066)		(0.068)	(0.070)
Obstacle: Corruption		0.034	0.035		0.003	0.004
		(0.025)	(0.024)		(0.009)	(0.008)
Obstacle: Private Racket		−0.024	−0.026		0.003	0.002
		(0.019)	(0.019)		(0.009)	(0.009)
Recent Growth		−0.007	−0.009		0.001	−0.001
		(0.007)	(0.007)		(0.005)	(0.006)
National Association Member		0.014	0.018		0.011	0.007
		(0.038)	(0.031)		(0.025)	(0.019)
Regional Association Member		0.023	0.023		0.014	0.012
		(0.040)	(0.041)		(0.038)	(0.040)
Sector Fixed Effects	No	No	Yes	No	No	Yes
Observations	625	515	515	623	515	515
R^2	0.066	0.183	0.221	0.037	0.176	0.218

*p<0.1; **p<0.05; ***p<0.01 The outcome variable in Columns 1–3 is whether a firm had a representative contest regional office, while the outcome in Columns 4–6 is whether that representative won their election. All models use OLS and cluster errors at the region level.

are not significant at conventional levels in all models. We should note that employment is not always the best proxy for the amount of financial resources a firm has at its disposal to invest in elections. A larger labor force does mean potentially more votes to mobilize,[44] but for many aspirants to regional office, money talks even louder. Party officials value the financial payoffs exchanged for a seat on the proportional representation list, and buying television ads, paying campaign staff, and distributing flyers requires cold, hard cash. As above, exporting firms run for office at higher rates, as do firms with federal or regional ownership (both results match to the analysis using the firm registration data).

Finally, there does not seem to be a strong relationship between membership of a business association and running for office. The point estimates on the indicator for being a member of either a national or regional trade association are basically zero in all models.[45] As Chapter 1 spelled out, because of their inability to corral members and effectively lobby collective interests, these institutions struggle to function as a substitute for direct political strategies in Russia. Similarly, greater experience with corruption and private rackets do not predict businessperson candidacy. At least for the firms surveyed, interest in running for office derives more from economic conditions than threats of expropriation and predation.

3.3 QUALITATIVE DATA

Finally, I draw on qualitative data from over seventy interviews with various individuals in Russian regions to fill out the narrative linking economic competition, party institutionalization, and businessperson candidacy. Over the course of 2013 and 2014, I spoke with businessperson candidates (winning and losing), deputies without direct business interests, journalists, academics, and civil society representatives from three regions: Tomsk, Ryazan, and Perm. When selecting these regions to focus on, I wanted to ensure variability along several dimensions of theoretical interest for explaining businessperson candidacy.

First, the three regions vary significantly in terms of economic structure. On one hand, Perm Region is marked by sizable natural resource wealth (oil, metals, etc.), important manufacturing facilities and fierce

44 Frye, Reuter, and Szakonyi (2014).

45 Collapsing the two indicators into a single dummy for any type of associational membership returns nearly identical results.

rivalries among big business groups. Tomsk has fewer natural resources than other regions (but is notable for its lumber) and some industry, while Ryazan is mostly dependent on agriculture and related industries for economic production. These differences allow me to gain insight into how different market conditions affect the interest of business in higher office. The political context in all three regions offers additional leverage. Perm is often considered one of the most open and democratic regions in Russia, with the ruling party United Russia fiercely competing with several systemic opposition parties for legislative influence. This contrasts with Ryazan, where UR controlled nearly 90 percent of the legislative seats by 2015, as well as Tomsk, where UR enjoyed a three-quarters majority. Although I do not use the interview data to explicitly test the above hypotheses, this variation across economic and political conditions helps provide confidence that the insights gleaned from talking with politicians are not specific to one specific type of region.

The interviews illuminate just how important market competition is for understanding when and why firms opt for businessperson candidacy. In Perm, firms rarely band together within a given sector to protect their individual interests. Few mechanisms exist to organize this cooperation so every firm ends up lobbying for its own individual interests.[46] A Perm legislative deputy remarked that in the legislature, there was a tradition of sectoral competition over redistribution.[47] Each sector received allocations and competed for budget transfers. One clear example has been conflicts over agricultural subsidies (such as for wheat and potato production), which have divided delegates and pitted rival firms directly against one another.[48] A long-time employee of the Perm regional legislature cited debates over the level of taxation imposed on natural resources companies as especially divisive between deputies from different economic backgrounds. As competition for resources increased, she remarked that more and more businesspeople began running for office.[49]

In the words of longtime analyst of Perm politics Oleg Podvintsev the thinking of a businessperson politicians is often "Everyone participates in the parliament, therefore I have to. I'd rather work with professional

46 Interview with Petr Panov, political scientist, Perm, Russia. October 3, 2013.

47 Interview with Elena Zyryanova, deputy, Perm Regional Duma, Perm, Russia, October 8, 2013.

48 Interview with Valeriye Mazanov, editor of the Kompanion Journal, Perm, Russia. October 3, 2013.

49 Interview with Nina Bayandina, Deputy Head of the Administration of the Perm Regional Legislature, Perm, Russia. October 7, 2013.

politicians but there are none."[50] Turovskii (2012) again referred to these dynamics as a kind of "chain reaction," whereby the electoral victories enjoyed by top managers in regional legislatures in places such as Perm and Primorskyi Krai have motivated others from the business community to seek the same status and benefits.

Some of this jockeying involves federal money, the implementation of anti-monopoly legislation, and importantly, state contracts. For example, in the Tomsk construction industry, fierce competition exists between firms based on the type of materials they used to build homes. Fierce competition arose between Shpeter's panel home building company, the Tomsk Housing Construction Company (TDSK), and a rival brick construction company led by Boris Maltsev, a longtime figure in both Tomsk and national politics. Maltsev himself remarked in an interview that "the state intervenes massively through regulation in order to construct barriers to entry, regulations, and laws."[51] He commented that TDSK abused its large market share and political connections to influence the opportunities available to competitors, especially the privatization of state land. Presumably Maltsev's own presence in the legislature helped him push back against this dominant firm in a very competitive sector.

Observers in Ryazan noted that failing to win a seat means that a firm cannot protect its interests, secure lucrative deals with other insiders, and withstand attacks from competitors who have placed directors as deputies.[52] Contributing to campaigns and lobbying do not measure up to a seat at the table. A local businessperson in Perm commented that "all relations need to occur on the same level"; to get ahead in politics, businesspeople need to be able to speak with an official eye-to-eye, and a deputy seat provides just that.[53] Interestingly, where firms occupy a monopoly position in their sector, some commentators noted that a seat in a legislature becomes less attractive. A newly elected deputy in the Perm legislature remarked that many monopolistic businesses in the region are "more concerned with foreign markets and protecting their interests from federal intrusion."[54] To them regional legislative office

[50] Interview with Oleg Podvintsev, political scientist, Perm, Russia. October 2, 2013.

[51] Interview with Boris Maltsev, deputy Tomsk Regional Duma, Tomsk, Russia. June 8, 2014.

[52] Interview with Aleksander Semenov, professor of the Ryazan branch of the Moscow State Art and Cultural University, Ryazan, Russia. November 18, 2013.

[53] Interview with Anton Tomachev, local businessperson, Perm, Russia, October 8, 2013.

[54] Interview with Andrei Starkov, businessperson and regional deputy, Perm, Russia. June 10, 2014.

offered few real advantages, as many of their most pressing business concerns ran through the federal center in Moscow. This helps explain why businessperson candidacy becomes much more frequent in locally competitive markets, where rival firms recognize the importance of proximate regulations for getting ahead.

Interviews with businesspeople and observers also supported the idea that strong political parties deter businessperson candidacy. Perm Region boasts high levels of party institutionalization: it ranks among the top 10 percent of regions in terms of overall party expenditures and nearly 5 percent more of all candidates there chose to run with a party affiliation than in the median Russian region. Strong parties helped adjudicate disputes behind closed doors and reassured competing firm interests that political parties would work to represent everyone who made financial contributions. Kovin remarked that, for example, although United Russia is "fragmented with lots of internal competition, problems and conflicts are resolved within the party itself."[55] Deputies remarked about overall ruling party discipline being high and outside groups' trust in politicians growing as a result.[56] In one deputy's words, United Russia was more "prone to dominate law-making and take the initiative to stay in power," making it the "best choice for business" as a permanent fixture on the political scene.[57] Having reliable, responsible political parties to represent one's interests helps reduce the attractiveness of running for political office.

In Tomsk, relationships with political parties were viewed as much more precarious. According to one leader of a systemic opposition party, "some parties have federal money so they do not need to rely too heavily on businessmen donations."[58] This often prevents them from providing adequate representation for their sponsors, since they are less dependent on the business community to win elections. As a local observer put it succinctly, in Tomsk, "businessmen need politicians more than politicians need businessmen."[59] This power imbalance means that parties value their reputation and relationship to the government more than

[55] Interview with Vitalii Kovin, professor and former representative of Golos, Perm, Russia. October 7, 2013.

[56] Interview with Lilia Shiraeva, Regional Deputy, Perm, Russia. October 2, 2013.

[57] Interview with Lilia Shiraeva, Regional Deputy, Perm, Russia. October 2, 2013.

[58] Interview with Galina Nemsteva, deputy of Tomsk Regional Duma, Tomsk, Russia. June 10, 2014.

[59] Interview with Sergey Schpagin, professor, Tomsk State University, Tomsk, Russia. June 9, 2014.

their responsibility to the business community. And even when agreements were struck, many local politicians were suspicious about parties' ability to commit to their word and foster trusting relationships with their candidates. One oft-recounted story involved a very wealthy businessperson in Tomsk who funded the majority of United Russia's national political campaign in 2011.[60] However, when it came time to distribute the spoils, the party betrayed the donor and withdrew its sponsorship of his efforts to secure a seat in national-level legislative bodies. Parties in Tomsk appeared more as a vehicle for narrow political interests than enduring actors that could aggregate disparate corporate interests.

In many interviews, business associations similarly failed to facilitate cooperation between politicians and businesspeople. Several interviewees commented on the weakness of business associations in Russia in exerting any real political influence.[61] The deputy chairperson of the Perm Regional Duma remarked that "business associations are not very involved in open lobbying," since deputies refrain from representing more than one set of economic interests while in office.[62] Some individuals were even more cynical. A local businessperson in Perm criticized the associations for not only failing to unite the business community, but also seeming to exist solely as a platform for association leaders to climb the political ladder.[63] The situation was all too similar in Ryazan. Regional business associations were run by former government officials who had no business experience and worked mainly to control businesses in the aims of the state, rather than independently represent it.[64] Business associations in Russia may prove more effective at helping business defend against capricious inspectors and tax collectors than coalescing into a cohesive political force that protects against politician shirking.

Anecdotal work on Russia casts further doubt that trade associations can act as a perfect substitute for businessperson candidacy. Few are engaged in open lobbying, and internal conflicts over policy directions undermine consensus-driven lobbying.[65] To quote a recent appraisal at

60 Interview with Aleksei Sokolov, journalist, Tomsk, Russia. June 11, 2014.
61 Interview with Olga Kolokolova, Yabloko Party Leader, Perm, October 6, 2013. Interview with Valeriye Mazanov, editor of the Kompanion Journal, Perm, Russia. October 3, 2013.
62 Interview with Igor Papkov, Deputy Chairperson, Perm Regional Duma. Perm. October 8, 2013.
63 Interview with Anton Tomachev, businessman, Perm, Russia. October 8, 2014.
64 Interview with Vladimir Avdonin, political scientist. November 11, 2014.
65 Interview with Igor Papkov, Deputy Chairperson, Perm Regional Duma. Perm. October 8, 2013.

the regional level, "chambers of commerce are not active lobbying actors, since they are not supported by the government and do not respond to the interests of business and society" (Murashhenkov, 2009, 132). These associations are often more concerned with running seminars to increase qualifications, such as in Lipetsk Oblast, or they defer to the governor to manage relations with the business community, as in Belgorod. A lack of legislation to structure relations between trade associations also limits their ability to get a seat at the table. Recent statistics suggest that Russian trade associations encompass no more than 5 percent of the total number of registered businesses in the country, giving them weak input on improving the investment climate.[66]

Business associations by definition represent collective interests, depending on the founding mission of the organization. Efforts coordinated through trade associations are unlikely to abate the effect of fierce within-sector competition on the need for direct representation. In Kostroma Oblast, different financial groups had already built their pathways into power and lobbied their interests independently, seeing no need to work together within an association.[67] Firms approached collective action cautiously, as many were burnt by associations which reneged on promises to come through politically. The leadership of these associations also prefer to participate in other types of public councils, rather than legislatures. By my rough count, there were less than thirty full-time employees of various business associations running for regional legislative office from 2004 to 2011, with only eight taking office. Associations do not appear to be supplanting direct candidacy as a way for firms to achieve political access.

In all, these conversations painted businessperson candidacy as an individualistic strategy available to wealthy elites looking both to shore up their firms' interests and stroke their ego. Petr Panov, a political scientist in Perm, remarked that "parliament is a club, a social institution for communication and the development of social ties. There is a symbolic attraction to it."[68] Local elites get addicted to the status offered by the position, perhaps motivated in some part by pride. Image is important for businesspeople who want deputy status, educational degrees, and other signals of success. These come at often exorbitant costs. To quote one campaign director from Perm, "businesses need to pay a ton of money

[66] Mashin (2016).
[67] Murashhenkov (2009).
[68] Interview with Petr Panov, political scientist, Perm, Russia. October 3, 2013.

to run for office; it is a very risky investment and you need to absorb the potential losses."[69] Firms must also make social contributions to stay in the good graces of government leaders, which increases the total cost of campaigning.[70] Collectively, running for and holding office can be an expensive affair, and only available to the wealthiest businesspeople in a region.

Beyond these three regions, Russian regional politics is full of examples of economic competition spilling over into legislative politics. Take, for example, Kamchatka, a region with a relatively high level of businessperson penetration into the legislature, mainly from its two leading industries: fishing and forestry. Fisheries depend on quotas allocated by state officials, especially the governor's office but also the legislature, to stay in business.[71] Smaller firms are especially vulnerable, since even though they make up the majority of entities working in the industry, they are often shut out of political access. In 2001, rival fishing companies each supported their own candidate for governor.[72] The campaign is the stuff of Russian regional lore. One candidate alleged that camouflaged men kidnapped him from his jeep, while his wife reported unknown figures threatening the family over the phone, trying to get the candidate to drop out of the race.

In Belgorod region, Elena Baturina, the wealthiest woman in Russia and wife of ex-mayor of Moscow Yuri Luzhkov, caused a scandal by aggressively expanding her business interests. State officials were less than welcoming, using an array of regulatory inspections and investigations, to halt her company Inteko's land acquisitions and fulfillment of state contracts. Some suspected that the powerful governor Evgeny Savchenko was acting to protect his own family's businesses from the threat of a Moscow firm intruding on his turf.[73] In the end, Baturina turned to legislative politics to defend her economic claims. To some degree, she co-opted the local branch of the Liberal-Democratic Party of Russia (LDPR), sending her own top managers and lawyers to run for the Belgorod Regional Duma and push back against local officials

[69] Interview with Oleg Borisenko, Political Technologist, Perm. October 7, 2013.

[70] Interview with Valeriy Mazanov, journalist. Perm, October 3, 2013.

[71] A similar situation is present in other coastal regions in the Far East, such as Primorskye Krai, where fisheries have funded rival candidates to secure access to quotas. (Chernyshev 2005; Blinov 2015).

[72] Fatullaev (2000).

[73] *AIS* (2016).

blocking her company's activities.[74] The 2005 legislative election exemplified rival business groups jockeying for power at the ballot box: Inteko representatives were even savagely beaten, and one killed, in the run-up.[75] Ultimately, the local Belgorod faction of United Russia dominated the elections and won the economic conflict.

3.4 DISCUSSION AND CONCLUDING REMARKS

Using both official firm financial data and survey responses, this chapter found that economic competition and weak political parties create incentives for firms to put forth candidates to elected office. Under these conditions, more conventional strategies for achieving policymaking influence become less effective. When they enjoy multiple suitors and only weak institutions to constrain them, politicians see little reason to comply with informal arrangements to represent firms' political interests. But not all firms can afford the resource-intensive strategy of placing representatives in political institutions such as parliaments. Only companies with substantial financial and labor resources, or that face lower campaign costs, will pay the cost of running for office.

Perhaps surprisingly, this chapter did not find consistent evidence that other institutional factors, such as opportunities to engage in collective action and the level of democratization, could help solve the commitment problem plaguing political access. Ceteris paribus, firms that participated in business associations did not refrain from running for office, nor did the level of businessperson candidacy fall in more democratic regions. The weakness of trade associations in contemporary Russia leaves firms on their own to deal with politicians on an individual, rather than collective, basis.

Perhaps more fundamentally, the median voter may not be as central to the decision-making of business elites as previously thought. When deciding whether to run for office, businesspeople evaluate their relationships with political officials, rather than the preferences and engagement of regular citizens. Part of this could be due to the type of office being pursued. Candidates to top executive positions may have to cater more intensively to the voting populace, given these more significant, public, and politically competitive elections. But firms seeking policy through the

74 *Kommersant* (2005).

75 RFE/RL Newsline (2005). "Lawyer's Death Linked to Feud Between Luzhkov's Wife and Belgorod Authorities" October 13, 2005.

legislative branch evaluate the effectiveness of various political strategies not based on the vulnerabilities they create with voters, but rather on the certainty they provide that lobbied politicians will follow through. Attempts to regulate the entry of businesspeople into political office must begin with this understanding of how institutions structure interactions between firms and other political elites.

4

Choosing Ballots, Parties, and Delegates

Igor Trubitsyin just could not commit. For this owner of a chain of supermarkets, an entertainment complex called Rock-City, and a food processing plant,[1] politics in his region of Ryazan was a game where political loyalties meant little. His considerable charitable work for the elderly and habit of handing out groceries right before elections have made him a political force to be reckoned with in his home district. By creating a powerful political machine of voters committed to his many candidacies, Trubitsyin has been able to coax partnerships out of just about any political grouping he wanted.

His autonomy has been astonishing, even by Russian standards. Trubitsyin first stood and won election to the Ryazan Regional Duma as an independent in 2001, and defended his seat in 2005. During that term, he helped put together and then head the list for the Patrioty Russia party for the 2008 Ryazan city council elections (Trubitsyin remained in the Regional Duma, giving his seat to another party member). By 2010 the tide had turned, as he coordinated with LDPR leaders at the federal level to take over the party's Ryazan office and lead their charge for the regional elections. That year, he again successfully defended his seat with an LDPR affiliation.[2] This arrangement didn't last long. Trubitsyin switched his support over to Just Russia mid-term before moving on to head United Russia's proportional representation list in the 2013 Ryazan city council elections (he would again remain in the regional legislature). His affinity for United Russia proved to have more staying power:

[1] Komarov (2003).
[2] Smirnov (2013).

he assumed leadership of the Ryazan chapter of the All-Russia People's Front, a social movement started in 2011 by Vladimir Putin to work alongside and reinvigorate United Russia. Finally, Trubitsyin officially ran as a member of United Russia in 2015 for the regional legislature, again winning his district.

Seventeen years in power (and counting): eight years as a nominal independent, followed by four successive political party affiliations. His autonomy made him politically uncontrollable, and a severe headache for whatever authorities were in charge. Trubitysin could change flags at a moment's notice, at times making deals with different political groupings at multiple levels, midway through his elected terms.[3] Politics was one everlasting set of calculations: which parties' fates were rising, or falling? What was the easiest path to electoral victory: running in a district or acquiring a spot on a party list?

The best path to win political office does not magically appear once a businessperson decides that a legislative seat is needed to promote firm interests. This chapter analyzes how businesspeople make several critical, and oftentimes difficult, choices about how to navigate the array of electoral rules, party affiliations, and delegation questions. As we will see, many candidates like Trubitsyin have the regional political world at their fingertips. For example, to quote Vladimir Avdonin on Trubitsyin's exploits, "the more independent, wealthy, and popular a businessman is, the more choices of political parties that they have."[4] But such resources are not available to all budding businessperson candidates, and tricky decisions await.

First, I explore how businesspeople decide which ballot to run on. The mixed member system in place in the majority of Russian regional legislatures leaves all candidates, including those with business ties, with a number of options. Businessperson candidates can first "go-it-alone" by assuming individual responsibility for contesting a plurality race in a single-member district. Traditionally, campaigns in these districts receive little to no material support from political parties and must be entirely self-financed. Alternately, candidates can try to secure a spot on some political party's list, hoping the party wins enough votes through the proportional representation ballot that his or her spot gets called into the legislature.[5] I discuss this option in greater detail below.

[3] Percev (2013).

[4] Interview with Vladimir Avdonin, political scientist. Ryazan, Russia. November 18, 2014.

[5] For some individuals, both options are available: candidates can both contest a plurality races and occupy a spot on the proportional representation system. Dual listing on both

The second decision pertains to party affiliation: which party, if any, will a businessperson candidate affiliate with? During the period analyzed, Russia saw the rise of a dominant ruling party, United Russia, which capitalized on the popularity of its national leader Vladimir Putin to capture a majority in all regional legislatures around the country. But the emergence of a ruling party regime did not spell the end for the opposition. Although significant consolidation occurred as the result of electoral reforms,[6] several national parties retained strong branches in the regions. The degree of their true opposition to ruling party governance varied considerably, with some challenging UR by threatening to protest,[7] while others acquiesced and remained docile junior partners. Candidates in plurality races could also run as independents, forgoing any party support for perceived autonomy and flexibility once in office.

Finally, businesses have to decide which representative of their firm to place on the ballot. As we saw in Chapter 1, high opportunity costs are one of the many barriers to entry for firms seeking direct representation within legislatures. Firms must decide whether sending their CEO to perform double duties in the public or private sector makes sense for their productivity and competitiveness. Many large firms in Russia have an array of qualified professionals to potentially represent their interests in office. When do firms send an individual other than their director to run for elected office?

All three decisions have significant consequences for a candidate's probability of getting elected as well as his or her ability to influence policymaking. For example, ballot choice is believed to influence the degree to which factions and parties can constrain deputies' behavior inside a legislature.[8] Deputies from single-member districts may enjoy more autonomy in pushing for their own narrow interests, since their electoral success is not contingent on toeing the party line. But affiliating with the ruling party means governing with the majority and accessing the multiple spoils that follow: better chances of winning committee chairmanships and an easier road to passing legislation are two prime examples. Finally, firm directors, rather than lower-level employees, enjoy greater clout within the legislature, given their public stature and recognizably from running their firms.

ballots provides a type of "insurance" that can dramatically increase the probability of winning a seat for politicians (Krauss, Nemoto, and Pekkanen, 2012).

[6] Greater detail on these rule changes can be found in the Chapter 3. The general effect was to reduce the number of viable parties that could contest regional elections nationwide.

[7] Reuter and Robertson (2015).

[8] Tavits (2009); Thames (2005).

Answering these three questions requires first bringing the analysis down to the firm level. Studying variation in firm characteristics, such as assets, ownership, and corporate governance structure, helps explain why firms choose to run candidates in plurality races, join up with specific political parties, and delegate representation to different types of executives. Overall, businesspeople prefer contesting deputy seats through the plurality system, with this route offering improved flexibility to deviate from the party line and push for firm-specific policy advantages. Larger firms can completely self-fund their candidates' campaigns in the SMDP races, while larger workforces help strengthen the "personal vote" by providing a pool of employees for voter mobilization.

Greater financial resources also allow businessperson candidates to join up with the ruling party if they so choose. Although the price of gaining a regime affiliation is undoubtedly higher, it brings with it a higher probability of election and better access to spoils and policymaking. Finally, firms opt for non-directors when they assess a high probability of that person both getting elected and becoming an effective advocate in the legislature. This depends on the strength of political parties and a specific candidate's legislative experience: when parties are strong or political incumbents can be found, firms are much more likely to delegate businessperson candidacy to individuals other than their CEO.

To provide evidence for these claims, I use the main dataset described in the last chapter, except the analysis is limited to only those firms that put forth a candidate to office (and thus expressed preferences for ballot, party, and individual to represent them). By looking at the costs and benefits involved with each decision, I again adopt the perspective of a firm trying to maximize its probability of winning office (and influencing policymaking), while minimizing the expenses involved.[9] To fill in the gaps, I draw on first-hand interviews with participants that illuminate how firms build their political campaigns and the difficult trade-offs with respect to all three decisions.

4.1 CHOOSING A BALLOT

In many countries around the world, voters cast two votes during elections to a given parliamentary body: one in a plurality race for a

[9] Interviews suggest that in the run-up to campaigns, firm directors use lavishly paid political consultants to crunch the numbers and walk them through the same decisions about the best way to win a seat in the legislature.

candidate to represent a geographic constituency and one for a party in on a proportional representation list system. In such mixed systems, this means candidates have a choice in deciding how they will pursue elected office, either in the plurality race to represent that constituency or through a spot on the party list. According to the Institute for Democracy and Electoral Assistance (IDEA), dozens of democracies use variants of these mixed member systems to select their legislators, both in the developed (Germany, Italy, and Japan) and developing (Pakistan, Thailand, and Venezuela) worlds.[10] In fact, much of our knowledge about the origins and effectiveness of mixed systems comes from countries in the former Communist bloc, such as Russia, Hungary, and Ukraine, where mixed systems were adopted en masse upon achieving independence.[11] Mixed systems have indeed gained in popularity in recent decades, offering institutional designers the "best of both worlds," as one common description has put it.[12] Although debates are still ongoing, mixed systems have the potential to generate both two-bloc, national party systems while also fostering local accountability and the development of minor parties, hence explaining their enduring appeal.

In Russia, the vast majority of regions have used a mixed system since 2005, with legislatures containing roughly an equal number of deputies elected from plurality races and the party-list system.[13] This is largely due to electoral reforms passed in 2004 that mandated that regions select at least 50 percent from legislators from a party list. A handful of regions saw that recommendation out to the fullest and moved to a completely proportional representation system. The situation is similar at the national level, again with some vacillation between systems: the State Duma has been elected using a mixed system since 1991, with the exception of the 2007 and 2011 elections, where a full proportional representation system was used.

[10] Institute for Democracy and Electoral Assistance, "Countries Using MMP Electoral System for National Legislature."

[11] Thames (2005); Turovsky (2018).

[12] Shugart and Wattenberg (2001).

[13] For more information, see Lyubarev (2011). Regions also vary somewhat in the specific rules and thresholds to select winning candidates and parties. The majority (70 percent) of convocations use an electoral threshold of 7 percent for parties to win seats in a legislature, with forty-five using a bar of less than 7 percent and only one using a threshold of 10 percent. All but three regional legislatures in the dataset used a closed-list system, whereby voters only select parties and not individual candidates on each party's list. Only one regional legislature requires candidates from single-member districts to win an absolute majority: plurality winners took seats in the rest.

When mixed electoral systems are in place, candidates face the first-order decision of deciding which ballot to seek office through. Clearly they care first and foremost about winning election, and primarily select the route into office that maximizes their probability of gaining a seat, while minimizing their costs. Plurality and party lists systems require different types of expenditures and investments, which can dictate an individual's propensity to choose one ballot over the other.

Beyond the requirements to get elected, the two ballots also offer different types of legislative influence once a candidate gets elected to a legislature. This section walks through these two dimensions in turn (cost and influence), before applying the theoretical framework and developing hypotheses about how businesspeople approach the set of costs and benefits involved with ballot choice.

First, the costs of running a campaign in a plurality race appear to far exceed those of gaining a seat on a party list. In Russia, candidates in single-member districts are largely left to their own devices, regardless of their party membership. Candidates need to personally fund their varied electoral expenses,[14] collect the number of signatures required to register with the electoral commission, and perhaps most importantly, build a campaign headquarters capable of winning a competitive election.[15] Some of this election machinery can be purchased off the shelf. Armies of expensive political strategists (or "polittechnologists") have descended on Russian regional politics, proffering their expertise and dirty tricks to the highest bidder. Interviews with candidates in Tomsk and Perm revealed that parties themselves offered little assistance, forcing candidates to both raise their own cash and oversee their own campaigns.[16] Plurality races become akin to the all-pay auctions present in the Egyptian system, as elites invest their own private resources into elections in order to signal their loyalty to the governing regime.[17] This drives

[14] Candidates must also self-finance in a number of developed democracies. The Comparative Candidates Survey of over 8,000 candidates to national parliaments in eighteen countries from 2005 to 2013 revealed that candidates drew on their own personal funds to pay for 47 percent of their campaign expenses, with party contributions covering 32 percent and donations covering just 21 percent (CCS, 2015).

[15] Interview with Vasiliy Yeremin, former deputy of Tomsk Regional Duma, Tomsk, Russia. June 10, 2014.

[16] Interview with Vasiliy Semkin, businessman and deputy of Tomsk Regional Duma, Tomsk, Russia. June 11, 2014; interview with Anton Tomachev, businessperson, Perm, Russia. October 8, 2013.

[17] Blaydes (2011).

candidates to seek the lowest cost races. Where there are fewer electoral competitors, the cheaper it is to win the election.[18]

Beyond the material resources required to run a campaign, winning a plurality race also requires at least some degree of likability, persuasive speaking talent, and networking skills. The ability to cultivate a personal vote also helps cut down on expenses. The more naturally likable a candidate it, the less he or she potentially has to buy off or threaten voters. Call it charisma, call it charm: SMDP candidates completely personify their campaign. Candidates are on the hook for the entire campaign, and sacrifice their time, investment, and potentially reputation if the election doesn't go their way. Politicians vary in both their visibility and popularity among constituents as well as willingness to invest in developing such intangible assets as might help their campaign. SMDP races are unpredictable undertakings, and unexpected electoral results, particularly in single-member districts, can cost candidates greatly.[19]

Running on a party list can help lower these costs and even increase the probability of getting elected. As discussed in Chapter 1, parties play an important role as gatekeepers in Russian regional legislatures: half the seats go to candidates on party lists. Although political parties themselves suffer from a variety of developmental problems (such as inconsistent ideologies and unstable member rolls), institutionally the electoral system ensures that parties will be in a position to allocate seats to individual candidates and win over some voters based on its brand.[20] Getting onto a party list surely does not come for free. Interviews with several candidates uncovered that the going rate for a competitive spot on a regional list can be up to $200,000.[21] But compared to the resources needed to singlehandedly win an SMDP race, this might be seen as inexpensive. Joining a party just requires an upfront investment, a one-time payment.

[18] Interview with Oleg Borisenko, political technologist, Perm, Russia. October 7, 2013.

[19] See Panov and Ross (2013). Take the very recent examples of a Communist governor unexpectedly winning in Irkutsk in 2015 (Zavadskaya et al., 2015) or the non-systemic opposition carrying an unexpected haul of seats during the local elections in Moscow in 2017.

[20] Which party is most attractive can depend on a variety of factors which I explore in more depth below, ranging from an ideological affinity for the party's goals to a much more cynically strategic approach that prioritizes getting into the legislature at any costs over any underlying set of policy preferences. For now, this theoretical discussion is limited to the binary choice of choosing a party or not.

[21] See below for a much more in-depth discussion of the process by which seats are allocated. Interview with Valeriy Otsipov, deputy of Tomsk Regional Duma, Tomsk, Russia. June 9, 2014.

A candidate's money does the talking during the campaign, placing their fate in the hands of the party.

Parties vary widely in their popularity and seats are not guaranteed. Less wealthy candidates may only be able to afford lower spots on the list and be left outside the parliament once the post-electoral lottery is complete.[22] Therefore, candidates going the PR route run the risk of losing their investment (i.e. their bid for a spot), but that uncertainty should be built into the price they pay (and the spot they receive). In a plurality race, that payoff is much more uncertain.

Beyond differences in the requirements to get elected, choosing the SMDP or PR route also has implications for a deputy's ability to influence policymaking while in office. Scholars have persuasively argued that the way legislators win seats affects their behavior while in elected office. According to the so-called "mandate divide," legislators elected from single-member districts focus on issues closer to the constituents who directly elected them (i.e. those geographically located in their districts).[23] On the other hand, those winning office through a party list tend to concentrate on more national issues. In addition, ballot type can also affect how leadership posts are distributed among deputies, with SMDP deputies more likely to gun for leadership positions related to distributive demands with direct effects on their constituencies.[24]

Deputies who rely on access to party lists for their seats are more vulnerable to pressure to toe the party line while in office. As discussed in Chapter 1, party leaders often have other image concerns and may be wary of allowing businesspeople to run amok and exploit the legislature for their own personal ends. That loss of autonomy can produce financial consequences. Parties can credibly continue to demand contributions from deputies long after a parliamentary convocation has begun, since politicians elected on the party list are more dependent on the party for their careers.[25] The case of Russia fits this pattern, where at least at the

[22] Some parties use midterm resignations to overcome the problem of limited capacity. Deputies are given half-terms in office, leaving their seat after two or three years to make room for a candidate who narrowly missed a spot during the previous election. Rotation increases the number of businesspeople that can be courted and assuages concerns about spots being bought but never received because of electoral difficulties. Interview with Aleksander Semenov, professor of the Ryazan branch of the Moscow State Art and Cultural University, Ryazan, Russia. November 18, 2013.

[23] Thames (2005); Sieberer (2010).

[24] Pekkanen, Nyblade, and Krauss (2006).

[25] Interview with Natalia Zubarevich, professor of geography at Moscow State University, Moscow, Russia. March 11, 2013.

national level, the adoption of a mixed-member system has generated a modest increase in defections among SMDP deputies from the official party lines.[26]

4.1.1 How Businesspeople Choose between Ballots

Applying this framework, I argue that ceteris paribus, businesspeople prefer to run for office through single-member districts. For firm directors, the attractiveness of winning a seat through the SMDP route builds off both dimensions: cost and influence. On one hand, firm directors are uniquely positioned to both dedicate significant financial sums to their campaigns, but also draw on the "personal vote" to directly persuade constituents to elect them (without needing help from political parties). If in many countries the primary limiting factor in reaching a legislature through an SMDP is cost, firms are well positioned to bear this burden and fund campaigns. We saw much of this in the previous chapter, as larger firms participated in dramatically higher rates in elections. Businesspeople politicians can draw on both their personal finances as well as firm resources to independently run their campaigns. Firm directors also have stronger connections to their districts than other types of politicians,[27] as often they are one of the major employers and contributors to the local tax base. As well-established names in their communities, businessperson candidates can appeal directly to voters using their record of financial success. These autonomous resources make them less reliant on political parties (and thus the party list) to win elections.[28]

Businessperson politicians are also very attracted to the independence and localized autonomy that winning a plurality race provides. Because these candidates are entering politics primarily to promote the interests of their own firm, representing a single-member district and bypassing any strenuous commitments to a political party allows for more flexibility in voting behavior, lawmaking, and using the perquisites of elected office, such as deputy requests, to their advantage. Tavits (2009) makes the broader argument that having strong local ties to constituents can enable a politician to capitalize on his or her own personal reputation and act as a maverick within a parliamentary body. Less dependent on the party for their political future, and wielding additional career options

[26] Kunicova and Remington (2008).
[27] Thames Jr (2001).
[28] Reuter and Szakonyi (2019).

outside the political system, this type of locally connected politician draws support from a nonpartisan electoral base to act more individualistically with respect to their lawmaking duties. The autonomy provided by SMDP races makes it easier for businessperson candidates to pursue their narrow firm-level interests that might be blocked or overruled by party leaders not wishing to allow such self-centered lawmaking.

Hypothesis 6. *Overall, businesspeople prefer to run for office in single-member districts.*

If this logic holds, we should also expect several comparative statics to hold true based on individual firm and candidate characteristics. For example, if businessperson candidates indeed prefer to run in SMDP races because of their superior ability to run (and finance campaigns), then firms with greater financial resources will be more likely to choose single-member district races over the party list. The flip side of this argument dictates that holding constant interest in seeking political office, smaller firms will more often seek office through the proportional representation route. Although these firms might prefer to run their own campaigns, resource constraints prevent them from shouldering the entire burden themselves, thus leaving open only the party list to access a regional legislature.

Hypothesis 7. *Firms with greater financial assets will be more likely to run directors in single-member districts.*

In Chapter 3, we also saw that the cost of elections in Russia can depend on the financial standing of voters. The costs of purchasing television airtime, printing and distributing flyers, arranging transportation to the polls, and paying consultants and campaign staffers are all closely correlated to the average income in a given region. Because many citizens are not sufficiently persuaded by a politician's ideological preferences or policy goals, material handouts, such as cash or foodstuffs, are often used to entice electoral support. Since candidates in single-member districts shoulder all of these expenses themselves, the appeal of this route into office will diminish when the costs of getting elected outweigh the expected private benefits. Where voters are wealthier and the economy is more developed, other avenues of influencing politics become more attractive.

Hypothesis 8. *Businesspeople are more likely to run in single-member districts in poorer regions.*

Indeed, some financial costs can be defrayed if candidates possess politically salient intangible assets, such as an ability to cultivate a personal vote among constituents. Money need not be spent informing and winning over voters if a politician has been deeply active in the local economy and community for a long period of time. One indicator of the strength of the local tie is the number of employees that a politician's firm has in a district: the more people directly working for the candidate, the more likely they can be mobilized cheaply to support them during a plurality race. Workplace mobilization during elections is a key asset for politicians at multiple levels in Russian politics, with a significant portion of the electorate reporting having been tapped by their managers and supervisors to act politically around election time.[29] Name recognition among voters may simply be a function of how long a candidate has been active in local politics. Older businesspeople candidates can use their longevity to build a personal base of support largely independent of cyclical electioneering.

Hypothesis 9. *Firms with larger workforces will be more likely to run directors in single-member districts.*

Hypothesis 10. *Firms led by older candidates will be more likely to run directors in single-member districts.*

Predicting interest in legislative autonomy creates some ambiguities. In many respects, all firms want the ability to operate freely and use their legislative seat to help their companies. But some variation could be tied to the industry in which a firm operates. For example, firms with highly immobile assets, such as those working in mining or manufacturing, may value a SMDP seat for its increased ability to center lawmaking demands on local constituents. Such enterprises may be more concerned about funneling state investment into physical infrastructure, such as roads and utilities, near their companies, and much less in the region-wide initiatives that political parties may push for. This narrow focus could lead them to pursue the autonomy of a SMDP seat. But these same factors

[29] Frye, Reuter, and Szakonyi (2014).

also contribute to a firm director's innate popularity and name recognition in an electoral district. Firms with factories that cannot be moved easily also inevitably provide large employment opportunities and contribute to social welfare in other ways. These are key electoral assets in any campaign. Therefore below, I hesitate to make strong claims that disentangle the cost-related factors to pursuing a seat from those related more directly to autonomy.

Finally, dual-listing in both a single-member district and on a party list offers another strategy to overcome the uncertainty of competitive elections. In the models below, I interpret candidates who occupy a spot in both systems as hedging their bets and thereby falling in between those that squarely choose either the single-member district or the party list route. We might expect firms that dual-list to be the largest in terms of size, reach, and stature since they are paying for access on two ballots. The middle way of dual-listing acts as an insurance policy for those firms not confident to contest only a single-member district race and the resources to test several different avenues to get into power.

4.1.2 Data and Empirical Strategy

All analysis in this chapter draws on the observational dataset on actual businessperson candidacies described in the preceding two chapters.[30] Information on the preferred ballot or party, for example, is not available for firms that chose not to put forth candidates. This requires within-group comparisons: holding constant their interest in running for office, I examine how individual firms make decisions about ballots, parties, and delegates.

The unit of analysis is again the firm. Specific firm characteristics help predict variation in how firms navigate electoral rules, and as analyzed in subsequent sections, select a party affiliation and top executive to represent them in office. The firm-level predictors on the right hand side of the regressions are identical to those described in the preceding chapter,

[30] Perhaps a better approach would involve surveying businesspeople who ran for office about their choices of ballot, party, and specific delegates to represent the firm. Unfortunately, the firm survey analyzed in the last chapter is underpowered, with less than a hundred businessperson candidates responding to the questions. Given this constraint (as well as the lack of questions directly related to these three decisions), I opt for the observational dataset here and supplement the quantitative parts with evidence from interviews.

capturing firm size, age, ownership, and importing and exporting activity.[31] In addition, because the dataset is subset to realized candidacies, I can bring in additional information on candidate traits, such as age, gender, and incumbency. Where appropriate, the models include region-level predictors, including proxies for population wealth and political party development.

I begin the analysis by looking at ballot structure. Three binary outcomes are defined as such: whether a firm ran its director on the (1) single-member district ballot, (2) party list, or (3) both (dual-listed). Because the key outcome of interest is the choice between these ballots, the sample is restricted to regions that used the mixed-member system to elect deputies. Firms that had multiple candidates and whose candidates ran on both the SMDP and party list slates are included in the dual-listed category, and analyzed separately. I use logistic models that include region, sector, and year fixed effects. This broad array of fixed effects helps account for cross-regional variation in the number of seats allocated to SMDP races and party lists, temporal factors such as concurrence with national elections,[32] and between-sector variation, both in size and the need for political representation. In addition, I build a categorical variable with values for each of three ballot choice outcomes, setting the dual-listed category as the reference. A multinomial logistic model that includes the same three sets of fixed effects is shown using this categorical variable.

4.1.3 Empirical Results

Table 4.1 presents summary statistics on candidates to regional office, based on both their choice of ballot and their business background. In support of Hypothesis 1, we see strong evidence that businesspeople are more likely to contest plurality races in single-member districts, than they are to acquire spots on the part list. Of the 10,282 SMDP candidates running from 2004 to 2011, half were businesspeople, compared to a much lower number of 37 percent of spots on party lists. Note that in real terms, the number of businesspeople running on party lists is far larger (9,666 versus 5,133), but as is the number of candidates listed on this

[31] In all of the analysis, I remove the forty-seven federal state-owned enterprises.

[32] Firm directors might for example be more inclined to run on party lists if they can ride national party coattails.

TABLE 4.1 *Ballot choice: Summary statistics*

Ballot Category	All Candidates	Businesspeople	%
Plurality (SMDP)	10,282	5,133	49.9
Party List (PR)	25,945	9,666	37.3
Dual-Listed	5,252	2,306	43.9
Total #	41,479	17,105	41.2

This table presents summary statistics about the percentage of candidates running on each ballot that are businesspeople.

route. Firms see both advantages in terms of winning office and influencing legislative decision-making by opting for SMDP races: remaining accountable directly to constituents, rather than party leaders (who assert control over spots on the party lists and political career trajectories) makes more business sense.

To further test the logic that campaign costs drive firms down different electoral paths, Table 4.2 presents logistic models that regress specific ballot choices on firm and region-level characteristics (Columns 1–6). Two models are shown for each of the three outcomes (SMDP, PR, and dual-listing): one that includes and one that excludes the variable of the logged number of employees in the firm. Although assets and employees are highly correlated (0.70), it is instructive to see the independent effects of both on ballot choice.[33] The table shows marginal effects for these logit models.

Several patterns emerge. First, we see a clear progression moving from the PR results to the SMDP results (left to right among the columns) that larger firms run more often on the SMDP ballot. This is the case measuring firm size using financial assets and the size of workforces, providing evidence in favor of Hypotheses 2 and 4. Larger firms are better able to afford the costs of personally financing races in single-member districts. A one standard-deviation increase in firm assets increases the probability of its directors running in a plurality race by roughly 10 percent.

In addition, we see that firms with older managers are more likely to choose the SMDP slate. Firms that can cultivate a personal vote, either due to the political experience and name recognition of their manager opt to seek office as a deputy from a single-member district. Here the result is quite strong too: candidates that are roughly ten years older than the

33 Interestingly, the variables remain statistically significant when both are included together in the models.

TABLE 4.2 *Ballot choice: Empirical models*

	Marginal Effects from Logit Models						Multinomial Logit Model	
	PR		Dual		SMDP		PR	SMDP
	(1)	(2)	(3)	(4)	(5)	(6)	(7)	(8)
Firm-Level Predictors								
Total Assets (logged)	−0.008**		−0.006***		0.014***		0.024	0.082***
	(0.003)		(0.002)		(0.003)		(0.018)	(0.018)
Number of Employees (logged)		−0.006		−0.012***		0.018***		
		(0.004)		(0.003)		(0.005)		
Top 5 Firm	0.002	−0.008	0.023*	0.030**	−0.025	−0.021	−0.147	−0.223**
	(0.019)	(0.019)	(0.012)	(0.013)	(0.016)	(0.017)	(0.098)	(0.100)
Firm Age (logged)	0.002	0.0005	0.016***	0.017***	−0.018***	−0.017**	−0.106***	−0.165***
	(0.007)	(0.007)	(0.005)	(0.005)	(0.006)	(0.007)	(0.038)	(0.039)
Regional SOE	0.014	0.012	0.008	0.002	−0.022	−0.016	−0.016	−0.113
	(0.053)	(0.052)	(0.037)	(0.038)	(0.057)	(0.058)	(0.234)	(0.236)
Municipal SOE	0.046	0.031	0.006	0.013	−0.054	−0.044	0.041	−0.235
	(0.037)	(0.036)	(0.028)	(0.028)	(0.034)	(0.034)	(0.190)	(0.204)
Importer	−0.002	−0.007	0.002	−0.001	0.001	0.008	−0.022	−0.014
	(0.019)	(0.020)	(0.014)	(0.014)	(0.017)	(0.018)	(0.098)	(0.100)
Exporter	0.002	−0.003	0.002	0.008	−0.006	−0.007	−0.017	−0.034
	(0.021)	(0.021)	(0.015)	(0.015)	(0.019)	(0.018)	(0.111)	(0.112)
Candidate-Level Predictors								
Candidate Age	−0.022	−0.030	−0.070***	−0.061**	0.098***	0.097***	0.419**	0.762***
	(0.037)	(0.039)	(0.026)	(0.027)	(0.034)	(0.036)	(0.165)	(0.174)
Male Candidate	−0.131***	−0.134***	0.042**	0.041**	0.096***	0.099***	−0.590***	−0.009
	(0.029)	(0.027)	(0.018)	(0.018)	(0.024)	(0.024)	(0.171)	(0.188)

Candidate was Incumbent	−0.179***	−0.173***	0.123***	0.121***	0.050**	0.046*	−1.164***	−0.556***
	(0.023)	(0.023)	(0.018)	(0.019)	(0.025)	(0.025)	(0.086)	(0.084)
Region-Level Predictors								
Gross Regional Product (logged)	−0.203	−0.178	−0.133	−0.119	0.314*	0.280*	0.888	2.130***
	(0.131)	(0.129)	(0.103)	(0.105)	(0.160)	(0.164)	(0.557)	(0.562)
Regional Population	−0.112	−0.020	0.876*	0.956*	−0.647	−0.789	−0.335	−1.799***
	(0.593)	(0.604)	(0.532)	(0.554)	(0.703)	(0.700)	(0.436)	(0.437)
Urbanization	−0.729	−0.583	−1.212	−1.110	1.928	1.692	−5.230***	−2.101*
	(1.996)	(1.867)	(1.301)	(1.302)	(2.132)	(2.133)	(1.174)	(1.214)
National Party Strength –	0.006	0.005	−0.030	−0.028	0.032	0.031	0.118	0.179
Expenditures	(0.030)	(0.030)	(0.019)	(0.019)	(0.032)	(0.031)	(0.157)	(0.159)
Sector FE	Yes	Yes	Yes	Yes	Yes	Yes	Yes	
Region FE	Yes	Yes	Yes	Yes	Yes	Yes	Yes	
Year FE	Yes	Yes	Yes	Yes	Yes	Yes	Yes	
Observations	8,947	8,467	8,947	8,467	8,947	8,467	8,947	

*p<0.1; **p<0.05; ***p<0.01 All models include sector, region, and year fixed effects. The sample only includes regions that used the mixed-member system. Columns 1–6 present marginal effects from separate logistic models with the outcome variable being a binary indicator for the type of ballot the businessperson candidate ran on (and the reference category being the other two potential ballot choices). Columns 7 and 8 present point estimates from a multinomial logistic model with the outcomes listed in the column header. The reference category is whether a business was dual-listed on both the PR and SMDP ballots. Errors are clustered on region.

mean run in plurality races at a 6 percent higher rate. The same logic is true for firms with larger workforces. Even controlling for total assets, firms that hire more employees are significantly more likely to run on plurality races, taking advantage of the additional votes at their disposal to mobilize in favor of the businessperson candidate.

The results on the outcome measuring whether a candidate was dual-listed for all three of these predictors fall in the middle of those for the PR and SMDP outcomes, lending support to the argument that this strategy is a middle way. Of particular interest are the point estimates for the Top 5 largest firms and Firm Age. Both results suggest that the economic heavyweights are most likely to contest both ballots. The firms with the longest presence in the region and that dominate the market have the resources to both acquire spots on the party list and finance plurality races. Older firms, relatively speaking, may also have had more opportunities to build relationships with parties, who are more likely to reward their loyalty with spots on the party list and endorsements in the party list. Younger firms, on the other hand, have not had the same time to develop those ties and prefer to try their hand in the plurality races. We also see that firms who send candidates with previous experience in the legislators (incumbents) are much more likely to dual-list. This makes sense given their pre-existing prominence and ability to both help the party win votes and carry a plurality race on their own.

At the regional level, I find that firms in wealthier regions are more likely to opt for the party list instead of single-member districts. This evidence supports Hypothesis 2 that firms make decisions about the ballot based on expectations of the cost of running. When candidates have to self-finance, as in plurality races, higher average income among potential voters can push campaign costs to unmanageable levels. Beyond this we see little evidence that other regional factors affect ballot choice.[34] Finally, the results from the multinomial logit in Columns 7 and 8 confirm the findings from above. Using dual-listed firms as a reference category, we again find that larger firms are more likely to run in single-member districts. Older managers are similarly more likely to go the single-member district route, as well as firms from poorer regions.

Figure 4.1 plots preferences for different ballots based on firm industry. Each point represents an industry-level coefficient from a model predicting the binary ballot choices that each firm director selects; the

[34] Not all region-level predictors are included in these models because of the region fixed effects, which would wash out time-invariant variables such as ethnic republic status and the presence of natural resources.

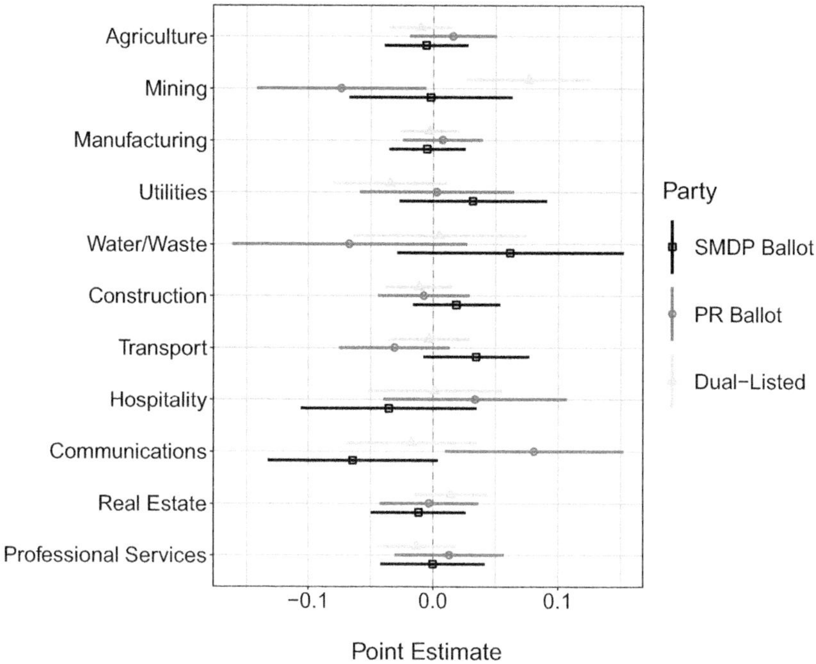

FIGURE 4.1: Ballot choice affiliation by sector
This figure presents point estimates on sector from three linear probability models for binary indicators capturing each of the ballot outcomes listed in the legend. The lines indicate 95 percent confidence intervals. The reference category is trade.

bands are 95 percent confidence intervals with the reference category being trade. The models are identical to those shown in Table 4.2 with all firm and regional characteristics (and fixed effects) included. The results are decidedly mixed. Some sections, such as hospitality and communications, see clearer advantages in placing candidates on the party lists. This could be either because these firms work in services and have weaker direct connections to geographically concentrated voters, or because they see less of a need to preserve autonomy in lawmaking. The opposite may be true for firms working in utilities and water/waste. One main takeaway is that after controlling for firm size, ownership, and director attributes, industry membership plays less of role in determining ballot choice. Moreover, neither sectoral turnover nor competition are strong predictors of ballot choice.

To briefly summarize, how businesspeople list their candidacy depends in large part on the type of firms they are representing. In general, businesspeople prefer running in plurality races over gaining seats on party lists. The results in Table 4.2 demonstrate that much of that decision is based on a firm's ability to cover the cost of campaigning: larger firms as well as those run by directors capable of cultivating a personal vote are better positioned to individually fund an electoral campaign without needing assistance from a political party.

4.2 CHOOSING A PARTY

After selecting a ballot to run on, businessperson candidates next must consider which party to affiliate with. To simplify, I focus in this section on candidates who choose to acquire a spot on party lists as their entry into the elections.[35] This ensures a between-party comparison of candidates running in the same types of races, especially in those regions which use proportional representation exclusively.[36] Much of the discussion below is specific to competitive authoritarian regimes, where a single ruling party dominates electoral competition.[37] Businesspeople weigh the costs and benefits of affiliating with this ruling party versus its alternatives, which control fewer seats and thus less legislative influence. To set the stage for this cost-benefit analysis, I first explore the trajectory of political party development in twenty-first-century Russia, before developing hypotheses about how the current party system affects businesspeople's political allegiances.

4.2.1 Party Membership in Putin-Era Russia

One of the many centralizing moves President Putin made upon taking power was to instill a modicum of order to a raucous party system.

[35] Candidates in SMDP races can affiliate with political parties, with some benefits offered, such as assistance collecting signatures and getting on the ballot. However, interviews suggest that party affiliation is significantly less important than local name recognition and individual financial support in these races. Indeed, 36 percent of SMDP candidates forewent any membership in their party and ran as independents. As a whole, this group fared better electorally than any party besides the ruling party, winning more seats as all of the systemic (and non-systemic) opposition parties *combined*.

[36] In both the main results here and in the Appendix, I include running as an independent as an outcome in the analysis, finding similar results to what is presented here about party choice.

[37] Furthermore, the decision to affiliate with the opposition also hinges somewhat on the particular nature of opposition parties in Russia. In the conclusion, I discuss the generalizability of the Russian context, and what the party choices made by businesspeople there can teach us about other political settings.

The late 1990s and early 2000s had been a period of intense fragmentation and disarray in the political system. Hale (2005) describes a setting where powerful substitutes arose to challenge the supremacy of political parties in elections to all levels of the Russian government. These substitutes took the form of financial-industrial groups and political machines, ideologically ambiguous but financially resourced to fund their own candidates and obstruct the development of nationwide political parties. Using surveys of candidates, Smyth (2005) finds that because of their access to alternative resources, many candidates did not view parties as essential for their pursuit of their political goals.

Soon after his election in 2000, Putin worked to limit the influence of such alternative political groupings and place the Russian government stably and perpetually in the orbit of a "party of power." His predecessor Boris Yeltsin had attempted a similar but unsuccessful experiment to cultivate a ruling party, but this time was different.[38] Putin's Kremlin restructured the incentives for powerful regional elites to join, offering tantalizing access to current and future spoils in return for loyalty.[39] This new ruling party United Russia ultimately helped bring obstinate regional governors into the Kremlin's fold and smoothed out the lawmaking process by co-opting legislators into a single faction. The new administration also passed laws to limit the proliferation of smaller political parties as well as undercut independents and party substitutes. A 2004 law mandated that at least half of the seats in regional legislatures be allocated through the proportional representation system. This dramatically increased the incentives for candidates to establish party affiliations. Later in 2006–2008, new registration rules required that all parties have official membership rolls of at least 50,000 individuals, a stringent demand that decimated the number of parties in existence by 2009.[40]

Putin's reforms helped crystallize the party system: by 2007, only four parties had won seats to the State Duma, and United Russia had built majorities in regional legislatures across the country. To date, a limited number of parties (the ruling party and three systemic opposition) act as gatekeepers into regional office, capitalizing on their control over party lists. Although candidates now had a clearer choice within their respective electoral markets, the political parties themselves had

[38] Reuter (2017).
[39] Reuter and Remington (2009).
[40] Golosov (2014).

only marginally developed their institutional capacity and discipline. In developed democracies, parties help elites solve key coordination problems and present a common agenda to voters.[41] Behind these agendas lie a nominally coherent ideology and policy platforms, backed up by material resources offered to candidates. In these settings, parties recruit strong, ideologically aligned candidates, implement internal procedures to determine those with the most electoral potential, and then throw their considerable financial and reputational support behind their preferred politicians.[42]

The role of parties in Russia is quite different from their Western counterparts. First, when it comes to selecting candidates, parties in Russia act more like auctioneers than democratic filters. Before each election, parties disseminate information to prospective candidates about the availability of spots on their list and the cost of accessing it. These candidates then hand over hefty sums of money in exchange for a designated number on the open list. Prices paid depend on normal forces of supply and demand within this electoral black market. The more candidates interested in a certain party, the higher the prices demanded by that party for a spot. Informal auctions are conducted, through which businesspeople compete in bidding wars for affiliation. Not all bids are completely monetary. Interviews from Perm suggest that demonstrated ability to mobilize votes or implement social and public works projects can substitute for a direct contributions to parties.[43]

Anecdotal evidence about bidding for seats is quite widespread in Russia. For example, at the national level, spots cost between $1.5 and $2 million for various parties contesting the State Duma convocation in 2003.[44] By 2007, those estimates had shot up to $7–10 million.[45] A member of United Russia was sentenced to five years in a prison colony and fined $700,000 in 2014 for attempting to sell a seat on the party's federal list for the 2011 State Duma elections for roughly $8 million.[46] Political scientist Alexander Morozov summed up the situation nicely, drawing on his experience working a leading political party:

41 Aldrich (1995); Kitschelt et al. (1999); Hale (2005).
42 Norris (1997); Hale (2005).
43 Interview with Valeriy Mazanov, editor of the Kompanion Journal, Perm, Russia. October 3, 2013.
44 Mereu, 2003.
45 BBC (2007); Beshley (2011).
46 Petukhova (2015); Chazan (2000).

> This system came about back in the late 1990s. From 2003 to 2008, I worked at the central headquarters of Just Russia. At the time, a practice was common of regional branches looking for some kind of "money bag" for financing party expenditures. Both regular expenses, and those around election time when things really got expensive. No attention was paid to political views. Just about the only requirement was that a candidate did not have a criminal past. This was closely researched.[47]

Selling spots on the party lists and endorsements in plurality races helps parties pay for the soaring costs of electoral campaigns, especially high-priced foreign and domestic consulting firms.[48] The party Just Russia was hit by a multiregion scandal in 2011 as members in Komi Republic, Udmurtiya Republic, Bryansk Oblast, and Nizhgorodskaya Oblast all complained of branch leaders openly selling seats on the party list to the highest payers.[49] The untimely death of a young deputy in Sverlodsk Oblast's regional legislature led to ample speculation about how much his seat would be sold for; prices ranged from 15 to 40 million rubles ($500,000 to $1.1 million). Such a practice was common for distributing spots on the party lists of Just Russia and United Russia in the previous elections.[50] The more popular parties are, the more seats they can sell during the next election, creating a positive feedback mechanism.[51] After elections, parties change their lists in order to reflect the highest bidder: those who pay the most have the best chance of getting in.[52]

Lost in these bidding wars is a place for ideology. Parties at the regional level do little to build ideologically coherent party platforms (or "ideational capital" as in Kitschelt et al., 1999). Gel'man (2008) succinctly describes the ideological ambiguity at the heart of the United Russia project:

> Top state officials needed UR as an instrument for the preservation of the status quo but not as an instrument of political change. No wonder that UR openly and deliberately manifested its loyalty to Russia's political regime and personally to Putin, while its position on major policy issues remained vague and indefinite. During the 2007 State Duma election campaign, UR's major slogan was "Vote for Putin's plan!" ("Golosui za plan Putina!"), without specific reference to the content of this "plan."

47 Murtazin (2013).
48 Hutcheson (2008).
49 Aleksandrov (2011).
50 Ura.Ru (2012).
51 BBC Monitoring (2007).
52 Interview with Oleg Podvintsev, political scientist, Perm, Russia. October 2, 2013.

By not declaring public positions on key left-right issues, United Russia left itself considerable room to maneuver and the opportunity to act as a big tent for powerful elites from around the country. The impossibility of dissecting exactly what United Russia stood for was exactly the point: the Putin-era electoral reforms and consolidation were designed to make electoral results solely based on who controlled what resources, be they administrative (such as the immense power of the bureaucracy to mobilize voters and support regime candidates) or financial (wealthy parties using rents to co-opt elites and win over recalcitrant voters). Whatever left-right programmatic competition existed during the 1990s gave way to party-centered clientelism by the mid-2000s. Indeed, conversations with political leaders in the regions suggest voters indeed may care more about candidates delivering pragmatic results than ideology.[53]

Examples of ideological inconsistency abound in systemic opposition parties as well. At the national level, the Communist Party of the Russian Federation has struggled to paper over internal divisions over the inclusion of prominent businesspeople on party lists, even expelling members who criticized the party's strategy of attracting support from millionaires instead of blue-collar workers.[54] As many as 24 percent of candidates on the Communist Party's list during the 2003 national elections were from big business, setting the standard for a muddled ideology in branches across the country.[55] National Communist Party leader Gennadiy Zyuganov even applauded the regional branch of the Communist Party in Nizhniy Novgorod for recruiting wealthy businesspeople into their ranks and filling party coffers with their contributions.[56] What won elections was not the Communist Party's plans for remaking government, but the resources it possessed to get out the vote.

The priority assigned to money over ideological coherence means that candidates adopt an instrumental approach to choosing party affiliations. My interviews suggest that political leanings are often inconsequential in determining which party candidates align with.[57] According to the deputy speaker of the Perm Regional Duma, which party a candidate

53 Interview with Vitalii Kovin, leader of Perm Golos organization, Perm, Russia. October 7, 2013.
54 Myers (2003).
55 Mereu (2003).
56 Zhmirikov (2005).
57 Interview with Valeriye Mazanov, editor of the Kompanion Journal, Perm, Russia. October 3, 2013; Interview with Natalia Zubarevich, professor of geography at Moscow State University, Moscow, Russia. March 11, 2013.

affiliates with simply does not matter.[58] Candidates care more about getting into office than the political grouping that gets them there. The practice of auctioning off seats also leads to weak, long-term allegiances between candidates and parties. Candidates can change party affiliations quite easily by just submitting a bid during the next election cycle. As consumers on the electoral market, they look for ways to maximize their ability to get into legislative office, while paying the lowest possible ticket price.

As gatekeepers to the lists, political parties act as vehicles for large financial interests to purchase access to political power. Party list candidates sponsor the electoral campaigns of regional party branches, hoping for a significant enough vote share to ensure that the full-time party leaders and the major donors can both find their way into the legislature. One scholar remarked that businesspeople have become "wallets" for political parties to draw upon in order to finance their expenditures.[59] Rank-and-file members often complained that these bidding wars undermined party discipline and organization by allotting top posts not to the most experienced or loyal, but to the most wealthy. In Primorsky Kray, for example, one commentator lamented how qualifications mattered little for selecting party leaders; instead selection processes resembled a "fight of the wallets."[60] In Chapter 3, I explored the consequences of weak party institutionalization for businesspeople's initial decision to enter politics and run for office. Below I discuss how this auction system affects which parties businessperson candidates look to affiliate with.

4.2.2 How Businesspeople Choose Between Parties

As the wallets backing party activities, businessperson candidates want to make sure they are getting their money's worth. Numerous interviewees remarked that the most advantageous party, and thus most coveted, to align with was United Russia.[61] Becoming a member of United Russia

58 Interview with Elena Zyryanova, deputy Perm Regional Duma, Perm, Russia, October 8, 2013.

59 Interview with Alla Chirikova, Institute of Sociology, Russian Academy of Sciences, Moscow, Russia. March 15, 2013.

60 Vasil'eva (2016).

61 Interview with Yuri Abramov, consultant at Ryazan office of the Central Election Commission, Ryazan, Russia. November 18, 2013; Interview with Petr Panov, political scientist, Perm, Russia. October 3, 2013.

offers exclusive benefits to candidates: better access to bureaucrats, faster escalators to achieve career ambitions at higher levels, and superior ability to get laws passed as a member of the legislative majority. These spoils do not run cheap. Possessing the potent combination of administrative resources and presidential coattails, United Russia is just about guaranteed a plurality of seats in each parliamentary convocation, no matter the region. Acquiring a high spot on the party list is a nearly guaranteed ticket to a deputy seat. That certainty of winning paired with the additional spoils inflates the price of making it onto the list. Not all firms are willing or able to bear these costs. Those with the more substantial financial assets will be much more likely to affiliate with UR.

Hypothesis 11. *Firms with more financial resources should run as members of the ruling United Russia party.*

But all parties, even the ruling one, have a limited number of seats they can sell on the market. A successful party campaign has to appeal to all of society to win high vote shares. Party lists thus need to somewhat reflect this diversity to broaden their appeal. Lawyers, doctors, teachers, and administrators collectively make-up the majority of candidates on most lists, with women much more likely to find spots on the proportional representation ballot. In regions such as Rostov and Nizhniy Novgorod, demand among businesspeople for seats can far outstrip supply, particularly for membership in United Russia.[62] Party leaders are concerned about conceding too much power to vested financial interests and acquiring a reputation of being solely vehicles for big business to capture legislative institutions.

When there isn't enough room under the umbrella of the ruling party, opposition parties can step in to fill the gap. As we saw in Chapter 1, parliamentary spots provide more than just opportunities to get legislation passed. For many businesspeople, just getting a seat is enough, no matter the party they will formally represent. In Nizhniy Novgorod region during the 2006 regional elections, well-financed candidates from the business sector began gravitating towards both the Russian Pensioners Party (RPP) and the Communist Party.[63] The influx of businesspeople into the RPP helped the party secure the second-most amount of seats

[62] Tagadryan (2007b).
[63] Zhmirikov, Aleksander (2005).

in the regional duma; it later was merged back into United Russia in exchange for significant political concessions.[64]

Opposition parties are less popular with the electorate and have fewer spots on party lists available to sell to businesspeople (as well as a weaker guarantee that a spot will lead to a deputy seat). Thus the price of joining an opposition party is lower. There may also be consequences for teaming up with the opposition, such as increased difficulties winning new state contracts or stopping payments placed on existing ones.[65] Businesses may face economic repercussions from bureaucrats, and some have rescinded their support for certain parties because of perceived threats.[66] Which opposition parties businesspeople choose is highly contingent on their regional political setting, particularly the price being offered. Overall though, we should expect smaller firms to join up with the opposition.

Beyond firm size, ownership structure can also play a big role in determining affiliation. Managers of state-owned enterprises (SOEs) may have different incentives to join parties than private firms. First, state enterprises (i.e. unitary enterprises) are fully controlled by governments at one of three levels: federal, regional, and municipal.[67] Their activities are governed by the corresponding ministry responsible for the sector in which they operate (i.e. an SOE working in farming would fall under the aegis of the Ministry of Agriculture). As pillars of the system of state capitalism promoted by the Putin regime, these enterprises should see greater benefits from joining and supporting the ruling party, which controls the majority of governorships as well as most cadre decisions in the wider bureaucracy.

Not many state enterprises though survived the wave of privatization during the 1990s in Russia, and those that did were often the smallest, least profitable, worst run, and least attractive to the private investors that might have bid on them. During the period studied in this project, municipal SOEs outnumbered their state and federal counterparts by nearly 2 to 1 across the country, a clear reversal of the situation in the 1990s.[68] Very often the directors of these municipal SOEs have not

[64] Zaytsev (2011).
[65] Interview with Andrei Starkov, deputy, Perm Regional Duma, Perm, Russia. October 7, 2013.
[66] Heyaskin (2012).
[67] Sprenger (2010).
[68] Sprenger (2010).

changed since the Soviet Union. We then might predict differences in party affiliation based on the specific governing structure of state-owned enterprises. Region-level SOEs, beholden to higher governing authorities for their benefits and regulation will be more likely to lean towards the ruling party, while municipal SOEs, as holdovers from privatization and less likely to have seen a change in directorship, will continue their allegiance to the successor party to CPSU, the Communist Party of the Russian Federation.

Hypothesis 12. *Regional state-owned enterprises will be more likely to support the ruling United Russia party.*

Hypothesis 13. *Municipal state-owned enterprises will be more likely to support the Communist Party.*

Lastly, the organization of the Russian economy into sectors has had profound implications for fiscal policy as well as political influence.[69] In Chapter 3, I found that firms in more competitive sectors are more likely to put forward directors as candidates to regional office. Sector may also matter when it comes to party affiliation. Joining the ruling party may make more sense for certain types of firms: for example, enterprises that are vulnerable to regulation may think it wise to align with the party of the bureaucracy. A common measure of vulnerability to regulation is the degree of asset mobility of a firm: those firms that can threaten to easily move their production facilities to a neighboring region or even country are able to better withstand pressure from unbridled bureaucrats looking to extract rents. The blurring of the line between the United Russia and the bureaucracy creates a situation where joining the ruling party can have specific benefits for certain types of firms. Though an imperfect measure in many respects, other sector-level measures of regulatory dependence are not available in Russia during this time period.

Hypothesis 14. *Firms operating in sectors marked by greater asset specificity will be more likely to support the ruling United Russia party.*

[69] Gehlbach (2006).

4.2.3 Data and Empirical Strategy

To analyze party choice, I first define five binary outcomes indicating which party a firm affiliated with during elections: United Russia (the ruling party), the Communist Party of the Russian Federation, Just Russia (a right-leaning party typically associated with businesspeople), the Liberal-Democratic Party of Russia (a far-right party known for espousing nationalism), and any of the smaller parties (liberal parties such as Yabloko and SPS, the Agrarian Party, etc.). The four individual parties analyzed are the only groupings to have representatives in the State Duma and generally have branches in all regions. Finally, I code a binary indicator for whether a firm was affiliated with multiple parties (or ran candidates both affiliated with a party and as an independent).

The main models shown here subset the sample of firms to only those connected to candidates running on party lists. The goal is to examine how firms decide between parties after the choice to run on the proportional representation ballot is made. That said, candidates running in plurality races often affiliate with a party in order to tap into the party's brand recognition or mobilizational support.[70] In the Appendix, I run the same models that include all candidates running in single-member districts or dual-listing, while controlling for ballot choice on the right hand side. The results are very similar when this larger sample is used. In addition, I show a multinomial model with two outcome variables – affiliating with United Russia and affiliating with a political party that is not United Russia – and using a reference category of running as an independent, while controlling for ballot choice. This model includes both SMDP and PR candidates. The predictors used are identical to those shown above in the models predicting ballot choice. Again all models include sector, region, and year fixed effects.

4.2.4 Empirical Results

First, Table 4.3 presents summary statistics on the breakdown of businessperson candidates among the leading four parties in Russia, as well as the smattering of smaller parties active in the regions. First, we

[70] For example, getting onto a ballot in Russia requires jumping through a number of administrative hoops, the most burdensome of which is collecting sufficient signatures; aligning with a political party can enable a candidate to tap into a body of party activists and mobilizers to spread the word about a candidacy. In her unique survey of regional deputies from nine regions in the late 1990s, Smyth (2005) finds that the promise of parties' material resources and popularity within districts attracted a minority of politicians in her sample.

TABLE 4.3 *Party choice: Summary statistics*

Political Party	All Candidates	Businesspeople	%
United Russia (UR)	7,508	3,389	45.1
Communist Party (KPRF)	6,054	1,597	26.4
Just Russia (SR)	4,932	2,189	44.4
Liberal-Democratic Party of Russia (LDPR)	4,972	1,912	38.5
Smaller Parties	7,729	2,884	37.3
Total #	31,197	11,972	38.4

This table presents summary statistics about the percentage of candidates running with each party who are businesspeople. The sample is limited to candidates running on party lists.

see that the ruling party United Russia has the largest percentage of businesspeople in its ranks at 45 percent, roughly 7 percent higher than the average among candidates on party lists. Given its dominant political position, it is not surprise that businesspeople covet this affiliation. Just behind United Russia comes Just Russia, a newer party created in 2006 after a merger between Rodina, the Russian Party of Life, and the Russian Pensioners Party.[71] In many regions, Just Russia has become a second home for wealthy businesspeople, adopting pro-market stances and pushing for an improved investment climate. The party's persistent courting of businesspeople left outside United Russia is evident, as 44 percent of its PR candidates come from the private sector. On the other side of the spectrum, the contrast is striking between the Communist Party's professed calls for nationalization of private enterprise, and businesspeople making up just over a quarter of its ranks. Winning elections requires financial backing, and the Communists are by no means immune to these economic pressures.

Specifications analyzing these specific party choices are shown in Table 4.4. As above, the first six columns of the table use logit specifications on binary outcome variables indicating party of choice (Columns 1–5) and whether a firm ran multiple candidates to office (Column 6). As predicted by Hypothesis 1, larger firms are much more likely to affiliate with the ruling United Russia party. The cost of acquiring a spot on the party list restricts the pool of potential firms to only those with sufficient financial assets. Similarly, larger firms are much more likely to run multiple candidates.

[71] March (2009).

TABLE 4.4 *Party choice*

	Marginal Effects from Logit Models						Multinomial Logit Model	
	UR	Communists	Just Russia	LDPR	Smaller	Multiple	Non-UR	UR
	(1)	(2)	(3)	(4)	(5)	(6)	(7)	(8)
Firm-Level Predictors								
Total Assets (logged)	0.043***	−0.006**	−0.009***	−0.005*	−0.014***	0.002**	−0.090***	0.196***
	(0.005)	(0.003)	(0.003)	(0.003)	(0.003)	(0.001)	(0.018)	(0.020)
Top 5 Firm	0.036	−0.021*	−0.010	−0.014	−0.034*	0.004	−0.182	0.039
	(0.027)	(0.011)	(0.024)	(0.018)	(0.019)	(0.005)	(0.112)	(0.107)
Firm Age (logged)	0.017**	0.003	−0.007	−0.004	−0.008	0.004*	0.027	0.054
	(0.008)	(0.005)	(0.006)	(0.006)	(0.007)	(0.002)	(0.038)	(0.039)
Regional SOE	0.122**	−0.018	−0.015	−0.065***	−0.063*	0.007	−0.053	0.234
	(0.050)	(0.025)	(0.035)	(0.015)	(0.035)	(0.021)	(0.249)	(0.241)
Municipal SOE	−0.082**	0.038	0.034	0.002	0.003	−0.009**	0.233	−0.252
	(0.038)	(0.037)	(0.025)	(0.022)	(0.028)	(0.004)	(0.189)	(0.207)
Importer	−0.005	−0.007	0.012	−0.004	−0.001	0.004	0.006	−0.050
	(0.019)	(0.012)	(0.017)	(0.017)	(0.018)	(0.004)	(0.107)	(0.106)
Exporter	−0.022	0.032*	−0.011	0.010	−0.014	−0.007**	0.036	−0.031
	(0.026)	(0.019)	(0.020)	(0.021)	(0.018)	(0.003)	(0.122)	(0.120)
Candidate-Level Predictors								
Candidate Age	0.183***	0.100***	−0.058**	−0.147***	−0.061**	−0.007	−0.067	1.238***
	(0.048)	(0.031)	(0.028)	(0.026)	(0.027)	(0.008)	(0.172)	(0.183)

(continued)

TABLE 4.4 *(continued)*

	Marginal Effects from Logit Models						Multinomial Logit Model	
	UR	Communists	Just Russia	LDPR	Smaller	Multiple	Non-UR	UR
	(1)	(2)	(3)	(4)	(5)	(6)	(7)	(8)
Male Candidate	0.019	0.022*	−0.008	−0.004	−0.041	0.013***	−0.343**	−0.248
	(0.042)	(0.013)	(0.030)	(0.026)	(0.026)	(0.0001)	(0.159)	(0.169)
Candidate was Incumbent	0.194***	−0.010	−0.054**	−0.012	−0.144***	0.012	−0.647***	0.630***
	(0.034)	(0.016)	(0.023)	(0.026)	(0.023)	(0.009)	(0.107)	(0.096)
Region-Level Predictors								
Gross Regional Product	0.106	0.221**	−0.035	−0.165*	−0.294	−0.049	−0.176	1.618***
(logged)	(0.145)	(0.098)	(0.160)	(0.096)	(0.213)	(0.040)	(0.600)	(0.596)
Regional Population	−1.282	0.089	−0.484	−0.107	2.160***	0.363	1.192**	−1.882***
	(0.992)	(0.515)	(0.683)	(0.446)	(0.649)	(0.235)	(0.505)	(0.500)
Urbanization	3.188	0.597	−2.145	−1.533	−2.733	−0.148	−6.993***	3.338***
	(2.218)	(1.872)	(2.441)	(1.328)	(2.599)	(0.267)	(1.102)	(1.102)
National Party Strength -	0.027	−0.013	0.017	0.028	−0.145	0.010	−0.636***	−0.394**
Expenditures	(0.045)	(0.029)	(0.075)	(0.029)	(0.122)	(0.014)	(0.193)	(0.187)
Sector FE	Yes	Yes	Yes	Yes	Yes	Yes	Yes	Yes
Region FE	Yes	Yes	Yes	Yes	Yes	Yes	Yes	Yes
Year FE	Yes	Yes	Yes	Yes	Yes	Yes	Yes	Yes
Observations	4,879	4,879	4,879	4,879	4,879	4,879	4,879	

*p<0.1; **p<0.05; ***p<0.01 All models include sector, region, and year fixed effects. The sample in Columns 1–6 includes candidates running on the proportional representation system, i.e. having a spot on the party list. Columns 1–6 present marginal effects from separate logit models with the outcome variable being a binary indicator for the specific political party the businessperson candidate affiliated with (and the reference category being all other political party choices). Columns 7 and 8 present point estimates from a multinomial logistic model with the outcomes listed in the column header (affiliating with United Russia or choosing an opposition party). The reference category is whether the candidate ran as an independent. The sample for this model includes all PR and SMDP candidates. Errors are clustered on region.

Next, we see that the choice of party also depends on firm ownership, and more specifically the level at which state-owned enterprises are given. Those operating at the regional level see greater benefits from joining the ruling party, while those at the municipal level, possibly with directors held over from the Soviet era, still retain their Communist allegiances. This latter result is also evident in the Appendix, which includes candidates running in single-member district races.

Several other results are of interest. Older candidates gravitate towards both United Russia and the Communist Party, perhaps because of their ability to cultivate a personal vote (in the former case) and ideological attachment to the Soviet Union (in the latter case). United Russia also attracts candidates with previous governing experience in the legislature. During this period of consolidation and party building, UR made concerted efforts to co-opt powerful regional elites. Moreover, the party's strong position in legislatures means that firms once aligned with the ruling party are more likely to stick with it. The multinomial results also uncover intriguing patterns on the regional predictors, particularly since the category of running as an independent is included. First we see that firms are much more likely to align with the ruling party in wealthier and more urbanized regions. One reason is that the ruling party can provide greater opportunities for rent-seeking when the pie is larger. Finally, we see that where party development is weaker, firms are much more likely to go it alone and run as independents.

4.2.5 Do Parties Coordinate Sectoral Interests?

Next, in Figure 4.2, I examine sectoral variation by plotting the point estimates on the sector fixed effects from six linear probability models with each of the following outcomes related to party choice: United Russia, Communists, Just Russia, Liberal-Democratic Party of Russia, Smaller Parties, or Independent. The point estimates on sector from each linear model are in different colors, and the reference category (the sector dropped from the analysis) is trade.

Several takeaways emerge from Figure 4.2. First, as predicted by Hypothesis 8, firms working in sectors with more immobile assets such as mining, manufacturing, and utilities are more likely to affiliate with the United Russia ruling party (excluding agriculture). Agricultural firms gravitate towards the "Smaller Parties" category, which includes the small Russian Agrarian party that later merged into United Russia in

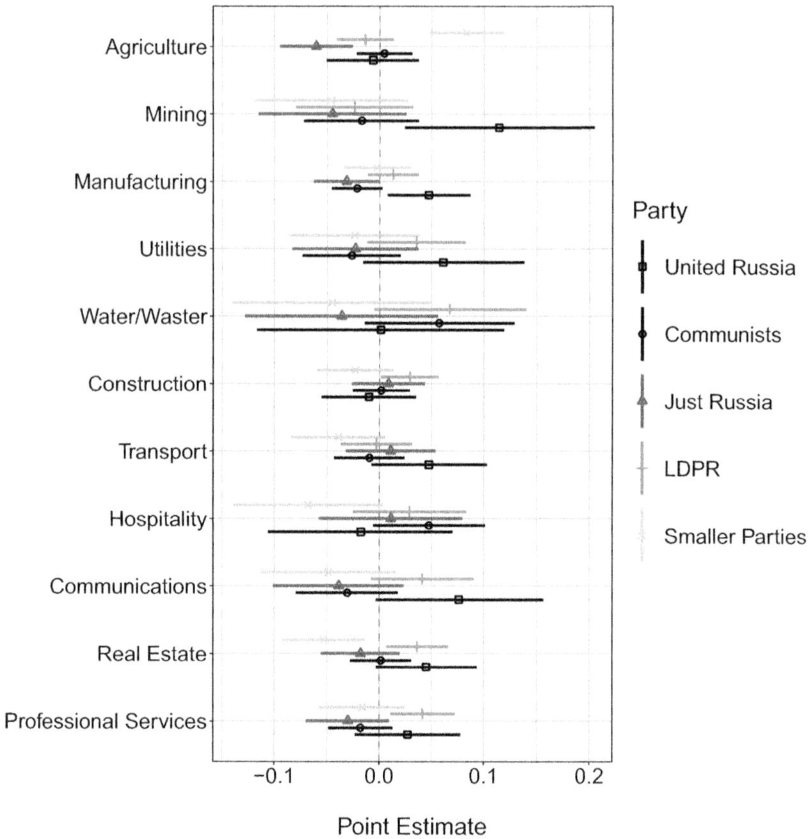

FIGURE 4.2: Party affiliation by sector
This figure presents point estimates on sector from five linear probability models for binary indicators capturing each of the party outcomes listed in the legend. The lines indicate 95% confidence intervals. The reference category is trade.

2008. Note there also seems to be a tendency for firms in services sectors as well as health and arts and recreation to affiliate with United Russia, although the variance on these estimates is quite large due to the small number of firms running from these industries. But the overall impression from this figure is that strong patterns of sector-party alliances are not present across the various Russian regions. With the exception of the higher probability of transportation and hospitality firms more likely to run as independents and the United Russia example above, we see little evidence that firms of a specific sector are more likely to find a home in a single political party.

This corresponds to descriptive evidence at the sectoral level that competing firms operating in a unique region tend to run candidates in different political parties. The dataset of businessperson candidates contains firms working in 2,977 unique region-sector-year combinations.[72] In other words, there is data on roughly 3,000 sectors that ran candidates to the same regional election in the same election. Sectors are defined using the two digit Russian OKVED code with fifty-three unique sectors represented in the data across the eighty-five regions and eight years. An example might be all businessperson candidates to the 2005 elections for Belgorod Regional Duma that represent agricultural firms.

Of these 2,977 region-sector-years, roughly 56 percent saw more than one firm put up a unique candidate to office in the same election (1,682 in total). The question then arises: did candidates representing different firms affiliate with the same party? If yes, this suggests political parties in Russia are acting as coordinating devices for sectoral interests, allowing them to band together under a single umbrella to push for collective demands. On the other hand, if firms in the same region-sector are running candidates in different parties, then political party (i.e. electoral) competition may be reflecting economic rivalry.

To answer the question, I create a new measure called *Effective Number of Parties per Sector*, or ENPS, measured at the region-sector-year level. The formula used is identical to that used to calculate the effective number of parties at the national level or the effective number of candidates per plurality race, except that the shares used as inputs are the percentage of firms in each region-sector-year that belong to each party. This gives the following equation:

$$ENPS = 1/\sum_{p}^{n} S_p^2 \tag{4.1}$$

where p indexes the 64 (n) unique parties with which candidates affiliated (it should be noted that 86 percent of all candidates ran under one of the four main parties or as independents) and S indicates the share of firms in a region-sector belonging to that party. As an illustration, take the example of the food processing industry in Kurskaya Oblast. Six candidates representing six different firms ran for office in the 2006 regional elections. Two candidates ran with a Communist Party affiliation (33.3 percent), two candidates ran as Independents (33.3 percent), and one

[72] For this exercise, I exclude the very small number of firms who ran multiple candidates or who affiliated with multiple parties.

candidate each ran with United Russia (16.7 percent) and the Agrarian Party (16.7 percent). According to the ENPS formula, there were 3.6 effective parties representing that sector for this regional election. For region-industries where all of the candidates ran under one party grouping, the ENPS would necessarily be 1. This formula therefore helps identify the degree to which businessperson candidates working in the same industry affiliate with the same political party during elections.

Across the entire sample, there are on average 2.138 Effective Number of Parties per region-sector. This means that candidates representing firms working in the same sector generally group into two different political parties. Of more interest is the role of sectoral competition. In Panel A, Figure 4.3, I plot all region-sectors according to their ENPS value on the y-axis and the level of sectoral competition on the x-axis (the reverse Herfindahl index measured in the previous chapter). Each dot represents a unique region-sector.

We see a positive correlation between the variables, estimated at roughly 0.25. As sectors become more competitive, businessperson candidates are more likely to affiliate with different parties. Panel B subsets this same data to just two industries with varying levels of internal competition: agriculture (weakly competitive, dark circles) and construction (highly competitive, light triangles). As indicated, firms working in construction tend to see their candidates join different political parties, while those in agriculture (where there tend to be more dominant players) group together in a small number of political parties.

Economic competition leads to a more fragmented party landscape. The lack of coordination within sector lends additional evidence of regional parliaments as sites of economic competition between firms. Rivals join opposing political parties in order to push for their own individual interests. Competitors in a single market see greater dividends from strengthening rival parties than trying to address their differences within single grouping.[73]

4.3 SELECTING A FIRM REPRESENTATIVE

Finally, firms vary with regard to which representative is sent to run for office. Most of the anecdotes presented so far in this book relate to owner-managers capitalizing on their name recognition and status to

73 Interview with Alla Chirikova, Institute of Sociology, Russian Academy of Sciences, Moscow, Russia. March 15, 2013.

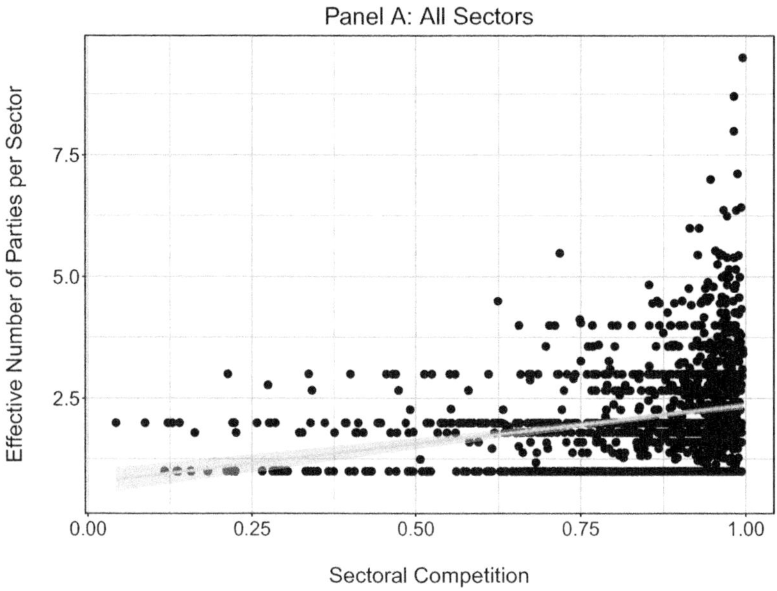

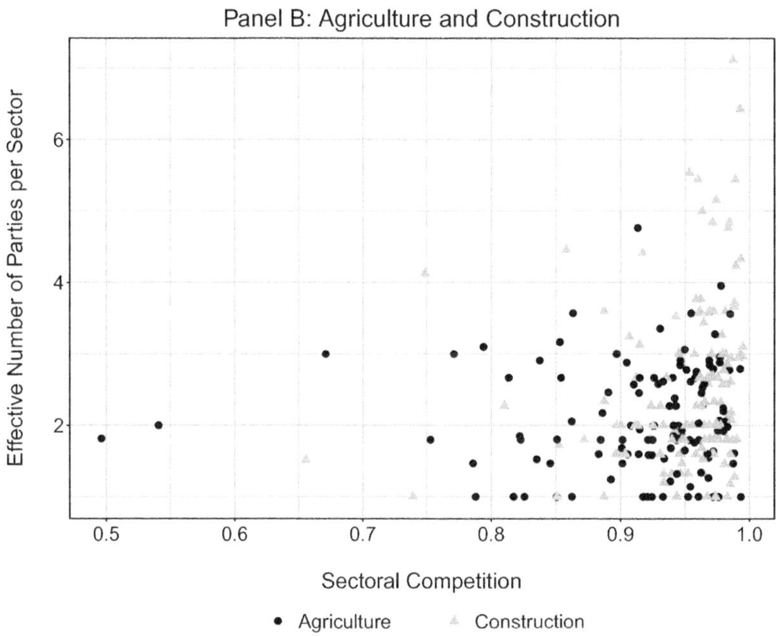

FIGURE 4.3: Competition splits firms between parties

Figure 4.3, Panel A plots region-sectors according to their values of Effective Number of Parties per Sector and the level of sectoral competition. The line represents the correlation between the two variables (0.25) with 95% confidence intervals. Panel B subsets this same data to just the agriculture and construction industries (with each dot indicating a region).

personally seek elected office. But larger firms have much more expansive boardrooms and C-suites. Beyond the CEO, there are multiple qualified, influential firm delegates that can effectively push for its interests in the public sphere. For example, in many companies, members of board of directors can play an integral role in raising investments, representing the companies in media, and using their contacts and expertise to further company objectives.[74]

How does a firm decide whether to send a delegate other than its director into public office? Firms face a different trade-off in approaching this decision. On one hand, having a non-director run for office frees up the actual CEO to remain a full-time physical presence in firm management.[75] As Chapter 1 argued, businessperson candidacy (including both the campaign and if successful, serving in office) diverts time away from a CEO's management functions. Businessperson politicians must attend committee meetings and plenary sessions, cater to the needs of their constituents, and spend time with strategists devising campaigns and public relations strategies. This stretches their ability to remain intimately involved with firm activities. By commissioning another member of the management team (e.g. a board member) to run for office in their stead, directors can access the spoils of direct political representation without losing sight of day-to-day firm operations.

Under certain conditions, sending a non-director may result in inadequate political representation. The ability to hammer out compromises and push for firm interests requires leverage backed by political, economic, or persuasive resources. By virtue of their position at the top of large companies, firm directors naturally thrive in this negotiating role. Their developed reputation as successful founders and managers of large enterprises help position them as political heavyweights who can contend for committee leadership roles and extract concessions from fellow lawmakers. The willingness of bureaucrats to respond to deputy requests also in part depends on their economic and political stature: the stature of firm directors allows them to press harder on bureaucrats to do their bidding. Sending a board member also can backfire electorally. As discussed earlier, winning candidate-centric elections (such as plurality races) often requires a personal touch and the direct involvement of a firm director.

74 Dass et al. (2013); Goldman, Rocholl, and So (2013).

75 I define a "non-director" as an individual other than the CEO tasked with management duties, such as deputy directors, other members of the C-suite, and members of the board of directors.

The general public may be unaffected by a relative or seemingly remote manager running for office.

This simple cost-benefit structure helps inform the set of conditions under which we might expect firms to delegate candidacy to non-directors. First, Chapter 1 argued that stronger political parties help alleviate concerns that firms may have about politician shirking as well as the effectiveness of other indirect strategies, such as making campaign contributions. This claim is probabilistic: there are still many firms who pursue businessperson candidacy even when political parties are relatively institutionalized. For example, fears over rivals gaining a competitive edge in a legislature may trump the benefits that developed political parties offer. Even when firms decide businessperson candidacy is a must, the strength of political parties affects the choice of delegate sent to run for office. Strong parties provide structure to legislative factions, helping to corral legislators and solve the many coordination problems involved with passing legislation. This can make a firm's legislative objectives more predictable and feasible, as well as less dependent on the individual personality and stature of the candidate designated to represent the firm. Popular parties can also lay out coattails for candidates to ride, reducing the necessity of cultivating a personal vote. Firms can feel more confident that the spots they buy on a party list will actually generate seats in the legislature. Non-directors can pursue the more affordable route into office through the PR system, rather than needing to invest in a more time- and resource-intensive plurality race.

Hypothesis 15. *Non-directors will be more likely to represent firms in regions where political parties are stronger and more institutionalized.*

Another important factor pertains to the candidate's political experience. Firms may feel more comfortable sending a non-director if that person already understands the lawmaking process and can use those connections to carve out political dividends in line with firm interests. Although some board members may have worked at some point in the executive branch, having direct experience in a legislature is much more attractive. Work on U.S. politics has found that the longer a legislator has served, the more effective they are at passing laws.[76] Firms may be more likely to entrust their political representation to board members who

[76] Miquel and Snyder Jr (2006).

have served in office before. They have already demonstrated an ability to juggle competing private sector and public sector duties effectively.

Hypothesis 16. *Firms will be more likely to select board members to run who have served in elected office previously.*

Other potential correlates of delegating to non-directors are of significant theoretical interest, but require much more detailed data on firm operations that is not conventionally available. For example, the effects of firm rivalry are not straightforward. On one hand, directors may see a pressing need to personally represent their firms in the legislature, calculating that throwing around their individual political weight is the only way to counter a rival's political influence. However, this can impose also significant costs on firm productivity, especially if the CEO's full-time physical presence is key to firm operations. In highly competitive markets, delegating elected office to a trusted subordinate may make more sense when a CEO's technical expertise is required on production sites. Similarly, Chapter 1 raised several examples of some firms running on autopilot, allowing their director to step away and pursue political office for reasons related to both firm interests and political ambitions. Detailed data on the day-to-day involvement of directors in firm activities would be needed to test such claims.

4.3.1 Data and Empirical Strategy

I test the hypotheses again by again using the observational data on businessperson candidates. The outcome variable analyzed is a binary indicator that takes a 1 if a firm's businessperson candidate is a member or chairperson of the firm's board of directors, and a 0 if that candidate worked as the firm's director or deputy director. Data on the candidate's position within the firm comes from one of two sources: (1) the field on his or her registration form with the Central Election Commission that lists place of work or (2) the entry in the SPARK database which lists his or her official affiliation with the firm. In the small number of cases where the two datasets gave conflicting information, I went with the coding from the official registration form. Overall, 15 percent of businessperson candidates served on their firm's board at the time of their election.

These data point masks important variation in the legal structures of firms that put forth candidates to elected office. Private Russian firms generally conform to one of three legal structures. The two types of

Joint-Stock Companies are distinguished by whether they are open (in Russian, OAOs), i.e. they are publicly traded, have an unlimited number of shareholders, and must have at least 100,000 rubles in charter capital, or whether they are closed (in Russian, ZAOs), i.e. they have a lower threshold of charter capital (10,000 rubles) and a maximum of 50 shareholders.[77] The remainder are considered Limited Liability Companies (in Russian, OOOs), meaning they are non-public, do not have to register with securities commissions and shares (or membership percentages) are less easily transferrable between parties. OOOs are by far the simplest and most cost-effective legal structure, and thereby popular among entrepreneurs.

According to Russian law, only companies with 50 or more voting shareholders must have a board of directors.[78] That is, only open-stock companies surpass this threshold. For ZAOs and OOOs, having a board is completely voluntary and few closed joint-stock companies (ZAOs) or limited liability companies (OOOs) comply.[79] For those companies with boards, several important restrictions apply. Other legal entities cannot become members of the board, and individuals from the company management team cannot constitute more than 25 percent of all members.[80]

Table 4.5 shows the distribution of board members as businessperson candidates across the three main types of legal structures. Roughly half of all businessperson candidates representing open joint-stock companies are members of the board, with the other half occupying roles as director or deputy director. The situation is different with regard to closed joint-stock companies, which are not required by law to convene boards. There only 13 percent of all candidates are board members. Registration data on which individual ZAOs have boards runs into problems of significant data missingness. Finally, we see that very few LLCs send board members, presumably because few of these companies have boards at all.

To control for this potential selection problems, I present logistic models that subset to either only the open joint-stock companies (OAOs), and to both open and closed joint-stock companies (OAOs and ZAOs). As above, the models include sector, region, and year fixed effects, though I also exclude sector fixed effects in two models to investigate the effect

[77] Another important difference is the way shares are distributed. For ZAOs, existing shareholders have a "right of first refusal" to purchase shares being offered by a fellow shareholder to a third party.

[78] Roundtable (2002).

[79] Teterevkova, Fedorov, and Dentons (2017).

[80] Roundtable (2002).

TABLE 4.5 *Delegate choice: Summary statistics*

Legal Form	All Candidates	Board Member as Candidate	%
Open Joint-Stock Companies (OAO)	2,807	1,377	49.1
Closed Joint-Stock Companies (ZAO)	1,434	191	13.3
Limited Liability Companies (OOO)	5,923	63	1.06

This table presents summary statistics for the percentage of businessperson candidates that are board members, conditional on the legal structure of the firms they work for.

sector size and competition on delegating businessperson candidacy to board members. As additional checks, I include standard firm covariates, particularly how long the firm has been operating, which should help predict the extent to which corporate governance measures have been instituted.

4.3.2 Empirical Results

Table 4.6 presents the results from these regressions. First, we see that firms are more likely to delegate businessperson candidacy to board members when political parties are stronger. The points estimates are consistently positive and statistically significant across all four models, which vary the sample and fixed effects used. Firms assess the ability of political parties to represent their interests not just when deciding whether to put forth a candidate in general to office, but also which individual will be tasked to run. Next, we see that the coefficients on Candidate was Incumbent are positive and statistically significant regardless of the sample used. Firms are much more likely to lean on board members with previous political experience to represent them in elected office. The coefficients are substantively large.

The point estimates on several control variables are also of interest. We see strong evidence that older firms are more likely to delegate businessperson candidacy to board members. Although in the case of closed joint-stock companies firm age could be an indicator of having a board of directors, we see effects of similar magnitude and statistical significance for those models that just look at open joint-stock companies. Russian law dictates that the board size is a function of the number

TABLE 4.6 *Board members as businessperson candidates*

	Board Member as Candidate			
	OAO	OAO + ZAO	OAO	OAO + ZAO
	(1)	(2)	(3)	(4)
Firm-Level Predictors				
Total Assets (logged)	−0.007	0.003	−0.010	0.002
	(0.009)	(0.006)	(0.008)	(0.006)
Top 5 Firm	−0.041	−0.052**	−0.027	−0.044*
	(0.026)	(0.021)	(0.031)	(0.023)
Firm Age (logged)	0.049***	0.048***	0.056***	0.052***
	(0.016)	(0.013)	(0.015)	(0.013)
Importer	0.015	0.014	0.022	0.014
	(0.029)	(0.024)	(0.030)	(0.024)
Exporter	−0.015	−0.011	0.032	0.029
	(0.029)	(0.022)	(0.028)	(0.023)
Candidate-Level Predictors				
Candidate Age	−0.071	0.015	−0.061	0.025
	(0.057)	(0.043)	(0.055)	(0.042)
Male Candidate	0.041	0.043	0.055	0.050
	(0.081)	(0.058)	(0.079)	(0.055)
Candidate was	0.047*	0.055**	0.053**	0.059**
Incumbent	(0.024)	(0.022)	(0.026)	(0.023)
Region-Level Predictors				
Gross Regional	0.187	0.100	0.198	0.097
Product (logged)	(0.124)	(0.091)	(0.123)	(0.098)
Regional Population	−0.143	0.260	0.074	0.431
	(0.814)	(0.600)	(0.786)	(0.605)
National Party	0.111***	0.083**	0.106***	0.082**
Strength –	(0.042)	(0.037)	(0.037)	(0.032)
Expenditures				
Sector-Level Predictors				
Total Sector Revenue			−0.008	−0.013**
(logged)			(0.008)	(0.006)
Sectoral Competition			0.024	−0.005
			(0.076)	(0.060)
Sector FE	Yes	Yes	No	No
Region FE	Yes	Yes	Yes	Yes
Year FE	Yes	Yes	Yes	Yes
Observations	2,685	4,007	2,685	4,007

*p<0.1; **p<0.05; ***p<0.01 All columns show marginal effects from separate logistic models with the outcome variable being a binary indicator for whether the businessperson candidate was a member of the firm's board of directors. Columns 1 and 3 subset the sample of only open joint-stock companies (OAOs), while Columns 3 and 4 include closed joint-stock companies (ZAOs) in addition to OAOs. Errors are clustered on region.

of unique shareholders;[81] for example, firms with more than 1,000 voting shareholders much have at least seven board members. Older firms may have more shareholders, and thus larger boards. This gives them a broader draw of potential businessperson candidates to choose from. Other firm-level characteristics have much less predictive power of delegating.

We also see that the degree of sectoral competition is not consistently related to delegating to board members. The signs on the coefficients from the two models fluctuate. This could be a function of the countervailing forces at work when rivalries are strong: firms may differ greatly on the touchy question of whether the best way to compete with rival firms is for a director to be in the legislature or working full-time at the firm.

4.4 DISCUSSION AND CONCLUDING REMARKS

Building on a growing body of literature,[82] this chapter presents evidence that the specific characteristics of formal institutions matter for understanding elite dynamics in competitive authoritarian regimes. It demonstrates that electoral rules, such as those allowing candidates to choose between ballots, structure how various individuals are drawn into politics, political parties secure financing and build capacity, and special interests are represented in policymaking circles. Ballot structure and party institutionalization have clear effects on the types of firms that put forth directors into politics.

Existing research argues that proportional representation systems may lead to greater corruption since the interests of political parties (which enjoy agenda-setting power) and business lobbies are more closely linked.[83] This chapter finds a different dynamic at work: businessperson candidates prefer running in single-member districts given the greater latitude offered in pushing for individual firm interests down the line. With regard to businessperson candidates, a SMDP seat may allow for more uninhibited and open lobbying since political parties wield less power to curb self-serving deputies that need only win the votes their geographic constituents and not the nod of party leaders. Measuring the level of corruption within legislative institutions involves not only paying attention

[81] Roundtable (2002).
[82] Gandhi and Lust-Okar (2009); Gandhi and Heller (2018); Ferree, Powell, and Scheiner (2014).
[83] Yadav (2011).

to electoral rules, but the types of elites (their backgrounds, interests, etc.) that run for office.

Moreover, the chapter sheds lights on the challenges economic interests face in coordinating representation in political institutions. At least with regard to businessperson candidates, politics is just another arena for direct competitors to protect their interests against one another. Unlike business or trade associations, political parties have few levers to bring together disparate or even competing firm interests under one roof.

That businesspeople do not necessarily coalesce under one party umbrella has implications for party system development. Greater economic competition over time may actually lead to more diverse and even stronger political institutions within society. If powerful economic elites cannot coordinate through a single political party, then their incentives are to build opposing ones, potentially altering the party system over time. Increasing economic competition between firms and sectors may facilitate the growth of alternative political parties that could, for example, challenge dominant ruling parties. This dispersion of wealth outside the hands of the central clique may be key for advancing plurality. A ruling party like United Russia has an interest then in promoting monopolistic behavior among firms, which if properly co-opted into party structures, will be easier to manage than a number of large, politically active firms supporting different political parties with their own ambitions. Political competition reflects the configuration of economic actors.

5

Firm-Level Returns from Businessperson Candidacy

This book opened by telling the story of Aleksander Shpeter, whose tenure in the Tomsk Regional Duma appeared to help his construction firm through the rocky straits of the 2008 financial crisis. Shpeter's firm, TDSK, had gotten the government bailouts it needed to unfreeze projects and replenish Tomsk's housing stock. But once the economy rebounded, some expected the cozy relationship between TDSK and regional authorities to die down. After all, the construction sector as a whole was back on its feet, why continue elevating one firm over all others?

Newspaper reports tell a different story. So long as Shpeter remained politically influential (as he did, winning re-election to the regional legislature in 2011), TDSK could access state procurement and win the rights to build on attractive plots once owned by the authorities. A new system of allocating contracts had been put into place: gaining access to the massive sums the Tomsk regional government wanted to invest in new housing construction now required getting onto the "white list," a list of preferred developers with strong political connections.[1] In 2013, leader of the local opposition political party Patriots of Russia Evgeny Krotov decried the consolidation that resulted in the construction sector, complaining that "practically all free plots in the city have been snatched up by ... (deputy) Shpeter."[2] Tomsk's beautiful architectural legacy from its

[1] A new system of allocating contracts had been put into place: gaining access to the massive sums the Tomsk regional government wanted to invest in new housing construction now required getting on to the "white list," a list of preferred candidates with strong political connections. Interview with Vasiliy Semkin, deputy of Tomsk Regional Duma. Tomsk, Russia June 11, 2014.

[2] Press Service (2013).

Tsarist past – an abundance of crumbling but striking wood homes in the city center – was also coming increasingly under threat from regional developers looking to build high rises. Taking the historical preservationists head-on, Shpeter declared "its time to build not only on the outskirts."[3] Local officials started to buy into these plans.

Since the crisis, the amount of public money TDSK has been able to tap borders on scandalous. An investigation by a leading anti-corruption watchdog uncovered that companies under the TDSK umbrella won 79 percent of all contracts handed out by local authorities, ultimately worth 2.3 billion rubles ($57.5 million).[4] Shpeter's TDSK was often the only bidder in some major auctions, receiving as their final payment basically the initial asking price set out by the government. Other tenders were specifically designed so that TDSK was the only local firm capable of executing the work, whether it be multiapartment complexes, swimming pools, or kindergartens. To again quote Shpeter himself, "Competitors don't bring money. They come to collect it."[5]

This chapter uses firm-level data to back up the wealth of anecdotal evidence we have about businessperson legislators helping their firms while in office. Though businesspeople occupy political office around the world, we have surprisingly little quantitative evidence about the economic consequences of politicians simultaneously working in the public and private sectors. Using the main dataset on regional legislators in Russia, this chapter thus shifts the focus to firm-level financial performance after connected deputies have taken office. Precisely measuring the returns to office is not straightforward. Previous chapters demonstrated that winning elected office is far from randomly assigned across Russian firms: first, firms vary greatly in their desire and ability to put forth directors to elected office, and second, myriad factors, not least their choice of ballot and party, affect a businessperson's chances of getting elected.

Taking advantage of close elections where the determination of the winner and runner-up is near randomly assigned,[6] this chapter adopts a regression discontinuity design (RDD) to solve this endogeneity problem and identify the causal effect of political connections on firm-level outcomes. Due to the discontinuity in the assignment to treatment, the

3 Sakharevich (2017).
4 Transparency International (2017).
5 Vygon (2006).
6 Lee (2008).

RDD can causally attribute any differences in profitability, revenue, or other measures of the firm performance to the effect of winning office. The analysis uses a subset of the main dataset introduced in Chapter 2: 2,706 politically connected firms connected to SMDP candidates. In addition, I draw upon qualitative interviews to help elucidate the mechanisms behind the effects found. My results indicate that firms connected to winning candidates increase their revenue by 60 percent and profit margin by 15 percent by the final year these candidates spend in office. These estimates are statistically significant, pass robustness checks that vary RDD specifications, and reflect a local average treatment effect for firms located near the winning threshold.

What drives these significant improvements in firm performance? One strand of research argues that political connections cast firms in a more favorable light among bank lenders. A director holding elected office may be taken as a strong signal of creditworthiness and government backing (such as guarantees) in the case of financial troubles.[7] But as we saw in Chapter 1, winning a seat in a legislature also opens doors to bureaucrats and favorable treatment with regard to regulations and winning access to state procurement.

Determining which channel is most important for rent-seeking has implications for designing reforms. If companies develop political ties primarily to secure loans, then equalizing access to finance for all firms should be paramount. Reforms might include mandating that banks appoint independent directors and empowering supervisory agencies to discipline lenders that prioritize political ties over adequate credit checks. Alternately, if connected politicians abuse access to state agencies, public service reform should come first. Measures should be taken to punish bureaucrats who offer preferential treatment to connected firms.

To test between the mechanisms, I collect data on ways legislative power could lead to firm benefits. I find that serving in office helps businesspeople win state contracts, but not increase their firms' financial leverage. Winning a seat in a regional legislature increases a firm's probability of accessing state procurement by approximately 40 percent, resulting in $700,000 of revenue. These findings suggest that connections do not alleviate credit constraints, but instead open up opportunities for firms to influence how state officials do their jobs.

I then examine how variation in structural and institutional characteristics affects the payoffs of holding elected office. First, winning

[7] Houston et al. (2014).

office is more valuable in richer regions and those endowed with natural resources. Counterintuitively, stronger democratic institutions do not constrain businessperson politicians from reaping rewards to their firms' revenue and profits. Instead, where the ruling party faces more serious challenges to its hold on power, connected firms enjoy more opportunities to redirect budgetary resources to private interests. More competitive legislatures are able to exert policymaking authority, thereby increasing the value of winning office. Winning candidates from opposition parties also secure rewards for their firms, suggesting that nondemocratic regimes employ political institutions not only to distribute rents to their supporters, but also their potential opponents. More intense political battles between parties require more government resources to buy off all connected firms.

What does seem to hold firm rent-seeking in check is whether their direct rivals also are able to place their directors into legislative office. Competitors monitor one another, preventing exploitative use of political privilege from spinning out of control. In fact, the presence in parliament of at least three firms from a single sector completely washes out the positive gains from winning office. These results suggest that access to parliament shares many features with market competition: as new players enter, the potential profits to be made shrink for all. For citizens and policymakers concerned with checking undue advantages accruing to businessperson politicians, the best solution involves empowering the actors most at financial risk from spoils going to connected firms. Equalizing access to government decision-making for all firms can help check those with representatives on the inside from skewing benefits too far in their favor.

5.1 RETURNS TO CORPORATE POLITICAL ACTIVITY

Fueled by concerns over corruption and fairness in political representation, the last two decades have seen a surge of both academic and journalistic interest in investigating whether the political investments that businesses make actually pay off for their bottom lines. These works cast a broad net, defining corporate political activity as lobbying, making financial campaign contributions, submitting regulatory opinions, and even mobilizing voters during elections. As we will see below, the firm-level outcomes analyzed are even more diverse.

For all this attention, definitive conclusions have yet to be reached about whether firms should expect a positive return on their political activity. A wealth of work has uncovered specific advantages accruing for companies that invest resources in gaining political access. For example, the more firms spend on lobbying the US Congress, the greater tax benefits they receive.[8] Although lobbying may have a somewhat small impact on policy enactment, the returns to getting desired laws through, say for US energy firms engaging Congress, are massive.[9] Similarly, campaign contributions made by firms in the United States help boost stock returns and win access to powerful committees.[10] Acquiring direct political connections, such as by bringing politicians into the firm, has been found to help firms lower their cost of capital, get access to advantageous credits and loans, increase their stock returns and profitability, secure preferred legislation,[11] and win state contracts.[12]

But engaging in corporate political activity may at times produce negative returns for some firms.[13] For example, lobbying in the United States in the financial sector often exposed firms to worse than normal stock returns once the financial crisis hit in 2008.[14] Similarly, Hadani and Schuler (2013) look at the most popular corporate political activities in the United States (campaign contributions, lobbying, and hiring former public officials) and find a negative effect of all three, except in cases where firms operated in highly regulated sectors. Other work has found little impact from contributing money and engaging in other political activities,[15] or that the effects are continent on specific institutional factors, such as the structure of government or degree of partisan competition.[16]

Developing direct political connections does not necessarily produce better outcomes for firms. Political connections can undermine a firm's competitiveness, investment behavior, and ability to innovate.[17] Successful politicians may not be effective firm managers, as government intervention into company management may lead to weak incentive

8 Richter, Samphantharak, and Timmons (2009).
9 Kang (2015).
10 Cooper, Gulen, and Ovtchinnikov (2010); Claessens, Feijen, and Laeven (2008); Powell and Grimmer (2016).
11 Hillman, Keim, and Schuler (2004).
12 Boubakri et al. (2012); Khwaja and Mian (2005); Carretta et al. (2012); Li et al. (2008); Truex (2014); Hillman, Keim, and Schuler (2004); Goldman, Rocholl, and So (2013).
13 Aggarwal, Meschke, and Wang (2012).
14 Igan, Mishra, and Tressel (2011).
15 Ansolabehere, Snyder Jr, and Ueda (2004).
16 Choi, Jia, and Lu (2014).
17 Desai and Olofsgard (2008).

systems and inadequate monitoring.[18] Given the often times illicit nature of the bargain, politicians may also require substantial contributions from firms, and can easily withhold their influence, costing firms valuable returns. As members of boards of directors, they can more easily extract resources and engage in rent-seeking.[19] If political circumstances change, a tie to the "wrong" type of politician can even impose a range of negative consequences on a firm.[20] Politically connected firms in France performed worse than their counterparts, given the political requirements to take on excess labor costs.[21] Similarly, institutions matter: in countries with strong rule of law, having direct political connections can hurt stock performance.[22] Cultivating direct ties can incur sizable risks for a firm with only contingent benefits.

Even work on post-Soviet legislatures has failed to reach definitive conclusions about whether legislatures are attractive fora for businesses to promote their interests. For example, work on national-level politics in Ukraine has found that winning seats in the Ukrainian Rada may not offer sufficient protection for an oligarch's financial assets.[23] In Russia, skepticism is also rife over whether authoritarian legislatures command sufficient political influence to actually affect firm performance. In the words of Tev (2016, p. 97), "the legislative branch in Russia, both at the national and the regional levels, is particularly weak and subordinated to administrative structures, and large businesspeople who enjoy access to the executive branch, may not feel a strong pull towards parliamentary representation."

One potential reason why consensus has been elusive is the relatively late move towards developing strong identification strategies to measure firm-level returns. To date, the wider literature on corporate political strategy has only recently begun to address the challenge of demonstrating causality.[24] Though the political connections are often correlated with firm-level benefits, many empirical designs fall prey to possible omitted variable bias driving these relationships.[25] Political influence is not

[18] Okhmatovskiy (2010).
[19] Faccio (2006).
[20] Siegel (2007).
[21] Bertrand et al. (2018).
[22] Brockman, Rui, and Zou (2013).
[23] Markus and Charnysh (2017).
[24] de Figueiredo and Richter (2014).
[25] Hillman, Keim, and Schuler (2004).

randomly assigned. Firms with strong political ties may have pre-existing advantages in the market that enable them to penetrate the political sphere. More concretely, Chapter 1 identified a whole host of factors affecting a firm's decision to send a businessperson to run for office. These selection effects undermine our ability to precisely estimate how much businessperson candidacy can actually benefit participant firms.

One exception is the use of natural experiments, a strategy which Fisman (2001) helped pioneer to measure the market value of political connections. Recent trends in this direction are especially encouraging. Boas, Hidalgo, and Richardson (2014) use an RDD to identify how campaign contributions can help Brazilian firms win state contracts, while Akey (2015) use a similar set-up to understand how stock markets react to politically active firms seeing their preferred candidates win office. Fisman, Schulz, and Vig (2012) also use an RDD to look at individual-level rent seeking among legislators in India. By identifying quasi-random variation in the way political access to allocated to firms, natural experiments offer our best hope for nailing down how strategies pay off for firm performance.

To briefly summarize, the wide variation in empirical results on the returns to corporate political activity strongly suggests a need for more refined approaches to analyzing firm political behavior. Although firm directors may be rational actors intent on improving market-based performance, their understanding of the political environment they are entering may be limited or flawed. The aim of this chapter will be to examine if, when and how the strategy of firm directors seeking and then winning elected political office pays off for their companies' bottom line.[26]

5.2 DATA AND RESEARCH DESIGN

To test the effect of having a director hold political office on firm performance, I adopt a regression discontinuity design (RDD) that exploits close elections. On average across a large sample, narrowly winning and losing candidates should be plausibly comparable, as if victory in the elections was randomly assigned. Close elections become akin to a coin

[26] Calculating the return on simply running for office, i.e. businessperson *candidacy*, requires a comparison of candidate and non-candidate firms. However, concerns about selection into candidacy undermine our ability to make causal claims about the relationship between running a director for office and firm performance.

flip, dependent on such circumstantial factors as the weather on election day.[27] RDDs using close elections have grown increasingly popular in the social sciences due to the clear assumptions required and their ability to identify a causal effect.[28] Here, I use the RDD to compare firm-level outcomes for those companies that are connected to candidates whose vote share falls close to the threshold required to win office. I compare firms connected to narrowly winning candidates to firms connected to narrowly losing candidates. If the assumptions of the RDD are met, this empirical strategy excludes the influence of unobserved differences over both candidates and firms and allows us to measure the economic effect of a firm having a connection to a legislator.

5.2.1 Data Description

I study the effect of political connections using the main observational dataset on businessperson candidates introduced in Chapter 2. Since the regression discontinuity design I use requires a majoritarian electoral system, I subset the dataset of elections to the approximately 41 percent of all legislative seats from 2004 to 2011 that were chosen using SMDP rules. This sample consists of elections to 114 regional legislative convocations in 78 regions from January 1, 2004 until March 3, 2011.[29]

My analysis compares only winners and losers in SMDP races, or 12,113 candidates running for office in 2,798 elections. In constructing the sample, I omit forty-five multi-member districts, as the probability of being above the cutoff score is no longer 50 percent. I also drop all firms connected to candidates from the sample that gained a seat in the legislature on the party list, whether or not they won or lost their single-member district race. The treatment is assigned at the level of the candidate, while the unit of analysis is the firm. All firms with a director, deputy director, board chair, or board member running for office in a SMDP are included in the sample. The treatment variable is electoral victory and takes a value of 1 if a firm is connected to a winning candidate and 0 otherwise. The forcing variable used is vote margin, with a cutoff point at zero. For firms connected to winning candidates (the treatment group), this value is the difference (positive in sign) from the first runner-up. For firms connected

27 Lee (2008).

28 Eggers et al. (2014).

29 During this period, eleven regions adopted full PR systems and thus did not enter the sample where the regression discontinuity design was adopted.

to losing candidates (the control group), this value is the difference (negative in sign) from the winner. This variable, *Vote Margin*, takes values from -1 to 1.

Both media and scholarly accounts of Russian politics raise concerns that elections to regional legislatures are not sufficiently competitive to allow for a RDD to be used. Although some falsification does occur at the regional level, there are reasons to believe that elites are truly competing for votes and not all electoral outcomes are pre-ordained. First, the average margin of victory is 30.1 percent with a median of 25.7 percent. Importantly, 634 elections were decided by less than 10 percentage points, roughly 23 percent of the total sample. This substantial sample size and the continuous forcing variable will allow us to isolate the RDD treatment effect right around the electoral threshold. Competitive elections are also distributed proportionately across Russia. Figure 5.1 presents the regional breakdown of elections decided by less than a 10 percent vote margin, as calculated as the proportion of the total number of SMDP elections per region.

Next, to preview discussion below, I examine balance along a range of covariates between winning and losing candidates in close elections and find no evidence that electoral manipulation favors a specific type of candidate or firm. Lastly, if authorities are indeed faking electoral competition to build legitimacy among the population, we should not expect financial benefits to accrue to the winners (or punishment inflicted on the losers). Any coordination between candidates would result in rent-sharing between complicit firms, and not advantages bestowed on

FIGURE 5.1: Percentage of SMDP elections decided by less than 10 Percent
Figure 5.1 maps the percentage of elections in single-member districts that were decided by a vote margin of less than 10 percent. Regions in white did not hold elections based on the majoritarian system during the period.

the anointed victor. I exclude the December 2011 election from the sample due to persistent concerns over vote fraud.[30]

The main outcome variables are total revenue (logged and measured in millions of rubles) and profit margin (net profits divided by total revenue) for each firm during the last year its connected political candidate held (if won the election) or would have held (if lost the election) office.[31] I only include firms that reported balance sheet data beginning the year prior to the election and spanning the term in office. In the Russian case, all firms are required to submit balance sheets and income statements to the state statistics agency Rosstat every year.

In addition to revenue and profit margin, I include firm covariates analyzed above. Below I show regression analysis with and without these controls, but given the myriad factors affecting firm performance beyond connections, the most refined models are those that include these covariates. The firm-level control variables include a dummy for foreign ownership, a dummy for any kind of state ownership, and logged total fixed assets (measured in millions of rubles) in the year prior to the election taking place. In addition, I use sector and region fixed effects, as well as year fixed effects for when the outcome variables were measured. Candidate controls include the age (logged), gender, a dummy for membership in the United Russia ruling party, and a dummy if the candidate was an incumbent from the previous convocation. With these data constraints in effect, the sample includes 2,706 firms connected to 1,930 candidates.

5.2.2 Regression Discontinuity Design

All analysis is done at the firm level, while the treatment is applied to candidates during the year of the election. Multiple candidates can also run in an election, creating potential for cross-unit dependence. To account for this, I use multiway clustered standard errors on both the candidate and the election level.[32] I also collapse the panel data into a cross-section and include the pre-election value of each outcome in every regression to account for differences in levels prior to the contested election. Because of midterm entries and exits, the average length of time a candidate spends in office is four years. For firms connected to losing candidates, the exit

30 Reuter and Szakonyi (2015).

31 The results are robust when outcomes are averaged over politicians' time in office.

32 Cameron, Gelbach, and Miller (2011).

year is the final year of the parliamentary session to which the candidates ran for office.

I follow Lee (2008) in adopting a regression discontinuity approach that maximizes my ability to control for any differences in observed and unobserved heterogeneity among firms. First, I show effects from a simple OLS regression using the global (full) sample of firms connected to candidates. This model estimates a correlation between a politically connected firm winning an election and performance outcomes. However, because of biases discussed above, we cannot interpret the point estimates as reflecting a causal effect. The following specifications are used in these OLS regressions (with and without controls):

$$Y_i = \alpha_i + \beta * z_i + Covariates_i + \epsilon_i \qquad (5.1)$$

where Y_i is the outcome variable for firm i (revenue and profit margin in the final year of the term), z_i is a binary treatment indicator for whether a candidate won or lost the election, $Covariates_i$ is the set of candidate and firm covariates from the pre-election year and region, sector and year fixed effects, and ϵ_i is a normally distributed error term.

Next, I use the regression discontinuity design to estimate a causal effect. The first approach narrows the estimation window and uses a simple OLS model, comparing observations located right at the threshold and weighing them equally. I present results using both 2 percent and 3 percent windows around the threshold to focus on very competitive elections.

The second approach also narrows the window, but includes a local-linear control functions to control for any correlation between the vote margin (the forcing variable) and the outcomes of interest. I use windows of 5 percent and the optimal bandwidth with bias-corrected robust confidence intervals calculated using the *rdrobust* package from Calonico, Cattaneo, and Titiunik (2014) (CCT) in order to more closely hone in around the threshold while retaining sufficient sample size.[33] Below is the specification estimated, with and without controls:

$$Y_i = \alpha_i + \beta * z_i + \gamma * f(Margin_i) + \eta * z_i * f(Margin_i) + Covariates_i + \epsilon_i \quad (5.2)$$

where Y_i is the outcome variable for firm i (revenue and profit margin in the final year of the term), z_i is a binary treatment indicator for whether a candidate won or lost the election, $f(Margin_i)$ is the local-linear control function that is interacted with the treatment variable to fit above

[33] This method generates a common bandwidth h to use on both sides of the cutoff.

and below the threshold, $Covariates_i$ is the set of candidate and firm covariates from the pre-election year and region, sector and year fixed effects, and ϵ_i is a normally distributed error term. These approaches help illustrate the effects of trade-offs made over the size of the window around the threshold and the type of control function adopted.

5.2.3 Balance Checks

Before moving on to the results, I run a series of checks to determine if any sorting is occurring around the cutoff point. Though regression discontinuity studies using close elections are becoming more common, concerns have been raised about their validity as a quasi-random design. If imbalances occur between winners and losers near the winning threshold, then the assumption that elections are decided randomly is violated. For example, incumbents running from the party in control of the electoral infrastructure may enjoy persistent advantages in close elections.[34]

In the case of Russia, the main cleavages around which sorting would most likely occur relate to the incumbent status and party affiliation of candidates. Incumbents from Putin's UR party may benefit from compatriot election officials and administrative resources to sway close electoral outcomes in their favor. First, I run McCrary (2008) density tests to formally assess the validity of the assumption of continuity around the threshold (see Appendix). In both cases, the estimated difference is small and the p-value returned is considerably above standard levels of statistical significance. Therefore, we cannot reject the null hypothesis of no sorting around the cutoff point of 0.

Next, I investigate whether any sorting occurs in both the types of candidates located around the winning threshold as well as the specific firms that these individuals are connected to. For example, recent research has shown that large, state-owned enterprises are more likely to mobilize their workers to vote during elections in Russia.[35] Similarly, candidates running on behalf of these firms may be able to marshal company resources to spend on campaigning or influencing officials. To capture the causal effect of winning office, the data must satisfy the assumption that both candidates and the firms they are connected to are similar across a set of baseline covariates.

34 Caughey and Sekhon (2011).
35 Frye, Reuter, and Szakonyi (2014).

To assess covariate balance among candidates and firms, I use two specifications: close margin and local linear regressions. The forcing variable in these specifications is again vote margin. I estimate the difference between winners and losers using two sample sizes for the close margin (bandwidths of 2 percent and 3 percent) and two sample sizes for the local linear (5 percent and the optimal bandwidth). Robust standard errors are clustered on the candidate level.

Figure 5.2 presents the t-statistics from a two-tailed test of the hypothesis that the difference between the comparison groups (winning versus losing candidates) for each of the 21 covariates is zero. We see little evidence of imbalance between winners and losers and their affiliated firms. In only one of the four specifications run does a t-statistic approach 2 (whether the candidate is a member of a systemic opposition party), the conventional level of statistical significance for rejecting the null hypothesis. Winning candidates are not more likely to run the type of firms most likely to participate in election campaigns nor do they have greater company resources to take advantage of to further their electoral campaigns. The 21 sets of regressions used to generate these t-tests are included in the Supplementary Appendix.

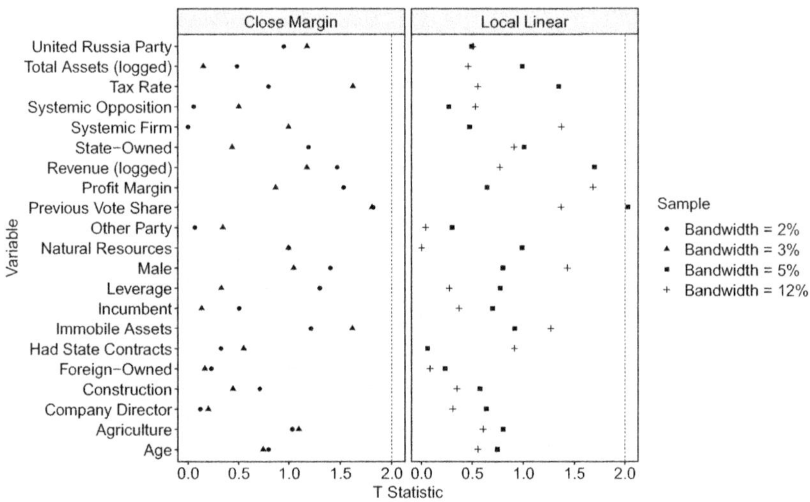

FIGURE 5.2: Balance statistics

Figure 5.2 depicts the t-statistics from a series of regressions of pre-treatment candidate and firm covariates on the treatment. The panel show results with and without a local linear control function.

5.3 RDD RESULTS

First, I present the graphic illustrations of the RDD treatment effect in Figure 5.3. I plot change in logged revenue (Panel A) and profit margin (Panel B) over the period against vote margin in bins of one percent, while limiting the interval of vote margin to elections decided by less than 10 percent to ease interpretation around the threshold. Each bin contains on average 24.2 observations. The plot includes line fit using a LOESS regression based on the tricubic kernal using the unbinned data, with the gray area indicating confidence intervals of 95 percent. The graphs are centered at the discontinuity cutoff point: a vote margin value of zero. The graphs show a positive jump for both revenue and profits around the threshold for winning elections. To calculate the size of this jump more precisely, I turn to regression analysis.

Results from regressions on end-of-term logged revenue on victory in single-member district elections, as indicated by the binary variable *District Win*, are presented in Table 5.1. As described above, Columns 1–2 present the results from simple OLS on the full sample of firms. The first model indicates that politically connected firms earn higher revenue over the term than their firms without connections. Next, I add firm-level (ownership type and logged total assets) and candidate-level controls (age, gender, incumbency, and membership of the United Russia party) as well as year, sector, and region fixed effects. The addition of these predictors reduces the effect of winning office, but the result is still statistically significant. Although we cannot claim that the point estimates from Models 1 and 2 present causal evidence, the correlation between political connections and firm performance is clearly positive in the Russian case.

Moving onto the RDD models, we see a consistent, positive, and statistically significant effect of directors winning election on firm revenue. In Columns 3 and 4, the bandwidth is narrowed to 2 percent and 3 percent respectively without covariates, and the point estimate on District Win indicates that firms connected to winning office enjoy an increase of revenue of between 40 percent and 55 percent. Including local-linear, widening the bandwidth used, and adding the full set of firm and candidate covariates and year, sector, and region fixed effects, returns consistently statistically significant point estimates on the treatment variable. In all, the coefficients on *District Win* from the varied set of RDD models range from roughly 30 percent to 70 percent, translating into a substantial effect of winning office on revenue. The range of

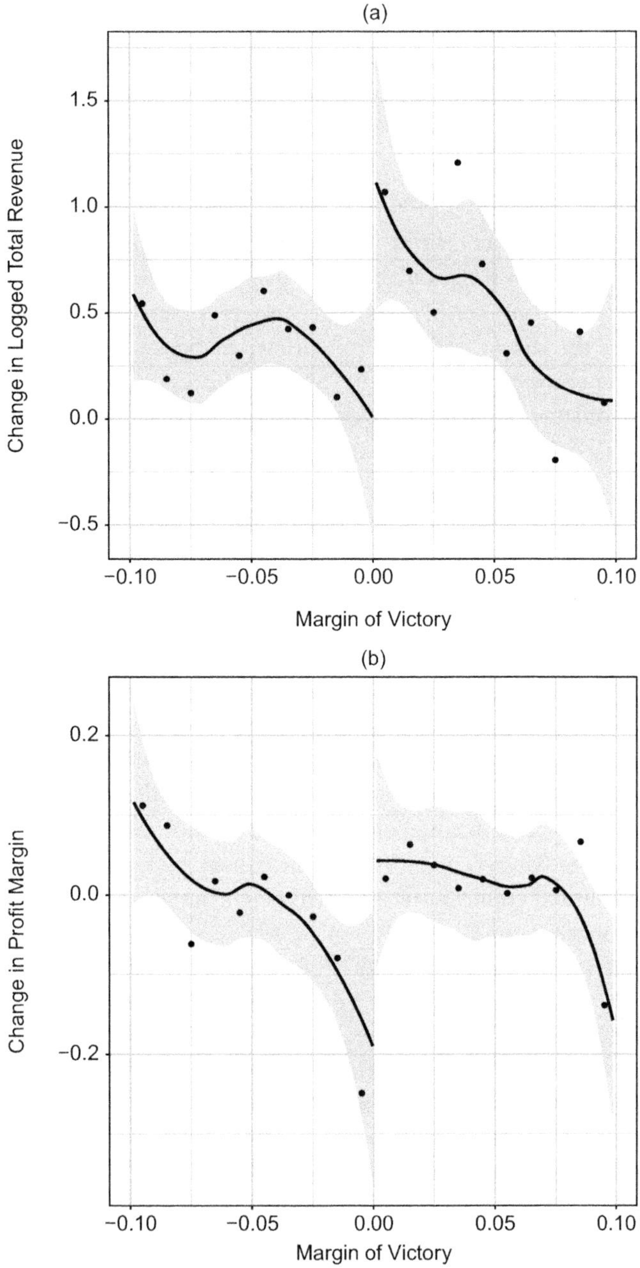

FIGURE 5.3: Firm-level returns: RDD plots

Figure 5.3 depicts the regression discontinuity using raw data binned at intervals of 1 percent vote margin for each of the two outcome variables. The regression line is estimated using LOESS, with the gray area indicating confidence intervals of 95 percent.

TABLE 5.1 *Political connections and firm revenue*

Control Function:	None				Local Linear			
Bandwidth:	Global		2%	3%	5%		Optimal	
	(1)	(2)	(3)	(4)	(5)	(6)	(7)	(8)
District Win	0.338***	0.240***	0.554**	0.416**	0.673**	0.707**	0.459**	0.446***
	(0.055)	(0.071)	(0.233)	(0.163)	(0.289)	(0.290)	(0.179)	(0.167)
Bandwidth	0.8	0.8	0.02	0.03	0.05	0.05	0.136	0.145
Firm and Cand. Covariates	No	Yes	No	No	No	Yes	No	Yes
Region, Sector, Year FE	No	Yes	No	No	No	No	No	Yes
Observations	2,410	2,410	87	134	202	202	610	646

*** $p<0.01$, ** $p<0.05$ The outcome variable is firm revenue in the final year of the connected candidate's term in office. Columns 1 and 2 present OLS results using the full dataset. Columns 3 and 4 also use OLS specifications, but restrict the bandwidth to close winning vote margins. Columns 5 to 8 are RDD specifications using local-linear control functions based on vote margin. Firm and candidate controls include age, gender, incumbency, ruling party membership, state ownership, foreign ownership, and logged total assets in the pre-election year. All models use bias-corrected robust standard errors clustered on the candidate level as well as include the pre-election value for the outcome.

specifications run strongly suggests large revenue advantages for a firm from having its director win elected office. Similar results emerge from the regressions on profit margin shown in Table 5.2. The order of the model specifications is identical to that from Table 5.1, except here the outcome variable is profitability. First, the results from the simple OLS models on the full sample indicate that politically connected firms do not see a higher profit margin over the term. When controls and fixed effects are added, the result increases but is only significant at the 10 percent level. Again, given the simple OLS regression, we cannot interpret these correlations as reflecting a causal effect.

The RDD results on profit margin present more persuasive causal evidence that winning office leads to more profitable firms. The coefficient on *District Win* is statistically significant across the different model specifications and windows used. Using both the close margin approach and local linear functions, as well as varying the bandwidth used and covariates used returns similar point estimates for the treatment. The difference in profit margin over the term that a winning firm director holds office ranges from 10 percent to 20 percent. The presence of a political connection can spell the difference between an impressively profitable firm and one that barely breaks into the black.

These results pass several robustness checks. First, the main results on revenue and profitability are robust to subsetting the sample to just candidates that were directors or deputy directors (as opposed to board members) and to candidates that only ran in a single-member district (as opposed to those that ran on the party list as well). Moreover, the RDD used above does not include a true control group; the firm performance outcomes are compared between so-called "winning" and "losing" firms. Firms that did not have a director run for political office are not analyzed. This leaves open the possibility that the treatment effect is driven not by the benefits of acquiring political ties, but by losing firms losing money due to the absence of political representation. To address this, I used Coarsened Exact Matching (CEM) technique to match firms with a director who ran for office with those that chose not to send a representative to participate in this process.[36] Though matching does not generate identification, I find that a substantial portion of the effect of having a political connection on firm performance is from the positive benefits of winning election. Firms losing elections also do better than

[36] Iacus, King, and Porro (2011).

TABLE 5.2 *Political connections and firm profitability*

Control Function:	None				Local Linear			
Bandwidth:	Global		2%	3%	5%		Optimal	
	(1)	(2)	(3)	(4)	(5)	(6)	(7)	(8)
District Win	−0.012	0.048	0.151***	0.107**	0.181***	0.198***	0.082**	0.094**
	(0.030)	(0.041)	(0.056)	(0.043)	(0.065)	(0.066)	(0.041)	(0.043)
Bandwidth	0.8	0.8	0.02	0.03	0.05	0.05	0.146	0.128
Firm and Cand. Covariates	No	Yes	No	No	No	Yes	No	Yes
Region, Sector, Year FE	No	Yes	No	No	No	No	No	Yes
Observations	2,390	2,390	86	133	201	201	646	564

*** $p<0.01$, ** $p<0.05$ The outcome variable is firm profitability in the final year of the connected candidate's term in office. Columns 1 and 2 present OLS results using the full dataset. Columns 3 and 4 also use OLS specifications, but restrict the bandwidth to close winning vote margins. Columns 5 to 8 are RDD specifications using local-linear control functions based on vote margin. Firm and candidate controls include age, gender, incumbency, ruling party membership, state ownership, foreign ownership, and logged total assets in the pre-election year. All models use bias-corrected robust standard errors clustered on the candidate level as well as include the pre-election value for the outcome.

their competitors down the road, but the revenue and profits they receive are lower.

5.4 CAUSAL MECHANISMS

What then is driving the results on increased revenue and profit margins for politically connected firms? I next investigate several channels by which firm directors in office can help their companies. One set of theories argues that political connections help firms by reducing uncertainty among financiers. When markets are underdeveloped, lenders have less information about potential clients and look for other signals of borrowing quality or property rights protection.[37] In a study of firms connected to parliamentarians in China, Truex (2014) finds little evidence of formal policy influence. Instead, investors interpreted membership in the National People's Congress as a "reputation boost," and lifted their share price. In Russia, signaling legitimacy in the absence of other market mechanisms may be especially important given the role of private banks in lending. A survey of 1,047 Russian firms in 2012 showed that roughly 70 percent received their most recent loan from a private financial institution.[38] Having a firm director serve as a legislator may be a powerful tool to secure financing.

Another theory asserts that corporate political activity opens doors to state bureaucrats who hold sway over lucrative public procurement and regulatory treatment. Winning a seat in parliament helps reduce the costs of acquiring information about state contracts and can help companies influence how bureaucrats design and conduct tenders. In Novgorod Region in 2005, a regional deputy and local firm director openly stated that winning a seat in the regional legislature would help his business achieve a necessary "understanding" with regional officials.[39] That year his company signed a memorandum of cooperation with the regional executive branch worth 35 million rubles ($1 million). A primary objective for Russian firms has also been to score tax breaks from regional governments.[40] Russian regions account for 40 percent (or $70 billion) of all annual public procurement in the country and assume responsibility for allocating contracts to suppliers. In Perm Region, a regional deputy

[37] Richter (2010).
[38] Russian Federation 2012 – World Bank Enterprise Survey (www.enterprisesurveys.org).
[39] Romanova (2006).
[40] Slinko, Yakovlev, and Zhuravskaya (2005).

and director of a large director of a large silicate panels factory came under investigation for underpaying his tax bill by 31 million rubles ($1 million) in 2003.[41]

Measuring all channels by which political connections operate is impossible. For example, data on subsidies is not available. Codifying influence over the regulatory process would involve drawing generalizations over the key rules affecting each industry across Russia over time, potentially a never-ending enterprise. Therefore, the analysis is limited to performance-improving activities where empirical data are available: taking on additional debt (evidence of signaling to private entities), and then receiving state contracts and paying lower taxes (evidence of achieving access). To measure financial leverage, I calculate a ratio of total liabilities (long-term and short-term liabilities) to total assets using SPARK data. To measure tax bills, I use a ratio of the annual profit tax paid divided by total profit before tax for each firm. Lastly, I collect data on all state procurement from the Federal Registry of State Contracts.[42] I code a binary variable to indicate whether firms connected to winning and losing candidates won any state contracts during the full legislative term they sought office in.[43] As above, the model specifications vary control functions, bandwidths, and covariates, as well as include the pre-election level of the outcome.

I present results from the set of regressions on tax rates, leverage, and state contracts in Table 5.3. Judging by the results from Columns 1–3, political connections may drive up the effective tax rate, though the coefficients fluctuate considerably and fall short of conventional levels of statistical significance. Winning elections may increase firms' public exposure and compel them to follow the letter of the law while their director is in office. More research is needed on how political connections might affect firms' legal compliance in places where the rule of law is generally weak.

Next, political connections are not being used to increase firms' leverage, as shown in Columns 4–6. The point estimates on *District Win* do not tell a consistent story across the model specifications. That leaves state contracts, the last mechanism for which data on firms is available. Columns 7–9 in Table 5.3 present evidence that firms connected to winning candidates indeed enjoy greater opportunities to sign

[41] Ura.ru News Agency (2008).

[42] Federal Procurement Portal, http://zakupki.gov.ru/epz/main/public/home.html.

[43] Analysis restricted to elections from 2008 onward, since data are not available prior.

TABLE 5.3 *Mechanisms*

Dependent Variable:	Tax Rate			Leverage			State Contracts		
Control Function:	Local Linear			Local Linear			Local Linear		
Bandwidth:	5%	Optimal		5%	Optimal		5%	Optimal	
	(1)	(2)	(3)	(4)	(5)	(6)	(7)	(8)	(9)
District Win	0.098	0.010	0.014	0.039	0.103	0.134	0.512*	0.177	0.382***
	(0.065)	(0.031)	(0.031)	(0.090)	(0.132)	(0.139)	(0.303)	(0.123)	(0.139)
Bandwidth	0.05	0.196	0.195	0.05	0.077	0.081	0.05	0.235	0.133
Firm and Cand. Covariates	No	Yes	Yes	No	Yes	Yes	No	Yes	Yes
Region, Year FE	No	No	Yes	No	No	Yes	No	No	Yes
Observations	90	255	228	216	705	620	48	168	152

*** $p<0.01$, * $p<0.1$ The outcome variable in Columns 1 to 3 is firm leverage, the outcome variable in Columns 4 to 6 is the tax rate paid to the government, and the outcome variable in Columns 7 to 9 is a binary indicator for whether the firm won any state contracts during its connected candidate's term in office. In the models analyzing state contracts, firms connected to candidates taking office prior to 2008 are excluded due to a lack of data. All models include a local linear control function, and use bandwidths of 5 percent or the optimal bandwidth (CCT). Controls include age, gender, incumbency, ruling party membership, state ownership, foreign ownership, and logged total assets in the year of the election. All models use bias-corrected robust standard errors clustered on the candidate and election levels as well as include the pre-election value for the outcome.

procurement contracts with the government. The estimates from the RDD specifications show that winning firms are roughly 30 to 50 percent more likely to win more state contracts than losing firms, amounting to roughly $700,000 in additional revenue from the state. Though the magnitude does not account for the entire increase in revenue as measured in Table 5.1, it does suggest that one way politically connected firms are able to increase both their revenue and profits is to tap into the largesse of public procurement.

5.5 HETEROGENEOUS TREATMENT EFFECTS

The value of political connections may also depend on institutional, economic, and convocational factors. First, the strength of democratic institutions may affect the rents businesspeople can extract from government. An underdeveloped civil society makes it harder to hold politicians accountable for their actions by applying pressure through public campaigns.[44] Weaker market institutions also make informal access to political power more advantageous, since avenues such as independent courts are unavailable to help protect property rights.[45] Where democracy has taken stronger root, politicians may be wary of abusing their public office for personal financial gain, knowing that they might be voted out of office by voters unhappy with their record of providing public goods.[46] Where media is less free, politicians face less scrutiny for manipulating legislation to their own advantage.

Alternately, greater political competition might increase the rents elites are able to extract while in office. High levels of competition could empower parliaments to play a more forceful role in regional policymaking. The executive branch no longer can push through its initiatives without resistance and must provide patronage to legislators in order to win their support. More assertive parliaments attract more attention from businesspeople, since the opportunities to actually wield political influence are greater. Since the early 2000s, the ruling United Russia party has enjoyed a formidable monopoly on political power across Russia. We might expect firms connected to representatives of the ruling party to fare better than their counterparts from the opposition. But if opposition parties are able to win and control legislative seats, ruling parties must

[44] Faccio (2006).
[45] Li et al. (2008).
[46] Gehlbach, Sonin, and Zhuravskaya (2010).

co-opt their members in order to build coalitions and get laws passed. This internal jockeying for power could result in more spoils being shared with all legislators, such as by providing benefits for connected firms.

Next, the ability of firms to reap benefits from connections may depend on the volume of government revenue that can be diverted. Richer regions, as well as those with natural resources, command larger budgets that may sweeten the pie available to policymakers. These additional funds attract attention from firms through the "pork" they offer for distribution. In addition, firms that are more vulnerable to regulatory sanction or expropriation may value access to politicians more than companies working in sectors less subject to the whims of local bureaucrats. The harder it is for a firm to redeploy its assets elsewhere (i.e. the level of asset specificity), the easier it is for government officials to engage in opportunistic behavior and extract excessive rents.

Lastly, the composition of the parliament that businesspeople win entry to may have an effect on their firms' performance. Legislators use their elected authority to make demands of bureaucrats and draft laws and regulations to benefit their individual firms. But their ability to turn their political power into financial returns for their firms, and their firms alone, requires that other political actors support their initiatives, remain in the dark, or look the other way.[47] This is especially true with regard to direct economic competitors: when multiple firms from the same sector are represented in the same parliament, each's ability to enact policy to the detriment of its rivals is limited. The more rivals that present to monitor and dissent, the less likely that an individual firm is able to dominate policymaking. When economic rivalry spills into legislatures, the potential political dividends to be reaped from holding office are competed away, just as they would when new firms enter the market and place pressure on the profit margins of their competitors.

To examine these mechanisms, I follow the literature by splitting the population of firms into subsets based on the median value of each dimension of theoretical interest. The models use a bandwidth of 5 percent vote margin and the optimal bandwidth (CCT) for each outcome variable (to retain adequate sample size in each group) and include candidate and firm covariates. To measure institutional quality, I first use the Carnegie Democracy Index that totals five-point expert assessments of ten different measures of democracy for Russia's regions for a

[47] For example, more public servants in office might serve as a check on firm directors' ability to craft legislation to aid their narrow interests (Braendle and Stutzer, 2013).

scale of 5 to 50, with higher scores indicative of more liberal democratic institutions.[48] I also measure the percentage of seats that United Russia controlled in each regional legislature, positing that stronger ruling party control is indicative of less political competition. Regional wealth is measured using gross regional product per capita and a dummy for the presence of natural resources (oil, natural gas, and metals). I code firms with immobile assets as those working in manufacturing, mining, energy/natural resources, construction, or agriculture. Finally, measures of businessperson presence in parliaments come from the analysis dataset. For each firm (winning and losing), I compute the number of other firms from the same sector that have firm directors serving in the regional legislature. I also calculate the percentage of legislative seats held by businesspeople in each convocation.

Table 5.4 presents the results from the regressions using the institutional variables to subset the sample. All models use a local linear control function, candidate and firm covariates, and sector and year fixed effects (Panel C also includes region fixed effects). These results first suggest a slightly positive relationship between the level of democracy (as measured by the Carnegie Index) and firm returns from political connections. In more democratic regions, firms appear to earn significantly larger profit margins and slightly greater revenue. Moreover, in parliaments where the ruling party faces more political rivals (Panel B), connected firms see substantially greater profit margins and revenue. These findings suggest firm directors who can gain entry into legislative institutions marked by greater competition and independence are able to extract more rents from the government. Furthermore, director membership in parties outside of the ruling coalition does not doom the performance of affiliated firms (Panel C). Although opposition candidates can expect smaller growth in revenue, their ability to bring home benefits is not diminished compared to those members of opposition parties that lost election. If anything, firms whose directors are aligned with the opposition do just as well as their counterparts in United Russia; the differences between the coefficients are not statistically significant. Rents are accruing to both ruling party and opposition members, the latter finding aligning with recent work by Reuter and Robertson (2015).

[48] I also run robustness checks that a) account for the importance of economic development in influencing democratization and b) hone in on those components connected most squarely with electoral democracy.

TABLE 5.4 *Institutional heterogeneity*

Dependent Variable:	Revenue		Profit Margin	
	(1)	(2)	(3)	(4)
	Panel A: Sample Split at Median of Democracy Score			
Sample:	Low Dem.	High Dem.	Low Dem.	High Dem.
District Win	0.223	0.434*	−0.003	0.140**
	(0.290)	(0.222)	(0.052)	(0.068)
Bandwidth:	0.145	0.145	0.128	0.128
Observations	269	377	232	332
	Panel B: Sample Split at Median of UR Control of Parliament			
Sample:	Low UR Control	High UR Control	Low UR Control	High UR Control
District Win	0.501**	−0.136	0.161***	−0.045
	(0.211)	(0.348)	(0.057)	(0.065)
Bandwidth:	0.145	0.145	0.128	0.128
Observations	457	189	410	154
	Panel C: Sample Split at Membership in UR Party			
Sample:	Non-UR	UR	Non-UR	UR
District Win	0.048	0.595	0.108	−0.006
	(0.259)	(0.434)	(0.087)	(0.072)
Bandwidth:	0.145	0.145	0.128	0.128
Observations	396	250	349	215

*** $p<0.01$, ** $p<0.05$, * $p<0.1$ This table displays heterogenous RDD treatment effects of winning office using the optimal bandwidth (CCT) and a local-linear control function. Panel A subsets on the median democracy score in the region. Panel B subsets on the median number of legislative seats the ruling party controlled. Panel C subsets on whether a candidate was a member of the ruling party. All models include firm-level and candidate-level covariates, use conventional robust standard errors clustered on the candidate level, and include the pre-election value for the outcome.

The ruling party sometimes grants rent-seeking opportunities to potential challengers to ensure support and prevent social unrest.

Next, in Table 5.5, politically connected firms may derive slightly greater revenue and profits in wealthier regions, especially where natural resources are fueling economic growth, but the evidence is not definitive. The point estimates regarding profitability are not quite statistically significant. Controlling for individual firm sector, size, and ownership, firms in economically developed and resource-rich regions make several-times-greater profits. Firms with immobile assets also may see increases in their profit margins are larger over the term, but the differences in the point estimates are not significant at conventional levels. Political access may be helping drive down the costs of business for these firms. Previous outlays on regulation or dealing with bureaucratic arbitrariness are no longer mandated if political ties can help clear up ties with officials.

On the other hand, competition between rent-seekers diminishes the return on running for office. As shown in Table 5.6, connected firms earn both greater revenue and larger profit margins when fewer of the rival firms also get their candidate into office. The return on winning elected office actually disappears completely as more and more firms from the same sector all win seats in a legislature. The more firm directors overall that become politicians, the smaller the payoff for their affiliated firms. The marketplace for rents that emerges within parliament offers reduced profit margins for participants. Businessperson politicians can serve as a check on each other in office, preventing the passing of policies that would advantage specific firms.

This result suggests that improving and expanding the representation of economic interests in political institutions could reduce rent-seeking and the distortion of political benefits to connected firms. Clearly just encouraging more businesspeople to run for office carries its own sense of problems, as legislatures cannot be expanded indefinitely and other groups in society would suffer from being deprived of their own descriptive representation. Instead, combating rent-seeking by businessperson politicians requires that competing firms have the means and opportunities to monitor actions that only benefit individual firms. Institutional design matters most. Ensuring free elections may be less important than creating more access points to institutions, holding open hearings and committee meetings, and reducing the barriers to entry to lobbying, such as the high costs and often times lack of a clear legal framework. As institutions become more transparent and inclusive of interest groups, the

TABLE 5.5 *Economic heterogeneity*

Dependent Variable:	Revenue		Profit Margin	
	(1)	(2)	(3)	(4)
Panel A: Sample Split at Median of Regional GRP per Capita				
Samples:	Low GRP	High GRP	Low GRP	High GRP
District Win	0.267	0.504*	0.044	0.171
	(0.222)	(0.298)	(0.032)	(0.141)
Bandwidth:	0.145	0.145	0.128	0.128
Observations	392	254	339	225
Panel B: Sample Split according to Presence of Natural Resources				
Samples:	No Resources	Resources	No Resources	Resources
District Win	0.296	0.468	0.066*	0.191
	(0.203)	(0.387)	(0.037)	(0.173)
Bandwidth:	0.145	0.145	0.128	0.128
Observations	453	193	393	171
Panel C: Sample Split at Firms with Immobile Assets				
Samples:	Mobile	Immobile	Mobile	Immobile
District Win	0.251	0.430*	0.030	0.124
	(0.343)	(0.224)	(0.054)	(0.079)
Bandwidth:	0.145	0.145	0.128	0.128
Observations	223	423	198	366

* $p<0.1$ This table displays heterogenous RDD treatment effects of winning office using the optimal bandwidth (CCT) and a local-linear control function. Panel A subsets on gross regional product per capita. Panel B subsets on whether the region possessed natural resources. Panel C subsets on whether a firm has immobile assets. All models include firm-level and candidate-level covariates, use conventional robust standard errors clustered on the candidate level, and include the pre-election value for the outcome.

TABLE 5.6 *Convocational heterogeneity*

Dependent Variable:	Revenue		Profit Margin	
	(1)	(2)	(3)	(4)
Panel A: Sample Split at Whether Firm has >1 Rival in Parliament				
Samples:	Few Rivals	Many Rivals	Few Rivals	Many Rivals
District Win	0.589**	−0.112	0.179	0.003
	(0.252)	(0.314)	(0.115)	(0.055)
Bandwidth:	0.145	0.145	0.128	0.128
Observations	251	220	208	197
Panel B: Sample Split at Median % of Businessperson Legislators				
Samples:	Low Bus. Parl	High Bus. Parl	Low Bus. Parl	High Bus. Parl
District Win	0.895***	−0.486*	0.164**	0.012
	(0.253)	(0.256)	(0.073)	(0.040)
Bandwidth:	0.145	0.145	0.128	0.128
Observations	341	305	294	270

* $p<0.1$ This table displays heterogenous RDD treatment effects of winning office using the optimal bandwidth (CCT) and a local-linear control function. Panel A subsets on whether a connected firm had one or fewer sectoral rivals connected to a legislator in the parliament versus three or more rivals. Panel B subsets on the median number of seats held by businessperson candidates in parliament. All models include firm-level and candidate-level covariates, use conventional robust standard errors clustered on the candidate level, and include the pre-election value for the outcome.

probability falls that one particular entity can dominate policymaking to its own advantage.

5.6 DISCUSSION AND CONCLUDING REMARKS

To summarize, using an RDD to estimate the causal effect of having an affiliated person win office, this chapter find that politically connected firms see an increase in revenue of approximately 60 percent and enjoy increased profit margins of roughly 15 percent. Such evidence suggests powerful incentives for firms to send directors into elected office. Because winning elections differs from making campaign contributions or lobbying, benchmarking across these strategies is difficult. Cingano and Pinotti (2013) show that firms in Italy that employ at least one official at the local level can see increases of roughly 6 percent in revenue and profitability. Amore and Bennedsen (2013) report that companies with family ties to politicians can increase their profits by 100 percent in low corrupt Denmark, similar to work on Thailand showing abnormal returns for connected companies of upwards of 200 percent.[49]

In Russia, gaining direct access to regional legislatures can make the difference between profitable and unprofitable firms. I demonstrate that the benefits of connections derive from lowered informational and regulatory costs for firms in their dealings with bureaucrats, and not from greater access to finance. Interviews with businesspeople deputies attest to this: companies whose directors were lost electoral campaigns were vulnerable to harassment from officials and the loss of market share.[50] Furthermore, deputies noted that corrupt state officials only wanted to work with people they already knew from being in office; a lost election meant a closed door to key policymakers and regulators.[51]

This chapter also provides a body of evidence to support a main assumption running through the book so far. Chapter 1 acknowledged that businesspeople may run for office for a variety of reasons behind seeking benefits for their companies. After all, prominent examples of businessperson politicians in the West, for example Donald Trump and Michael Bloomberg, suggest ideological, ego and other personal motivations play a strong role. By demonstrating that Russian firms benefit

49 Bunkanwanicha and Wiwattanakantang (2009).

50 Interview with Elena Zyryanova, deputy Perm Regional Duma, Perm, Russia. October 8, 2013.

51 Interview with Lilia Shiraeva, Regional Deputy, Perm, Russia. October 2, 2013.

immensely from having directors hold elected office, the results in this chapter assert the importance of corporate strategy for explaining these candidacies. If businesspeople were not seeking elected office to help their firms, then we should not have found any firm-level returns on their investment.

The finding that connected firms draw greater revenue and profits in more democratic regions also contributes to our understanding of how the value of political connections is shaped by political institutions.[52] Gehlbach, Sonin, and Zhuravskaya (2010) argue that rent-seeking businesspeople should be less likely to seek elected office when institutions are more democratic, since they fear being voted out by the median voter. This chapter alternately uncovers that businesspeople value more politically competitive parliaments that are able to pass more encompassing legislation and allow more voices to be heard.[53] When parliaments are weak, businesspeople prefer to lobby the executive branch. When parliaments can exert influence on regulations and budgets, businesspeople instead view them as key, possibly by occupying the seats themselves. Parliaments become fora through which business demands are negotiated and private favors exchanged, with rents accrued to the special interests represented. Firms and other groups left outside these networks lose their ability to influence policy.

52 Faccio (2006).
53 Pyle (2009); Govorun, Marques, and Pyle (2016); Szakonyi (2018*a*).

6

Businesspeople as Policymakers

In 1876, the Prussian brewer Karl Kruger entered into an agreement with the Tomsk City Duma on a ten-year real estate lease for quite a significant sum at the time – 100 rubles a year. In less than twelve months, Kruger's factory was churning out Viennese-style lagers for thirsty local residents. The next century was a time of tumult – evictions and relocations, dry laws, world wars, nationalization – yet the historical threads linking Kruger's small enterprise and the Soviet-renamed "Tomsk Brewery No. 1" remained unbroken: a rich tradition of beermaking and genuine consumer loyalty. Just when Gorbachev was taking power as General Secretary in 1985, a fresh graduate of a local polytechnic university named Ivan Klein found work at the brewery as a mechanic. Over the next decade, Klein rose to become head engineer, and then general director, ultimately taking a majority stake during the brewery's privatization in 1994. The privatized company grew rapidly, winning prizes and expanding production to become the region's most popular line of beers.

But beyond becoming "beer king," Klein also had political ambitions. After serving in the regional legislature, in 2013 he turned his sights on the elections to become Tomsk's mayor, a new vacancy following the resignation of the previous officeholder. Propelled by strong name recognition and visible charitable works, Klein also impressed voters with his success in the business world.[1] During a largely colorless campaign, Klein made vague promises to balance the budget and reduce the obstacles to doing business; he won office easy with over 60 percent of the vote. Improving the business environment and cutting government

[1] RIA Novosti (2013).

spending became signature themes for his first foray as mayor: early on he swapped out the expensive government car of his predecessor for a simple sedan and invited local businesspeople to participate in a variety of city projects.[2] At the same time, he ramped up spending on road construction, nearly quadrupling the city's budget for repairs and acquiring new equipment. Five years later, with the city still running a large deficit, Klein coasted to re-election.

Klein's political objectives as mayor of Tomsk's succinctly illustrate what businesspeople more generally try to accomplish while in office. On one hand, Chapter 5 revealed the lengths businesspeople go to help their own firms. Legislators use their time in office to unlock access to state procurement contracts and beneficial regulations, both of which contribute to significant improvements in their own firms' financial performance. This can lead to dramatic distortions in the way winners and losers emerge from economic competition: firms that pursue direct access to policymaking prosper, while their competitors languish without political representation.

On the other hand, businesspeople in political office also have to govern. Their election is not simply a free pass to exploit the government for their own personal interests. Businessperson politicians take on responsibility for many other issues facing their constituents, from educating the next generation of citizens, to providing health care to the sick and elderly to basic infrastructure for economic activity to flourish. How we evaluate whether businesspeople in public office contribute to prosperity and public welfare must not only encompass their own efforts to benefit their firms, but the decisions they make regarding the provision of key public services.

This chapter investigates the policies businessperson politicians adopt while in office. It draws on existing theoretical work on the importance of politicians' background to develop testable hypotheses about how and why businessperson politicians could behave differently in public office. First, these leaders may possess superior knowledge of and interest in solving issues important to the wider business community. Motivated by this set of preferences, politicians coming from the private sector may push for pro-business policies, particularly those that improve the business environment and promote economic growth. But drawing on their experience managing enterprises, businesspeople may also be uniquely positioned to improve the way government works. We might expect

[2] Shestopalova (2014). RIA Tomsk (2014).

them to use their private sector know-how to increase the quality and lower the cost of public service delivery, for example, by eliminating wasteful spending. The question then arises: do businesspeople shape government to run *for* business (i.e. by adopting pro-business policies) or *like* a business (i.e. by increasing government efficiency)?

My two-part research design first uses another regression discontinuity design (RDD) on a new dataset of 68,169 businessperson candidates for mayor across Russia from 2007 to 2016. The design compares budget and procurement outcomes between municipalities where businesspeople barely won office to those where they barely lost. By switching to the analysis to an executive office, I am better able to isolate the effect of private sector background on individual policymaking. Mayors in Russia enjoy more autonomy to unilaterally push for their own policy goals than legislators, who must work within coalitions to pass legislation. But to test that the results hold for different branches, I also present analysis using the dataset from Chapter 2 on regional deputies to investigate how businessperson politicians affect regional budget spending. Though this secondary analysis is not causally identified, it helps illustrate the importance of a private sector background across institutional arrangements and political positions.

The analysis reveals that businessperson politicians in Russia adopt primarily pro-business policies while serving in government. I find that as both mayors and regional deputies, businessperson politicians increase expenditures on economic infrastructure, dedicating additional money to the construction of roads, rails, and ports. Levels of spending on health care and education do not change under businessperson mayors, nor does the size of government decrease. And at the regional level, more businesspeople in office is are associated with lower levels of corporate tax revenue. Prioritizing economic over social infrastructure brings immediate benefits to firms and opens up opportunities for rent-seeking, while holding back long-term accumulation of human capital. These results are robust to controlling for financial dependency between governments and party affiliation, with extensions showing that specific institutional arrangements play little role in preventing businesspeople from imposing their preferences on policymaking.

Next, even given their managerial expertise, businesspeople in elected office do little to improve government efficiency. The RDD results indicate that municipalities run by businesspeople do not run smaller deficits; at the regional level, I even uncover evidence that more businessperson legislators results in larger deficit spending and higher levels of debt.

Moreover, using detailed data on state procurement, I find that mayoral administrations run by businesspeople are less likely to adopt the most transparent, competitive mechanisms for choosing contractors: open auctions. This is particularly true for procurement in the construction sector, where opportunities for corruption are most favorable. Taken together, this chapter reveals that politicians coming from the private sector refashion government to work for the business community, which may come at the expense of more lasting economic growth and improved government performance.

6.1 DEMOGRAPHIC DETERMINANTS OF POLICYMAKING

Where politicians worked prior to entering government can have profound effects on their decision-making and priorities. Individuals are often politically socialized in the workplace, developing shared perspectives and even policy preferences within their profession.[3] Politicians not only bring these attitudes with them into office, but also management skills, financial connections and allegiances to employers. Empirical work has done much to link officials' careers in the private sector with their behavior in office. Adolph (2013) shows the previous career trajectory of central bankers helps explain variation in their conservatism. Relatedly, legislators with a background in insurance push for laws more favorable to their former industry.[4]

This section argues that as a discrete professional category, businesspeople may behave differently from politicians with different career pasts. Drawing on literatures from urban studies and management together with public opinion data, I argue that businesspeople possess both distinct political preferences and management skills that could influence their political priorities. The aim is to generate a set of testable hypotheses about the observable policy areas where businesspeople might diverge from other types of politicians in elected office.

6.1.1 Adopting Pro-Business Policies

First, businesspeople may have different preferences for government action and care about solving different problems facing society. Economic

[3] Peterson (1992).
[4] Hansen, Carnes, and Gray (2018).

policy figures to be at the top of the list. The Life in Transition Survey (LiTS) of over 50,000 citizens across thirty-four countries shows that the political preferences of businesspeople generally conform to those held by the rest of the population, except with regards to economic issues (shown in the Appendix). Businesspeople generally agree about social issues but express qualitatively different views on redistribution, state intervention in the economy, and what spending items government should prioritize (discussed more below). Carnes (2018) similarly shows that US legislators who own businesses have more conservative opinions on a range of economic issues, such as the need to reduce inequality or fund social programs.

Although there are many other plausible hypotheses about other issues where businesspeople might hold different preferences, differences over economic policies provide a good starting point for theorizing about what businesspeople might do in elected office. Given their firsthand experience bringing goods and services to market, businesspeople may view their time in government as an opportunity to develop an economic environment more hospitable for entrepreneurship and with a smaller, more effective government footprint. They also may understand which specific government actions are required to attract investment, create employment, and spur consumption. Concerns over these policy issues can drive them to enter politics in the first place.[5]

The notion that politicians with personal links to the private sector will prioritize pro-growth policies draws heavily on work on urban politics in the United States. Capitalizing on shared policy interests, businesspeople united around reshaping government to create "growth machines."[6] By devoting their slack resources to politics, they joined municipal governing coalitions and implemented a number of pro-growth policies and development plans.[7] Politicians coming from the private sector may try to promote economic growth by easing the costs of and obstacles to doing business. In other words, they try to make government work *for* business.

Which specific pro-growth policies might these politicians adopt? Clearly many are at their disposal. On balance, we should expect that as a professional class, businesspeople most influence policies that will have

[5] Li, Meng, and Zhang (2006).
[6] Hunter (2017); Logan and Molotch (1987).
[7] Stone (1989).

an immediate and generalizably positive impact on the larger business community. That is, we should see them devote greater attention to policies which provide the median firm with the greatest short-term benefits, while imposing the lowest costs. Not all pro-growth policies qualify. Whereas upgrading human capital can increase employment, earnings, and technological innovation, such changes requires years of investment and often impose substantial financial costs. Other issues are divisive. For example, businesspeople may split on free trade depending on the international competitiveness of their firms or industry. The type of regulatory policy an elected official advocates may be contingent on whether they want to promote competition or protect market incumbents.

But there are other areas where the preferences of businesspeople appear to coalesce more strongly. First, given firms' concern over access to key inputs, suppliers, and markets, increasing government spending on economic infrastructure, such as roads, railroads, and utilities, becomes very attractive. Infrastructure spending drives up overall demand, reduces transportation and other costs, and creates lucrative opportunities for companies to sell directly to the state. Survey evidence suggests that businesspeople express consistent support for this type of intervention. The LiTS survey (discussed above and in the Appendix in more detail) asked respondents to choose among seven issue areas where extra government spending should be prioritized. Businesspeople were much more likely to rank infrastructure as their top issue, whereas health care and pensions ranked at the bottom. Per surveys of almost 300,000 respondents over the last decade, Russian businesspeople feel just strongly about prioritizing economic infrastructure over other issues (see Appendix).

Parsing out exactly why businesspeople hold such different preferences is necessarily more complicated: individuals with strong preferences may select into management roles or entrepreneurship, or their time in the private sector may independently shape their worldview. Answering this question requires fine-grained panel data and a sharp identification strategy. But importantly for this chapter, the distinct preferences of businesspeople observed in the survey analysis come through controlling for individual wealth. Experience in the private sector seems to have distinct effect on one's views of government priorities. As an occupational class, businesspeople are considerably more concerned about upgrading infrastructure than the average citizen, who prioritizes investments in health care and education.

Hypothesis 17. *Businessperson politicians will prioritize spending on economic infrastructure.*

Spending choices can impact growth. Cross-national work suggests that shifting spending from economic to social infrastructure can place an economy on a stronger and more equitable footing and increase growth rates.[8] In addition, rent-seeking tends to accompany spending on infrastructure projects, especially in places with weak institutions that fail to hold politicians accountable.[9] Many politicians may be driven by personal self-interest and run for office precisely to take advantage of these opportunities. We saw in Chapter 5 just how much Russian firms could profit from having their directors become regional deputies.

Next, experience in the business world may predispose politicians to reduce the size of government and lower their own tax burden. This motivation could stem from an ideological opposition among businesspeople towards excessive government intervention. Cutting taxes and red tape facilitate market entry, production and entrepreneurship, to the possible detriment of government finances and even consumer safety.

Preferences for a smaller government footprint appear to be shared by businesspeople worldwide. Judging from World Bank BEEPS Surveys (2002, 2005, and 2009) of nearly 20,000 firms across twenty-six transitioning countries, managers rank tax rates as their biggest obstacle to doing business. Cohesive business groups have successfully blocked government attempts to raise revenue in a variety of contexts.[10] The situation is similar in Russia. In recent surveys, businesspeople are much more likely to support a reduction in the size of the state and lessened burdens placed on private firms. Again controlling for income, entrepreneurs consistently advocated privatizing assets, cutting taxes and drawing down government programs.[11]

Hypothesis 18. *Businesspeople in office will reduce government spending and cut corporate taxes.*

[8] Acosta-Ormaechea and Morozumi (2017).
[9] Robinson and Torvik (2005).
[10] Fairfield (2010).
[11] Levada Center surveys of 1,600 respondents from July 2007 to September 2016.

Improving Government Efficiency

Next, experience in the private sector may endow businesspeople with management skills that set them apart from other types of politicians. Directors in the corporate world have to oversee diverse teams, organize information flows, manage budgets and physical resources, and delegate responsibilities, all with aim of maximizing efficiency, productivity, and profitability. Scholars have even argued that the key social skills required to succeed in business – persuasion, negotiation, and manipulation – may find relevant applications in political life.[12] Such organizational abilities and insights distinguish businesspeople from politicians coming from professions where management duties play a secondary role to applying one's specialized expertise, such as medicine, engineering, or law. Businesspeople may be more effective managers, and therefore better able to improve how government works.

We might then expect businesspeople to make government run *like* a business. They may take steps to increase efficiency in bureaucratic service delivery, particularly by cutting down on wasteful spending. Work on public administration argues there are instructive lessons to be transferred from the private to the public sector.[13] Running a successful business, generally speaking, requires delivering quality customer service and achieving profitability. By importing know-how from their private sector careers, businesspeople may be uniquely capable of cleaning up the bureaucracy and increasing public sector productivity.

That commitment to improving government performance may extend to rooting out corruption. Companies often bear the brunt of extortionate bureaucrats. As directors take office, their priority may lie in combatting different types of rent-seeking that plague the business environment. In Italy and Brazil, some of the loudest voices for anti-corruption measures have come directly from the business community.[14] But firms' interest in rooting out corruption can vary, and some businesspeople may view government service as an opportunity to help themselves at the public's expense.[15] There may be a risk that businesspeople put their management prowess to work in making government work solely for their own firms, including engaging in corruption to do so.

[12] Ferris et al. (2007).
[13] Box (1999).
[14] Mantovani (2014); Compact (2006).
[15] Dixit (2018).

How would we know if businesspeople are genuinely committed to improving government performance? For example, running a business more efficiently can mean many things, from re-allocating resources to high-performing units to maximizing supply chain efficiency. In the corporate world, calculating firm-level productivity is somewhat straightforward: both inputs (i.e. capital, labor, and materials) and outputs (i.e. sales, profits) are mostly observable.[16] On the other hand, measuring public sector productivity runs into several methodological challenges, particularly concerning the quality of outputs and usage of collective goods.

I argue there are several observable implications of businesspeople acting to increase government efficiency. First, politicians coming from the private sector may impose budget constraints and put government finances in order. Excessive government spending can be a symptom of bad political management and fragmented policy leadership.[17] Since running a deficit is akin to a company making a loss, we might expect businesspeople to institute an ethos of fiscal responsibility. Although taking on reasonable debt loads may help finance investment, businesses generally are more sensitive to the demands of their shareholders who require profits to sustain interest in their firms.

Hypothesis 19. *Businessperson politicians will run smaller budget deficits.*

Another approach on the rise in economics uses administrative data on public procurement to capture how well governments achieve value for money spent.[18] Public procurement accounts for 13 percent of domestic GDP worldwide, and bureaucrats often have incredible discretion in deciding how contracts are allocated. Properly designing procurement systems can dramatically limit waste and improve the quality of deliverables. For example, introducing electronic procurement in India and Indonesia led to better road quality and fewer delays.[19] By prioritizing best practices and closely monitoring spending, businesspeople politicians can reduce the price that the government pays to deliver key goods and services.

[16] Syverson (2011).
[17] Alesina and Perotti (1995).
[18] Lau, Lonti, and Schultz (2017).
[19] Lewis-Faupel et al. (2016).

Hypothesis 20. *Businessperson politicians will push for more efficient public procurement.*

This overall drive towards efficiency often features prominently in the campaigns of businessperson politicians worldwide. In his party's manifesto, Finnish businessman Juha Sipila promised to remake the government in the private sector's image. His economic program calls for "tightened public sector expenditures, improvements in productivity, the removal of excessive regulations and, if necessary, a savings of two billion in spending."[20] During his 2012 presidential campaign, former investment banker Mitt Romney declared, "the key to balancing the budget–having spent 25 years in business, I know something about taking waste out of enterprises – I'd love to do that to the federal government."[21]

Businesspeople holding political offices in Russia outlined the same plans for remaking government. In his 2018 race for the mayorship of Nizhniy Novgorod, businessman Roman Koshelov declared the need to "optimize the work of municipal institutions, and reduce budget expenditures without sacrificing quality."[22] Just after his appointment as governor in 2004, businessman Oleg Chirkunov quickly announced that he viewed Perm Region as a "corporation." Contemporary media accounts described him changing the deputy leadership, firing workers who "did not like to neglect the lunch break and regularly took tea breaks several times a day," and optimizing the budget reporting system.[23] A self-organized group of entrepreneurs running for office in the city of Saransk similarly called for introducing more efficiency into government operations and cutting programs.[24] Beyond these promises though, we know little about whether businesspeople actually follow through and improve government performance.

6.2 DATA AND RESEARCH DESIGN

I first investigate the effect of politicians' private sector experience on policymaking using data on budgets and public procurement at the municipal level in Russia from 2007 to 2015. As a federal state, Russia is

20 Keskusta, Centre Party of Finland, 2011. Center Party Election Platform.
21 Romney (2011).
22 Zercalo.org (2018).
23 Kravcova (2005).
24 SGS (2012).

divided approximately 23,000 municipalities.[25] Municipal governments provide for preschool, primary, and secondary education, the majority of all health care, public transportation, utilities, and local road construction.[26] Total spending at this administrative level accounting for roughly 6 percent of Russian GDP.[27] Revenue comes from land and personal property taxes, tax-sharing agreements with higher-level units, and intergovernmental transfers.

Fiscal decision-making at the municipality level is concentrated in the hands of the local executive, or mayor. Recent reforms have limited the size of the mainly unpaid legislative council and endowed the executive with strong veto powers.[28] The mayoral administration prepares economic prognoses and drafts the budget for the local council, which then approves it. The administration also executes the budget activities, submitting only annual reports to the local council. This gives mayors disproportionate ability to influence the size and composition of spending, and effectively sidelines the legislative branch.

Mayors in Russia can either be elected through a popular vote (council-mayor model) or appointed by council deputies (council-manager model). Unfortunately, Russian authorities (through the Central Election Commission, or CEC) only make available information on elected mayors. No systematic data are available on even the names of the managers appointed by the council deputies, much less their professional background. Therefore the analysis is limited to municipalities for which mayoral elections are held, with data coming from the CEC.[29] Whether

[25] I exclude closed cities (ZATOs) from the analysis. The number of municipalities is constantly changing due to unit merges and proliferation. Each region classifies subordinate municipalities into four types: municipal rayons and city okrugs (upper tier) and rural and urban settlements (lower tier). See the Appendix for summary statistics across the different types.

[26] De Silva et al. (2009).

[27] See a more detailed breakdown of spending across line-items for regional and municipal governments in the Appendix.

[28] Ross (2007).

[29] In a small number of "dual" cases, a municipality could have both a popularly elected "head of municipality" and an appointed "head of administration," or city manager. The mayor has few powers, while the manager runs the government. Information on the distribution of responsibilities is not made available, and I cannot determine which municipalities fall into this category. I include all municipalities where a mayoral election was held, recognizing that the inclusion of these dual arrangement cases should bias the estimates downward since elected mayors have less policy influence.

a municipality uses an election or an appointment system depends on its region; to account for this selection, I include region fixed effects.[30]

I first collected information on 19,886 municipal plurality elections in 13,308 municipalities, or 58 percent of the total across Russia. Mayoral elections attract interest from an average of 3.4 candidates; 18 percent of elections are decided by 10 percent of the vote share or less. Municipal elections in Russia are not only competitive, but can lead to unpredictable outcomes. With an average of 4,000 ballots cast per election, a small number of votes can tip the scales.[31] Although candidates from the ruling United Russia (UR) party won two-thirds of mayorships, political independents and members of systemic opposition parties, such as the Communists, often defeat regime-connected candidates and wield power at the local level.

6.2.1 Measuring Private Sector Experience

Key to this analysis is that businesspeople participate in and win mayoral elections. To identify experience in the private sector, I adopt a similar identification approach to that used in Chapter 2. First, I code each candidate's place of work on their registration form. Using this information, I code a binary indicator for whether a candidate worked as a firm director, deputy director, or a member of the board of directors at the time of their candidacy. Although this approach captures a majority of businessperson politicians, it misses some candidates who might not want to draw attention to their private sector activities. To account for this, I match each candidate based on their full name and region to the SPARK database. Candidates registered as an individual entrepreneur prior to their election were also coded as businesspeople.[32] This variable thus denotes candidates whose primary profession during the election campaign is in the private sector, and not professional politicians who draw on some outside income from their business interests.

[30] The type of municipality, size, and dependence on subsidies do not predict whether elections are used, but including region fixed effects explains over 65 percent of the variation.

[31] Average turnout was just under 60 percent, a relatively high figure for Russia.

[32] Because the size of the firms connected to city mayors is much smaller, it is impossible to conduct the same kind of firm-level analysis as shown in previous chapters. These connected firms are less likely to submit detailed financial data to the authorities, precluding in-depth investigations of heterogeneity across different types of business people. This question is ripe for future research.

TABLE 6.1 *Candidate summary statistics*

	All Cands.	Businesspeople	Non-Business people
(1) Total No.	68,169	10,904	57,265
(2) Mean Age	46.3	44.8	46.6
(3) Female (%)	26.7	16.3	28.7
(4) Education Level	5.5	5.6	5.5
(5) Political Independents (%)	59.7	63.7	59.0
(6) Ruling Party Member (%)	25.8	12.9	28.2
(7) Elections Won (%)	29.2	17.0	31.5

This table presents summary statistics on candidates running for mayoral election. The middle column subsets to only businessperson candidates, while the right column looks at those without a private sector background.

Roughly 35 percent of elections (7,058) saw at least one businessperson run, with approximately one-sixth seeing candidacies from two or more. For elections with multiple businesspeople, I dropped the municipality completely to ensure a clean comparison between the municipalities where businesspeople won and lost. Businesspeople won 22.5 percent of the elections they contested; overall, 8 percent of mayors during the period came directly from the private sector.

Table 6.1 compares mayoral candidates with private sector experience to those without across a number of other demographic characteristics. Businessperson candidates are somewhat younger than the rest of the candidate pool and less likely to be female; gender imbalances across occupations in general are large in Russia, with women more often finding employment in the public sector. On the other hand, businesspeople have just as much formal education as those coming from other occupations, based on a six-point scale of the highest level of education that ranges from one (primary school education) to six (postgraduate education). Businessperson mayors affiliate less often with the ruling party, UR, than for example, candidates from the private sector running for regional deputy office (see Chapter 2). Part of this effect may be mechanical: UR often imposes quotas on the number of businesspeople allowed to affiliate in order to maintain a veneer of descriptive representation.

More importantly for this analysis, in contrast to the regional level, municipal elections in Russia see little programmatic competition between parties. While the ruling party UR controlled 68 percent of municipalities during the period, non-partisan independents controlled nearly all of the rest (28 percent). Independents represent views from across the spectrum and are often those for whom no room was left under the ruling party umbrella. Opposition parties, such as the left-leaning Communists or the right-leaning Just Russia, have little to no established presence at the local level.

The combination of inactive systemic opposition parties and elections to executive roles may mean that affiliating with a party becomes less critical. As mayors, businesspeople do not need to enter party-aligned coalitions to get their decisions through. They can retain their autonomy and use their own resources to win election. In that regard, mayoral elections resemble the contests to single member districts explored in Chapter 4.

That said, I take several steps to account for the potential role of partisanship in explaining the behavior of businesspeople in office. First, in the Research Design section, I show that businessperson candidates from UR are not more likely to win close elections; party affiliation does not confer electoral advantages to this group of candidates. Second, robustness checks in the Appendix show that the policy decisions of businessperson mayors do not vary based on membership in ruling party. Finally, I include an indicator for party membership in RDD specifications as an additional control for possible ideological affinity among partisans.

6.2.2 Outcome Data

To test whether businesspeople implement "pro-business" policies, I collect data on municipal budgets from the Russian State Statistics Agency. I measure spending on economic infrastructure through expenditures on the "national economy"; at this level, this money goes to public transport and railroads, roads, water transport, and telecommunications.[33] For social infrastructure, I collect data on education and health care spending. Each of these budget subcategory outcomes are measured as a fraction of the total expenditures for that year and take values between 0 and 1. I test the second hypothesis using a logged measure of total

[33] This category is officially divided into four subcategories. Public transport covers the development and maintenance of bus and light rail systems in the municipality. Roads cover the expansion and maintenance of road infrastructure, including traffic signaling and safety measures. Water transport covers the purchase of hydrotechnic equipment and port maintenance. Telecommunications expenditures go to maintaining phone and television networks.

expenditures for each municipality. Unfortunately, municipal authorities have little authority to set tax rates or influence tax collection; in the next section I show analysis using regional data on corporate tax revenue. Municipalities vary considerably as to the money they spend overall and on different types of infrastructure (see Appendix).

To test whether businessperson politicians improve government efficiency, I look at two sets of outcomes. First, I calculate each municipality's budget deficit by dividing total expenditures by total revenue. In an effort to restrain government spending, Russian law punishes municipal governments that run high deficits by suspending intergovernmental grants. Even with these measures in place, 16 percent of municipalities ran a deficit of more than 5 percent of their total revenue, while over 40 percent ran surpluses of the same amount. Fiscal responsibility varies across municipalities.

The next measure looks at how municipalities select contractors within public procurement. International organizations and scholars argue that holding open, competitive auctions helps enforce transparency, reduce opportunities for corruption, and limit budget expenditures.[34] Research on Czech Republic and Italy has shown that the alternate approach – giving bureaucrats discretion to negotiate with suppliers on factors other than price – leads to worse outcomes.[35] When bureaucrats can avoid using open, competitive auctions in favor of negotiated approaches, fewer bidders participate, more contracts are awarded to politically connected and anonymous firms, and higher prices are paid for the same goods and services. Work on Russia has uncovered similar findings: governments that use open auctions pay lower prices for the same goods and see less collusion among bidders.[36]

For all purchases, Russian bureaucrats have a choice about whether to use a competitive, "electronic auction" rather than an open tender. Auctions are held online in realtime and are used to procure roughly 50 percent of all government contracts. Favoritism is harder to carry out since supplier registration procedures are more transparent, bids are submitted anonymously, and contracts are awarded solely based on the lowest bid. One the other hand, many mayors prefer negotiated tenders, since they offer greater scope for accepting bribes to ensure

[34] Beth (2007).
[35] Palguta and Pertold (2017); Baltrunaite et al. (2018).
[36] Yakovlev et al. (2016).

certain contractors or blackmailing winners.[37] Russian mayors appoint the bureaucrats who decide which mechanisms will be used to select suppliers as well as oversee the bidding over and implementation of the contract. Mayors bent on corrupting the process would avoid electronic auctions wherever possible so that their preferred suppliers could be selected more easily.

To detect whether mayoral administrations are more likely to use auctions, I use public procurement data from the Russian procurement portal. Using the tax identification codes for 20,581 mayoral administrations, I then built a dataset of all 1,427,288 contracts signed from 2011 to 2016 by these local executive branches, totaling $124 billion in procurement. This covers 92 percent of the total amount with some administrations missing due to problems identifying their location in the portal's database. I code a binary indicator for whether an electronic auction was used for each contract, and then calculate the percentage of all contracts that used auctions for each mayoral term.[38] This outcome "Competitive Procurement" takes values from 0 to 1. Mayoral administrations that use electronic auctions are maximizing competition between bidders and procedural transparency, while paying the lowest prices for goods or services.

I also coded contracts by their official two-digit product code, and calculated the percentage of contracts within the top five categories procured by mayoral administrations: construction, cars, furniture, office supplies, and food. Collectively these five categories account for 75 percent of all procurement; other expenditures get routed through schools, hospitals, and other agencies where the mayor has weaker oversight over procurement practices. Below I show results specifically on construction procurement, where extra investment in economic infrastructure would be directed. The construction sector is generally viewed as among the most ripe for corruption not just in Russia, but also cross-nationally.[39] The Appendix shows results for the other four categories.

37 Filippovskii (2018); Zaitseva (2014).

38 Note that price thresholds regulate the types of negotiated mechanisms available to procurers in Russia. For all purchases under 500,000 rubles ($17,000), only sealed-bid auctions or electronic auctions can be used. For purchases above that threshold, either tenders (which use criteria including but not only price) and electronic auctions. Per the literature, I exclude all contracts under 10,000 rubles ($300), when auctions are not used.

39 Kyriacou, Muinelo-Gallo, and Roca-Sagalés (2015).

One final concern with studying Russian budget and procurement data relates to the level of centralization within Russia's federal structure. The Russian government during the Putin era has concentrated fiscal power within the federal center, relying on elaborate formulas to allocate transfers to lower governments. Municipal governments are particularly dependent on these subsidies to fund their expenditures.[40]

However, interpreting budget expenditures and procurement outcomes as reflective of the preferences of local politicians is valid for several reasons. First, even controlling for region, year, and municipality "type," there is significant variation between municipalities on every spending category, from deficits and procurement outcomes to spending on different types of goods and services. This variation suggests that other political factors beyond the centralized formulas must be taken into account. Second, recognizing that transfers from the center may be accompanied by strict dictates, I include a control for lower-level dependence on subventions and intergovernmental grants as well as region fixed effects. Finally, if all spending and procurement decisions for the thousands of municipalities were being made in Moscow, we should not expect any effect of the identity of local mayors on different outcomes. A fully centralized state should bias against finding statistically significant results on a municipality having a businessperson candidate.

6.2.3 Research Design and Balance Checks

For the municipal analysis, I again use a regression discontinuity design (RDD) based on close elections.[41] This time I compare outcomes in municipalities which saw a businessperson candidate narrowly win office with those that saw one narrowly lose office. Budget outcomes are averaged over the term a businessperson mayor either held office (if he or she won) or would have held office (if he or she lost).[42] I include the

[40] For example, an estimate in 2018 by the Russian Ministry of Finance suggested that municipalities generated 37 percent of their revenue from local taxation.

[41] Lee (2008).

[42] See the Appendix for more detail on sample construction. Nearly all mayoral terms last five years and outcomes are averaged over the full calendar years a mayor was in office. For a term to be included in the analysis, a mayor must serve for at least two full years. If a mayor served consecutive terms, then each term is considered a separate observation. Budgets are passed in November and December for the following year, with supplementary spending passed in June, September, and December of each year. All budget outcomes are measured in terms of actual spending and officially released four months after the budget year concludes.

initial (pre-election) level for each budget outcome, as well as the pre-election total expenditures per year (logged). Unfortunately, such detailed procurement data on selection mechanisms are available only starting in 2011: for these models, I include only a control for pre-election total expenditures per year (logged).[43] The unit of analysis is a mayoral term and the forcing variable is the vote margin of the businessperson candidate, which ranges from -1 to 1 with a cutoff point of zero.

The model set-up is nearly identical to that used in Chapter 5. I show simple OLS models on the full sample, not restricting based on businessperson margin of victory, while alternately including covariates and fixed effects. The point estimates reflect basic correlations between having a businessperson serve as mayor and not, while excluding all municipalities that saw no businessperson candidates. Next, I restrict the sample to very close elections and show difference-in-means specifications among only those municipalities with intense electoral competition, including municipality type fixed effects included and standard errors clustered on region and year.

The RDD models estimate a local average treatment effect using a local-linear control function and two bandwidths on each side of the threshold: 5 percent and the optimal bandwidth $\hat{h}$ with bias-corrected robust confidence intervals calculated according to Calonico, Cattaneo, and Titiunik (2014). The specifications take the following form:

$$Y_i = \alpha_i + \beta * z_i + \gamma * f(Margin_i) + \eta * z_i * f(Margin_i) + Covariates_i + \epsilon_i \quad (6.1)$$

where Y_i is the outcome variable for municipality i, z_i is a binary treatment indicator for whether a businessperson mayoral candidate won or lost, $f(Margin_i)$ is the local-linear function interacted with the treatment to fit above and below the threshold, and *Covariates* is a vector of factors that influence government spending, including pre-election values. I calculate the municipality's dependence on subventions to fund the local budget, as dependence may constrain local political autonomy. I control for population size using the size of the voter list (logged), and include electoral turnout, the logged number of candidates, an indicator for the incumbent status of the businessperson candidate, and candidates' party membership. Municipal type fixed effects are included in all models, while region and year fixed effects (end of term) are used alongside covariates to capture differences in institutional arrangements and time shocks.

43 See the Appendix for summary statistics.

We saw in Chapter 5 that for the RDD to return a valid causal estimate, observations located around the cutoff point should not display signs of sorting. In other words, municipalities where businesspeople barely won and lost should not differ substantively beyond the outcome of the election. This assumption would, for example, be violated if businessperson candidates in certain municipalities engaged in fraud to tip close elections in their favor.

Just like at the regional level, anecdotal evidence suggests that such manipulations can occur in Russian mayoral elections, and largely take the form of administrative pressure directed against candidates from opposition parties.[44] For electoral fraud to undermine a design where professional background is the treatment, systematic evidence would be needed of businesspeople, regardless of partisanship, co-opting electoral processes. To test that this balance also holds for municipal elections, I run several validity checks. First, results from McCrary (2008) tests indicate that the assumption of continuity around the cutoff point of 0 is met. Although some mayoral candidates may benefit from electoral manipulations, these opportunities are not disproportionately allotted to businesspeople.

Next, I investigate whether there are specific characteristics of municipalities that predict whether businesspeople win or lose close elections. These placebo tests use the same specifications as above, except that the initial (election year) values of the outcome variables and covariates are regressed on the treatment. In the Appendix, I show the t-statistics from regressions on twenty placebo covariates using four model specifications. The covariates capture the size of municipality (budget expenditures and population), the economic situation at election time (given the lack of municipal GDP data, I use change in annual revenue and expansion of housing stock), the desirability of mayoral office (number of candidates), candidate characteristics and party membership, and pre-treatment budget subcategory spending. The t-statistics in the left panel are from specifications using OLS on narrow bandwidths while those in the right panel come from local-linear specifications using a 5 percent bandwidth for each outcome.

In none of the four specifications do the t-statistics exceed, or even approach, a value of two, which is generally accepted as the lower bound of statistical significance. In other words, businessperson politicians do not enjoy special advantages in close elections. This is not to claim that

44 Ross (2007).

elections at the municipal level are completely free and fair. But with regards to close elections involving businesspeople, the placebo specifications demonstrate that the continuity assumption required to validate the RDD is met. We do not see discontinuities related to deteriorating economic conditions nor specific political characteristics of municipalities around close elections involving businessperson candidates.

6.3 EMPIRICAL RESULTS

Figure 6.1 presents a graphical representation of the RDD treatment effects for the main outcomes: budget deficits, competitive procurement (all purchases), competitive procurement (construction purchases), and spending on economic infrastructure, health, and education. Each panel plots the residuals from a regression of the outcome averaged over the mayor's term controlling for pre-election values and municipality type fixed effects. The x-axis shows a 20 percent vote margin on each side of the threshold, with observations collapsed into bins of 1.5 percent (on average, bins include 30.6 observations). The solid lines represent the fitted values of a local linear regression estimated on each side of the threshold (zero margin of victory), with 95 percent confidence intervals shown in gray. The plots indicate two clear discontinuities: municipalities with mayors with private sector experience see greater spending on economic infrastructure and a smaller percentage of construction-related procurement being conducted using open auctions. The other outcomes are much more evenly distributed around the cutoff, suggesting that the absence of an effect from businessperson mayors.

To investigate further, Table 6.2 shows the regression results testing whether businessperson mayors adopt pro-business policies. In each panel, Columns 1 and 2 present simple OLS results for the full sample (shown as a benchmark for the RDD estimates), Column 3 narrows the bandwidth to 3 percent to calculate differences-in-means, and Columns 4 to 6 show local-linear RDD specifications using the 5 percent and the optimal CCT bandwidth (with and without controls). In other words, the left half of each panel uses simple OLS, while the right half shows causal estimates from the RDD specifications.

As shown in Panel A, Table 6.2, businessperson mayors increase spending on economic infrastructure. The magnitudes of the point estimates are large, statistically significant, and reflect a local average treatment effect. On average, municipalities led by a businessperson mayor spend an additional 6 to 7 percent of their budget on economic

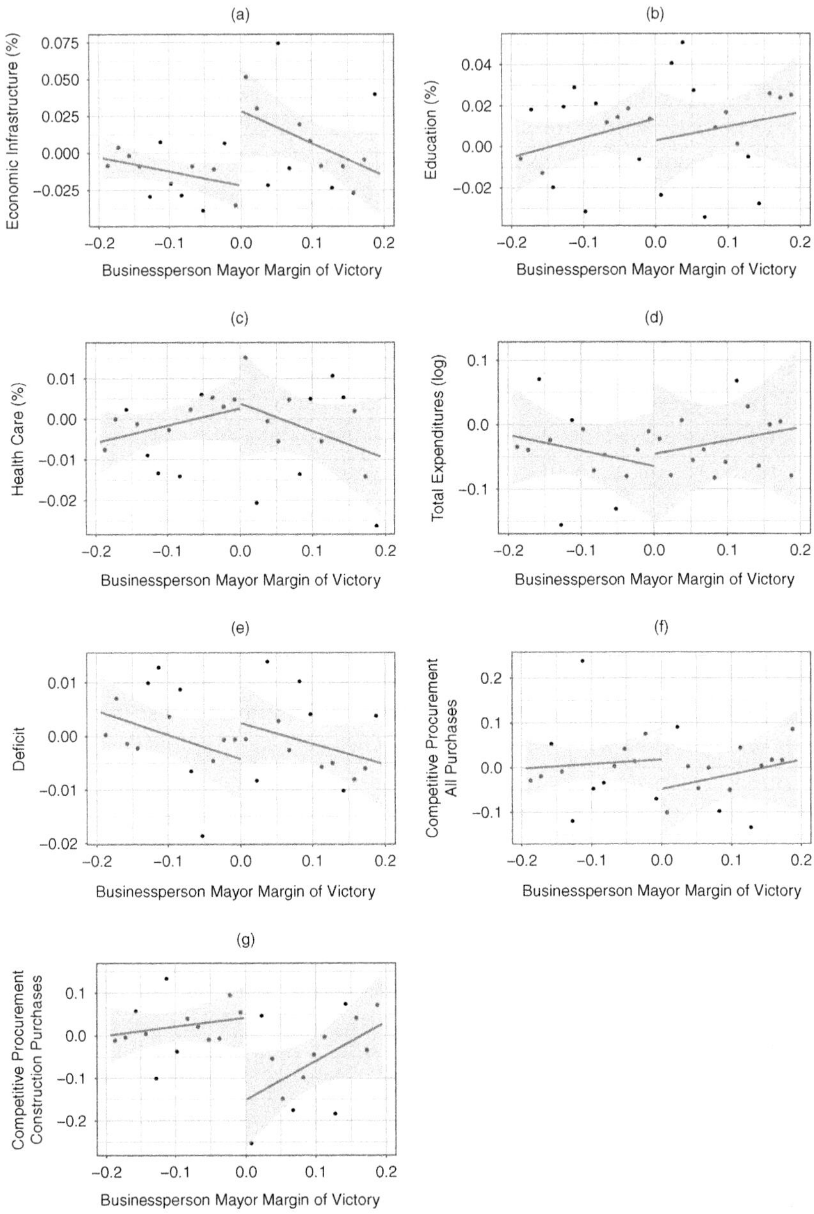

FIGURE 6.1: Municipal outcomes: RDD plots

The figure plots the binned residuals from regressing each outcome (averaged over the mayoral term) on pre-election values and municipality fixed effects; bins are calculated at 1.5% vote margin intervals. The solid lines represent the fitted values of a local linear regression estimated on each side of the threshold (zero margin of victory), with 95% confidence intervals shown in grey.

TABLE 6.2 *Adopting pro-business policies*

Panel A: Economic Infrastructure						
Control Function:	None (OLS)			Local Linear (RDD)		
Bandwidth:	Global		3%	5%	Optimal	
	(1)	(2)	(3)	(4)	(5)	(6)
Businessperson Mayor	0.003	0.005	0.061**	0.145**	0.067**	0.060***
	(0.004)	(0.005)	(0.024)	(0.062)	(0.026)	(0.023)
Bandwidth	1	1	0.03	0.05	0.2	0.21
Municipality Type FE	Yes	Yes	Yes	Yes	Yes	Yes
Covariates; Region, Year FE	No	Yes	No	No	No	Yes
Observations	1,548	1,525	54	86	406	417

Panel B: Education						
Control Function:	None (OLS)			Local Linear (RDD)		
Bandwidth:	Global		3%	5%	Optimal	
	(1)	(2)	(3)	(4)	(5)	(6)
Businessperson Mayor	0.004	0.004	−0.006	−0.006	−0.017	−0.009
	(0.005)	(0.006)	(0.020)	(0.053)	(0.019)	(0.018)
Bandwidth	1	1	0.03	0.05	0.24	0.25
Municipality Type FE	Yes	Yes	Yes	Yes	Yes	Yes
Covariates; Region, Year FE	No	Yes	No	No	No	Yes
Observations	1,075	1,063	44	67	361	368

(continued)

TABLE 6.2 *(continued)*

Panel C: Health

Control Function:	None (OLS)			Local Linear (RDD)		
Bandwidth:	Global		3%	5%	Optimal	
	(1)	(2)	(3)	(4)	(5)	(6)
Businessperson Mayor	0.001	−0.001	−0.007	0.006	−0.0001	0.002
	(0.003)	(0.003)	(0.010)	(0.021)	(0.009)	(0.009)
Bandwidth	1	1	0.03	0.05	0.2	0.21
Municipality Type FE	Yes	Yes	Yes	Yes	Yes	Yes
Covariates; Region, Year FE	No	Yes	No	No	No	Yes
Observations	1,069	1,045	46	73	299	298

Panel D: Total Expenditures

Control Function:	None (OLS)			Local Linear (RDD)		
Bandwidth:	Global		3%	5%	Optimal	
	(1)	(2)	(3)	(4)	(5)	(6)
Businessperson Mayor	−0.038	0.014	−0.024	0.232	0.036	0.055
	(0.023)	(0.023)	(0.115)	(0.262)	(0.096)	(0.099)
Bandwidth	1	1	0.03	0.05	0.25	0.26
Municipality Type FE	Yes	Yes	Yes	Yes	Yes	Yes
Covariates; Region, Year FE	No	Yes	No	No	No	Yes
Observations	2,260	2,204	90	149	802	797

**$p<0.05$; ***$p<0.01$ The panels examine the percentage of municipal expenditures dedicated to economic infrastructure (A), education (B), and health (C). Column D examines total municipal expenditures (logged in thousands of rubles). Columns 1–3 use standard OLS, while Columns 4–6 show RDD specifications with bias-corrected robust standard errors per Calonico, Cattaneo, and Titiunik (2014). Bandwidths are applied to each side of the threshold and standard errors are clustered on region.

infrastructure.[45] Businessperson mayors prioritize spending on issues that immediately help the broader business community.

Panels B and C of Table 6.2 then look at expenditures on social infrastructure, specifically health and education, finding that businessperson politicians do not prioritize investments in human capital. Expenditures on health care are generally unchanged upon a businessperson taking office, while there is only suggestive evidence that businesspeople cut spending on education. Similarly, businessperson mayors do not affect the total size of government (Panel D). The models return positive and negative point estimates that vary depending on specification and the controls included.

Table 6.3 examines whether businesspeople mayors improve government efficiency, as measured by budget deficits (Panel A), the percentage of all procurement using electronic auctions (Panel B), and the percentage of construction procurement using auctions (Panel C). First, there is no clear evidence that businesspeople impose more fiscal responsibility in their municipalities. Across the specifications, the point estimates fluctuate from positive to negative and none of the RDD estimates are statistically significant. The coefficients are not large, while using a binary indicator for a large deficit does not return substantively different estimates (see the Appendix). Businessperson mayors neither reduce the size of government, nor increase deficits. Moreover, there is no definitive evidence that they draw down spending on one area exclusively, such as education, health care, or culture. Instead, to fund economic infrastructure, businessperson mayors reallocate money from several other different subcategories, depending on the municipality.

The estimates in Panel B suggest that perhaps mayoral administrations run by businesspeople may be less likely to use electronic auctions to procure all their goods and services. The point estimates are mostly negative, but not statistically significant. However, when we analyze construction procurement (Panel C), the largest spending category and that most associated with corruption, we see a different story. When businesspeople become mayor, the percentage of corruption procurement conducted using electronic auctions falls roughly 20 percent. Businessperson mayors are not prioritizing transparency and competition in this

45 The point estimates on the OLS models may be smaller than those from the RDD may be because municipalities where businesspeople win with large margins may already spend more on economic infrastructure so the marginal effect is smaller from having a mayor with such a background win.

TABLE 6.3 *Improving government efficiency*

Panel A: Budget Deficit

Control Function:	None (OLS)			Local Linear (RDD)		
Bandwidth:	Global		3%	5%	Optimal	
	(1)	(2)	(3)	(4)	(5)	(6)
Businessperson Mayor	−0.002	−0.001	−0.001	0.001	0.004	0.007
	(0.002)	(0.002)	(0.008)	(0.018)	(0.006)	(0.007)
Bandwidth	1	1	0.03	0.05	0.24	0.2
Municipality Type FE	Yes	Yes	Yes	Yes	Yes	Yes
Covariates; Region, Year FE	No	Yes	No	No	No	Yes
Observations	2,148	2,104	84	141	716	556

Panel B: Competitive Procurement – All Purchases

Control Function:	None (OLS)			Local Linear (RDD)		
Bandwidth:	Global		3%	5%	Optimal	
	(1)	(2)	(3)	(4)	(5)	(6)
Businessperson Mayor	−0.018	0.001	−0.012	0.013	−0.001	−0.022
	(0.018)	(0.021)	(0.082)	(0.165)	(0.072)	(0.067)
Bandwidth	1	1	0.03	0.05	0.17	0.23
Municipality Type FE	Yes	Yes	Yes	Yes	Yes	Yes
Covariates; Region, Year FE	No	No	No	No	No	No
Observations	1,903	1,861	75	121	418	598

Panel C: Competitive Procurement – Construction Purchases

Control Function:	None (OLS)			Local Linear (RDD)		
Bandwidth:	Global		3%	5%	Optimal	
	(1)	(2)	(3)	(4)	(5)	(6)
Businessperson Mayor	−0.027	−0.014	−0.155**	−0.356*	−0.185***	−0.210***
	(0.019)	(0.023)	(0.074)	(0.197)	(0.063)	(0.063)
Bandwidth	1	1	0.03	0.05	0.22	0.22
Municipality Type FE	Yes	Yes	Yes	Yes	Yes	Yes
Covariates; Region, Year FE	No	No	No	No	No	No
Observations	1,662	1,625	65	101	495	477

*p<0.1; **p<0.05; ***p<0.01 Panel A examines the budget deficit in each municipality (the ratio of expenditures to revenue), Panel B examines the percentage of all contracts procured using electronic auctions, while Panel C examines the percentage of construction contracts procured using electronic auctions. Columns 1–3 use standard OLS, while Columns 4–6 show RDD specifications with bias-corrected robust standard errors per Calonico, Cattaneo, and Titiunik (2014). Bandwidths are applied to each side of the threshold and standard errors are clustered on region.

sector, instead giving bureaucrats discretion to use alternative selection mechanisms more prone to collusion and rent-seeking. As shown in the Appendix, the lower utilization of auctions is specific to procurement in the construction sector, and not evident among purchases of office supplies, food, or furniture, where available rents are lower.

The municipal analysis demonstrates that businessperson mayors do more to push a pro-business agenda than to improve government performance. These results are robust to controlling for the municipality's dependence on transfers as well as the party membership of the businessperson candidate. In the Appendix, I show additional evidence that institutional arrangements, such as the strength of democratic institutions and partisan alignment with governors, do little to constrain businessperson mayors from pushing their pro-business agendas. The absence of strong heterogenous effects suggests that businesspeople are adeptly able to navigate different types of government structures.

6.3.1 Robustness: Spending by Regional Legislatures

As an additional test of the main hypotheses, I also analyze data on Russian regional legislators. The advantages of studying a second level of government are multiple. Unlike municipalities, regional legislative and executive branches work together to pass budgets. Legislative committees have the resources and capacity to hold open hearings with stakeholders, reject line-items, add their own amendments, and even send budgets bill back to the executive for further changes.[46] Moreover, although regional legislatures engage in relatively little public procurement themselves, more detailed budget data are available, allowing me to investigate more precisely where money is directed and whether businesspeople affect the size of government through tax collection.

Greater parity between the two branches enables us to explore whether the ability of businesspeople to affect policy is specific to a certain institutional arrangement or role within government. When compelled to work together to pass legislation, businesspeople may not be able to solve key collective action problems involved with pushing for their shared interests. The previous chapter found that having multiple businesspeople in a single convocation served as a check on their individual ability to carve out rents for their firms. This section tests the related

[46] The chairman of the legislature in the Republic of Karelia noted that over 150 amendments to the budget are reviewed each year Levin (2003).

hypothesis that in these settings, a greater number of businesspeople in the legislator instead leads to more cooperative work to achieve community-wide goals of interest to firms across many sectors.

Data on annual regional budgets comes from the Federal Treasury and runs from 2008 to 2015.[47] First, I measure deficits through the ratio of expenditures to revenue. Regions have the added ability to issue commercial loans and bonds backed by state guarantees.[48] In the Appendix, I show results using data on this regional borrowing, including bond and loan issuances, to further probe how businesspeople affect deficit spending.

To measure pro-business policies, I look at how much money was spent on the subcategories of the national economy, health care, and education, as well as logged total expenditures. Each subcategory outcome is measured as a fraction of total expenditures (or for property taxes, total revenue) and take a values between 0 and 1. As the Appendix shows, regional legislatures vary in how they allocate money to different areas. Each of these budget outcomes is measured as a fraction of total expenditures (or for property taxes, total revenue) for that year and takes values between 0 and 1. Roughly equal shares of expenditures are devoted to the economy, health care, and education. I measure efficiency again through deficits, or the ratio of expenditures to revenue. Due to space constraints, I also show models in the Appendix that look at macro-level outcomes, such as the unemployment rate and public and private investment.

To measure the extent that businesspeople participate in the budget process, I combine the dataset analyzed in Chapter 2 (which covers the period of 2004–2011) with a database of candidacies for 2011–2016. For all legislators (either having won office pre- or post-2011), I first code whether they had a professional background in the private sector using data from their official registration forms. Next, I match legislators to entries they may have in an offline database on individual entrepreneurs that contains entries on whether they were active in the private sector. Unfortunately, because of the limitations on using the algorithm, I can only detect whether candidates from 2011 to 2015 worked in the private

[47] The period is restricted to these years due to changes in accounting in 2008. Chechnya and Ingushetia are excluded due to abnormal variability and unreliability in their budget data. There is significant variation in the way regional legislatures allocate money to different issue areas. The Appendix shows plots of spending distributions and summary statistics. Roughly equal shares of expenditures are devoted to the economy, health care, and education (between 15 and 20 percent per annum).

[48] Remington (2016).

sector, and not their individual firm connections. The main predictor is the percentage of all legislators that are businesspeople.

The unit of analysis is the region-year, with the main predictor lagged since budgets are set in the previous calendar year. Identifying exogenous sources of variation in successful businessperson candidacy at the regional level in Russia is challenging, if not impossible. Well-identified approaches that study legislator background take advantage of quota systems or quirks in proposal rules that introduce exogenous variation in the politicians that govern. No such institutions are present in Russia. Instead, I run OLS models with both region and year fixed effects. The estimates are underidentified, but account for between-region variation and time shocks that affect spending across Russia. In addition, I control for the lagged value for each outcome, total expenditures, gross regional product, population, urbanization, dependency on federal subsidies, indicators for the governor's party and business background, and the percentage of seats controlled by the ruling party. All models show standard errors clustered on region and year.

The results from the region level specifications echo the municipal analysis. A greater number of businessperson legislators is associated with additional money allocated to economic infrastructure, but not to health care or education. Further analysis breaks down national economy expenditures into subcategories and finds that the majority of the effect comes from more spending on transportation infrastructure. Although they only reflect correlations, the point estimates in Table 6.4 indicate a substantively large, statistically significant increase in spending on the economy (Columns 1 and 2) when more businesspeople take office. To put this number in perspective, take the median regional legislature in the dataset, made up of 45 legislators. For every additional businessperson in office, total spending on economic infrastructure increases by 1 percent (0.2 percentage points). This translates into an additional $950,000 in economic expenditures (at 31 rubles/dollar). A one standard deviation increase in the number of businessperson legislators, i.e. an extra six deputies with private sector experience, is associated with an increase in spending on the economy by roughly $5.7 million. Businesspeople serving in the legislative branch individually may exert less influence on the budget process than those who take up mayoral office, but collectively can get their interests heard.

Businesspeople also do little to make government run more efficiently (Columns 9 and 10), even potentially running up higher budget deficits. Since regional governments can tap credit markets for financing,

TABLE 6.4 *Region level: Budget size, deficit, and operational expenditures*

	Pro-Business								Pro-Efficiency	
	Econ. Expend. (%)		Education (%)		Health (%)		Total Spending (log)		Deficit (%)	
	(1)	(2)	(3)	(4)	(5)	(6)	(7)	(8)	(9)	(10)
Perc. Businesspeople	0.076***	0.064***	−0.022	−0.028	−0.014	−0.015	−0.056	−0.083	0.109*	0.110*
	(0.023)	(0.022)	(0.021)	(0.022)	(0.025)	(0.025)	(0.170)	(0.176)	(0.058)	(0.057)
Total Expenditures (log)	0.151***	0.147***	−0.065***	−0.067***	−0.031**	−0.027*			0.192***	0.205**
	(0.019)	(0.017)	(0.017)	(0.019)	(0.014)	(0.015)			(0.070)	(0.087)
GRP (log)		−0.009		0.026		−0.007		0.240***		−0.155*
		(0.019)		(0.025)		(0.016)		(0.080)		(0.090)
Population (log)		0.052		−0.105		0.0003		−0.203		−0.144
		(0.136)		(0.196)		(0.133)		(0.556)		(0.281)
Urbanization		−0.321		0.076		0.127		0.888		0.178
		(0.218)		(0.281)		(0.192)		(0.910)		(0.566)
Held Regional Election		−0.001		0.001		0.001		−0.00002		−0.0003
		(0.001)		(0.001)		(0.001)		(0.004)		(0.002)
Dependence on Subsidies		0.059		−0.059*		−0.034		0.205		−0.026
		(0.038)		(0.032)		(0.026)		(0.137)		(0.113)
UR Governor		−0.0002		0.004		−0.0005		−0.014		−0.003
		(0.007)		(0.007)		(0.005)		(0.019)		(0.010)
Businessperson Governor		0.010		0.009		0.003		0.032		0.005
		(0.007)		(0.006)		(0.004)		(0.020)		(0.011)
UR Control of Legislature		0.002		−0.003		−0.030		0.118**		0.034
		(0.018)		(0.024)		(0.025)		(0.059)		(0.026)
Region, Year Fixed Effects	Yes	Yes	Yes	Yes	Yes	Yes	Yes	Yes	Yes	Yes
Observations	640	640	640	640	640	640	640	640	640	640

*p<0.1; **p<0.05; ***p<0.01 Columns 1–6 examine ratios of different types of expenditures to revenue (the column headers indication the category), while Columns 7 and 8 examine total regional expenditures (thousands of rubles, logged). Columns 9 and 10 examine the deficit ratio as measured by

businessperson legislators take advantage and issue bonds. A greater presence of businessperson politicians may increase private and public investment, but the effects, though large, are not precisely estimated. Having businesspeople take office also does not lower the unemployment rate. Businessperson legislators favor the private sector by reducing the tax burden on all firms, as measured by revenue from the corporate property tax, one of the three taxes that regional governments have the authority over. In sum, the regional analysis confirms the findings from the municipal RDD: businessperson politicians do not change the size of government but find money (in this case, through bond issuances) to invest in economic rather than social infrastructure.

6.4 CONCLUDING REMARKS

Citizen-candidate models argue that voters take into account the personal characteristics of candidates when making their vote choice.[49] This chapter demonstrated that their reasoning is correct: having experience in the private sector results in politicians setting priorities that advantage the business community, while doing little to improve how government works. This raises significant questions about representation and accountability:[50] are voters' interests being properly represented when businesspeople help themselves in power? Interpreted in isolation, the results presented here could suggest that businessperson politicians are allocating spending towards the issues that voters care about and are truly focused on improving the economy. For example, roads in Russia are of particularly low quality and voters may be electing these businesspeople precisely to pass budgets that fix the problem.

Taken together, the evidence in this chapter suggests a different dynamic at work: businessperson politicians in Russia are prioritizing policies of most importance to their own community. Large-N surveys from 2009 to 2011 indicate that roads rank no higher than seventh on a ranking of the fifteen most pressing local problems, trailing issues like housing, health care, alcoholism and drugs, corruption, high prices, and unemployment (see the Appendix). Another 2016 survey of 400,000 companies revealed that poor road construction was one of three primary obstacles to doing business (alongside corruption and bureaucratic

49 Besley and Coate (1997); Osborne and Slivinski (1996).
50 Pitkin (1967); Przeworski, Stokes, and Manin (1999).

inspections). Businesspeople in Russia see government service as an opportunity to fix the problems they care most about.

In line with research on US cities,[51] this chapter also finds that different types of governing institutions do little to affect how mayors and legislators affect policy. The cohesive preferences and outcomes achieved by businesspeople are even more impressive considering the heterogeneous set of industries and financial interests they represent. Although businessperson deputies may check each another's ability to secure individual rents from office, collectively a greater proportion of deputies from the private sector leads to policy more aligned with the overall business community. From a corruption standpoint, this is an improvement. But from a political representation standpoint, businesspeople are still potentially putting their own interests about their constituents. The final chapter explores potential policy recommendations for solving that problem.

[51] de Benedictis-Kessner and Warshaw (2016).

7

Conclusion and Policy Recommendations

My primary motivation for writing this book grew out of observing the sharply intertwined fates of Russian companies and politicians in the post-Soviet period. Success in one world seemed to depend on success in the other, with often times the line in between so blurry as to be invisible. In the case of Aleksandr Shpeter and the Tomsk Housing Construction Company, the absence of that line was essential to surviving and prospering under intense competition and an existential financial crisis. My goal has not just been to show that political connections matter for firms, but to investigate who tries to acquire them, how they go about doing so, and how this affects the lives of regular citizens. All said and done, the news is not encouraging. Firms benefit substantially from their directors entering political institutions, while voters' priorities get upstaged by those of the business community.

Businesspeople recognize and seize these opportunities to directly influence policymaking partly because so-called professional politicians have let them down in the past. The large number of businesspeople running for elected office express genuine frustration with elected politicians failing to adequately represent their interests. As economic competition grows fierce and parties fail to constrain unreliable politicians, the best way to gain and protect political advantages is for a CEO to become a politician herself. This book has introduced and unpacked a strategy available to firms that previous work on representation of economic interests mostly ignores, i.e., directly holding political office rather than using the more conventional (and studied) avenues for gaining favorable policies. When professional politicians cannot be trusted to hold up their end of the representation bargain, outsider candidates see a chance to supplant them in elected office.

This concluding section serves two functions. First, I explore the potential for the book's main arguments to travel to countries beyond Russia and the post-Soviet world. In the Introduction, I made the case that Russia offers a series of compelling advantages for studying issues related to businessperson candidacy. This book drew on extensive subnational variation to develop a general theory of the how and why of businessperson candidacy. However, we have close to zero theoretical nor empirical studies of this phenomenon from other countries around the world. And for all its advantages, Russia still displays several unique features that may limit the external validity of the main analysis. Below I draw out the main scope conditions for when interest groups will be most likely to face risks of politician shirking as well as the settings under which businesspeople are most capable of reshaping government to work for their own interests.

Finally, the book concludes with an extended discussion of the actions policymakers and citizens can take to manage the conflicts of interests that businesspeople bring with them into political office. In doing so, I lay out a menu of policy options, both new and old, drawing on the literature on revolving door politics.[1] Which policies best balance the trade-off between attracting qualified businesspeople to run for election and curbing their ability to misuse their office?

I argue that priority should be placed on creating distance between businesspeople and their firms when they take office. This can best be achieved by prohibiting outside jobs or income among active politicians, forcing divestiture of ownership stakes in firms, and requiring recusals when public duties and private interests overlap. But the regulation of conflicts of interest cannot stop after a politician has taken office. Annual disclosures must go beyond individual assets and encompass all companies politicians were connected to beforehand. Standards need to be developed for connected companies to make public their financial statements and relations with government when previous directors are in political office. These measures would still allow businesspeople to run for office, but help select out those that are there for the wrong reasons, and prevent the misuse of political power.

[1] I use Transparency International's definition of the revolving door as the "movement of individuals from government to the private sector and from the private sector to government" David-Barrett (2011).

7.1 TAKING THE ARGUMENTS TO THE ROAD

The central argument in this book is that businesspeople run for political office when the risk of politician shirking is high. Developing the trust required to enforce informal agreements requires repeated interactions over time between stable actors,[2] something that is hard to develop where politicians regularly change parties and care little about long-term reputations. As a result, we should expect businesspeople candidacy to be a more prevalent non-market strategy in countries where cooperation between firms and politicians breaks down.

Several types of institutions fit the bill for such a scenario. For example, countries undergoing political and/or economic transitions, for example from closed to open societies (and vice versa), often see a parade of political actors and parties, and a high degree of political uncertainty about future governments.[3] Politicians shift easily from one grouping to another, depending on which direction the political winds are headed. The list of countries witnessing such unstable allegiances is long, including Brazil, Italy, Japan, Ecuador, Nepal, and the Philippines.[4] On the other hand, the development of strong parties helps provide assurances to interest groups of all types that they can expect reliable representation. We should see the severity of the commitment problem lessened in countries where political parties are concerned with their longterm reputations and ideological cohesion, and that take steps to block outsider candidates from reaching the ballot.[5]

Other forms of collective action also could do much to deter politician shirking. When firms can pool their financial resources and reach consensus on collective political objectives, politicians have a much harder time defecting from agreements and deploying a divide-and-conquer strategy towards the business community. Theoretically, business associations could play a leading role in building trust and long-term relationships between companies and individual leaders. A key scope condition is then the degree to which economic elites can act as a cohesive bloc to channel their instrumental power to influence economy policymaking.[6] Although many business associations operate on paper in Russia, the

[2] Großer, Reuben, and Tymula (2013).

[3] Kenyon and Naoi (2010); Petrova and H. Bates (2012); Schedler (2013).

[4] See for example: Desposato (2006); Heller and Mershon (2005); Mershon and Shvetsova (2008). Countries undergoing economic transitions also may see political connections increase in value (Hellman, 1998; Szakonyi and Urpelainen, 2014).

[5] Levitsky and Ziblatt (2018).

[6] Fairfield (2015); Hacker and Pierson (2011).

level of interfirm coordination is still rather low, especially among small and medium-sized businesses working outside of urban centers. Similar weaknesses in organizing collective action among firms have been noted in prominent emerging markets across Latin America, Africa, and Southeast Asia.[7] On the other hand, Yadav and Mukherjee (2015) and Fairfield (2015) identify a number of countries where businesses have enjoyed much more success banding together to push for their collective interests. By preventing market competition from spilling over into the political arena, firms can economize on political expenditures and keep their directors in the roles they are best suited for: management.

Another view holds that strengthening democracy and improving electoral accountability could deter businessperson candidacy. This book has challenged this story, arguing that relations between politicians and firms matter more than those between politicians and voters. Indeed, a variety of evidence demonstrates that the level of subnational democratization in Russia is unrelated to business participation in elections. This variation in democratic institutions needs to be taken seriously. Although Russia has become undoubtably more authoritarian under Vladimir Putin, the businesspeople analyzed here are clearly not plucked into power by an autocrat from above. We have seen them expend vast resources to win competitive, unpredictable elections at multiple levels, and often join political parties genuinely opposed to Putin's rule.

For broader comparison, roughly 10 to 15 percent of the legislatures studied in this book are located in Russian regions classified as electorally democratic as the Philippines.[8] This suggests that businesspeople are not deterred by having to compete in fair elections or conform to stronger democratic norms. In fact, the cross-national statistics shown in the Introduction indicate that democracy and businessperson candidacy are by no means incompatible. Kohli (2012, p. 42) writes that severe concentration of wealth in India "enables businessmen to 'buy' politicians, shape decision-making through the media, and even enter politics themselves." That influence has co-opted the state to slant pro-business rather than pro-market. And recent work on the United States has uncovered not only substantial numbers of corporate executives serving in high-level national office, but stock

[7] Schneider (2013).

[8] See Saikkonen (2015). Parliaments in regions considered more democratic are even slightly more likely to be populated by businessmen, at a rate of about 40 percent compared to that of 36 percent in the non-democratic sample.

markets rewarding firms for their connections to these policymakers.[9] How broadly democratic a country is may matter less than the varieties of collective action available to constrain politicians and organize business.

Much of this discussion so far has concerned the many incentives for businesspeople to run for office. But costs matter as well. With popular membership declining and official state funding often inadequate, political parties are looking more and more to wealthy individual patrons to finance campaign activities. The presence of wealthy businesspeople in higher office may even be trending upwards, as the increased costs of mounting campaigns limit the number of private citizens who can afford to fund them.[10] Much may depend on how readily countries pass laws mandating public financing of political parties. If parties are relieved of the burden of raising money from private individuals and corporations, fewer deputies spots need be allotted in exchange. The more countries rely on private financing for elections, the higher the likelihood that economic elites will seize the opportunities to outspend their opponents and catapult themselves into office on the back of their financial resources.

Yet there may be limits to this luxurious spending, and another scope condition comes in the form of economic development. As countries grow richer, the opportunity costs of running for office may lead to decreased interest among businesspeople in running for office. Serving in office can be very taxing on individual firm directors in terms of time and money, not to mention the added political pressure and media exposure from occupying a public position. Companies may begin outsourcing their political needs to lobbying firms not only because of the perceived effectiveness of such efforts to influence politicians, but because firm directors can no longer play so many roles simultaneously. Complicated management duties combined with attractive executive compensation could lessen both the feasibility and appeal for businesspeople to play politician. Therefore, we should expect the prevalence of businessperson candidacy to be most prominent in middle and low-income countries, where the costs of running for office are not prohibitively high, and the structure of electoral systems incentivizes the entry of high net worth individuals.

[9] Babenko, Fedaseyeu, and Zhang (2018).
[10] Barndt (2014); Yadav (2011).

7.2 DESIGNING EFFECTIVE POLICY

Businesspeople entering politics generate clear conflicts of interest. In office, they regularly make policy decisions that affect the financial performance of both their individual assets and their firms. Just the presence of a conflict of interest need not result in impartial decision-making or wrongdoing. What matters is how the political actor addresses the degree of incompatibility. As Gong and Ren (2013, p. 5) write, a conflict of interest is a "necessary rather than sufficient condition of corruption." Some businessperson politicians voluntarily take steps to prevent their own personal interests from bleeding over into policymaking. The commitment of these "good types" is to uphold and promote the public good. But as we have seen, many capitalize on the political access they have secured to help themselves.

Countries around the world have acknowledged the pitfalls that conflicts of interest present for governance. As of 2017, nearly all national governments have instituted some kind of system to identity situations that present a risk of actual or perceived conflict of interest for politicians, following a frenzied diffusion worldwide in the 2000s.[11] Conflict of interest (COI) systems "seek to prohibit legislators from receiving any benefit that may clash with their service of the public interest."[12] Policy approaches generally aim to achieve two main prophylactic objectives: (1) preventing individuals' conflicts of interest from influencing policy and (2) preventing illegal self-enrichment. Below I connect our knowledge about how the handful of these policies work with the specific challenge of designing regulations to weed out the "good" from the "bad" types of businessperson politicians.[13]

Attracting the right kind of businesspeople to run for office raises all sorts of issues. Simply elevating the barriers to entry for businesspeople running for office can be counterproductive. If the aim is to reduce self-serving behavior among politicians, then placing obstacles in front of all businesspeople risks throwing the baby out with the bathwater. Even if individuals with private sector experience do not have all the answers for solving problems within the bureaucracy, this by no means suggests they have no place in political office. Government has become more specialized and complicated over time, requiring skilled individuals to run it.

[11] Rossi, Pop, and Berger (2017).
[12] NDI (1999).
[13] Besley (2005); Caselli and Morelli (2004); Mansbridge (2009).

Businesspeople bring with them real knowledge about the way the economy works, much of which could theoretically lead to improvements in governance. Having proximate expertise to issues helps an individual identify the highest quality ideas and methods, even if some bias leaks into the decision-making process.[14] From government investment strategy to restructuring bureaucracy, businesspeople have the potential to make solid contributions to public service and facilitate better communication between the public and private sectors. The challenge is identifying individuals who will not also approach government service with purely selfish motives.

7.2.1 Cooling-Off versus Moonlighting

The first question that arises in debates about regulating businesspeople in politics concerns what to do with their formal roles within companies. Businesspeople are often attached to the firms they have helped build and only reluctantly give up the strings to pursue other career goals. Countries vary widely in how they approach this delicate subject. Some err on the side of strict caution, passing laws that effectively block managers of certain firms from holding elected office. Others adopt a much more lenient approach and allow outside jobs and income. This section outlines the different ways governments handle this delicate issue of deciding what private sector connections businessperson politicians can keep. Although empirical studies about the effectiveness of all the approaches are still few, I develop a set of recommendations that best navigate the trade-off of attracting qualified candidates, while managing their conflicts of interest.

In some respects, businessperson political candidacy is the odd man out in the growing literature on the revolving door in politics. Very little attention is paid to "pre-public employment," e.g. the background of candidates prior to entering government. Instead, the academic and policy worlds tend to focus on "post-public employment," that is, the career choices of political officials after they leave office.[15] Private companies and lobbying outfits greatly value former government workers for their expertise and personal contacts inside of government.[16] In the United States, congressional staffers and regulators enjoy incredible demand

[14] Li (2017).
[15] Martini (2015).
[16] LaPira and Thomas (2014); Blanes i Vidal, Draca, and Fons-Rosen (2012); Coen and Vannoni (2016); Lucca, Seru, and Trebbi (2014).

from private sector employers who dangle salaries twice those offered by the government as well as much more comfortable working conditions.[17] A growing body of research demonstrates that the returns to hiring former lawmakers and regulators can be immensely profitable for private companies.[18]

Some lessons for businessperson candidacy can be learned from all this attention given to post-public employment. The most common policy thought to throw a wrench in the revolving door is the "cooling-off period." Cooling-off periods designate a set amount of time (generally 1–3 years) whereby public officials must delay taking private sector positions that are directly related to the responsibilities they held in government. Not surprisingly, governments vary considerably in the type of restrictions they place on former officials. Norwegian politicians cannot enter the private sector for six months after leaving office, while politicians in the United Kingdom must only refrain from all lobbying activities for two years.[19] China has gone even further, prohibiting government officials from engaging in any business related to their official responsibilities for a three year period following their departure from government.[20] By requiring lawmakers to "cool off" from government service, the hope is that the value of their political connections and knowledge will decay and not unjustly benefit the companies that would like to immediately capitalize on their experience in power. There is emerging evidence that these laws have some impact: the one-year cooling-off period passed under the Honest Leadership and Open Government Act (HLOGA) in 2007 reduced the number of former U.S. congressional staffers that went on to become lobbyists.[21]

Laws regulating the opposite movement – businesspeople into politics – could draw on these experiences. For example, any candidate to office would have to demonstrate that they have not worked for a for-profit entity for some designated amount of time prior to beginning their campaign. A cooling-off period for businesspeople would enforce the boundary between an individual's private sector interests and political

[17] Cain and Drutman (2014).

[18] Luechinger and Moser (2014).

[19] Martini (2015).

[20] Gong and Ren (2013).

[21] See Cain and Drutman (2014). In addition, no fewer than 30 US states have passed variants of cooling-off period legislation that require lawmakers and staffers to step away from politics and delay registering as lobbyists after leaving public office (Wang, 2016). Evidence about the effectiveness of these laws is still lacking.

public sector obligations,[22] helping to select out candidates that sought political access to benefit companies in which they retained an active role. This type of move would not be without precedent. Countries such as Austria, France, and Greece explicitly block directors and board members from running for parliament if their firms have any transactions with the state.[23] The OECD counts six other member countries which closely monitor the recruitment of individuals coming from the private sector and block certain candidates if conflicts of interests carry too much liability.[24]

Requiring businesspeople to completely step away from their companies, either for a set amount of time or through divestment, would create a strong deterrent for businesspeople expressing interest in politics, both those with noble intentions of public service and those seeking to use politics to help their companies. Although a cooling-off period might enable businesspeople to gain political experience before embarking on a political career (such as by working for a think tank or non-governmental organization), it would be unrealistic to expect prominent CEOs to give up their business empires just for the opportunity to run for election. No matter how experienced or wealthy these businessperson candidates may be, these resources are no guarantee of electoral victory. Who would sacrifice their past business success for an electoral lottery ticket?

Implementing a cooling-off period for businesspeople also raises many questions about enforcement. How would experience in the private sector be evaluated during the "pre-public" period? Many of the most pointed critiques of the current US laws on cooling off bemoan the abundance of loopholes available to crafty political officials looking to avoid "post-public" bans, from manipulating their salary to carefully managing their lobbying behavior.[25] European countries have not fared much better, as more and more officials have learned how to evade bans and enter the private sector immediately after their terms in government are over.[26] Governments that enter the perilous game of regulating individuals' labor choices can become exceptionally bureaucratic and overcomplicated.

In all, asking businesspeople to step back completely from their economic activities *prior to* entering politics would be both impractical and misguided. Enforcement would create potentially insurmountable

[22] Wang (2016).
[23] Braendle and Stutzer (2016).
[24] OECD (2015).
[25] Lipton and Protess (2014).
[26] Martini (2015); Zinnbauer (2015).

headaches. And banning businesspeople completely from running would lead to a scarcity of human capital working in government, especially in countries without established civil services.[27] Both absolute bans and cooling-off periods run the real risk of deterring the best people from entering public service. The requirements to enter government would be too burdensome.

Milder approaches are available. Some countries have tried allowing politicians to maintain their connections to businesses, but under government supervision. Businesspeople are not the only political figures who want to remain connected to their profession while in government. Politicians often receive outside earnings by practicing law, giving speeches or lectures, or serving on the boards of associations or unions. Geys and Mause (2013, p. 1) employ the term "moonlighting" to refer to "any paid or honorary outside job executed by a politician in addition to his/her 'job' inside parliament and/or government." In the United States, incompatibility laws introduced first during the Kennedy administration allow outside jobs but only if they do not conflict with officials' duties.[28] Many European countries treat moonlighting similarly.[29] Cross-national evidence suggests a substantial proportion of national-level legislators moonlight, ranging from 48 percent of the Norwegian parliament to nearly 100 percent of MPs in the two houses of the Swiss Federal Assembly.[30] Nolan (1992) cautions that prohibitions on outside income may punish the innocent, who rely on moonlighting to make ends meet.

However, allowing businesspeople to continue to operate their businesses without constraint raises real risks of self-enrichment running amok. This is the case in places such as New York State, where lax rules about outside work may have contributed to outrageous corruption scandals involving the former speaker of the State Assembly Sheldon Silver, among others.[31] And as Chapter 5 showed, altogether ignoring the reality that unmonitored businesspeople will work to help their firms while in office can lead to astonishingly biased outcomes in favor of the politically connected. Survey evidence suggests that the public (at least in the UK)

[27] Feintzeig (2014). *The Economist* (2016).

[28] See Koffsky (1995); Nolan (1992). Only certain high-level employees are prohibited from earning any outside earned income, largely due to concerns about side jobs distracting from their primary roles.

[29] Fedele and Naticchioni (2016); Staat and Kuehnhanss (2017).

[30] Geys and Mause (2013).

[31] Kolhatkar (2016).

comes out strongly against allowing politicians to work as firm directors while in office.[32]

If the goal is to continue to attract the most qualified candidates, then governments have to demonstrate both flexibility with regards to backgrounds, but also stringency about how conflicts of interest are managed. Here Russia, at least on paper at the federal level, has made a step in the right direction. Businesspeople are allowed to run for office for the national parliament (the State Duma), but they must halt all connections with their firms upon taking office. Being caught directing any business activities is grounds for removal from office. Questions about the selective enforcement of that law still linger, but the motivation behind it is warranted. Deputies simply do not respond in commendable ways to being allowed to take on second jobs. Their attention to lawmaking suffers,[33] and their commitment to upholding the public interest falls. Keeping one foot in the private sector may provide some "survival insurance" after they leave office,[34] but also may lay the groundwork for much of the corruption feared in their post-public employment.[35]

Therefore, best practice would be to allow businesspeople to run for office, but place strict limitations on what they can do with their time while in office. Strong incompatibility rules need to create obstacles that limit the extent conflicts of interest (and time) can corrupt how officials make decisions and provide public services. At a minimum, officials must step down from any positions in companies, whether as manager or on the board of directors. No lawmaker should be allowed to simultaneously hold positions in the private and public sectors. Accordingly, elected officials should be not be allowed to earn outside income that originates in private companies, whether it be through consulting contracts, honoraria from speeches, or other avenues. Because of the difficulties identifying whether compensation is being offered for political favors, state officials in general should not be allowed to earn income on the side while in office, no matter the source of their employment. Anything less invites opportunities for moonlighting and special interest representation that fuels corrupt exchanges.

While in office, businesspeople should also abide by stronger rules on disqualification that require them to step aside from decision-making

32 Campbell and Cowley (2015).

33 Arnold, Kauder, and Potrafke (2014); Hurka, Obholzer, and Daniel (2019).

34 Geys and Mause (2013); Norris (1996).

35 Eggers and Hainmueller (2009); Palmer and Schneer (2016).

that could affect potentially their former employers. For example, businessperson deputies should not be allowed to chair committees that address legislation directly related to their firms' business activities. Officials should be forced to recuse themselves from any decision that affects firms they have had a financial interest in, as is the case of some executive branch officials in the United States.[36] For example, ethics officials in Canada required Finance Minister Paul Martin to disqualify himself from any decisions pertaining to maritime transportation; before taking office, Martin had built a massive private shipping company, which was placed in a trust run by relatives.[37] Enforcing these rules will not be simple, but I discuss more below about how mandating disclosures and strengthening sanctions together may help tilt the scales towards ethics offices.

7.2.2 Divesting Assets

Beyond debates about how businessperson deputies should spend their time in office, an even thornier question arises with what to do with their assets. Once again, opinions diverge about how best to approach the subject, and we have surprisingly little empirical evidence to date about what works. In general, policy approaches fall into two camps. On one end, some countries force officials to divest their ownership stakes in any companies deemed to present a conflict of interest with their future responsibilities in government. Other governments take a gentler tact and advise incoming officials to place their assets in blind trusts or even do nothing beyond disclosing them.[38] Which approach better fulfills the dual objectives of attracting qualified professionals to serve in government, while also limiting the potential fallout of the inevitable conflicts of interest that arise? First, I articulate both sides of the debate.

Divestiture laws require that candidates submit pre-election forms that detail their financial assets in privately and publicly held companies. Ethics offices review these documents, identify assets that could create conflicts of interest, and require officials to sell them before taking office. In the United States, these requirements are usually only applicable to

36 Cain, Alisson, and Mark (2008).

37 Stark (2008).

38 Members of the US Congress are under no obligation to either divest or use blind trusts, but must submit documentation every year under the STOCK act about their securities trading (Hall et al., 2017).

appointed executive branch officials such as cabinet members,[39] while Australia, New Zealand, and Canada apply the statute to a much broader set of public officials.[40] Many other occupations place such demands on their members. Business journalists and bankers in the United States, for example, abide by strict regulations about the type of securities that can own to allay concerns that their reporting and analysis is self-motivated. A candidate stepping away and divesting from their business interests would demonstrate to the public that conflicts of interest do not influence their policy decisions. This commitment would let business-people send a strong signal that they are entering politics for the right reasons.

The main alternative to complete divestiture takes the form of a blind trust. Rather than forcing politicians to sell their assets, blind trusts freeze their access to them. Blind trusts require officials to place ownership stakes into a fund run by independent trustees who make investment decisions on the officials' behalf but without their knowledge or input. Officials cannot act on potentially economically valuable information they are privy to in their public role, but which is not available more broadly.[41] In the United States, for example, the legislative foundation for blind trusts was formalized in 1978 under the Ethics in Government Act, which stipulates that executive branch officials will receive no information about the trusts' financial performance except for quarterly updates on cash value needed for tax purposes.[42] To some experts, blind trusts are "the best way to avoid the appearance of a conflict of interest between a politician's personal investments and the public interest that an official is charged to serve."[43]

Our understanding of whether blind trusts achieve their objective is limited. What we know comes from the federal level in the United States where most presidents (and would-be presidents) have used some kind of trust to hold their assets since the 1960s. Skepticism about their effectiveness is rife. Take the case of former Presidential Candidate Mitt Romney, whose personal lawyer and longtime friend Bradford Malt was put in charge of running the blind trust.[44] Did that relationship demonstrate

39 Maskell (2014).
40 Stark (2008); Bertók (2003).
41 Stark (2008).
42 Purdum (2012).
43 Purdum (2007). Center for Responsive Politics (2007).
44 Romney was also quoted himself as declaring "The blind trust is an age-old ruse." As cited in Purdum (2012).

enough distance from the politician? Blind trusts also shield the public from knowing their contents and how their being managed, another potential drawback if concerns over the independence of trustees arise.[45] The more public that information is, the more the politicians that benefit from blind trusts would have an idea about how their money is being managed. For example, for well-known politicians, the sales of many of their most high-profile assets would be widely covered in the media, thereby violating the "blind" in blind trust.[46] And less than 4 percent members of the US Congress choose to employ them at all, giving use a weak evidence base for evaluation.[47]

Given these drawbacks, the best solution is to require divestiture of ownership stakes. Indeed, many countries have already started down this track, requiring high-level elected and appointed officials to sell any individual assets they own that could be directly related to their official duties. The US ethics code, which generally is viewed as the strongest among developed countries, already outlines specific prohibitions on owning assets for administrators in the Federal Aviation Administration (ban on financial interests in aeronautical enterprises), National Indian Gaming Commission (ban on financial interests in gambling enterprises), and Office of Surface Mining Reclamation and Enforcement (ban on financial interests in coal mining enterprises).[48] Even without specific laws, many high-level officials divest voluntarily from asses that might present conflicts. John Kerry sold nearly 100 investments in foreign assets upon taking office as Secretary of State.[49] Perhaps after having received criticism for hypocrisy between his rhetoric over campaign finance and personal behavior,[50] President Obama restructured his investment portfolio to only include index funds and treasury bills.[51] Mandating divestitures of other appointees based on their future duties would be both practical and effective. Forcing politicians to divest ownership stakes could may result in some personal financial losses, but this is a reasonable price to pay to ensure that politicians only act in the public's, and not their own, interest.

45 Rosica (2014).
46 Casselman (2017).
47 Vandermey and Rapp (2012). "Who Needs a Blind Trust?" Fortune. October 22.
48 Maskell (2014).
49 Bender (2013).
50 McIntire and Drewmarch (2007).
51 Shear (2010).

7.2.3 Mandating Transparency and Calling Citizens to Action

Bans on working in the private sector are a clear and urgent necessity. Businesspeople should be required to step back from all management positions upon taking office, as well as divest from companies upon taking office. But even with these laws, strong transparency requirements are needed to ensure that they are not skirting enforcement, identifying loopholes, and engaging in self-enrichment. Only by demanding full and regularly updated information from politicians about their financial dealings can the general public have any chance at mitigating the risks of state capture. Around the world, the most prevalent way to impose this transparency are income and asset disclosures (IAD) systems. IAD laws generally cover both causes of concern for businessperson politicians. First, they require officials to report all sources of income and business ties, which would bring to the surface any paid directorships or board memberships. Second, many countries also require disclosure of personal assets, liabilities, and expenditures, as well as sometimes those of family members.[52] As of 2017, 161 of 176 countries have instituted some kind of asset declaration law, up from 109 in 2010.[53] Several factors explain their diffusion across states and governments, from scandals that prompt government action to policy learning, diffusion, and the growing strength of the global anti-corruption movement.[54]

Asset disclosures help mitigate the damage caused by conflicts of interest through two mechanisms: prevention and enforcement. By compelling officials to open up their finances before taking office, these laws highlight areas where action needs to be taken immediately (e.g. by requiring divestitures or individuals to step down from their private sector positions). Secondly, IAD systems facilitate the "detection and prosecution of illegal enrichment by public officials" by providing unique evidence to authorities to bring corrupt officials to justice.[55] Officials can flag changes in wealth over time and cross-check the information in disclosures against other independent sources, such as car and real estate registries or tax statements.[56] These high hopes for

52 Habershon and Trapnell (2012); Rossi, Pop, and Berger (2017); Szakonyi (2020).
53 Djankov et al. (2010).
54 Mackenzie (2002); Rosenson (2005); OECD (2011).
55 Habershon and Trapnell (2012).
56 Bank (2013).

asset declarations lead some experts to believe that "the single most important preventive tool for combating money laundering and corruption is the registering of officials' assets and income."[57] Leading international institutions have developed a set of best practices for countries to adapt to their own context, from determining which officials should be covered to how sanctions for non-compliance should be administered.[58]

Citizens must also be able to track how the performance of politically connected firms and identify potential abuses of privilege. This implies that for businesspeople taking office, the firms they managed beforehand should be liable to additional reporting requirements. The US Stop Trading on Congressional Knowledge (STOCK) Act, although imperfect, provides a good starting point for how such a disclosure system could be constructed. The STOCK Act not only prohibits insider trading among nationally elected US officials, but also mandates lawmakers to file regular reports (available online) about any trades they make. Research has shown that even considering the law's many weaknesses and loopholes, it significantly reined in transaction volumes among sitting Congressmen and women, many of whom raised eyebrows before the additional transparency measures were taken.[59] Instituting similar requirements for all firms, publicly and privately owned, managed by sitting politicians could have similarly beneficial effects. We should require politically connected firms to report similarly detailed data on their performance and contracting with government agencies when current and former politicians are in office.

But more fundamentally, there must be receptive audiences ready to use this information to achieve their own goals. Without active monitoring, just mandating transparency can enable "moral licensing" whereby individuals who reveal potential of conflicts feel more emboldened in their behavior since they have come clean initially.[60] For corrupt officials, this unshackling may be even greater if they believe authorities are incapable of expertly analyzing the disclosures and holding them accountable. Information quickly falls by the wayside when no one pays attention: a government can require millions of its officials to declare

57 Chaikin and Sharman (2009).
58 OECD (2011); Habershon and Trapnell (2012).
59 Public Citizen (2017).
60 Cain, Loewenstein, and Moore (2005).

their assets, but if no one processes and analyzes the data, this heightened level of transparency is useless.

The media and even regular citizens play a huge role in using disclosures to keep officials honest. Disclosure forms are a "mother lode" for investigative reporting.[61] But legislation in many countries does not even require disclosures to be made available to the wider public.[62] Even when declarations are made public, citizens also express alarmingly little interest in their contents, as evidence by the puny number of requests filed to view the forms of top US officials.[63] Efforts must be taken to make disclosure information as quickly and effortlessly as possible for people to access, analyze, and use.

The primary "end users" of the data do not necessarily have to be voters in society. Relevant government authorities require resources and permission to cross-check between various sources, and bureaucratic rules are often underspecified to facilitate these information flows.[64] Tax agencies should use the information to identify instances where politicians are evading the law and hiding income. Civil society activists should flag instances of unexplained income or firm performance, helping draw attention to abuses of power. And political parties should invest their own resources into opposition research that helps uncover illicit behavior of both candidates to and politicians currently serving in office. The information revealed in the asset disclosures is highly compatible with each of these end users' decision-making routines,[65] providing a catalyst for tough sanctions for corrupt politicians, whether through the legal system or the ballot box.

The public appeal of candidates boasting of their business credentials has never been higher. Many candidates are campaigning hard on the connection between their private sector know-how and their ability to generate economic growth in elected office. In recent years, businesspeople have taken the reins of many national government running on platforms of stimulating slumping national economies by running government like a business.[66] And the public is often positively disposed to electing candidates with such experience.

[61] Dobel (1993).
[62] Djankov et al. (2010).
[63] Mackenzie (2002).
[64] Burdescu et al. (2010); Szakonyi (2020).
[65] Fung, Graham, and Weil (2007).
[66] Bershidsky (2015); Gardner and Martinez (2010).

There is no single solution for preventing these politicians from abusing public office. Countries will need to adapt these proposed "best" practices to their own political and economic contexts. But the time to experiment with policy solutions is already at hand. Businesspeople running as outsider candidates will continue to enjoy unprecedented popular support in elections around the world. Without strengthened protections and vigilant monitoring of conflicts of interest, governments face heightened risks of being completely captured by private sector interests, to the detriment of citizens everywhere.

Appendix

A DATA SOURCES

A.1 Introduction to SPARK Database

The primary method this book uses to identify businessperson candidacies takes advantage of official firm registration data. All Russian firms are required to submit basic company information, balance sheets, and income statements to the state statistics agency Rosstat every year. This database of registration details is known as the Uniform Register of Legal Entities (EGRUL). The majority of companies comply in order to maintain good relations with the authorities.[1] I collect this firm-level data from the SPARK Professional Market and Company Analysis System (SPARK), which is administered by the well-known press agency Interfax. SPARK is a subscription-based service that purchases, aggregates, and organizes data from Rosstat for use by outside users.

The SPARK firm data includes registration details, company contacts, information on management and corporate structure, and financial statements, for nearly 9 million firms and organizations in Russia, Kazakhstan, and Ukraine over the last 15 years. According to the company's website (www.spark-interfax.ru), SPARK's clients include bank risk departments, financial monitoring services, marketing agencies, insurance and auditing firms, media outlets, and educational institutions. My access was granted through my affiliation with the Higher School of Economics in Moscow, Russia. During this work, I only collected data

[1] Mironov and Zhuravskaya (2016).

on officially registered entities in Russia, which are uniquely identified using their ten digit tax identification number (INN) and their eight digit All-Russian Classifier of Firms and Organizations code (OKPO). Each firm has an individual page as well as numerous subpages that contain data on registration history, licenses, and balance sheets, depending on availability.

SPARK also houses a directory of individuals that is based on the Uniform State Register of Individual Entrepreneurs (EGRIP). This directory contains data on all people officially registered with the government with the status of "private entrepreneurs" or "entrepreneurs not having formed a legal entity." These are official classifications designed to help simplify registration and tax reporting requirements for small businesses. EGRIP collects registration data on almost 12 million of these individual entrepreneurs who are uniquely identified through a twelve digit tax identification number (INN). Data on entrepreneurs include personal demographic information (name, birthdate, and registration date) as well as entries for every legal entity that they had ever had an official affiliation with (firm director, member of the board of directors, etc.). SPARK also organizes data for all individual businesspeople that are not registered in EGRIP (such as firm directors and members of boards of directors), but no information on birthdate or registration date is available; these businesspeople appear like their counterparts in EGRIP as individual entries in the database.

One of the advantage of using SPARK to identify the business ties of politicians in Russia is that the system creates a unique homepage for each individual containing information on all companies they have either managed or sat on the board of directors at any time since 1998. These homepages are created for everyone, regardless of whether they have an entry in EGRIP, and include all identifying information for connected firms (INN, OKPO, etc.), an individual's position in the firm, the date they began their affiliation with the firm, and whether the affiliation was still active.

A.2 Description of Algorithm

The process of identifying businessperson candidates first required locating this homepage for every candidate to regional office during 2004–2011. First, I wrote a Python script to collect information on all candidates from the Central Election Commission of the Russian Federation (CEC) and collected by the Center in Support of Democracy and Human Rights Helix. The Helix Center has systematized election results from the CEC and uploaded the data to a centralized database. I collected the election data from the Helix site, filling in any missing data from the primary CEC website.[2] These data included the first, middle and last names, birthdate, region, gender, last place of work, legislative organ, and political party for all candidates. For those running in single-member districts, the data include the candidate's total vote count and vote share; for candidates on the party list, the candidate's list number is available.

Next, using a programming script, I matched each candidate to his or her homepage in the SPARK database if one existed, using their first name, last name, middle name, and region as identifying information. The script entered the candidate's names and region into the "manager" box of SPARK's search function for querying its database. If this query returned results, the script then navigated SPARK to locate the individual's homepage. All the data on that homepage was then scraped into a database. Lastly, the script located the firm's page and collected data on basic company characteristics, the board of directors (if one existed), and all financial data.

Roughly 76 percent of these candidates had homepages in the SPARK system.[3] Next, I manually matched firms to all candidates who listed a company as their place of work on their ballot registration form but who were not located in the SPARK database; these manual matches accounted for an additional 9 percent of the sample. The final dataset includes firms that candidates directed at the time of their electoral campaign or where they sat on the board of directors.

A.3 Data Quality and Limitations

This official financial data from SPARK has been widely used by academics and journalists alike studying firm-level performance, as well as malfeasance, in Russia. Data from the SPARK system have been used in investigations of shadow election campaign financings,[4] firm-level tax

[2] Located at: www.vybory.izbirkom.ru/region/izbirkom.

[3] This, however, does not mean that 76 percent of all candidates are entrepreneurs: SPARK includes a considerable amount information on a number of occupational characteristics of individuals in Russia, including time worked in public institutions, such as hospitals, schools, and political parties.

[4] Mironov and Zhuravskaya (2016).

evasion,[5] bureaucratic efficiency,[6] and nepotistic corruption,[7] as well as by journalists looking at firms exerting influence on politicians.[8] Using reported financial data to analyze organizational performance may introduce some biases. For example, companies may avoid submitting accurate information about their profitability for fear of exposing themselves to greater tax liabilities or unwanted attention from hostile takeovers. Given the sensitivity of politicians to unwanted public scrutiny of their financial dealings while in office, we might expect that politically connected firms would be more likely to hide their above-normal profits. This downward bias would make any identification of an effect of political ties on firm financial outcomes a lower bound. We simply do not have sources of data on firm accounting or company characteristics beyond limited firm surveys.

Another concern would be data missingness, which can arise from two situations. First, I am unable to identify whether other candidates not listed as directors ran for office on behalf of a specific firm. Examples include friends or relatives of the firm director who operate as proxies of firm management in office, but have no official designation in the firm and thus do not appear in records of directorships. While I fully acknowledge the possibility of such scenarios, I do not believe the use of proxies significantly undermines the quality of the data and research design used in the book for several reasons. First, employing friends and family to run for office on behalf of a firm carries a significant set of risks related to electoral uncertainty. By virtue of their personal standing at the top of their firm and community, businessperson candidates have intangible assets related to their electability that cannot simply be transferred to kin and associates. Therefore, in order to win elections, a businessperson needs to stand for office himself or herself and appeal to voters using the "personal vote." Second, this book focuses on individuals who simultaneously combine private and public sector activities in order to benefit their firms through political access. It is thus interested in a specific subset of political connections, of which there are many types in the Russian context, one where an individual must make trade-offs in their time and resources between two competing occupations. Therefore, although proxies and other types of political ties may be rife in Russia,

[5] Mironov (2013).
[6] Best, Hjort, and Szakonyi (2017).
[7] Szakonyi (2019).
[8] Beshley (2012).

they constitute a different and equally valid research endeavor. Any type of delegation to an individual whose interests may not completely align with the firm introduces the same reneging problem described in the first part of this book.

The last concern relates to the possibility of businessperson candidates taking steps to hide their connections to firms at the time of the election. Unfortunately it is impossible to gauge in any meaningful way the extent of this evasion of reporting requirements using only publicly available election and firm-level data. For analysis on the determinants of businessperson candidacy, this creates problems with the underreporting of firms running candidates, since some number of firms are actually represented in electoral campaigns to regional office but go undetected by the algorithm. Within-sample comparisons using the dataset, such as measuring the benefits of holding office using the regression-discontinuity design, would be affected by this missingness if it was correlated with whether candidates won or lost office. Given the uncertainty of fierce electoral competition in the single-member districts, there is less concern that one or the other type of candidates would systematically hide their connections across the sample.

B CHAPTER 2: DESCRIPTIVE STATISTICS

B.1 Descriptive Statistics

- Table B1 presents descriptive statistics for the main firm-level dataset based on registrations submitted to the Russian State Statistics Agency. Table B2 presents correlations between the main indicators used to measure democracy. Table B3 provides similar summary information for the cross-sectional firm survey conducted in 2017.

TABLE B1 *Descriptive statistics: Firm registration data*

Statistic	N	Mean	St. Dev.	Min	Pctl(25)	Pctl(75)	Max
Firm had Businessperson Candidate	1,166,164	0.01	0.10	0	0	0	1
Firm had Serious Businessperson Candidate	1,166,164	0.01	0.09	0	0	0	1
Total Assets (thous rub.)	1,158,618	89.38	4,225.76	0	0.22	13.65	2,793,132
Firm Age	1,166,164	5.42	6.13	0	1	8	307
Importer	1,166,164	0.09	0.28	0	0	0	1
Exporter	1,166,164	0.06	0.23	0	0	0	1
Number of Subsidiaries	1,166,164	0.18	1.48	0	0	0	871
Municipal State-Owned Enterprise	1,166,164	0.02	0.13	0	0	0	1
Regional / Federal State-Owned Enterprise	1,166,164	0.01	0.08	0	0	0	1
Total Sector Revenue (logged)	1,166,030	18.32	2.62	1.39	16.57	20.01	23.32
Sectoral Oligopoly	1,164,720	0.34	0.21	0.08	0.20	0.43	1
Regional GRP (logged)	1,166,164	13.65	1.45	8.13	12.47	15.24	15.78
Total Population (logged)	1,166,164	15.12	0.91	10.64	14.50	16.20	16.24
Level of Urbanization	1,166,164	0.82	0.15	0	0.74	1	1
Natural Resources	1,166,164	0.29	0.45	0	0	1	1
National Party Strength – Expenditures	1,163,771	17.19	0.79	12.83	16.67	17.80	18.46
National Party Strength – Nominations	999,004	0.65	0.18	0.15	0.58	0.81	0.98
Regional Press Freedom	1,165,507	3.55	0.90	1	3	4	5
Aggregate Accountability (Minimal)	1,165,507	10.29	1.97	4	9	12	14
Aggregate Accountability (Maximal)	1,165,507	20.33	4.06	9	18	23	29
Ethnic Republic	1,166,164	0.07	0.26	0	0	0	1

TABLE B2 *Descriptive statistics: Correlations*

	(1)	(2)	(3)
(1) National Party Strength – Expenditures			
(2) National Party Strength – Nominations	0.532*		
(3) Aggregate Accountability (Maximal)	0.307*	−0.012	
(4) Aggregate Accountability (Minimal)	0.3*	−0.029	0.975*

*p<0.05

TABLE B3 *Descriptive statistics: Firm survey*

Statistic	N	Mean	St. Dev.	Min	Pctl(25)	Pctl(75)	Max
Regional Competition	639	2.32	0.77	1	2	3	3
Firm Age (log)	654	2.81	0.96	0	2.30	3.30	5.46
No. Employees (log)	654	5.51	0.88	3.93	4.79	5.86	9.31
Exporter	652	0.28	0.45	0	0	1	1
Regional/Federal SOE	619	0.06	0.24	0	0	0	1
Municipal SOE	619	0.06	0.24	0	0	0	1
Obstacle: Corruption	605	2.35	1.35	1	1	3	5
Obstacle: Private Racket	615	1.48	0.96	1	1	2	5
Recent Growth	648	4.35	2.27	1	3	5	9
Sales to State	642	1.19	0.53	1	1	1	4
National Association Member	619	0.24	0.42	0	0	0	1
Regional Association Member	619	0.21	0.41	0	0	0	1
Candidate from Firm Ran	640	0.11	0.31	0	0	0	1
Candidate from Firm Won	638	0.08	0.27	0	0	0	1

C CHAPTER 3: ROBUSTNESS CHECKS

C.1 Firm Registration Data: Extensions

- Table C1 presents another series of robustness checks for the main results using the firm registration data. Because of the difficulties presenting so many covariates, I do not show the coefficients on the set of firm-level characteristics included in all models (age, importing status, exporting status, etc.). First, I show the baseline model from the main text in Column 1. In Column 2, I subset to only private firms, thereby removing state-owned enterprises from the analysis. We see that the main effects are still present: economic competition and weak party institutions both lead to greater businessperson candidacy among *only* private firms. The interaction between being a top 5 firm and sectoral competition remains positive. Column 3 uses an alternate measure for defining party strength through nominations. I include the party affiliation of businessperson candidates in the measure (in the main text, the nominations measure excluded them). The point estimate remains negative and statistically significant: regions with more established parties see fewer businessperson candidates.
- Next, in Column 4, I show that the main results are robust to including alternate measures of political competition in the region, including whether the governor is a member of United Russia and the popularity of the ruling party in national elections. Column 5 provides another robustness check on the result showing a positive relationship between democratization and businessperson candidacy, this time using the "minimal accountability" measure.
- Columns 6 and 7 vary the non-parametric threshold used to define the large firms: instead of top 5 membership, I code firms according to whether they were in the top 10 or the top 20 firms in their sector. Here again we see that not only does sectoral competition stimulate interest in businessperson candidacy, large firms defined using these alternate thresholds are even more incentivized to run their directors in competitive environments.

C.2 Candidate Data

- Table C2 looks at the determinants of businessperson candidacy, but runs analysis at the candidate level. The goal is to further probe the robustness of the findings using predictors measured at the regional

TABLE C1 *Determinants of businessperson candidacy: Firm registration data extensions*

	Firm Had Candidate						
	(1)	(2)	(3)	(4)	(5)	(6)	(7)
Firm-Level Predictors							
Top 5 Firm	0.030***	0.029***	0.026***	0.030***	0.030***		
	(0.002)	(0.002)	(0.002)	(0.002)	(0.002)		
Top 10 Firm						0.026***	
						(0.002)	
Top 20 Firm							0.026***
							(0.002)
Sector-Level Predictors							
Total Sector Revenue (logged)	0.004***	0.004***	0.004***	0.004***	0.004***	0.004***	0.004***
	(0.0002)	(0.0002)	(0.0002)	(0.0002)	(0.0002)	(0.0002)	(0.0002)
Sectoral Competition	0.007***	0.007***	0.007***	0.007***	0.007***	0.009***	0.009***
	(0.001)	(0.001)	(0.001)	(0.001)	(0.001)	(0.001)	(0.001)
Sectoral Competition* Top 5 Firm	0.028***	0.030***	0.036***	0.028***	0.028***		
	(0.003)	(0.003)	(0.003)	(0.003)	(0.003)		
Sectoral Competition* Top 10 Firm						0.016***	
						(0.002)	
Sectoral Competition* Top 20 Firm							0.003
							(0.002)
Region-Level Predictors							
Gross Regional Product (logged)	−0.013***	−0.013***	−0.015***	−0.010***	−0.013***	−0.013***	−0.013***
	(0.002)	(0.002)	(0.002)	(0.002)	(0.002)	(0.002)	(0.002)
Total Population (logged)	0.005**	0.004*	0.005*	0.003	0.005**	0.005**	0.005*
	(0.002)	(0.002)	(0.003)	(0.002)	(0.002)	(0.002)	(0.002)
Level of Urbanization	−0.006	−0.011	0.001	−0.014	−0.010	−0.007	−0.007
	(0.013)	(0.012)	(0.014)	(0.012)	(0.013)	(0.013)	(0.013)
Natural Resources	0.002	0.002	0.001	0.0004	0.002	0.002	0.002
	(0.004)	(0.004)	(0.004)	(0.004)	(0.004)	(0.004)	(0.004)

Ethnic Republic	0.008**	0.009**	0.012***	0.010**	0.008*	0.008*	0.007*
	(0.004)	(0.004)	(0.004)	(0.004)	(0.004)	(0.004)	(0.004)
National Party Strength – Expenditures	−0.004***	−0.004***		−0.005***	−0.004***	−0.004***	−0.004***
	(0.001)	(0.001)		(0.001)	(0.001)	(0.001)	(0.001)
National Party Strength – Nominations (w. bus)			−0.005**				
			(0.002)				
Aggregate Accountability (Maximal)	0.001***	0.001***	0.001***	0.001***		0.001***	0.001***
	(0.0002)	(0.0002)	(0.0002)	(0.0002)		(0.0002)	(0.0002)
Aggregate Accountability (Minimal)					0.001***		
					(0.0003)		
Governor is UR Member				−0.001			
				(0.001)			
UR National Vote Share (logged)				−0.011***			
				(0.003)			
Other Firm Characteristics	Yes	Yes	Yes	Yes	Yes	Yes	Yes
Region, Sector Effects	Random	Random	Random	Random	Random	Random	Random
Year Effects	Fixed	Fixed	Fixed	Fixed	Fixed	Fixed	Fixed
Observations	940,149	913,510	802,175	940,149	940,149	940,149	940,149

*p<0.1; **p<0.05; ***p<0.01 The dependent variable is a binary indicator for whether a firm was connected to a businessperson candidate. All models include random effects at the region and sector level, and year fixed effects. Column 2 subsets the sample to only private firms (excluding SOEs). Other Firm Characteristics include age, importing status, exporting status, log assets, and whether the firm was owned by federal, regional, or municipal governments. Errors are clustered at the region level.

TABLE C2 *Determinants of businessperson candidacy: Candidate level*

	Candidate was Businessperson			
	(1)	(2)	(3)	(4)
Male	0.210***	0.211***	0.212***	0.210***
	(0.010)	(0.006)	(0.008)	(0.006)
SMD Ballot	0.079***	0.069***	0.070***	0.066***
	(0.010)	(0.005)	(0.009)	(0.005)
Age (logged)	−0.061***	−0.063***	−0.061***	−0.061***
	(0.010)	(0.009)	(0.011)	(0.009)
Incumbent	0.094***	0.094***	0.111***	0.108***
	(0.015)	(0.008)	(0.011)	(0.008)
Total Population (logged)	0.051***	0.043***	0.056***	0.062***
	(0.013)	(0.014)	(0.010)	(0.012)
Gross Regional Product (logged)	−0.001	0.003	−0.017	−0.014
	(0.011)	(0.013)	(0.011)	(0.012)
Ethnic Republic	−0.046***	−0.032*	−0.023*	−0.011
	(0.015)	(0.018)	(0.013)	(0.016)
Aggregate Accountability (Maximal)	0.001	0.005	0.006**	0.008**
	(0.003)	(0.004)	(0.003)	(0.003)
Natural Resources	0.012	−0.005	−0.006	−0.014
	(0.012)	(0.017)	(0.013)	(0.014)
Urbanization	0.057	0.066	0.090	0.067
	(0.070)	(0.070)	(0.067)	(0.062)
National Party Strength – Expenditures	−0.033**	−0.002		
	(0.017)	(0.011)		
National Party Strength – Nominations			−0.063*	−0.084**
			(0.035)	(0.034)
Year Effects	Fixed	Random	Fixed	Random
Observations	39,317	39,317	36,256	36,256
R^2	0.055		0.056	

*p<0.1; **p<0.05; ***p<0.01 The dependent table is a binary indicator for whether a candidate was identified as a businessperson. The sample includes all candidates to office from 2004 to 2011. Models alternate between random and fixed effects at the region and year levels. For fixed effects models, standard errors are clustered at the region and year level.

level, especially the strength of party institutions. The dataset includes every candidate to regional legislative office from 2004 to 2011, bringing together data on both individual and regional-level characteristics.

The outcome variable is a binary indicator for whether a candidate was connected to a businessperson at the time of their election.

- Again the results indicate that stronger party institutions lead to fewer businessperson candidacies. The point estimates on the two variables measuring national party strength are negative, large in magnitude, and for the most part statistically significant. These results hold even controlling for the number of firms in each region and alternating between random and fixed-effects models (at the region and year levels).

D CHAPTER 4: ROBUSTNESS CHECKS

D.1 Party Choice: All Candidates

- In the main text, the models predicting party choice subset to the sample of candidates running on the proportional representation system. There the goal was to examine variation across parties, conditional on candidates to choosing to run with some kind of party affiliation. However, candidates running in plurality districts also have the choice to join a political party, or stay independent. In Table D1, I show results that include all SMD and PR candidates, with indicators for each of the ballot choices included on the right hand side in all models.
- The results marginally change when the sample is broadened in this way. Larger firms are still more likely to affiliate with the United Russia ruling party, as are those with older directors who have served in office before. Similarly, older businessperson candidates are more likely to join up with the Communists. The only real differences from Table D1 in the main text concern the statistical significance of several of the point estimates related to state-owned enterprises. Although being a regional SOE director is positively correlated with joining United Russia, this result is no longer statistically significant.

	Marginal Effects from Logit Models						
	UR	Communists	Just Russia	LDPR	Smaller	Independent	Multiple
	(1)	(2)	(3)	(4)	(5)	(6)	(7)
Firm-Level Predictors							
Total Assets (logged)	0.047***	−0.008***	−0.007***	−0.006***	−0.007***	−0.005***	0.006***
	(0.004)	(0.002)	(0.002)	(0.002)	(0.002)	(0.002)	(0.001)
Top 5 Firm	0.029*	−0.012	−0.018	−0.011	−0.035***	0.002	−0.002
	(0.016)	(0.008)	(0.011)	(0.010)	(0.010)	(0.008)	(0.006)
Firm Age (logged)	0.008	0.004	−0.002	−0.003	−0.005	0.008*	0.009***
	(0.006)	(0.004)	(0.004)	(0.003)	(0.004)	(0.004)	(0.003)
Regional SOE	0.059	−0.005	−0.008	−0.013	−0.046**	−0.009	−0.015***
	(0.042)	(0.018)	(0.022)	(0.024)	(0.020)	(0.020)	(0.005)
Municipal SOE	−0.080**	0.033	0.027*	0.011	−0.001	−0.004	0.002
	(0.031)	(0.023)	(0.017)	(0.016)	(0.020)	(0.018)	(0.014)
Importer	−0.007	−0.007	0.006	0.001	−0.002	−0.003	0.002
	(0.014)	(0.009)	(0.011)	(0.011)	(0.010)	(0.010)	(0.005)
Exporter	−0.015	0.019	−0.007	0.001	−0.005	0.011	0.001
	(0.019)	(0.014)	(0.010)	(0.012)	(0.013)	(0.009)	(0.006)
Candidate-Level Predictors							
Candidate Age	0.222***	0.115***	−0.049***	−0.126***	−0.051***	−0.099***	−0.020***
	(0.034)	(0.025)	(0.018)	(0.021)	(0.019)	(0.021)	(0.007)
Male Candidate	0.017	0.015	−0.013	0.005	−0.019	0.007	0.030***
	(0.031)	(0.010)	(0.017)	(0.017)	(0.017)	(0.020)	(0.0001)
Candidate was Incumbent	0.215***	−0.011	−0.053***	−0.031***	−0.066***	−0.018	0.033***
	(0.020)	(0.009)	(0.011)	(0.011)	(0.012)	(0.013)	(0.006)

(continued)

TABLE D1 *(continued)*

	Marginal Effects from Logit Models						
	UR	Communists	Just Russia	LDPR	Smaller	Independent	Multiple
	(1)	(2)	(3)	(4)	(5)	(6)	(7)
Region-Level Predictors							
Gross Regional Product	0.305**	0.028	−0.010	−0.063	−0.257	−0.217**	−0.045
(logged)	(0.153)	(0.059)	(0.096)	(0.062)	(0.162)	(0.094)	(0.031)
Regional Population	−0.150	−0.296	−0.804*	0.143	1.507***	−0.099	0.230
	(0.883)	(0.306)	(0.430)	(0.306)	(0.446)	(0.502)	(0.171)
Urbanization	2.356	0.487	−2.089	−0.334	−2.079	−0.018	0.719**
	(2.151)	(0.875)	(1.677)	(1.058)	(1.861)	(1.424)	(0.312)
National Party Strength –	0.0004	−0.014	0.015	0.027	−0.161*	0.016	−0.014
Expenditures	(0.040)	(0.018)	(0.035)	(0.018)	(0.093)	(0.026)	(0.014)
Sector FE	Yes	Yes	Yes	Yes	Yes	Yes	Yes
Region FE	Yes	Yes	Yes	Yes	Yes	Yes	Yes
Year FE	Yes	Yes	Yes	Yes	Yes	Yes	Yes
Observations	9,633	9,633	9,633	9,633	9,633	9,633	9,633

*p<0.1; **p<0.05; ***p<0.01 All models include sector, region, and year fixed effects. The sample includes candidates whether they ran in a plurality race or won a spot on the party list. Columns 1–6 present marginal effects from separate logistic models with the outcome variable being a binary indicator for the specific political party the businessperson candidate affiliated with (and the reference category being all other political party choices). Errors are clustered on region.

E CHAPTER 5: ROBUSTNESS CHECKS

E.1 Digging into the Democracy Mechanism

- Heterogeneity analysis using regression discontinuity designs is conventionally done by subsetting the sample along single dimensions of interest. This may introduce problems if mechanisms are identified along some dimension that could be plausibly endogenous to another unaccounted for dimension. With regard to this chapter, that involves finding that the value of winning office decreases in more democratic regions. In Russia, democratic regions may be more economically developed. The heterogeneous effect on democracy may be then capturing the effect of regional wealth, rather than the quality of democratic institutions.
- To address this issue, I first ran a regression of the Carnegie Center's democracy score that was used in the chapter on regional GDP per capita, the level of urbanization in the region, and an indicator for the presence of natural resources. These factors are widely thought to be associated with the quality of democratic institutions, not just in Russia, but around the world. The sample used was all regions that entered the dataset for the years 2003–2011, with the unit of analysis being the region-year. Democracy is indeed slightly positively correlated with economic development. I also ran the same regression with the percentage of seats belong to ruling United Russia members as the outcome.
- Next, I merged the region-year-level residuals from these regressions into the firm-level database upon which the regression discontinuity was run. These residuals reflect the variation in democratic development and in United Russia control over the legislature between regions that are unexplained by economic development, urbanization, and resource wealth. Using the median of these residuals, I subset the RDD sample, the same approach used in the chapter that subset along the median of the raw scores. I then ran the same RDD specifications as those in the heterogeneity tables in the chapter.
- The results are shown in Table E1. Even when accounting for the level of economic development, the heterogeneous effects on the level of democracy from the main text hold. Firms that are connected to candidates in more (residualized) democratic regions perform better in terms of revenue and profitability. Similarly, the results subsetting on the (residualized) percentage of United Russia members in a legislature conform to the main results in the chapter. The value of winning a seat in places with a stronger opposition presence increases.

TABLE E1 *Institutional residualized heterogeneity*

Dependent Variable:	Revenue		Profit Margin	
	(1)	(2)	(3)	(4)
Panel A: Sample Split at Median of Residualized Democracy Score				
Sample:	Low Dem.	High Dem.	Low Dem.	High Dem.
District Win	0.232	0.495**	0.023	0.154**
	(0.281)	(0.221)	(0.057)	(0.070)
Bandwidth:	0.145	0.145	0.128	0.128
Observations	290	353	251	310
Panel B: Sample Split at Median of Residualized UR Control of Parliament				
Sample:	Low UR Control	High UR Control	Low UR Control	High UR Control
District Win	0.549***	−0.162	0.157***	−0.046
	(0.212)	(0.371)	(0.058)	(0.066)
Bandwidth:	0.145	0.145	0.128	0.128
Observations	437	192	398	153

*** $p<0.01$, ** $p<0.05$ This table displays heterogenous RD treatment effects of winning office using the optimal bandwidth (CCT) for vote share and a local-linear control function. Panel A subsets on the median (residualized) democracy score in the region. Panel B subsets on the median (residualized) number of legislative seats the ruling party controlled. All models include firm-level and candidate-level covariates, use robust standard errors clustered on the candidate and election levels, and include the pre-election value for the outcome.

F CHAPTER 6: DESCRIPTIVE STATISTICS AND ROBUSTNESS CHECKS

F.1 Descriptive Statistics: Overview of Regional and Municipal Spending

- Table F1 gives an item-by-item breakdown of spending by regional and municipal governments, totaled across all the units at each administrative level. Data come from the Russian Ministry of Finance. The top rows display the expenditures for each item in USD billions in 2015, and then as a percentage of the total expenditures, the last row in the table. The left section of the table shows data for regional governments, while the right shows it for municipal governments.
- The table clearly shows that municipal spending is spread across several important subcategories: education (accounting for nearly 50 percent of all expenditures), followed by housing, national economy, government, and social policy. Note that these are summed across the four municipality types. More detail on the breakdown by different types can be found in the next section.

F.2 Municipality Level: Other Outcome Variables

- Tables F2–F4 use the same regression discontinuity design to analyze several other variables of interest at the municipal level. Panel A in Table F2 uses as an outcome a binary indicator for whether a municipality, on average, ran a budget deficit of more than 5 percent over each mayoral term. In line with the results in the main table, we do not see consistent evidence that businessperson mayors are more likely to run larger (or for that matter smaller) deficits. The point estimates are statistically indistinguishable from zero. The outcome in Panel B measures the percentage of municipal revenue that comes from upper-level transfers, i.e. intergovernmental grants and subventions from the federal or regional government that fund municipal budget activities. In all the models shown in the main text, this value is included as a control. Panel B puts it on the left hand side of the regression. The results suggest that municipalities run by businesspeople may be somewhat more likely to depend on these transfers, but the point estimates do not reach statistical significance.

TABLE F1 *Regional and municipal expenditures by line item (2015)*

Item	Regional	% of Total	Municipal	% of Total
Common Government Expenses	4.76	3.51	5.57	9.39
Defense	0.06	0.05	0.06	0.11
Law Enforcement	1.44	1.06	0.42	0.70
Economy	27.68	20.40	5.80	9.76
Housing and Communal Services	10.05	7.41	7.71	12.98
Environmental Protection	0.33	0.24	0.06	0.09
Education	30.35	22.36	28.60	48.15
Culture	2.53	1.86	3.03	5.10
Health Care	22.52	16.59	0.31	0.51
Social Policy	24.39	17.98	4.86	8.18
Physical Culture and Sport	2.45	1.80	1.05	1.76
Mass Media	0.62	0.46	0.11	0.19
Debt Payments	2.14	1.58	0.37	0.62
Transfers	6.38	4.70	1.46	2.46
Total Deficit	−1.80		−1.06	
Total Expenditures	135.70		59.40	

All figures are from the year 2015 and shown in billions USD, using an exchange rate of 60 rubles per dollar. The percentage columns show the portion of total regional (Column 3) or municipal (Column 5) spending for each line item, that is, divided by the total expenditures line at the bottom of the table. Deficit calculates total income minus total expenditures. Data come from www.budget.gov.ru.

- Table F3 uses the same main RDD specification to analyze how businessperson mayors allocate spending to the top seven subcategories, accounting for 96 percent of all municipal spending (the results on education, health care, and economy are the same as those in Table 6.2 of the main text). We see that spending appears to drop for the categories of education, social policy (transfers to the elderly and disabled), and general bureaucratic agencies, such as the legislative body and the judicial system. This suggests that businessperson mayors find money from many different areas of government to fund their policy priorities, but there is not one single category that bears the brunt of the reallocation.
- Next, Table F4 analyzes outcomes that capture the percentage of procurement in the five largest product categories (procured by mayoral

TABLE F2 *Municipality level: Budget size and dependency*

Panel A: Large Budget Deficit (binary)

Control Function:	None (OLS)			Local Linear (RDD)		
Bandwidth:	Global		3%	5%	Optimal	
	(1)	(2)	(3)	(4)	(5)	(6)
Businessperson Mayor	−0.006	−0.007	−0.025	−0.095	−0.012	−0.010
	(0.005)	(0.007)	(0.026)	(0.110)	(0.018)	(0.019)
Bandwidth	1	1	0.03	0.05	0.31	0.29
Municipality Type FE	Yes	Yes	Yes	Yes	Yes	Yes
Covariates; Region, Year FE	No	Yes	No	No	No	Yes
Observations	2,150	2,106	84	141	963	887

Panel B: Revenue from Upper-Level Transfers

Control Function:	None (OLS)			Local Linear (RDD)		
Bandwidth:	Global		3%	5%	Optimal	
	(1)	(2)	(3)	(4)	(5)	(6)
Businessperson Mayor	0.003	0.004	0.026	−0.023	0.002	0.001
	(0.006)	(0.007)	(0.029)	(0.066)	(0.031)	(0.031)
Bandwidth	1	1	0.03	0.05	0.17	0.17
Municipality Type FE	Yes	Yes	Yes	Yes	Yes	Yes
Covariates; Region, Year FE	No	Yes	No	No	No	Yes
Observations	2,200	2,200	86	142	513	516

Panel A examines whether a municipality ran a large budget deficit in each year, as measured using a binary indicator. Panel B examines the percentage of municipal revenue coming from transfers from higher level goverment bodies. The RDD models used include a linear control function and use an optimal bandwidth with bias-corrected robust standard errors per Calonico, Cattaneo, and Titiunik (2014). All errors are clustered on region.

TABLE F3 *Municipality level: All budget subcategories*

	Economy (1)	Education (2)	Health (3)	Housing (4)	Social Policy (5)	Gov. Affairs (6)	Culture (7)
Businessperson Mayor	0.067** (0.026)	−0.017 (0.019)	−0.0001 (0.009)	0.004 (0.020)	−0.010 (0.008)	−0.024 (0.024)	0.022 (0.024)
Bandwidth	0.2	0.24	0.2	0.18	0.15	0.21	0.21
Municipality Type FE	Yes	Yes	Yes	Yes	Yes	Yes	Yes
Covariates; Region, Year FE	No	No	No	No	No	No	No
Observations	406	361	299	536	258	648	488

*p<0.1; **p<0.05; ***p<0.01 The panels examine the percentage of expenditures dedicated to the outcome listed in the column headers. The regression models used include a linear control function and use an optimal bandwidth with bias-corrected robust standard errors per Calonico, Cattaneo, and Titiunik (2014). All errors are clustered on region.

administrations) that use electronic auctions to select suppliers. The first two columns are the same as Table 6.3 in the main text, looking at electronic auctions in construction procurement. However, beyond construction, we do not see evidence that businessperson mayors influence the selection mechanisms for car, food, office supplies, or furniture procurement. This potentially due to the fewer opportunities to engage in rent-seeking when procuring goods and services in these categories.

F.3 Region Level: Other Outcome Variables

- One advantage of conducting the regional analysis is the more finely grained budget and loan data to analyze. First, Table F5 runs the same region-level models to analyze the various subcategories under the "national economy" line-item, which we saw businessperson legislators devote more money towards in the main text (shown again here in Columns 1 and 2). Looking at the three main subcategories, we see that the vast majority of the increased budget allocation in economic infrastructure goes specifically to roads and transport (Columns 7 and 8), and not agriculture or utilities. Moreover, Columns 9 and

TABLE F4 *Municipality level: Procurement*

	Construction		Cars		Food Products		Office Supplies		Furniture	
	(1)	(2)	(3)	(4)	(5)	(6)	(7)	(8)	(9)	(10)
Businessperson Mayor	−0.185***	−0.210***	0.271**	0.210	−0.111	−0.366	−0.287	0.165	−0.174	−0.147
	(0.063)	(0.063)	(0.126)	(0.149)	(0.321)	(0.370)	(0.290)	(0.286)	(0.222)	(0.224)
Bandwidth	0.22	0.22	0.15	0.15	0.25	0.16	0.22	0.19	0.17	0.12
Municipality Type FE	Yes	Yes	Yes	Yes	Yes	Yes	Yes	Yes	Yes	Yes
Covariates; Region, Year FE	No	Yes	No	Yes	No	Yes	No	Yes	No	Yes
Observations	495	477	181	177	48	29	117	67	151	84

**p<0.05; ***p<0.01 This table analyzes the percentage of procurement contracts where suppliers are selected through electronic auctions, breaking down procurement into five categories (as indicated by the column labels). The two models for each outcome alternate including covariates, and region and year fixed effects. The regression models include a linear control function and use an optimal bandwidth with bias-corrected robust standard errors per Calonico, Cattaneo, and Titiunik (2014). All errors are clustered on region.

TABLE F5 *Region level: Economic infrastructure broken down*

	Economic Expenditures (%)		Agriculture (%)		Fuel and Utilities (%)		Roads / Transport (%)		Corporate Property Tax (% Rev.)	
	(1)	(2)	(3)	(4)	(5)	(6)	(7)	(8)	(9)	(10)
Perc. Businesspeople	0.076***	0.064***	0.001	−0.004	0.009	0.008	0.082***	0.074***	−0.017	−0.020
	(0.023)	(0.022)	(0.014)	(0.014)	(0.006)	(0.006)	(0.021)	(0.018)	(0.024)	(0.024)
Total Expenditures (log)	0.151***	0.147***	0.020	0.019*	−0.002	−0.004	0.046***	0.043***		
	(0.019)	(0.017)	(0.012)	(0.011)	(0.005)	(0.006)	(0.017)	(0.012)		
Total Revenue (log)									−0.053***	−0.050***
									(0.011)	(0.010)
GRP (log)		−0.009		0.014		0.017*		−0.020		−0.012
		(0.019)		(0.010)		(0.010)		(0.016)		(0.015)
Population (log)		0.052		−0.044		−0.0001		−0.092		−0.187***
		(0.136)		(0.078)		(0.026)		(0.148)		(0.052)
Urbanization		−0.321		−0.269***		−0.007		−0.019		−0.038
		(0.218)		(0.095)		(0.059)		(0.245)		(0.112)
Held Regional Election		−0.001		0.001		0.00001		−0.001		0.0004
		(0.001)		(0.001)		(0.0001)		(0.001)		(0.001)
Dependence on Subsidies		0.059		0.003		0.005		0.070***		−0.018
		(0.038)		(0.015)		(0.012)		(0.024)		(0.019)
UR Governor		−0.0002		0.001		−0.0003		0.009*		−0.001
		(0.007)		(0.002)		(0.002)		(0.005)		(0.006)

Businessperson Governor		0.010		0.001		0.001		0.007		0.002
		(0.007)		(0.003)		(0.001)		(0.006)		(0.004)
UR Control of Legislature		0.002		0.002		−0.001		−0.006		0.003
		(0.018)		(0.007)		(0.004)		(0.018)		(0.015)
Region, Year Fixed Effects	Yes	Yes	Yes	Yes	Yes	Yes	Yes	Yes	Yes	Yes
Observations	640	640	640	640	628	628	640	640	640	640

*p<0.1; ***p<0.01 This table examines the percent of budget expenditures devoted to the total "national economy" (Columns 1–2), agriculture (Columns 3–4), fuel and utilities (Columns 5–6), and roads and transport (Columns 7–8). Columns 9 and 10 look at the percentage of revenue coming from corporate property tax, one of three taxes that regional legislatures can set independently. All models use OLS and cluster errors on region and year.

10 suggest that businessperson legislators may also act to reduce corporate taxes, one of three taxes that can be set by regional legislators. In all, this table provides additional evidence that businessperson politicians devote more money to items of specific interest to their community, and may even act to reduce tax burdens, while also providing a strong robustness check for the municipal level analysis.

- Table F6 similarly breaks down different types of social policy investments in regional budgets. Overall, we see considerably less money dedicated to health, education, and housing, though the point estimates generated by these models are not statistically significant. Adding up these three policy area into an umbrella "social policy" category (Columns 7 and 8) returns some evidence that businessperson politicians reduce spending on social infrastructure as a whole.
- Finally, Table F7 examines other region-level outcome economic variables that could be affected by the presence of businessperson politicians active in the regional legislature. Columns 1 and 2 examine the level of private investment (thousands of rubles, logged), Columns 3 and 4 examine the level of government investment, Columns 5 and 6 look at the unemployment rate, and Columns 7 and 8 look at the change in bond debt from year to year. Regions have the added ability to issue commercial loans and bonds backed by state guarantees.[9]
- The point estimates on the percentage of legislators coming from the private sector are large both for explaining private and public investment. However, none of the coefficients are statistically significant, making it difficult to claim that having more businesspeople in power actually affects investment outcomes. Unemployment also appears unchanged when more businesspeople are in office. In general, businesspeople have a larger direct effect on budget allocations, a policy decision which they have control over, rather than indirect effects on other economic indicators.
- In line with the results in the main text on deficits, we see that having more businesspeople sit in the regional legislature results in generally larger debt levels over time. We see that year on year changes in debt levels are greater when businesspeople are in elected office, indicating that they are using debt to finance the larger budget deficits.

[9] Remington (2016).

TABLE F6 *Region level: Social infrastructure broken down*

	Health (%)		Education (%)		Housing (%)		All Social Policy (%)	
	(1)	(2)	(3)	(4)	(5)	(6)	(7)	(8)
Perc. Businesspeople	−0.014	−0.015	−0.022	−0.028	−0.021	−0.018	−0.081*	−0.085*
	(0.025)	(0.025)	(0.021)	(0.022)	(0.034)	(0.032)	(0.042)	(0.044)
Total Expenditures (log)	−0.031**	−0.027*	−0.065***	−0.067***	0.072***	0.075***	−0.073***	−0.070***
	(0.014)	(0.015)	(0.017)	(0.019)	(0.020)	(0.020)	(0.026)	(0.025)
GRP (log)		−0.007		0.026		−0.045		−0.046
		(0.016)		(0.025)		(0.034)		(0.046)
Population (log)		0.0003		−0.105		0.174		0.243
		(0.133)		(0.196)		(0.176)		(0.304)
Urbanization		0.127		0.076		−0.067		0.359
		(0.192)		(0.281)		(0.327)		(0.411)
Held Regional Election		0.001		0.001		−0.00004		0.0003
		(0.001)		(0.001)		(0.001)		(0.001)
Dependence on Subsidies		−0.034		−0.059*		0.004		−0.071
		(0.026)		(0.032)		(0.051)		(0.061)
UR Governor		−0.0005		0.004		−0.0002		0.020*
		(0.005)		(0.007)		(0.006)		(0.011)
Businessperson Governor		0.003		0.009		−0.003		0.014
		(0.004)		(0.006)		(0.005)		(0.012)
UR Control of Legislature		−0.030		−0.003		0.028		0.004
		(0.025)		(0.024)		(0.025)		(0.034)
Region, Year Fixed Effects	Yes	Yes	Yes	Yes	Yes	Yes	Yes	Yes
Observations	640	640	640	640	640	640	640	640

*p<0.1; **p<0.05; ***p<0.01 This table examines the percent of budget expenditures devoted to health (Columns 1–2), education (Columns 3–4), and housing (Columns 5–6). Columns 7 and 8 look at aggregated spending on social issues. All models use OLS and cluster errors on region and year.

TABLE F7 *Region level: Other economic outcomes*

	Private Investment		Government Investment		Unemployment Rate		Gov. Bond Issuances	
	(1)	(2)	(3)	(4)	(5)	(6)	(7)	(8)
Perc. Businesspeople	0.642	0.570	0.404*	0.440*	−0.016	−0.014	0.045***	0.038**
	(0.394)	(0.382)	(0.218)	(0.232)	(0.010)	(0.010)	(0.017)	(0.016)
GRP (log)	0.673**	0.549**	1.678***	1.689***	−0.001	−0.001	0.022*	0.019*
	(0.265)	(0.262)	(0.182)	(0.192)	(0.006)	(0.006)	(0.012)	(0.011)
Population (log)		1.301***		0.111		−0.018**		0.029
		(0.335)		(0.278)		(0.008)		(0.026)
Urbanization		−2.725		−0.780		0.085**		0.055
		(2.003)		(1.481)		(0.043)		(0.149)
Held Regional Election		−3.120		0.685		0.209**		−0.151
		(2.791)		(3.235)		(0.105)		(0.200)
Dependence on Subsidies		−0.011		0.001		−0.0005*		−0.00004
		(0.012)		(0.009)		(0.0003)		(0.001)
UR Governor		−0.317		0.261		−0.004		−0.018
		(0.372)		(0.440)		(0.009)		(0.022)
Businessperson Governor		0.114		0.042		−0.001		0.001
		(0.078)		(0.080)		(0.002)		(0.005)
UR Control of Legislature		0.030		−0.047		0.001		0.007**
		(0.084)		(0.058)		(0.002)		(0.003)
Total Expenditures (log)		−0.011		−0.177		−0.004		−0.014
		(0.288)		(0.330)		(0.006)		(0.009)
Region, Year Fixed Effects	Yes	Yes	Yes	Yes	Yes	Yes	Yes	Yes
Observations	556	556	556	556	640	640	640	640

*p<0.1; **p<0.05; ***p<0.01 Models examine private investment in Columns 1 and 2 (thousands of rubles, logged), government investment in Columns 3 and 4 (thousands of rubles, logged), the unemployment rate in Columns 5 and 6, and the change in bond issuances (Columns 7 and 8). All models use OLS and cluster errors on both region and year.

F.4 Public Opinion Data on Businesspeople's Preferences: Life in Transition Survey

- To examine whether businesspeople have different preferences for government action, I draw on data from the latest round of the Life in Transition Survey (LiTS) conducted in 2016. Run by the World Bank and the European Bank for Reconstruction and Development (EBRD), LiTS polled 51,206 households from thirty-four countries across Europe. The sample for each country is nationally representative with face-to-face interviews conducted with a member of each household selected at random. The complete data can be found at http://litsonline-ebrd.com/.
- There are several key advantages to using LiTS to compare the political preferences of businesspeople (executives, entrepreneurs, etc.) to the rest of the population. First, LiTS includes both twenty-nine countries undergoing economic transition throughout Eastern Europe, the Caucasus, and Central Asia (including Russia) as well as more developed economies for comparison located in Western and Southern Europe: Germany, Italy, Greece, Cyprus, and the Czech Republic. This broad scope improves our ability to generalize across different political and economic settings.
- Second, the survey includes several direct questions about an individual's entrepreneurial and management activities in the private sector. I code an individual as a businessperson if (a) they self-described their occupation as a "employer" in the private-sector (in contrast to a wage employee, intern/apprentice, etc.) or (b) they answered they had set up their current business (from a separate question). Together these two questions capture people working either in executive positions or as entrepreneurs; 6.7 percent of all respondents qualify as businesspeople. Surprisingly, LiTS is one of the only cross-national surveys that asks respondents explicitly about their entrepreneurial activities: the Afrobarometer and Latinobarometer, for example, use more skills-based occupational categories without referencing running a business.
- Third, LiTS includes questions about both broad political attitudes and specific preferences for types of government spending. First, in Table F8, I compare the political attitudes of businesspeople to everyone else by asking their degree of support for nine different policy statements, as indicated by each column:

1. Incomes should be made more equal (10-point scale)
2. Government ownership of business and industry should be increased (10-point scale)
3. Competition is harmful. It brings out the worst in people (10-point scale)
4. Immigrants make a valuable contribution to the national economy of our country (binary)
5. Free and fair elections are important for [your] country (5-point scale)
6. Law and order is important for [your] country (5-point scale)
7. Freedom of speech is important for [your] country (5-point scale)
8. A press that is independent from the government is important for [your] country (5-point scale)
9. Free and fair elections are important for [your] country (5-point scale)
10. Equal rights for women as citizens is important for [your] country (5-point scale)

- The models in Table F8 include basic demographic characteristics as controls as well as country fixed effects. The drop in sample size from the overall number of respondents comes from missingness in the income variable; the results are robust to excluding this measure. Standard errors are clustered by country. The results indicate first that the political attitudes of businesspeople only differ from other citizens with regards to economic questions. Businesspeople are much less likely to support redistribution of income and a large role for the government in the economy. Otherwise, there are no statistically significant differences on other policy issues related to political liberties, immigration, or women's rights. Given these preferences we might expect businesspeople to pursue different policies mainly in the economic realm.
- Next, Table F9 examines differences over budgetary preferences between businesspeople and other citizens. All LiTS respondents were asked which issue area should be the first priority for extra government spending. The column headers indicate the seven categories given as possible responses, with "Infrastructure" being described as "Public infrastructures (e.g. public transport, roads, etc.)." Businesspeople across the thirty-four countries express much stronger support for additional government spending on infrastructure, and somewhat

TABLE F8 *Life in transition survey: General policy preferences of businesspeople*

	Incomes Equal (1)	Increase Gov. Own. (2)	Reduce Competition (3)	Immigrants Good (4)	Free Elections (5)	Law and Order (6)	Freedom of Speech (7)	Free Press (8)	Equal Rights Women (9)
Male	−0.090***	−0.155***	−0.041	0.0005	−0.025**	−0.015	−0.017*	−0.010	−0.106***
	(0.034)	(0.050)	(0.046)	(0.007)	(0.012)	(0.010)	(0.009)	(0.012)	(0.014)
Education	−0.157***	−0.026	−0.063***	0.012***	0.024***	0.023***	0.024***	0.028***	0.025***
	(0.019)	(0.022)	(0.019)	(0.004)	(0.006)	(0.006)	(0.006)	(0.007)	(0.006)
Age (log)	0.165***	0.331***	−0.178***	−0.055***	0.040**	0.033**	−0.006	−0.0005	0.008
	(0.062)	(0.075)	(0.055)	(0.016)	(0.018)	(0.016)	(0.017)	(0.020)	(0.020)
Urban Resident	0.059	−0.100	−0.129*	0.017	−0.016	−0.016	−0.020	−0.0004	0.002
	(0.080)	(0.084)	(0.073)	(0.012)	(0.029)	(0.027)	(0.027)	(0.028)	(0.023)
Employed	0.139**	−0.100	−0.112*	−0.020	0.046*	0.058***	0.034	0.033	0.059***
	(0.058)	(0.075)	(0.065)	(0.014)	(0.025)	(0.022)	(0.023)	(0.023)	(0.017)
Income (log)	−0.232***	−0.233***	−0.242***	0.011	0.028	0.023	0.016	0.012	0.017
	(0.046)	(0.068)	(0.071)	(0.007)	(0.018)	(0.017)	(0.020)	(0.023)	(0.018)
Businessperson	−0.436***	−0.238***	−0.088	0.002	0.0002	−0.004	0.008	0.025	0.007
	(0.076)	(0.075)	(0.068)	(0.010)	(0.019)	(0.017)	(0.022)	(0.026)	(0.015)
Country FE	Yes	Yes	Yes	Yes	Yes	Yes	Yes	Yes	Yes
Observations	38,764	36,734	38,306	27,673	39,494	39,639	39,471	38,694	39,454
R^2	0.127	0.049	0.054	0.381	0.055	0.054	0.059	0.044	0.052

*p<0.1; **p<0.05; ***p<0.01 This table examines respondent support for nine policy positions (outlined in the text, with scales). A respondent is coded as a businessperson if they either self-identify as a private-sector employer or they run their own business. All models include country fixed effects and cluster standard errors on country.

TABLE F9 *Life in transition survey: Preferences for government spending*

	Education (1)	Health (2)	Housing (3)	Pensions (4)	Poor People (5)	Environment (6)	Infrastructure (7)
Male	0.004	−0.025***	0.003	−0.007*	0.001	0.003**	0.015***
	(0.006)	(0.007)	(0.002)	(0.004)	(0.006)	(0.002)	(0.003)
Education	0.026***	0.003	−0.002***	−0.016***	−0.018***	0.002***	0.003***
	(0.002)	(0.003)	(0.001)	(0.002)	(0.002)	(0.0005)	(0.001)
Age (log)	−0.079***	0.054***	−0.052***	0.204***	−0.105***	−0.007***	−0.013***
	(0.009)	(0.011)	(0.008)	(0.016)	(0.011)	(0.002)	(0.003)
Urban Resident	0.007	0.022*	−0.011***	−0.016**	−0.003	0.003	0.001
	(0.008)	(0.011)	(0.004)	(0.006)	(0.011)	(0.002)	(0.003)
Employed	−0.004	−0.0003	0.007*	−0.013*	−0.0001	0.002	0.005*
	(0.009)	(0.010)	(0.004)	(0.007)	(0.008)	(0.002)	(0.003)
Income (log)	0.025***	0.015***	0.001	−0.023***	−0.029***	0.003*	0.008***
	(0.006)	(0.006)	(0.003)	(0.006)	(0.007)	(0.002)	(0.002)
Businessperson	0.013	−0.027***	−0.001	−0.015*	−0.015	0.009**	0.025***
	(0.009)	(0.009)	(0.005)	(0.009)	(0.009)	(0.004)	(0.006)
Country FE	Yes	Yes	Yes	Yes	Yes	Yes	Yes
Observations	39,723	39,723	39,723	39,723	39,723	39,723	39,723
R^2	0.060	0.031	0.031	0.085	0.050	0.014	0.023

*p<0.1; **p<0.05; ***p<0.01 This table examines respondent support for government spending across seven different categories indicated in the column headers. A respondent is coded as a Businessperson if they either self-identify as a private-sector employer or they run their own business. All models include country fixed effects and cluster standard errors on country.

less so protecting the environment. On the other hand, extra spending on health care and pensions rank as lower priorities for businesspeople. These results come through controlling for basic demographics, including logged income.

- The analysis of public opinion data in LiTS demonstrates not only do businesspeople express distinct preferences on economic questions, they also support more government intervention in areas of particular interest to the business community, such as roads and public transportation. It then follows that while in elected office, they may act on these preferences when deciding which policies to pursue.

Bibliography

Acemoglu, Daron, Simon Johnson, Amir Kermani, James Kwak, and Todd Mitton. 2013. "The Value of Connections in Turbulent Times: Evidence from the United States." *NBER Working Paper Series* (w19701).

Acosta-Ormaechea, Santiago, and Atsuyoshi Morozumi. 2017. "Public Spending Reallocations and Economic Growth across Different Income Levels." *Economic Inquiry* 55 (1): 98–114.

Adolph, Christopher. 2013. *Bankers, Bureaucrats, and Central Bank Politics: The Myth of Neutrality*. Cambridge: Cambridge University Press.

Aggarwal, Rajesh, Felix Meschke, and Tracy Wang. 2012. "Corporate Political Contributions: Investment or Agency?" *Business and Politics* 14 (1): 1–38.

Ainsworth, Scott, and Itai Sened. 1993. "The Role of Lobbyists: Entrepreneurs with Two Audiences." *American Journal of Political Science* 37 (3): 834–866.

AIS. 2016. "Belgorodskogo Gubernatora Evgeniya Savchenko Okruzhili Korruptsionery," September 12.

Akey, Pat. 2015. "Valuing Changes in Political Networks: Evidence from Campaign Contributions to Close Congressional Elections." *The Review of Financial Studies* 28 (11): 3188–3223.

Akhmedov, Akhmed, and Ekaterina Zhuravskaya. 2004. "Opportunistic Political Cycles: Test in a Young Democracy Setting." *The Quarterly Journal of Economics* 119 (4): 1301–1338.

Albin-Lackey, Chris. 2007. *Criminal Politics: Violence, "Godfathers" and Corruption in Nigeria*. Vol. 19 Human Rights Watch. Nigeria: Human Rights Watch.

Aldrich, John H. 1995. *Why Parties?: The Origin and Transformation of Political Parties in America*. Chicago: University of Chicago Press.

Alesina, Alberto, and Roberto Perotti. 1995. "The Political Economy of Budget Deficits." *Staff Papers* 42 (1): 1–31.

Aleksandrov, Aleksandr. 2011. "Sudebnaia Proverka Eserov." *Moskovskii Komsomolets*, November 08.

Amore, Mario Daniele, and Morten Bennedsen. 2013. "The Value of Local Political Connections in a Low-Corruption Environment." *Journal of Financial Economics* 110 (2): 387–402.

Ansolabehere, Stephen, James M. Snyder Jr, and Michiko Ueda. 2004. "Did Firms Profit from Soft Money?" *Election Law Journal* 3 (2): 193–198.

Arnold, Felix, Björn Kauder, and Niklas Potrafke. 2014. "Outside Earnings, Absence, and Activity: Evidence From German Parliamentarians." *European Journal of Political Economy* 36: 147–157.

Arriola, Leonardo. 2012. *Multi-Ethnic Coalitions in Africa: Business Financing of Opposition Election Campaigns*. Cambridge: Cambridge University Press.

Arter, David. 2016. "When New Party X has the 'X Factor': On Resilient Entrepreneurial Parties." *Party Politics* 22 (1): 15–26.

Artés, Joaquín, and Enrique García Viñuela. 2007. "Campaign Spending and Office-seeking Motivations: An Empirical Analysis." *Public Choice* 133 (1–2): 41–55.

Babenko, Ilona, Viktar Fedaseyeu, and Song Zhang. 2018. "Executives in Politics." *BAFFI CAREFIN Centre Research Paper* 2017-62: 1–42.

Baltrunaite, Audinga, Cristina Giorgiantonio, Sauro Mocetti, Tommaso Orlando et al. 2018. *Discretion and Supplier Selection in Public Procurement*. Technical report, Bank of Italy, Economic Research and International Relations Area.

Bandiera, Oriana, Stephen Hansen, Andrea Prat, and Raffaella Sadun. 2017. *CEO Behavior and Firm Performance*. Technical Report w23248, United States National Bureau of Economic Research.

Barndt, William T. 2014. "Corporation-Based Parties: The Present and Future of Business Politics in Latin America." *Latin American Politics and Society* 56 (3): 1–22.

Barnett, Michael L. 2007. "Stakeholder Influence Capacity and the Variability of Financial Returns to Corporate Social Responsibility." *Academy of Management Review* 32 (3): 794–816.

Baron, David P. 1989. "Service-Induced Campaign Contributions and the Electoral Equilibrium." *The Quarterly Journal of Economics* 104 (1): 45–72.

Baron, David P. 1995*a*. "Integrated Strategy: Market and Nonmarket Components." *California Management Review* 37 (2): 47–65.

Baron, David P. 1995*b*. "The Nonmarket Strategy System." *Sloan Management Review* 37 (1): 73.

Baron, David P. 2009. *Business and Its Environment*. Englewood Cliffs, NJ: Prentice Hall.

Barova, Yekaterina. 2014. "Ne Khvataet Na Zhizn: Kak Deputaty Torguyut Svoim Statusom." *Argumenty i Fakty*, February 12.

Barsukova, Svetlana. 2006. "Vlast' i Biznes: Novye Pravila Igry." *Polis: Politicheskiye Issledovaniye* (6): 135–144.

Barsukova, Svetlana. 2011. "Tenevye Pravila Vzaimootnoshenij Politikov I Predprinimatelej." *Journal of Institutional Studies* 3 (3): 40–56.

Barsukova, Svetlana Yurevna, and Vasilii Ivanovich Zvyagintsev. 2006. "Mehanizm Politicheskogo Investirovaniya, Ili Kak I Zachem Rossiiskiy Biznes Uchastvuet v Vyborah i Oplachivaet Partiinuyu Zhizn'." Polis. *Politicheskie Issledovaniya* 2: 110–121.

Bartels, Larry. 2008. "The Irrational Electorate." *Wilson Quarterly* 32: 44–50.

Baumgartner, Frank R., Christian Breunig, Christoffer Green-Pedersen, Bryan D. Jones, Peter B. Mortensen, Michiel Nuytemans, and Stefaan Walgrave. 2009.

"Punctuated Equilibrium in Comparative Perspective." *American Journal of Political Science* 53 (3): 603–620.
Baysinger, Barry D. 1984. "Domain Maintenance as an Objective of Business Political Activity: An Expanded Typology." *Academy of Management Review* 9 (2): 248–258.
BBC Monitoring, 2007. RenTV News Report, "Independent Russian MPs Allege Sale of State Duma Seats," July 6.
Beazer, Quintin H. 2014. "Political Centralization and Economic Performance: Evidence from Russia." *The Journal of Politics* 77 (1): 128–145.
Bekbulatova, Taisiya. 2018. "Russia's Invisible, Ubiquitous Lobbyists." *Meduza*, January 8.
Bender, Bryan. 2013. "Kerry to Divest Some Financial Holdings." *Boston Globe*, January 23.
Berkowitz, Daniel, and David N. DeJong. 1999. "Russia's Internal Border." *Regional Science and Urban Economics* 29 (5): 633–649.
Bershidsky, Leonid. 2015. "Another Wealthy Businessman Takes a Crack at Running a Country." *National Post*, April 20.
Bertók, János. 2003. *Managing Conflict of Interest in the Public Service: OECD Guidelines and Overview*. Paris: OECD Publishing.
Bertrand, Marianne, Francis Kramarz, Antoinette Schoar, and David Thesmar. 2018. The Cost of Political Connections. *Review of Finance* 22(3): 849–876.
Beshley, Olga. 2011, "Ohotniki do Ohotnogo Ryada." *The New Times*, November 15.
Besley, Timothy. 2005. "Political Selection." *The Journal of Economic Perspectives* 19 (3): 43–60.
Besley, Timothy, and Stephen Coate. 1997. "An Economic Model of Representative Democracy." *The Quarterly Journal of Economics* 112 (1): 85–114.
Besley, Timothy, Jose G. Montalvo, and Marta Reynal-Querol. 2011. "Do Educated Leaders Matter?" *The Economic Journal* 121 (554): F205–F227.
Best, Michael, Jonas Hjort, and David Szakonyi. 2017. "Individuals and Organizations as Sources of State Effectiveness (April 2017)." NBER Working Paper No. w23350.
Besley, Timothy, and Stephen Coate. 1997. "An Economic Model of Representative Democracy." *The Quarterly Journal of Economics* 112 (1): 85–114.
Beth, Elodie. 2007. *Integrity in Public Procurement: Good Practice from A To Z*. Organisation for Economic Co-operation and Development (OECD). Available at SSRN: https://ssrn.com/abstract=987026
Bizzarro, Fernando, John Gerring, Carl Henrik Knutsen, Allen Hicken, Michael Bernhard, Svend-Erik Skaaning, Michael Coppedge, and Staffan I. Lindberg. 2018. "Party Strength and Economic Growth." *World Politics* 70 (2): 275–320.
Blanes i Vidal, Jordi, Mirko Draca, and Christian Fons-Rosen. 2012. "Revolving Door Lobbyists." *American Economic Review* 102 (7): 3731–3748.
Blau, Benjamin M., Tyler J. Brough, and Diana W. Thomas. 2013. "Corporate Lobbying, Political Connections, and the Bailout of Banks." *Journal of Banking & Finance* 37 (8): 3007–3017.

Blaydes, Lisa. 2011. *Elections and Distributive Politics in Mubarak's Egypt*. Cambridge: Cambridge University Press.

Blinov, Andrey. 2015. "Politika. Nekassovyi Schet." *Moskovskie Novosti*, May 15.

Boas, Taylor C., F. Daniel Hidalgo, and Neal P. Richardson. 2014. "The Spoils of Victory: Campaign Donations and Government Contracts in Brazil." *Journal of Politics* 76 (2): 415–429.

Bocharova, Svetlana. 2007. "Saratovskie Stradanija." *Nezavisimaia Gazeta*, July 31.

Bonardi, Jean-Phillipe, Amy Hillman, and Gerald Keim. 2005. "The Attractiveness of Political Markets: Implication for Firm Strategies." *Academy of Management Review* 30 (2): 397–413.

Borisova, Elena. 2004. "Russkij Biznes Master-Klass Iz Zhizni Biznesmena-Oppozicionera." *Ekspert*, July 12.

Boubakri, Narjess, Omrane Guedhami, Dev Mishra, and Walid Saffar. 2012. "Political Connections and the Cost of Equity Capital." *Journal of Corporate Finance* 18 (3): 541–559.

Bowornwathana, Bidhya. 2004. "Thaksin's Model of Government Reform: Prime Ministerialisation Through 'A Country Is My Company' Approach." *Asian Journal of Political Science* 12 (1): 135–153.

Box, Richard C. 1999. "Running Government Like A Business: Implications For Public Administration Theory And Practice." *The American Review of Public Administration* 29 (1): 19–43.

Braendle, Thomas. 2016. "Do Institutions Affect Citizens' Selection Into Politics?" *Journal of Economic Surveys* 30 (2): 205–227.

Braendle, Thomas, and Alois Stutzer. 2013. "Political Selection of Public Servants and Parliamentary Oversight." *Economics of Governance* 14 (1): 45–76.

Braendle, Thomas, and Alois Stutzer. 2016. "Selection of Public Servants into Politics." *Journal of Comparative Economics* 44 (3): 696–719.

Braggion, Fabio, and Lyndon Moore. 2013. "The Economic Benefits of Political Connections in late Victorian Britain." *The Journal of Economic History* 73 (01): 142–176.

Brancati, Dawn. 2014. "Democratic Authoritarianism: Origins and Effects." *Annual Review of Political Science* 17: 313–326.

Bryansk Today. 2018. "Eks-Deputata Bryanskoy Obldumy Panteleeva Osudili Za Afery Na 12 Mln Rubley." April 11.

Brezis, Elise S., and Joël Cariolle. 2019. "The Revolving Door, State Connections, and Inequality of Influence in the Financial Sector." *Journal of Institutional Economics* 15(4): 595–614.

Brockman, Paul, Oliver M. Rui, and Huan Zou. 2013. "Institutions and the Performance of Politically Connected M&As." *Journal of International Business Studies* 44 (8): 833–852.

Bruno, Randolph Luca, Maria Bytchkova, and Saul Estrin. 2013. "Institutional Determinants of New Firm Entry in Russia: A Cross-Regional Analysis." *Review of Economics and Statistics* 95 (5): 1740–1749.

Bryk, Anthony S., and Stephen W. Raudenbush. 1992. *Hierarchical Linear Models: Applications and Data Analysis Methods*. Thousand Oaks: Sage Publications, Inc.

Buckley, Noah, and Ora John Reuter. 2019. "Performance Incentives Under Autocracy: Evidence from Russia's Regions." *Comparative Politics* 51(2): 239–266.

Bunkanwanicha, Pramuan, and Yupana Wiwattanakantang. 2009. "Big Business Owners in Politics." *Review of Financial Studies* 22 (6): 2133–2168.

Burden, Barry C. 2007. *Personal Roots of Representation*. Princeton: Princeton University Press.

Burdescu, Ruxandra, Gary J. Reid, Stephanie E. Trapnell, and Daniel W. Barnes. 2010. *Income and Asset Disclosure Systems: Establishing Good Governance Through Accountability*. Washington DC: World Bank Publications.

Buribayev, Aidar. 2012. "How Russian Elections Are Financed." *Forbes Russia*, October 11.

Bush, Jason. 2003. "Russia. Why Business Is Rushing Into Politics." *Bloomberg*, December 7.

Cain, Bruce E., and Lee Drutman. 2014. "Congressional Staff and the Revolving Door: The Impact of Regulatory Change." *Election Law Journal* 13 (1): 27–44.

Cain, Bruce, Gash Alisson, and Oleszek Mark. 2008. "Conflict of Interest Legislation in the United States: Origins, Evolution and Inter-Branch Differnces." In *Conflict of Interest and Public Life: Cross-National Perspectives*, ed. Christine Trost, and Alison L. Gash. Cambridge: Cambridge University Press pp. 101–124.

Cain, Daylian M., George Loewenstein, and Don A. Moore. 2005. "The Dirt on Coming Clean: Perverse Effects of Disclosing Conflicts of Interest." *The Journal of Legal Studies* 34 (1): 1–25.

Calder, Kent E. 1989. "Elites in an Equalizing Role: Ex-Bureaucrats as Coordinators and Intermediaries in the Japanese Government–Business Relationship." *Comparative Politics* 21 (4): 379–403.

Calonico, Sebastian, Matias D. Cattaneo, and Rocio Titiunik. 2014. "Robust Nonparametric Confidence Intervals for Regression-Discontinuity Designs." *Econometrica* 82 (6): 2295–2326.

Cameron, A. Colin, Jonah B. Gelbach, and Douglas L. Miller. 2011. "Robust Inference with Multiway Clustering." *Journal of Business & Economic Statistics* 29 (2): 238–249.

Campbell, Rosie, and Philip Cowley. 2015. "Attitudes to Moonlighting Politicians: Evidence from the United Kingdom." *Journal of Experimental Political Science* 2 (1): 63–72.

Carnes, Nicholas. 2012. "Does the Numerical Underrepresentation of the Working Class in Congress Matter?" *Legislative Studies Quarterly* 37 (1): 5–34.

Carnes, Nicholas. 2013. *White-Collar Government: The Hidden Role of Class in Economic Policy Making*. Chicago: University of Chicago Press.

Carnes, Nicholas. 2018. *The Cash Ceiling: Why Only the Rich Run for Office–and What We Can Do about It*. Princeton: Princeton University Press.

Carnes, Nicholas, and Noam Lupu. 2015. "Rethinking the Comparative Perspective on Class and Representation: Evidence from Latin America." *American Journal of Political Science* 59 (1): 1–18.

Carretta, Alessandro, Vincenzo Farina, Abhishek Gon, and Antonio Parisi. 2012. "Politicians 'on Board': Do Political Connections Affect Banking Activities in Italy?" *European Management Review* 9 (2): 75–83.

Caselli, Francesco, and Massimo Morelli. 2004. "Bad Politicians." *Journal of Public Economics* 88 (3): 759–782.

Casselman, Ben. 2017. "No One Has A Good Plan To Get Rid of Trump's Conflicts, Including Trump." *Five Thirty Eight*, January 11.

Caughey, Devin, and Jasjeet S. Sekhon. 2011. "Elections and the Regression Discontinuity Design: Lessons from Close US House Races, 1942–2008." *Political Analysis* 19 (4): 385–408.

CCS. 2015. "Comparative Candidates Survey Module I - 2005–2013 [Dataset – cumulative file]." *Distributed by FORS, Lausanne* .

Center for Responsive Politics. 2007. "Q&A: Government Officials' Blind Trusts. Interview with Dan Auble." March 8.

Chaikin, David, and Jason Sharman. 2009. *Corruption and Money Laundering: A Symbiotic Relationship*. New York: Springer.

Chaisty, Paul. 2013. "The Preponderance and Effects of Sectoral Ties in the State Duma." *Europe-Asia Studies* 65 (4): 717–736.

Chattopadhyay, Raghabendra, and Esther Duflo. 2004. "Women as Policy Makers: Evidence From a Randomized Policy Experiment in India." *Econometrica* 72 (5): 1409–1443.

Chazan, Guy. 2000. "Votes for Sale in the Duma, says Russian Banker." *Telegraph*, September 10.

Chebankova, Elena. 2010. "Business and Politics in the Russian Regions." *Journal of Communist Studies and Transition Politics* 26 (1): 25–53.

Chernyshev, Aleksey. 2005. "Regional'naya Politika. Primorskie Deputaty Rashodyatsya Po Frakcijam." *Kommersant*, June 8.

Chernyshev, Aleksey. 2007. "Primorskaya Edinaya Rossija Lishilas Edinstva." *Kommersant*, August 3.

Chernykh, Lucy. 2008. "Ultimate Ownership and Control in Russia." *Journal of Financial Economics* 88 (1): 169–192.

Chernokoz, Olga. 2013. "Pochemu v Regionalynih Parlamentah Otkryto Sidit Bisnesmeni?" *Regioni Online*, February 12.

Chistyakova, Svetlana. 2005. "Taynaya Vechera." *Zolotoye Koltso* (Yaroslavl), January 14.

Choi, Seong-Jin, Nan Jia, and Jiangyong Lu. 2014. "The Structure of Political Institutions and Effectiveness of Corporate Political Lobbying." *Organization Science* 26 (1): 158–179.

Chong, Alberto, and Mark Gradstein. 2009. "Firm-Level Determinants of Political Influence." *Economics & Politics* 22 (3): 233–256.

Chowdhury, Farah Deeba. 2009. "Problems of Women's Participation in Bangladesh Politics." *The Round Table* 98 (404): 555–567.

Cingano, Federico, and Paolo Pinotti. 2013. "Politicians At Work: The Private Returns and Social Costs of Political Connections." *Journal of the European Economic Association* 11 (2): 433–465.

Claessens, Stijn, Erik Feijen, and Luc Laeven. 2008. "Political Connections and Preferential Access to Finance: The Role of Campaign Contributions." *Journal of Financial Economics* 88 (3): 554–580.

Coase, Ronald H. 1937. "The Nature of the Firm." *Economica* 4 (16): 386–405.

Coen, David, and Matia Vannoni. 2016. "Sliding Doors in Brussels: A Career Path Analysis of EU Affairs Managers." *European Journal of Political Research* 55 (4): 811–826.

Coen, David, Wyn Grant, and Graham Wilson. 2012. "Political Science: Perspectives on Business and Government." In *The Oxford Handbook of Business and Government*, ed. David Coen, Wyn Grant, and Graham Wilson. Oxford: Oxford University Press pp. 9–34.

Colignon, Richard, and Chikako Usui. 2001. "The Resilience of Japan's Iron Triangle." *Asian Survey* 41 (5): 865–895.

Compact, UN Global. 2006. "Business Against Corruption-Case Stories and Examples." *UN Global Compact Reports* 1 (1): 25–207.

Cooper, Michael J., Huseyin Gulen, and Alexei V. Ovtchinnikov. 2010. "Corporate Political Contributions and Stock Returns." *The Journal of Finance* 65 (2): 687–724.

Corstange, Daniel. 2016. *The Price of a Vote in the Middle East*. Cambridge: Cambridge University Press.

Croissant, Aurel, and Daniel Pojar Jr. 2005. "Quo Vadis Thailand? Thai Politics after the 2005 Parliamentary Elections." *Strategic Insight* 4 (6).

Dalton, Russell J., and Steven Weldon. 2007. "Partisanship and Party System Institutionalization." *Party Politics* 13 (2): 179–196.

Damania, Richard. 2002. "Influence in Decline: Lobbying in Contracting Industries." *Economics and Politics* 14 (2): 209–223.

Dass, Nishant, Omesh Kini, Vikram Nanda, Bunyamin Onal, and Jun Wang. 2013. "Board Expertise: Do Directors From Related Industries Help Bridge The Information Gap?" *The Review of Financial Studies* 27 (5): 1533–1592.

David-Barrett, Elizabeth. 2011. *Cabs for Hire? Fixing the Revolving Door Between Government and Business*. Project Report. Transparency International UK.

Dayen, David. 2015. "Wall Street Pays Bankers to Work in Government and it Doesn't Want Anyone to Know." *The New Republic*, February 4.

de Benedictis-Kessner, Justin, and Christopher Warshaw. 2016. "Mayoral Partisanship and Municipal Fiscal Policy." *The Journal of Politics* 78 (4): 1124–1138.

de Figueiredo, John M., and Brian Kelleher Richter. 2014. "Advancing the Empirical Research on Lobbying." *Annual Review of Political Science* 17: 163–185.

De Silva, Migara O., Galina Kurlyandskaya, Elena Andreeva, and Natalia Golovanova. 2009. *Intergovernmental Reforms in the Russian Federation: One Step Forward, Two Steps Back?* Washington, DC: World Bank.

DeBacker, Jason. 2012. "Political Parties and Political Shirking." *Public Choice* 150 (3–4): 651–670.

Deng, Guosheng, and Scott Kennedy. 2010. "Big Business and Industry Association Lobbying in China: The Paradox of Contrasting Styles." *The China Journal* (63): 101–125.

Denisov, Dmitry. 2010. "Business Lobbying and Government Relations in Russia: The Need for New Principles." *Reuters Institute Fellowship Paper*.

Desai, Raj, and Anders Olofsgard. 2008. "Do Politically Connected Firms Undermine Their Own Competitiveness? Evidence from Developing Countries." *Brookings Global Economy and Development Working Paper* (18).

Desposato, Scott W. 2006. "Parties for Rent? Ambition, Ideology, and Party Switching in Brazil's Chamber of Deputies." *American Journal of Political Science* 50 (1): 62–80.

Di Bella, Gabriel, Oksana Dynnikova, and Francesco Grigoli. 2017. Fiscal Federalism and Regional Performance. Working Paper WP/17/265 International Monetary Fund.

Dickson, Bruce J. 2007. "Integrating Wealth and Power in China: The Communist Party's Embrace of the Private Sector." *China Quarterly* 192: 827–854.

DiMaggio, Paul, and Walter Powell. 1983. "The Iron Cage Revisited: Institutional Isomorphism and Collective Rationality in Organizational Fields." *American Sociological Review* 48 (2): 147–160.

Dmitriev, Igor. 2009. "Prodai Zapros: Kak Deputaty Gosdumy Delayut Biznes na Sobstvenniye Zaprosy." *Versiya.Ru*, December 7.

Dixit, Avinash. 2018. "Anti-Corruption Institutions: Some History and Theory." In *Institutions, Governance and the Control of Corruption*. Springer pp. 15–49.

Djankov, Simeon, Rafael La Porta, Florencio Lopez-de Silanes, and Andrei Shleifer. 2010. "Disclosure by Politicians." *American Economic Journal: Applied Economics* 2 (2): 179–209.

Dobel, Patrick. 1993. "The Realpolitik of Ethics Codes: An Implementation Approach to Public Ethics." In H George Frederickson (Ed.), *Ethics and Public Administration*. Armonk, NY: M. E. Sharpe. pp. 158–174.

Doner, Richard F., and Ben Ross Schneider. 2000. "Business Associations and Economic Development: Why Some Associations Contribute More Than Others." *Business and Politics* 2 (3): 261–288.

Dreher, Axel, Michael J. Lamla, Sarah M. Lein, and Frank Somogyi. 2009. "The Impact of Political Leaders' Profession and Education on Reforms." *Journal of Comparative Economics* 37 (1): 169–193.

Drokova, Yuliya and Mikhail Rudnyev. 2008. "TDSK Deneg Ne Nashla." *Vedomosti*, November 24.

Drucker, Joshua. 2015. "An Evaluation of Competitive Industrial Structure and Regional Manufacturing Employment Change." *Regional Studies* 49 (9): 1481–1496.

Drutman, Lee. 2015*a*. *The Business of America is Lobbying: How Corporations Became Politicized and Politics Became More Corporate*. Oxford: Oxford University Press.

Drutman, Lee. 2015*b*. "How Corporate Lobbyists Conquered American Democracy." *Atlantic*, April 20.

Dunaev, Daniil. 2015. "Omsky Edinorossy Gotovyat' K Chistke Ryadov." *Nezavisimaia Gazeta*, July 23.

Duvanova, Dinissa. 2013. *Building Business in Post-Communist Russia, Eastern Europe, and Eurasia: Collective Goods, Selective Incentives, and Predatory States*. Cambridge: Cambridge University Press.

Earle, John S., and Scott Gehlbach. 2015. "The Productivity Consequences of Political Turnover: Firm-Level Evidence from Ukraine's Orange Revolution." *American Journal of Political Science* 59 (3): 708–723.

The Economist. 2016. "Mandarin Lessons." March 10.

Eggers, Andrew, Anthony Fowler, Jens Hainmueller, Andrew Hall, and James M. Snyder. 2014. "On the Validity of the Regression Discontinuity Design for Estimating Electoral Effects: New Evidence from Over 40,000 Close Races." *American Journal of Political Science* 59 (1): 259–274.

Eggers, Andrew C., and Jens Hainmueller. 2009. "MPs for Sale? Returns to Office in Postwar British Politics." *American Political Science Review* 103 (04): 513–533.

Engvall, Johan. 2014. "Why are Public Offices Sold in Kyrgyzstan?" *Post-Soviet Affairs* 30 (1): 67–85.

Enikolopov, Ruben, and Ekaterina Zhuravskaya. 2007. "Decentralization and Political Institutions." *Journal of Public Economics* 91 (11–12): 2261–2290.

Enikolopov, Ruben, and Sergey Stepanov. 2013. "Corporate Governance in Russia." In *The Oxford Handbook of the Russian Economy*, ed. Michael Alexeev, and Shlomo Weber. Oxford: Oxford University Press pp. 242–220.

Ezrow, Natasha M., and Erica Frantz. 2011. *Dictators and Dictatorships: Understanding Authoritarian Regimes and Their Leaders*. Bloomsbury Publishing USA.

Facchini, Giovanni, Anna Maria Mayda, and Prachi Mishra. 2011. "Do Interest Groups Affect US Immigration Policy?" *Journal of International Economics* 85 (1): 114–128.

Faccio, Mara. 2006. "Politically-Connected Firms." *The American Economic Review* 96 (1): 369–386.

Faccio, Mara, Ronald W. Masulis, and John McConnell. 2006. "Political Connections and Corporate Bailouts." *The Journal of Finance* 61 (6): 2597–2635.

Fafchamps, Marcel. 1996. "The Enforcement of Commercial Contracts in Ghana." *World Development* 24 (3): 427–448.

Fairfield, Tasha. 2010. "Business Power and Tax Reform: Taxing Income and Profits in Chile And Argentina." *Latin American Politics and Society* 52 (2): 37–71.

Fairfield, Tasha. 2015. *Private Wealth and Public Revenue: Business Power and Tax Politics*. Cambridge: Cambridge University Press.

Fang, Lee. 2013. "The Reverse Revolving Door: How Corporate Insiders Are Rewarded Upon Leaving Firms for Congress." *The Nation*, May 4.

Fatullaev, Milrad. 2000. "Komu Vlast' - Tomu I Rybki Vslast'." *Nezavisimaja Gazeta*, October 14.

Fedele, Alessandro, and Paolo Naticchioni. 2016. "Moonlighting Politicians: Motivation Matters!" *German Economic Review* 17 (2): 127–156.

Feintzeig, Rachel. 2014. "U.S. Struggles to Draw Young, Savvy Staff." *Wall Street Journal*, July 10.

Ferguson, Thomas, and Hans-Joachim Voth. 2008. "Betting on Hitler—the Value of Political Connections in Nazi Germany." *The Quarterly Journal of Economics* 123 (1): 101–137.

Ferraz, Claudio, and Frederico Finan. 2008. "Exposing Corrupt Politicians: the Effects of Brazil's Publicly Released Audits on Electoral Outcomes." *The Quarterly Journal of Economics* 123 (2): 703–745.
Ferree, Karen E., G. Bingham Powell, and Ethan Scheiner. 2014. "Context, Electoral Rules, and Party Systems." *Annual Review of Political Science* 17: 421–439.
Ferris, Gerald R., Darren C. Treadway, Pamela L. Perrewé, Robyn L. Brouer, Ceasar Douglas, and Sean Lux. 2007. "Political Skill in Organizations." *Journal of Management* 33 (3): 290–320.
Filippovskii, Ernest. 2018. "Vziatku mera naukograda sochli moshennichestvom." *Kommersant*, July 7.
Fisman, Raymond. 2001. "Estimating the Value of Political Connections." *The American Economic Review* 91 (4): 1095–1102.
Fisman, Raymond, Florian Schulz, and Vikrant Vig. 2012. "Private Returns to Public Office." *Journal of Political Economy* 122 (4): 806–862.
Fox, Richard L., and Jennifer L. Lawless. 2011. "Gaining and Losing Interest in Running for Public Office: The Concept of Dynamic Political Ambition." *The Journal of Politics* 73 (02): 443–462.
Fredriksson, Per G., and Jim R. Wollscheid. 2014. "Political Institutions, Political Careers and Environmental Policy." *Kyklos* 67 (1): 54–73.
Freinkman, Lev, and Alexander Plekhanov. 2009. "Fiscal Decentralization in Rentier Regions: Evidence from Russia." *World Development* 37 (2): 503–512.
Freytes, Carlos. 2015. "The Cerrado is Not the Pampas: Explaining Tax and Regulatory Policies on Agricultural Exports in Argentina and Brazil (2003–2013)." *Doctoral Thesis, Northwestern University, USA.*
Frye, Timothy. 2002. "Capture or Exchange? Business Lobbying in Russia." *Europe-Asia Studies* 54 (7): 1017–1036.
Frye, Timothy. 2006. "Original Sin, Good Works, and Property Rights in Russia." *World Politics* 58 (4): 479.
Frye, Timothy, and Andrei Shleifer. 1997. "The Invisible Hand and the Grabbing Hand." *The American Economic Review* 87 (2): 354–358.
Frye, Timothy, Andrei Yakovlev, and Yevgeny Yasin. 2009. "The 'Other' Russian Economy: How Everyday Firms View the Rules of the Game in Russia." *Social Research: An International Quarterly* 76 (1): 29–54.
Frye, Timothy, Ora John Reuter, and David Szakonyi. 2014. "Political Machines at Work: Voter Mobilization and Electoral Subversion in the Workplace." *World Politics* 66 (2): 195–228.
Frye, Timothy, Ora John Reuter, and David Szakonyi. 2019. "Hitting Them with Carrots: Voter Intimidation and Vote Buying in Russia." *British Journal of Political Science* 49(3): 857–881.
Frye, Timothy, Ora John Reuter, and David Szakonyi. 2019. "Vote Brokers, Clientelist Appeals, and Voter Turnout: Evidence from Russia and Venezuela." *World Politics* 71(4): 710–746.
Fung, Archon, Mary Graham, and David Weil. 2007. *Full Disclosure: The Perils and Promise of Transparency*. Cambridge: Cambridge University Press.
Gagliarducci, Stefano, Tommaso Nannicini, and Paolo Naticchioni. 2010. "Moonlighting Politicians." *Journal of Public Economics* 94 (9–10): 688–699.

Gandhi, Jennifer. 2008. *Political Institutions under Dictatorship*. Cambridge: Cambridge University Press.

Gandhi, Jennifer, and Abigail L. Heller. 2018. "Electoral Systems in Authoritarian States." *The Oxford Handbook of Electoral Systems* p. 387.

Gandhi, Jennifer, and Ellen Lust-Okar. 2009. "Elections Under Authoritarianism." *Annual Review of Political Science* 12 (1): 403–422.

Gans-Morse, Jordan. 2012. "Threats to Property Rights in Russia: From Private Coercion to State Aggression." *Post-Soviet Affairs* 28 (3): 263–295.

Gardner, Simon, and Rodrigo Martinez. 2010. "Chile's Pinera Unveils Business-Heavy Cabinet." *Reuters*, February 9.

Gehlbach, Scott. 2006. "The Consequences of Collective Action: An Incomplete Contracts Approach." *American Journal of Political Science* 50 (3): 802–823.

Gehlbach, Scott, Konstantin Sonin, and Ekaterina Zhuravskaya. 2010. "Businessman Candidates." *American Journal of Political Science* 54 (3): 718–736.

Gehlbach, Scott, and Philip Keefer. 2011. "Investment Without Democracy: Ruling-Party Institutionalization and Credible Commitment in Autocracies." *Journal of Comparative Economics* 39 (2): 123–139.

Gehlbach, Scott, and Philip Keefer. 2012. "Private Investment and the Institutionalization of Collective Action in Autocracies: Ruling Parties and Legislatures." *The Journal of Politics* 74 (02): 621–635.

Gelman, Andrew, and Jennifer Hill. 2006. *Data Analysis Using Regression and Multilevel/Hierarchical Models*. Cambridge: Cambridge University Press.

Gel'man, Vladimir. 2008. "Party Politics in Russia: From Competition to Hierarchy." *Europe-Asia Studies* 60 (6): 913–930.

Gerber, Theodore P. 2001. "Paths to Success: Individual and Regional Determinants of Self-Employment Entry in Post-Communist Russia." *International Journal of Sociology* 31 (2): 3–37.

Gerber, Theodore P., and Olga Mayorova. 2006. "Dynamic Gender Differences in a Post-Socialist Labor Market: Russia, 1991–1997." *Social Forces* 84 (4): 2047–2075.

Geys, Benny, and Karsten Mause. 2013. "Moonlighting Politicians: A Survey and Research Agenda." *The Journal of Legislative Studies* 19 (1): 76–97.

Gibson, James L., Cornelius P. Cotter, John F. Bibby, and Robert J. Huckshorn. 1983. "Assessing Party Organizational Strength." *American Journal of Political Science* 27(2): 193–222.

Gibson, James L., Cornelius P. Cotter, John F. Bibby, and Robert J. Huckshorn. 1985. "Whither The Local Parties?: A Cross-Sectional and Longitudinal Analysis of the Strength of Party Organizations." *American Journal of Political Science* 29(1): 139–160.

Gilens, Martin, and Benjamin I. Page. 2014. "Testing Theories of American Politics: Elites, Interest Groups, and Average Citizens." *Perspectives on Politics* 12 (3): 564–581.

Gimpel, James G., Frances E. Lee, and Michael Parrott. 2014. "Business Interests and the Party Coalitions: Industry Sector Contributions to us Congressional Campaigns." *American Politics Research* 42 (6): 1034–1076.

Godwin, Erik K., R. Kenneth Godwin, and Scott Ainsworth. 2007. "Is Corporate Lobbying Rational or Just a Waste of Money." In *Interest Group Politics*, ed. A.J. Cigler, and B.A. Loomis. Washington: Congressional Quarterly Press pp. 256–278.

Goldman, Eitan, Jorg Rocholl, and Jongil So. 2013. "Politically Connected Boards of Directors and the Allocation of Procurement Contracts." *Review of Finance* 17 (5): 1617–1648.

Goldstein, Rebecca, and Hye Young You. 2017. "Cities as Lobbyists." *American Journal of Political Science* 61 (4): 864–876.

Golosov, Grigorii. 2011. "Russia's Regional Legislative Elections, 2003-2007: Authoritarianism Incorporated." *Europe-Asia Studies* 63 (3): 397–414.

Golosov, Grigorii. 2014. "Co-optation in the Process of Dominant Party System Building: the Case of Russia." *East European Politics* 30 (2): 271–285.

Gong, Ting, and Jianming Ren. 2013. "Hard Rules and Soft Constraints: Regulating Conflict of Interest in China." *Journal of Contemporary China* 22 (79): 1–17.

Gordon, Sanford C., and Catherine Hafer. 2007. "Corporate Influence and the Regulatory Mandate." *Journal of Politics* 69 (2): 300–319.

Gordon, Sanford C., Catherine Hafer, and Dimitri Landa. 2007. "Consumption or Investment? On Motivations for Political Giving." *Journal of Politics* 69 (4): 1057–1072.

Gormley Jr, William T. 1979. "A Test of the Revolving Door Hypothesis at the FCC." *American Journal of Political Science* 23 (4): 665–683.

Govorun, Andrei, Israel Marques, and William Pyle. 2016. "The Political Roots of Intermediated Lobbying: Evidence from Russian Enterprises and Business Associations." *Business and Politics* 18 (4): 395–433.

Grashhenkov, Il'ja, and Maksim Mejer. 2016. "Faktor Vlijanija Finansovo-Promyshlennyh Grupp Na Regional"nuju Politiku." *Vlast'* 86: 85–89.

Gray, Stephen, Iman Harymawan, and John Nowland. 2016. "Political and Government Connections on Corporate Boards in Australia: Good for Business?" *Australian Journal of Management* 41 (1): 3–26.

Greve, Henrich R. 1998. "Managerial Cognition and The Mimetic Adoption of Market Positions: What You See Is What You Do." *Strategic Management Journal* 19(10): 967–988.

Grier, Kevin B., Michael C. Munger, and Brian E. Roberts. 1994. "The Determinants of Industry Political Activity, 1978-1986." *American Political Science Review* 88 (4): 911–926.

Großer, Jens, Ernesto Reuben, and Agnieszka Tymula. 2013. "Political Quid Pro Quo Agreements: An Experimental Ctudy." *American Journal of Political Science* 57 (3): 582–597.

Grossman, Gene M., and Elhanan Helpman. 1994. "Protection for Sale." *American Economic Review* 84 (4): 833–850.

Haber, Stephen. 2006. "Authoritarian Government." In *The Oxford Handbook of Political Economy*, ed. Donald Wittman Barry Weingast. Oxford: Oxford University Press pp. 693–707.

Habershon, Alexandra, and Stephanie Trapnell. 2012. *Public Office, Private Interests: Accountability Through Income and Asset Disclosure*. Washington DC: World Bank Publications.

Hacker, Jacob S., and Paul Pierson. 2011. *Winner-Take-All Politics: How Washington Made the Rich Richer–and Turned its Back on the Middle Class*. New York: Simon and Schuster.

Hadani, Michael. 2007. "Family Matters: Founding Family Firms and Corporate Political Activity." *Business and Society* 46 (4): 395–428.

Hadani, Michael, and Douglas A Schuler. 2013. "In Search of El Dorado: The Elusive Financial Returns on Corporate Political Investments." *Strategic Management Journal* 34 (2): 165–181.

Hale, Henry. 2005. *Why Not Parties in Russia?: Democracy, Federalism, and the State*. Cambridge: Cambridge University Press.

Hale, Henry E. 2003. "Explaining Machine Politics in Russia's Regions: Economy, Ethnicity, and Legacy." *Post-Soviet Affairs* 19 (3): 228–263.

Hall, Andrew. 2015. "The Candidate Supply: How the Costs and Benefits of Running for Office Shape the Democratic Process." PhD thesis Harvard University.

Hall, Joshua C., Serkan Karadas, and Minh Tam Tammy Schlosky. 2017. "Abnormal Returns from Joining Congress? Evidence from New Members." *Journal of Financial Economic Policy* 9 (4): 450–474.

Hall, Richard L., and Alan V. Deardorff. 2006. "Lobbying as Legislative Subsidy." *American Political Science Review* 100 (01): 69–84.

Han, Li. 2007. "Marketing Politics? Economic Reforms and the Selection of Political Elites in China." Department of Economics Job Market Paper. Cambridge, MA: Harvard University.

Hansen, Eric R., Nicholas Carnes, and Virginia Gray. 2018. "What Happens When Insurers Make Insurance Laws? State Legislative Agendas and the Occupational Makeup of Government." *State Politics & Policy Quarterly* 19(2): 155–179.

Hansen, Wendy, and Neil Mitchell. 2000. "Disaggregating and Explaining Corporate Political Activity: Domestic and Foreign Corporations in National Politics." *American Political Science Review* 94 (4): 891–903.

Harstad, Bård, and Jakob Svensson. 2011. "Bribes, Lobbying, and Development." *American Political Science Review* 105 (01): 46–63.

Hart, David M. 2001. "Why Do Some Firms Give? Why Do Some Give a Lot?: High-Tech PACs, 1977–1996." *The Journal of Politics* 63 (04): 1230–1249.

Haveman, Heather A. 1993. "Follow the Leader: Mimetic Isomorphism and Entry into New Markets." *Administrative Science Quarterly* pp. 593–627.

Heyaskin, Georgii. 2012. "Bourgeoisie in Power: Rules of the Game of Business in Politics." *Uhhan Sire*, June 4.

Healy, Andrew, and Neil Malhotra. 2009. "Myopic Voters and Natural Disaster Policy." *American Political Science Review* 103 (3): 387–406.

Healy, Andrew, and Neil Malhotra. 2013. "Retrospective Voting Reconsidered." *Annual Review of Political Science* 16: 285–306.

Heinz, John P. 1993. *The Hollow Core: Private Interests in National Policy Making*. Cambridge, MA: Harvard University Press.

Heller, William B, and Carol Mershon. 2005. "Party Switching in the Italian Chamber of Deputies, 1996–2001." *The Journal of Politics* 67 (2): 536–559.

Hellman, Joel S. 1998. "Winners Take All: The Politics of Partial Reform in Postcommunist Transitions." *World Politics* 50 (2): 203–234.

Hellman, Joel S., Geraint Jones, and Daniel Kaufmann. 2003. "Seize the State, Seize the Day: State Capture and Influence in Transition Economies." *Journal of Comparative Economics* 31 (4): 751–773.

Henisz, Witold J. 2000. "The Institutional Environment for Economic Growth." *Economics and Politics* 12 (1): 1–31.

Herron, Erik S., and Nazar Boyko. 2015. "Horizontal Accountability During Political Transition: The Use of Deputy Requests in Ukraine, 2002–2006." *Party Politics* 21 (1): 131–142.

Hertel-Fernandez, Alex. 2019. *State Capture: How Conservative Activists, Big Businesses, and Wealthy Donors Reshaped the American States–and the Nation*. Oxford: Oxford University Press.

Hertel-Fernandez, Alexander. 2017. "American Employers as Political Machines." *The Journal of Politics* 79 (1): 105–117.

Hicken, Allen, and Erik Martínez Kuhonta. 2011. "Shadows from the Past: Party System Institutionalization in Asia." *Comparative Political Studies* 44 (5): 572–597.

Hill, Matthew D., G. Wayne Kelly, G. Brandon Lockhart, and Robert A. Ness. 2013. "Determinants and Effects of Corporate Lobbying." *Financial Management* 42 (4): 931–957.

Hillman, A J. 2005. "Politicians on the Board of Directors: Do Connections Affect the Bottom Line?" *Journal of Management* 31 (3): 464–481.

Hillman, A.J., and M.A. Hitt. 1999. "Corporate Political Strategy Formulation: A Model of Approach, Participation, and Strategy Decisions." *Academy of Management Review* 24(4): 825–842.

Hillman, Amy J., Gerald D. Keim, and Douglas Schuler. 2004. "Corporate Political Activity: A Review and Research Agenda." *Journal of Management* 30 (6): 837–857.

Hillman, Arye L. 1982. "Declining Industries and Political-Support Protectionist Motives." *The American Economic Review* 72 (5): 1180–1187.

Hiscox, Michael J. 2004. "International Capital Mobility and Trade Politics: Capital Flows, Coalitions and Lobbying." *Economics & Politics* 16 (3): 253–285.

Hojnacki, Marie, Kathleen M. Marchetti, Frank R. Baumgartner, Jeffrey M. Berry, David C. Kimball, and Beth L. Leech. 2015. "Assessing Business Advantage in Washington Lobbying." *Interest Groups & Advocacy* 4 (3): 205–224.

Hopkins, Daniel J., and Katherine T. McCabe. 2012. "After It's Too Late: Estimating the Policy Impacts of Black Mayoralties in US Cities." *American Politics Research* 40 (4): 665–700.

Horiuchi, Akiyoshi, and Katsutoshi Shimizu. 2001. "Did Amakudari Undermine The Effectiveness Of Regulator Monitoring In Japan?" *Journal of Banking & Finance* 25 (3): 573–596.

Hou, Yue. 2019. *The Private Sector in Public Office*. Cambridge: Cambridge University Press.

Houston, Joel F., Liangliang Jiang, Chen Lin, and Yue Ma. 2014. "Political Connections and the Cost of Bank Loans." *Journal of Accounting Research* 52 (1): 193–243.

Hunter, Floyd. 2017. *Community Power Structure*. Garden City: Ancher Books.
Huntington, Samuel P. 1970. "Social and Institutional Dynamics of One-Party Systems." In *Authoritarian Politics in Modern Society: The Dynamics of Established Party Systems*, ed. Samuel P. Huntington, and Clement H. Moore. New York: Basic Books.
Hurka, Steffen, Lukas Obholzer, and William T. Daniel. 2018. "When Time Is Money: Sideline Jobs, Ancillary Income and Legislative Effort." *Journal of European Public Policy* 25(5): 651–669.
Hutcheson, Derek. 2008. "Russia: Electoral Campaigning in a 'Managed Democracy'." In *The Routledge Handbook of Political Management*. London/New York: Routledge pp. 98–121.
Hutcheson, Derek S. 2012. "Party Finance in Russia." *East European Politics* 28 (3): 267–282.
Iacus, Stefano M., Gary King, and Giuseppe Porro. 2011. "Causal Inference without Balance Checking: Coarsened Exact Matching." *Political Analysis* 20 (1): 1–24.
Igan, Deniz, Prachi Mishra, and Thierry Tressel. 2011. "A Fistful of Dollars: Lobbying and the Financial Crisis." *NBER Working Paper Series* (w17076).
Issacharoff, Samuel, and Daniel R. Ortiz. 1999. "Governing through Intermediaries." *Virginia Law Review* pp. 1627–1670.
ITAR-TASS. 2012. "Gosduma Prekratila Deputatskie Polnomochiya Knyshova S 22 Oktyabrya."
Ivonina, Alla. 2009. "Tomskii Stroitelniy Kompleks: Otkat Let Na Pyat' Nazad." *Vsyo Delo V Tomske*, April 30.
Iwasaki, Ichiro. 2017. "Corporate Governance System and Regional Heterogeneity: Evidence from East and West Russia." *RRC Working Paper Series* (72).
John, Anna, Tazeeb S. Rajwani, and Thomas C. Lawton. 2015. "Corporate Political Activity." In *The Routledge Companion to Non-Market Strategy*, ed. Thomas C. Lawton and Tazeeb S. Rajwani. New York: Routledge pp. 103–150.
Johnson, Chalmers. 1982. *Miti and the Japanese Miracle: The Growth of Industrial Policy: 1925-1975*. Palo Alto: Stanford University Press.
Jones, Benjamin F., and Benjamin A. Olken. 2005. "Do Leaders Matter? National Leadership and Growth since World War II." *The Quarterly Journal of Economics* 120 (3): 835–864.
Josefsson, Cecilia. 2014. "Who Benefits From Gender Quotas? Assessing the Impact of Election Procedure Reform on Members of Parliament's Attributes in Uganda." *International Political Science Review* 35 (1): 93–105.
Junisbai, Barbara. 2012. "Improbable but Potentially Pivotal Oppositions: Privatization, Capitalists, and Political Contestation in the Post-Soviet Autocracies." *Perspectives on Politics* 10 (04): 891–916.
Kang, Karam. 2015. "Policy Influence and Private Returns from Lobbying in the Energy Sector." *The Review of Economic Studies* 83 (1): 269–305.
Karhunen, Päivi, and Svetlana Ledyaeva. 2010. "Determinants of Entrepreneurial Interest and Risk Tolerance Among Russian University Students: Empirical Study." *Journal of Enterprising Culture* 18 (03): 229–263.
Katsourides, Yiannos. 2012. "Composition, Recruitment and Career Patterns of the Political Elite in Cyprus (1988–2010)." *The Cyprus Review* 24 (1): 15–37.

Kazun, Anton. 2015. "Violent Corporate Raiding in Russia: Preconditions and Protective Factors." *Demokratizatsiya: The Journal of Post-Soviet Democratization* 23 (4): 459–484.

Kennedy, Scott. 2009. "Comparing Formal and Informal Lobbying Practices in China: The Capital's Ambivalent Embrace of Capitalists." *China Information* 23 (2): 195–222.

Kenyon, Thomas, and Megumi Naoi. 2010. "Policy Uncertainty In Hybrid Regimes: Evidence From Firm-Level Surveys." *Comparative Political Studies* 43 (4): 486–510.

Kersh, Rogan. 2000. "State Autonomy & Civil Society: The Lobbyist Connection." *Critical Review* 14 (2–3): 237–258.

Khwaja, Asim, and Atif Mian. 2005. "Do Lenders Favor Politically Connected Firms? Rent Provision in an Emerging Financial Market." *Quarterly Journal of Economics* 120 (4): 1371–1411.

Kim, Jin-Hyuk. 2008. "Corporate Lobbying Revisited." *Business and Politics* 10 (2): 1–23.

Kitschelt, Herbert, Zdenka Mansfeldova, Radoslaw Markowski, and Gabor Toka. 1999. *Post-Communist Party Systems: Competition, Representation, and Inter-party Cooperation.* Cambridge: Cambridge University Press.

Koffsky, Daniel L. 1995. "Coming to Terms with Bureaucratic Ethics." *Journal of Law and Politics* 11: 235.

Kohli, Atul. 2012. *Poverty Amid Plenty In The New India.* Cambridge: Cambridge University Press.

Kokoshkina, Elena. 2018. "Nepomerniye Zaprosi: Kak Deputaty Predstavlyayut Interesy Izbirateleu Vtaine ot Nikh." *Team29*, February 2.

Kolhatkar, Sheelah. 2016. "Trump's Conflict-of-Interest Problem." *New Yorker*, November 14.

Komarov, Mikhail. 2003. "Podrobnosti. Gosbrigady." *Novaia Gazeta* No.56, August 4.

Kommersant. 2005. "Istorija Konflikta Belgorodskih Vlastej S 'Inteko." October 11.

Kommersant. 2011. "Businessmen in Big Politics." September 16.

Kopevcek, Lubomír. 2016. "'I'm Paying, So I Decide' Czech ANO as an Extreme Form of a Business-Firm Party." *East European Politics and Societies* 30 (4): 725–749.

Kornai, Janos. 1986. "The Soft Budget Constraint." *Kyklos* 39 (1): 3–30.

Koter, Dominika. 2017. "Costly Electoral Campaigns and the Changing Composition and Quality of Parliament: Evidence from Benin." *African Affairs* 116 (465): 573–596.

Krasno, Jonathan S., Donald Philip Green, and Jonathan A. Cowden. 1994. "The Dynamics of Campaign Fundraising in House Elections." *The Journal of Politics* 56 (2): 459–474.

Krauss, Ellis, Kuniaki Nemoto, and Robert Pekkanen. 2012. "Reverse Contamination Burning and Building Bridges in Mixed-Member Systems." *Comparative Political Studies* 45 (6): 747–773.

Kravcova, Marija. 2005. "Politika Regiony. Perezagruzka Regional'nyh Jelit." *Expert*, October 24.

Kroeger, Alex. 2018. "Dominant Party Rule, Elections, and Cabinet Instability in African Autocracies." *British Journal of Political Science*. Forthcomings.

Kryshtanovskaya, Olga, and Stephen White. 2005. "The Rise of the Russian Business Elite." *Communist and Post-Communist Studies* 38 (3): 293–307.

Kuenzi, Michelle, and Gina Lambright. 2001. "Party System Institutionalization in 30 African Countries." *Party Politics* 7 (4): 437–468.

Kunicova, Jana, and Thomas Frederick Remington. 2008. "Mandates, Parties and Dissent Effect of Electoral Rules on Parliamentary Party Cohesion in the Russian State Duma, 1994–2003." *Party Politics* 14 (5): 555–574.

Kyriacou, Andreas P., Leonel Muinelo-Gallo, and Oriol Roca-Sagalés. 2015. "Construction Corrupts: Empirical Evidence from a Panel of 42 Countries." *Public Choice* 165 (1–2): 123–145.

LaPira, Timothy M., and Herschel F. Thomas. 2014. "Revolving Door Lobbyists and Interest Representation." *Interest Groups & Advocacy* 3 (1): 4–29.

Lau, Edwin, Zsuzsanna Lonti, and Rebecca Schultz. 2017. "Challenges in the Measurement of Public Sector Productivity in OECD Countries." *International Productivity Monitor* 32: 180–195.

Lawton, Thomas, Steven McGuire, and Tazeeb Rajwani. 2013. "Corporate Political Activity: A Literature Review and Research Agenda." *International Journal of Management Reviews* 15 (1): 86–105.

Ledeneva, Alena. 2011. "Can Medvedev Change Sistema? Informal Networks and Public Administration in Russia." In *Russia as a Network State*, ed. Vadim Kononenko, and Arkady Moshes. London: Palgrave Macmillan: pp. 39–61.

Lee, David S. 2008. "Randomized Experiments from Non-Random Selection in US House Elections." *Journal of Econometrics* 142 (2): 675–697.

Lee, Seungjoo, and Sang-Young Rhyu. 2008. "The Political Dynamics of Informal Networks in South Korea: The Case of Parachute Appointment." *The Pacific Review* 21 (1): 45–66.

Levin, Nikolay. 2003. "Role and Significance of the Regional Legislative Branch in the Formation and Perfection of Budget-Financial Policy." In *Budget Policy of Regions, Cities and Communes in Europe*, ed. Petrozavodsk State University. Petrozavodsk: pp. 4–8.

Levitsky, Steven, and Daniel Ziblatt. 2018. *How Democracies Die*. New York: Crown.

Lewis-Faupel, Sean, Yusuf Neggers, Benjamin A. Olken, and Rohini Pande. 2016. "Can Electronic Procurement Improve Infrastructure Provision? Evidence from Public Works in India and Indonesia." *American Economic Journal: Economic Policy* 8 (3): 258–283.

Li, Danielle. 2017. "Expertise versus Bias in Evaluation: Evidence from the NIH." *American Economic Journal: Applied Economics* 9 (2): 60–92.

Li, Hongbin, Lingsheng Meng, and Junsen Zhang. 2006. "Why Do Entrepreneurs Enter Politics? Evidence from China." *Economic Inquiry* 44 (3): 559–578.

Li, Hongbin, Lingsheng Meng, Qian Wang, and Li-An Zhou. 2008. "Political Connections, Financing and Firm Performance: Evidence from Chinese Private Firms." *Journal of Development Economics* 87 (2): 283–299.

Li, Julie Juan, Laura Poppo, and Kevin Zheng Zhou. 2008. "Do Managerial Ties in China Always Produce Value? Competition, Uncertainty, and Domestic vs. Foreign Firms." *Strategic Management Journal* 29 (4): 383–400.

Li, Xu-Hong, and Xiaoya Liang. 2015. "A Confucian Social Model of Political Appointments among Chinese Private-firm Entrepreneurs." *Academy of Management Journal* 58 (2): 592–617.

Libman, Alexander, and Anastassia V. Obydenkova. 2015. "CPSU Legacies and Regional Democracy in Contemporary Russia." *Political Studies* 63 (1): 173–190.

Libman, Alexander, Tatiana G. Dolgopyatova, and Andrei A. Yakovlev. 2014. "The Birth of an Entrepreneurial Board in Emerging Markets: A Russian Case." Higher School of Economics Research Paper No. WP BRP 29/MAN/2014.

Lieberman, Marvin B, and Shigeru Asaba. 2006. "Why do Firms Imitate Each Other?" *Academy of Management Review* 31 (2): 366–385.

Lindblom, Charles Edward. 1977. *Politics and Markets: The World's Political Economic Systems*. New York: Basic Books.

Lipton, Eric, and Ben Protess. 2014. "Law Doesn't End Revolving Door on Capitol Hill." *New York Times*, February 1.

Litvinova, Yekaterina. 2009. "TDSK Polushila Podkrepleniye Ot Minoborony." *Kommersant*. August 21.

Logan, John, and Harvey Molotch. 1987. *Urban Fortunes*. Berkeley: University of California Press.

Lowery, David, and Kathleen Marchetti. 2012. "You Don't Know Jack: Principals, Agents and Lobbying." *Interest Groups & Advocacy* 1 (2): 139–170.

Lucca, David, Amit Seru, and Francesco Trebbi. 2014. "The Revolving Door and Worker Flows in Banking Regulation." *Journal of Monetary Economics* 65: 17–32.

Luechinger, Simon, and Christoph Moser. 2014. "The Value of the Revolving Door: Political Appointees and the Stock Market." *Journal of Public Economics* 119: 93–107.

Lupu, Noam. 2016. *Party Brands In Crisis: Partisanship, Brand Dilution, and the Breakdown of Political Parties in Latin America*. Cambridge: Cambridge University Press.

Lust, Ellen. 2009. "Competitive Clientelism in the Middle East." *Journal of Democracy* 20 (3): 122–135.

Lux, S., T. R. Crook, and D. J. Woehr. 2011. "Mixing Business With Politics: A Meta-Analysis of the Antecedents and Outcomes of Corporate Political Activity." *Journal of Management* 37 (1): 223–247.

Lyubarev, Arkady. 2011. "Electoral Legislation in Russian Regions." *Europe-Asia Studies* 63 (3): 415–427.

Macher, Jeffrey T., and John W. Mayo. 2015. "Influencing Public Policymaking: Firm, Industry-, and Country-level Determinants." *Strategic Management Journal* 36 (13): 2021–2038.

Mackenzie, G. Calvin with Michael Hafkin. 2002. *Scandal Proof: Do Ethics Laws Make Government Ethical?* Washington DC: Brookings Institution Press.

Maestas, Cherie D., Sarah Fulton, L. Sandy Maisel, and Walter J. Stone. 2006. "When to Risk It? Institutions, Ambitions, and the Decision to Run for The US House." *American Political Science Review* 100 (2): 195.

Magaloni, Beatriz. 2006. *Voting for Autocracy: Hegemonic Party Survival and its Demise in Mexico*. Cambridge: Cambridge University Press.

Mainwaring, Scott, and Mariano Torcal. 2006. "Party System Institutionalization and Party System Theory After the Third Wave of Democratization." *Handbook of Party Politics* 11 (6): 204–227.

Makkai, Toni, and John Braithwaite. 1992. "In and Out of the Revolving Door: Making Sense of Regulatory Capture." *Journal of Public Policy* 12 (01): 61–78.

Mansbridge, Jane. 2009. "A 'Selection Model' of Political Representation." *Journal of Political Philosophy* 17 (4): 369–398.

Mantovani, Massimo. 2014. "The Private Sector Role in the Fight against Corruption." In *Preventing Corporate Corruption. The Anti-Bribery Compliance Model*, ed. Stefano Manacorda, Francesco Centonze, and Gabrio Forti. Cham, Springer: Switzerland, pp. 35–42.

March, Luke. 2009. "Managing Opposition in a Hybrid Regime: Just Russia and Parastatal Opposition." *Slavic Review* 68 (3): 504–527.

Markus, Stanislav. 2012. "Secure Property as a Bottom-Up Process: Firms, Stakeholders, and Predators in Weak States." *World Politics* 64 (02): 242–277.

Markus, Stanislav, and Volha Charnysh. 2017. "The Flexible Few: Oligarchs and Wealth Defense in Developing Democracies." *Comparative Political Studies* 50 (12): 1632–1665.

Marques, Israel. 2017. "Political Connections and Non-Traditional Investment: Evidence from Public-Private Partnerships in Vocational Education." *SSRN Working Paper* .

Marques, Israel, Andrei Govorun, and William Pyle. 2014. "The Political Roots of Intermediated Lobbying: Evidence from Russian Firms and Business Associations." *Higher School of Economics Research Paper* (WP BRP 46/EC/2013).

Martini, Maira. 2015. Cooling Off Periods: Regulating The Revolving Door. Technical Report 40 Transparency International.

Mashin, D. V. 2016. "Pomoshh' Torgovo-Promyshlennyh Palat V Lobbirovanii Interesov Biznesa: Regional'nyj Vzgljad." *Pravozashhitnik* 1: 17–22.

Maskell, Jack. 2014. Financial Assets and Conflict of Interest Regulation in the Executive Branch. Technical Report R43365 Congressional Research Service.

Massini, Silvia, Arie Y. Lewin, and Henrich R. Greve. 2005. "Innovators and Imitators: Organizational Reference Groups and Adoption of Organizational Routines." *Research Policy* 34 (10): 1550–1569.

Maury, Benjamin, and Eva Liljeblom. 2009. "Oligarchs, Political Regime Changes, and Firm Valuation." *Economics of Transition* 17 (3): 411–438.

McCarty, Nolan, and Lawrence S. Rothenberg. 1996. "Commitment and the Campaign Contribution Contract." *American Journal of Political Science* 40 (3): 872–904.

McCrary, Justin. 2008. "Manipulation of the Running Variable in the Regression Discontinuity Design: A Density Test." *Journal of Econometrics* 142 (2): 698–714.

McIntire Drewmarch. 2007. "In '05 Investing, Obama Took Same Path as Donors." *New York Times*, March 7.

McMenamin, Ian. 2012. "If Money Talks, What Does It Say? Varieties of Capitalism and Business Financing of Parties." *World Politics* 64 (1): 1–38.

McMillan, John, and Pablo Zoido. 2004. "How to Subvert Democracy: Montesinos in Peru." *Journal of Economic Perspectives* 18 (4): 69–92.

Medvedev, Yuri. 2010. "Institut Vyborov I Jelektoral"nye Processy V Sovremennom Mire." *Vestnik Permskogo Universiteta* 1 (9): 5–12.

Mereu, Francesca. 2003. "Business Will Have Big Voice in Duma." *Moscow Times*, November 11.

Mershon, Carol, and Olga Shvetsova. 2008. "Parliamentary Cycles and Party Switching in Legislatures." *Comparative Political Studies* 41 (1): 99–127.

Mezias, Stephen J. 1990. "An Institutional Model of Organizational Practice: Financial Reporting at the Fortune 200." *Administrative Science Quarterly* 35 (3): 431–457.

Miller, Gary J. 2005. "The Political Evolution of Principal-agent Models." *Annual Review of Political Science* 8: 203–225.

Mikhailov, Vladislav. 2012. "Stroika Posle Nokdouna." *Ekspert Sibir*, April 30. No. 17–18.

Mikhailov, Vladislav. 2013. "Raveneniye Na Million." *Ekspert Online*, March 11.

Milyo, Jeffrey, David Primo, and Timothy Groseclose. 2000. "Corporate PAC Campaign Contributions in Perspective." *Business and Politics* 2 (1): 75–88.

Minor, Dylan. 2016. "The Organization of Nonmarket Strategy." In *Strategy Beyond Markets*. Emerald Group Publishing Limited pp. 413–436.

Miquel, Gerard Padro I., and James M. Snyder Jr. 2006. "Legislative Effectiveness and Legislative Careers." *Legislative Studies Quarterly* 31 (3): 347–381.

Mironov, Maxim. 2013. "Taxes, Theft, and Firm Performance." *The Journal of Finance* 68 (4): 1441–1472.

Mironov, Maxim, and Ekaterina Zhuravskaya. 2016. "Corruption in Procurement and the Political Cycle In Tunneling: Evidence from Financial Transactions Data." *American Economic Journal: Economic Policy* 8 (2): 287–321.

Mizoguchi, Tetsuro, and Nguyen Van Quyen. 2012. "Amakudari: The Post-Retirement Employment of Elite Bureaucrats in Japan." *Journal of Public Economic Theory* 14 (5): 813–847.

Molokaeva, Oksana. 2014. "Formy Dejatel"nosti Deputatov Parlamentov Subjektov Rossijskoj Federacii, Uchastvujushhih V Rabote Komitetov I Komissij." *Vedomosti Moskovskoj Gorodskoj Dumy* 1: 50–54.

Morton, Rebecca, and Charles Cameron. 1992. "Elections and the Theory of Campaign Contributions: A Survey and Critical Analysis." *Economics & Politics* 4 (1): 79–108.

Murashhenkov, Sergej Viktorovich. 2009. "Formirovanie Lobbistskih Otnoshenij Na Regional"nom Urovne: Institucional"nyj Aspekt." *Izvestija Tul'skogo Gosudarstvennogo Universiteta. Gumanitarnye Nauki* 2.

Murtazin, Irek. 2013. "Deputatom Mozhet Stat' Kazhdyi." *Novaya Gazeta*, May 15.

Musacchio, Aldo, and Ian Read. 2007. "Bankers, Industrialists, and their Cliques: Elite Networks in Mexico and Brazil During Early Industrialization." *Enterprise & Society* 8 (4): 842–880.

Myers, Steven Lee. 2003. "Big Business Plays Largest Role in Current Russian Vote." *New York Times*, December 2.

Naoi, Megumi, and Ellis Krauss. 2009. "Who Lobbies Whom? Special Interest Politics Under Alternative Electoral Systems." *American Journal of Political Science* 53 (4): 874–892.

Naurin, Elin. 2011. *Election Promises, Party Behaviour and Voter Perceptions*. Basingstoke: Palgrave Macmillan.

Nawrocki, David, and William Carter. 2010. "Industry Competitiveness Using Herfindahl and Entropy Concentration Indices with Firm Market Capitalization Data." *Applied Economics* 42 (22): 2855–2863.

NDI. 1999. Legislative Ethics: A Comparative Analysis. Research paper 4 National Democratic Institute for International Affairs Washington DC.

Noble, Ben. 2017. "Amending Budget Bills in the Russian State Duma." *Post-Communist Economies* 29 (4): 505–522.

Nolan, Beth. 1992. "Public Interest, Private Income: Conflicts and Control Limits on the Outside Income of Government Officials." *Northwestern University Law Review* 87: 57.

Norris, Pippa. 1996. "The Nolan Committee: Financial Interests and Constituency Service." *Government and Opposition* 31 (4): 441–448.

Norris, Pippa. 1997. *Passages to Power: Legislative Recruitment in Advanced Democracies*. Cambridge: Cambridge University Press.

Norris, Pippa, and Andrea Abel Van Es. 2016. *Checkbook Elections?: Political Finance in Comparative Perspective*. Oxford: Oxford University Press.

North, Douglass C. 1991. "Institutions." *Journal of Economic Perspectives* 5 (1): 97–112.

Novoselov, Sergey, and Marina Lepina. 2005. "Pobeg. Deputat Ushel S Zaimom." *Kommersant*, December 16.

Nownes, Anthony J. 2013. *Interest Groups in American Politics: Pressure and Power*. Hoboken: Routledge.

OECD. 2011. *Asset Declarations for Public Officials: A Tool to Prevent Corruption*. Paris: OECD Publishing.

OECD. 2015. *Government at a Glance 2015*. Paris: OECD Publishing.

Okhmatovskiy, Ilya. 2010. "Performance Implications of Ties to the Government and SOEs: A Political Embeddedness Perspective." *Journal of Management Studies* 47 (6): 1020–1047.

Olken, Benjamin A. 2007. "Monitoring Corruption: Evidence from a Field Experiment In Indonesia." *Journal of political Economy* 115 (2): 200–249.

Olson, Mancur. 1965. *The Logic of Collective Action: Public Goods and the Theory of Groups*. Cambridge, MA: Harvard University Press.

Orttung, Robert W., and Sufian Zhemukhov. 2014. "The 2014 Sochi Olympic Mega-Project and Russia's Political Economy." *East European Politics* 30 (2): 175–191.

Osborne, Martin J., and Al Slivinski. 1996. "A Model of Political Competition with Citizen-Candidates." *The Quarterly Journal of Economics* 111 (1): 65–96.

Ozer, Mine, and Seung-Hyun Lee. 2009. "When Do Firms Prefer Individual Action to Collective Action in The Pursuit of Corporate Political Strategy? A New Perspective on Industry Concentration." *Business and Politics* 11 (1): 1–23.

Palda, Filip. 1992. "The Determinants of Campaign Spending: The Role of the Government Jackpot." *Economic Inquiry* 30 (4): 627–638.

Palguta, Ján, and Filip Pertold. 2017. "Manipulation of Procurement Contracts: Evidence from the Introduction of Discretionary Thresholds." *American Economic Journal: Economic Policy* 9 (2): 293–315.

Palmer, Maxwell, and Benjamin Schneer. 2016. "Capitol Gains: The Returns to Elected Office from Corporate Board Directorships." *The Journal of Politics* 78 (1): 181–196.

Pan, Yigang, Lefa Teng, Atipol Bhanich Supapol, Xiongwen Lu, Dan Huang, and Zhennan Wang. 2014. "Firms' FDI ownership: The Influence of Government Ownership and Legislative Connections." *Journal of International Business Studies* 45: 1029–1043.

Paniagua, Victoria. 2017. "Elites, Portfolio Diversification, and Business Influence." APSA 2017 Conference Paper.

Panov, Petr, and Cameron Ross. 2013. "Patterns of Electoral Contestation in Russian Regional Assemblies: Between 'Competitive' and 'Hegemonic' Authoritarianism." *Demokratizatsiya: The Journal of Post-Soviet Democratization* 21 (3): 369–399.

Pasmi.Ru 2017. "V Sverdlovskoy Oblasti Byvshego Deputata Osudyat Za Moshennichestvo." November 1.

Pekkanen, Robert, Benjamin Nyblade, and Ellis S. Krauss. 2006. "Electoral Incentives in Mixed-Member Systems: Party, Posts, and Zombie Politicians in Japan." *American Political Science Review* 100 (02): 183–193.

Pepinsky, Thomas. 2014. "The Institutional Turn in Comparative Authoritarianism." *British Journal of Political Science* 44 (03): 631–653.

Pepinsky, Thomas B. 2009. *Economic Crises and the Breakdown of Authoritarian Regimes: Indonesia and Malaysia in Comparative Perspective*. Cambridge: Cambridge University Press.

Percev, Andrey. 2013. "V Kremle Ob Yetom Bespredele Znayut." *Gazeta.Ru*, September 9.

Pérez, Silvia Guerra, Carolina Bona Sánchez, and Domingo Javier Santana Martín. 2015. "Politically Connected Firms in Spain." *BRQ Business Research Quarterly* 18 (4): 230–245.

Petersen, Mitchell A., and Raghuram G. Rajan. 1995. "The Effect of Credit Market Competition on Lending Relationships." *The Quarterly Journal of Economics* 110 (2): 407–443.

Peterson, Steven A. 1992. "Workplace Politicization and its Political Spillovers: A Research Note." *Economic and Industrial Democracy* 13 (4): 511–524.

Petrov, Ilya. 2008. "Ryad Tomskiy Stroitelniy Kompanii Stolknulis s Nedobrosovestniyi Konkurentsii." *Chas Pik, Tomsk 2 TV*, November 11.

Petrova, Maria, and Robert H. Bates. 2012. "Evolution of Risk and Political Regimes." *Economics & Politics* 24 (2): 200–225.

Petukhova, Ekaterina. 2015. "Guba ne Duma." *Lenta.ru*, February 6.

Phongpaichit, Pasuk, and Chris Baker. 2004. "Pluto-Populism in Thailand: Business Remaking Politics." In *Populism and Reformism in Southeast Asia: The Threat and Promise of New Politics*, ed. Eva-Lotta E. Hedman, and John T. Sidel. New Haven Yale University Council Southeast Asia Studies Monograph Series.

Pistor, Katharina. 1996. "Supply and Demand for Contract Enforcement in Russia: Courts, Arbitration, and Private Enforcement." *Review of Central and East European Law* 22: 55–87.

Pitkin, Hanna F. 1967. *The Concept of Representation.* Berkeley: University of California Press.

Pittman, Russell. 1977. "Market Structure and Campaign Contributions." *Public Choice* 31 (1): 37–52.

Porter, Michael E. 1980. *Competitive Strategy: Techniques for Analyzing Industries and Competition.* New York: Free Press.

Powell, Eleanor Neff, and Justin Grimmer. 2016. "Money in Exile: Campaign Contributions and Committee Access." *The Journal of Politics* 78 (4): 974–988.

Press Service of the Tomsk Regional Branch of the "Patriots of Russia" Political Party. 2013. "Evgeny Krotov Calls for Competition in the Construction Sector." September 24.

Proshu Slova! 2004. Uralsykie Obschvestvenniye Vedomosti. December 1.

Przeworski, Adam, Susan C. Stokes, and Bernard Manin. 1999. *Democracy, Accountability, and Representation.* Cambridge: Cambridge University Press.

Public Citizen. 2017. "The Impact of the STOCK Act on Stock Trading Activity by U.S. Senators, 2009–2015." Technical report, Public Citizen Washington.

Purdum, Todd. 2012. "An Age-Old Ruse." *Vanity Fair*, July.

Pyle, William. 2009. "Organized Business, Political Competition, and Property Rights: Evidence from the Russian Federation." *The Journal of Law, Economics, & Organization* 27 (1): 2–31.

Querubin, Pablo, and James M. Snyder Jr. 2011. "The Control of Politicians in Normal Times and Times of Crisis: Wealth Accumulation by US Congressmen, 1850–1880." *NBER Working Paper Series* (w17634).

Quraishi, S.Y., and Sam Van Der Staak. 2015. "Asia's Big Democracies Are Drowning in Campaign Cash." *Foreign Policy*, April 27.

Ragozina, Yelena. 2007. "Shhedrye, No Skrytnye." *Vedomosti*, March 13.

Rastorguyev, Sergey. 2012. "Biznes I Predstavitel"naja Vlast" V Central"nom Federal"nom Okruge Rf V 2000–2011 Gg." *Vlast"* pp. 146–152.

Rastorguyev, Sergey. 2014. "Vzaimootnoshenija Vlasti I Biznesa V Regionah Rossii: Stereotipy I Real'naja Praktika." *Obozrevatel" Observer* 1: 103–109.

Remington, Thomas. 2008. "Patronage and the Party of Power: President–Parliament Relations under Vladimir Putin." *Europe-Asia Studies* 60 (6): 959–987.

Remington, Thomas. 2016. "Here's How Alexander Hamilton Would Understand Russia's Regional Debt Crisis." *Washington Post*, March 24.

Reuter, Ora John. 2017. *The Origins of Dominant Parties*. Cambridge: Cambridge University Press.

Reuter, Ora John, and David Szakonyi. 2015. "Online Social Media and Political Awareness in Authoritarian Regimes." *British Journal of Political Science* 45(1): 29–51.

Reuter, Ora John, and David Szakonyi. 2019. "Elite Defection under Autocracy: Evidence from Russia." *American Political Science Review* 113 (2): 552–568.

Reuter, Ora John, and Graeme B. Robertson. 2012. "Subnational Appointments in Authoritarian Regimes: Evidence from Russian Gubernatorial Appointments." *The Journal of Politics* 74 (4): 1023–1037.

Reuter, Ora John, and Graeme B. Robertson. 2015. "Legislatures, Cooptation, and Social Protest in Contemporary Authoritarian Regimes." *The Journal of Politics* 77 (1): 235–248.

Reuter, Ora John, and Rostislav Turovsky. 2014. "Dominant Party Rule and Legislative Leadership in Authoritarian Regimes." *Party Politics* 20 (5): 663–674.

Reuter, Ora John, and Thomas F Remington. 2009. "Dominant Party Regimes and the Commitment Problem: The Case of United Russia." *Comparative Political Studies* 42 (4): 501–526.

RFE/RL Newsline. 2005. "Lawyer's Death Linked to Feud Between Luzhkov's Wife and Belgorod Authorities." October 13.

Rhoades, Stephen A. 1993. "The Herfindahl-Hirschman Index." *Federal Reserve Bulletin* 79: 188.

RIA Novosti. 2005. "V Tule Za Moshennichestvo Zaderzhan Deputat Gorodskoj Dumy." April 25.

RIA Novosti. 2013. "Problemy Vybora U Izvestnyh Tomichey Net: Mnogie Golosovali Za Kleina." October 13.

RIA Tomsk. 2014. "God U Vlasti: Kak Tomichi Ocenivajut Pervye Itogi Raboty Mjera Klyaina." *RIA Novosti*, October 16.

Richter, Brian Kelleher. 2010. "The Role Political Connections Play in Access to Finance: Evidence from Cross-Listing." *SSRN Working Paper 1503542*.

Richter, Brian Kelleher, Krislert Samphantharak, and Jeffrey F. Timmons. 2009. "Lobbying and Taxes." *American Journal of Political Science* 53 (4): 893–909.

Roberts, Andrew. 2018. "Millionaires and the Public in Czech Politics." *Post-Soviet Affairs* 34 (6): 353–366.

Robinson, James A., and Ragnar Torvik. 2005. "White Elephants." *Journal of Public Economics* 89 (2): 197–210.

Rochlitz, Michael. 2014. "Corporate Raiding and the Role of the State in Russia." *Post-Soviet Affairs* 30 (2–3): 89–114.

Romanova, Lyudmila. 2006. "Revolution of the Governing." *Vedomosti Smart Money*, November 11.

Romney, Mitt. 2011. "2011 GOP Debate in Tampa, Florida, Sponsored by the Tea Party Express." *CNN*. September 22.

Rose, Richard. 2000. "A Supply-Side View of Russia's Elections." *East European Constitutional Review* 9: 53.

Rose, Richard, and William Mishler. 2010. "A Supply-Demand Model of Party-System Institutionalization: The Russian Case." *Party Politics* 16 (6): 801–821.

Rosenson, Beth A. 2005. *The Shadowlands of Conduct: Ethics and State Politics.* Washington DC: Georgetown University Press.

Rosenson, Beth A. 2006. "The Impact of Ethics Laws on Legislative Recruitment and the Occupational Composition of State Legislatures." *Political Research Quarterly* 59 (4): 619–627.

Rosenthal, Alan. 2001. *The Third House: Lobbyists and Lobbying in the States.* Washington: Congressional Quarterly.

Rosica, James. 2014. "Suit Asks Court to Stop Politicians' Use of Blind Trusts." *Tribune/Scripps Capital Bureau.* May 14.

Ross, Cameron. 2007. "Municipal Reform in the Russian Federation and Putin's 'Electoral Vertical'." *Demokratizatsiya* 15 (2): 191.

Ross, Cameron, and Adrian Campbell. 2008. *Federalism and Local Politics in Russia.* New York: Routledge.

Rossi, Ivana Maria, Laura Pop, and Tammar Berger. 2017. *Getting the Full Picture on Public Officials: A How-to Guide for Effective Financial Disclosure.* Washington DC: World Bank Publications.

Roth, Andrew. 2013. "Russian Legislator's Body Is Found in a Barrel Filled With Concrete." *New York Times*, February 18.

Roundtable, OECD Russian Corporate Governance. 2002. "White Paper on Corporate Governance in Russia."

Saikkonen, Inga A-L. 2015. "Variation in Subnational Electoral Authoritarianism: Evidence from the Russian Federation." *Democratization* 23 (3): 437–458.

Sakaeva, Maria. 2014. "Politicheskoe Uchastie Malogo Biznesa Kak Strategija Zashhity Sobstvennosti V Rossijskih Regionah." *Terra Economicus* 12 (3): 152–161.

Sakaeva, Maria. 2015. "Biznesmeny V Organah Zakonodatel'noj Vlasti: Ispol'zovanie Deputatskogo Statusa V Predprinimatel'skoj Dejatel'nosti." PhD thesis Higher School of Economics, Moscow, Russia.

Sakaeva, Maria. 2016. "Biznesmeny V Zakonodatel'nyh Sobranijah Regionov-Status Kak Zashhita I Preferencija." *Sociologicheskie Issledovanija* 4: 142–146.

Sakharevich, Galina. 2017. "Tomsk Bez Granits." *Russkii Reporter, No. 19*, October 23.

Savage, Dean. 1974. "Patterns of Access to Business Leadership in France." *International Studies of Management & Organization* 4 (1–2): 115–137.

Savkin, Aleksej. 2009. "Deputatskij Zanos." *Russkye Newsweek*, June 1.

SGS. 2012. Press Conference. "Elections and Businessperson Participation: Interview with Lev Novikov." February 7.

Scheck, Justin, and Charles Forelle. 2014. "The Business of Lords: How the House of Lords Mixes Politics and Business." *Wall Street Journal*, November 21.

Schedler, Andreas. 2013. *The Politics of Uncertainty: Sustaining and Subverting Electoral Authoritarianism.* Oxford: Oxford University Press.

Schlesinger, Joseph A. 1966. *Ambition and Politics: Political Careers in the United States.* Chicago: Rand McNally.

Schneider, Ben Ross. 2010. "Business Politics and Policy Making in Contemporary Latin America." In *How Democracy Works: Political Institutions,*

Actors and Arenas in Latin American Policymaking, ed. by Carlos Scartascini, Ernesto Stein, and Mariano Tommasi. Cambridge: Inter-American Development Bank and David Rockefeller Center for Latin American Studies, Harvard University, pp. 217–246.

Schneider, Ben Ross. 2012. "Business Politics in Latin America: Patterns of Fragmentation and Centralization." In *The Oxford Handbook of Business and Government*, ed. David Coen, Wyn Grant, and Graham Wilson. Oxford: Oxford University Press pp. 307–329.

Schneider, Ben Ross. 2013. *Hierarchical Capitalism in Latin America*. Cambridge: Cambridge University Press.

Schuler, Douglas A., Kathleen Rehbein, and Roxy D. Cramer. 2002. "Pursuing Strategic Advantage Through Political Means: A Multivariate Approach." *Academy of Management Journal* 45 (4): 659–672.

Sedlak, Alena. 2007. "Mandates for the Business Class." *Yuzhniy Reporter*, April 23.

Semenova, Elena. 2012. "Patterns of Parliamentary Representation and Careers in Ukraine: 1990–2007." *East European Politics & Societies* 26 (3): 538–560.

Semykina, Anastasia, and Susan J. Linz. 2007. "Gender Differences in Personality and Earnings: Evidence from Russia." *Journal of Economic Psychology* 28 (3): 387–410.

Sergeev, Anatoliy. 2009. "Stroisya, Kto Mozhet." *Noviye Izvestiye*, No. 82, May 20.

Sergeyev, Sergey. 2017. "Delo Tabak." *Kommersant*, June 22.

Sharafutdinova, Gulnaz. 2006. "When do Elites Compete? The Determinants of Political Competition in Russian Regions." *Comparative Politics* 38 (3): 273–293.

Sharafutdinova, Gulnaz. 2010. *Political Consequences of Crony Capitalism Inside Russia*. Notre Dame: University of Notre Dame Press.

Sharafutdinova, Gulnaz, and Rostislav Turovsky. 2017. "The Politics of Federal Transfers in Putin's Russia: Regional Competition, Lobbying, and Federal Priorities." *Post-Soviet Affairs* 33 (2): 161–175.

Sharafutidnova, Gulnaz. 2013. "Getting the Dough and Saving the Machine: Lessons from Tatarstan." *Demokratizatsiya* 21 (4): 507.

Shear, Michael D. 2016. "For Obama, Lack of Huge Stock Portfolio Helps Avoid Need for Blind Trust." *Washington Post*, April 16.

Shestopalova, Nelli. 2014. "Ne Ponravilas' Posadka. Dorogoy Sedan Mjera Tomska Pomenayut Na Dorozhnuyu Tehniku." *Smart News*, January 5.

Shleifer, Andrei, and Daniel Treisman. 2014. "Normal Countries: The East 25 Years After Communism." *Foreign Affairs* 93 (6).

Shleifer, Andrei, and Robert W Vishny. 1993. "Corruption." *The Quarterly Journal of Economics* 108 (3): 599–617.

Shugart, Matthew, and Martin P. Wattenberg. 2001. *Mixed-Member Electoral Systems: The Best of Both Worlds?* Oxford: Oxford University Press.

Sieberer, Ulrich. 2010. "Behavioral Consequences of Mixed Electoral Systems: Deviating Voting Behavior of District and List MPs in the German Bundestag." *Electoral Studies* 29 (3): 484–496.

Siegel, Jordan. 2007. "Contingent Political Capital and International Alliances: Evidence from South Korea." *Administrative Science Quarterly* 52 (4): 621–666.

Sjöberg, Fredrik. 2011. *Competitive Elections in Authoritarian States. Weak States, Strong Elites, and Fractional Societies in Central Asia and Beyond.* Upsala: Statsvetenskapliga Institutionen.

Slinko, Irina, Evgeny Yakovlev, and Ekaterina Zhuravskaya. 2005. "Laws for Sale: Evidence from Russia." *American Law and Economics Review* 7 (1): 284–318.

Smilov, Daniel, and Jurij Toplak. 2008. *Political Finance and Corruption in Eastern Europe the Transition Period.* Farnham: Ashgate Publishing, Ltd.

Smirnov, Konstantin. 2013. "Deputat I Ego Krysha." *Vid Sboku*, March 3.

Smirnov, Sergei. 2010. "Zachem Biznesmenam Deputatstvo?" *Delo.ru*, October 28.

Smyth, Regina. 2005. *Candidate Strategies and Electoral Competition in the Russian Federation: Democracy Without Foundation.* Cambridge: Cambridge University Press.

Snyder Jr, James M. 1990. "Campaign Contributions as Investments: The US House of Representatives, 1980–1986." *Journal of Political Economy* 98 (6): 1195–1227.

Snyder Jr, James M. 1992. "Long-term Investing in Politicians; or, Give Early, Give Often." *Journal of Law and Economics* 35 (1): 15–44.

Spector, Regine A. 2008. "Securing Property in Contemporary Kyrgyzstan." *Post-Soviet Affairs* 24 (2): 149–176.

Spiller, Pablo T., and Sanny Liao. 2006. Buy, Lobby or Sue: Interest Groups' Participation in Policy Making-A Selective Survey. Technical Report National Bureau of Economic Research.

Sprenger, Carsten. 2010. "State Ownership in the Russian Economy: Its Magnitude, Structure and Governance Problems." *ICEF Working Paper* .

Staat, Christian, and Colin R. Kuehnhanss. 2017. "Outside Earnings, Electoral Systems and Legislative Effort in the European Parliament." *JCMS: Journal of Common Market Studies* 55 (2): 368–386.

Stark, Andrew. 2008. "Conflict of Interest in Canada." In *Conflict of Interest and Public Life: Cross-National Perspectives*, ed. Christine Trost, and Alison L. Gash. Cambridge: Cambridge University Press pp. 125–155.

Stephenson, Matthew C. 2003. "'When the Devil Turns...': The Political Foundations of Independent Judicial Review." *The Journal of Legal Studies* 32 (1): 59–89.

Stephenson, Matthew C., and Howell E. Jackson. 2010. "Lobbyists as Imperfect Agents: Implications for Public Policy in a Pluralist System." *Harvard Journal on Legislation* 47: 1.

Stone, Clarence. 1989. *Regime Politics: Governing Atlanta, 1946–1988.* Lawrence: University Press of Kansas.

Stone, Walter J., and L. Sandy Maisel. 2003. "The Not-So-Simple Calculus of Winning: Potential US House Candidates' Nomination and General Election Prospects." *Journal of Politics* 65 (4): 951–977.

Stratmann, Thomas. 1998. "The Market for Congressional Votes: Is Timing of Contributions Everything?" *The Journal of Law and Economics* 41 (1): 85–114.

Susman, Thomas M., and Margaret H. Martin. 2006. "Contingent Fee Lobbying: Inflaming Avarice or Facilitating Constitutional Rights." *Seton Hall Legislative Journal* 31: 311.

Svinin, Viktor. 2008. "V Tomske Zhdut Defolta." *Nezavisimaya Gazeta*, No. 219, October 10.

Svolik, Milan W. 2012. *The Politics of Authoritarian Rule*. Cambridge: Cambridge University Press.

Syverson, Chad. 2011. "What Determines Productivity?" *Journal of Economic Literature* 49 (2): 326–365.

Szakonyi, David. 2018*a*. "Businesspeople in Elected Office: Identifying Private Benefits from Firm-Level Returns." *American Political Science Review* 112 (2): 322–338.

Szakonyi, David. 2020. "Indecent Disclosures: Anti-Corruption Reforms and Political Selection." *Available at SSRN 3101123*.

Szakonyi, David. 2019. "Princelings in the Private Sector: The Value of Nepotism." *Quarterly Journal of Political Science* 14 (4): 349–381.

Szakonyi, David, and Johannes Urpelainen. 2014. "Who Benefits from Economic Reform? Firms and Distributive Politics." *The Journal of Politics* 76 (3): 841–858.

Tagadryan, Tsiala. 2007*a*. "Na Krjuchke U Minfina." *Yuzhniye Reporter*, April 23.

Tagadryan, Tsiala. 2007b. "OOO Vybory." *Yuhnyie Reporter*, April 23.

Takiye Delo. 2018. "V Krasnoyarske Deputat Pered Vyborami Otkryl Blagotvoritel'nyj Proekt Za Schet Biznesmena, Kotorogo Zapugal." April 5.

Tarakanova, Tatyana. 2008. "Chekista I Deputata Obvinjajut V Moshennichestve." *Rossiiskaia gazeta*, May 17.

Tausanovitch, Chris, and Christopher Warshaw. 2014. "Representation in Municipal Government." *American Political Science Review* 108 (3): 605–641.

Tavits, Margit. 2009. "The Making of Mavericks Local Loyalties and Party Defection." *Comparative Political Studies* 42 (6): 793–815.

Teterevkova, Evgenia, Sergey Fedorov, and Viacheslav Gareev Dentons. 2017. "Corporate Governance And Directors' Duties." *Practical Law – Global Guide*, pp. 1–10.

Tev, Dmitriy. 2016. "Jekonomicheskaja Jelita Rf: Opyt Raboty V Politiko-Administrativnoj Sfere." *Zhurnal Politicheskoj Filosofii I Sociologii Politiki «Politija. Analiz. Hronika. Prognoz»* 2 (81): 89–108.

Thames, Frank C. 2005. "A House Divided Party Strength and the Mandate Divide in Hungary, Russia, and Ukraine." *Comparative Political Studies* 38 (3): 282–303.

Thames Jr, Frank C. 2001. "Legislative Voting Behaviour in the Russian Duma: Understanding the Effect of Mandate." *Europe-Asia Studies* 53 (6): 869–884.

Tomz, Michael, and Robert P. Van Houweling. 2012. "Political Pledges as Credible Commitments." Unpublished Manuscript. Available at: https://dl.dropboxusercontent.com/u/24724021/Pledges.pdf.

Transparency International. 2017. "Kak Zarabatyvayut Na Goskontraktah Krupneyshie Donory Politicheskih Partiy." Altai Regional Office Report. March 27.

Traynor, Ian. "Europa: 30,000 Lobbyists and Counting: Is Brussels Under Corporate Sway?" *Guardian*, May 8, 2014.

Treisman, Daniel. 2000. "The Causes of Corruption: A Cross-National Study." *Journal of Public Economics* 76 (3): 399–457.

Treisman, Daniel. 2007. "What Have We Learned about the Causes of Corruption from Ten Years of Cross-national Empirical Research?" *Annual Review of Political Science* 10: 211–244.

Truex, Rory. 2014. "The Returns to Office in a 'Rubber Stamp' Parliament." *American Political Science Review* 108 (02): 235–251.

Turovskii, Rostislav. 2004. Regional'nye Modeli Vzaimodejstvija Mezhdu Delovymi I Vlastnymi Jelitami: Sovremennye Processy I Ih Social'no-Politicheskie Posledstvija. Technical report Institut Obshhestvennogo Proektirovanija: Itogovyj Analiticheskij Doklad.

Turovskii, Rostislav. 2008. "The Representation of Business Elites in Regional Politics: Étatism, Elitism and Clientelism." In *Federalism and Local Politics in Russia*, ed. Cameron Ross, and Adrian Campbell. London: Routledge pp. 200–222.

Turovskii, Rostislav F. 2012. Regional Models of Cooperation Between Business and Political Elites: Modern Processes and Their Socio-Political Consequences. Technical report Center for Political Technologies, Russia.

Turovsky, Rostislav. 2007. "The Influence of Russian Big Business on Regional Power: Models and Political Consequences." In *Politics in the Russian regions*, ed. Graeme J Gill. London: Springer pp. 138–161.

Turovsky, Rostislav. 2018. "Institutionalization Versus Personalization: Electoral Effects of the Mixed-Member Electoral System in Russia." *European Politics and Society* pp. 1–28.

Vandermey, Anne, and Nicolas Rapp. 2012. "Who Needs a Blind Trust?" *Fortune*. October 22.

Udal'tsov, Vitalij. 2015. "Dolgova 'Kidayut'. Sponsor Kprf Ostaetsya Bez Korochki Deputata." *Rupor73*, September 18.

Ura.Ru. 2012. "Deputat Zaksobranija Sverdlovskoj Oblasti Skonchalsja Ot Peredozirovki Narkotikov." March 6.

Ura.ru News Agency. 2008. "Permskiy Deputat-Biznesmen Podozrevaetsya V Uklonenii Ot Uplaty Nalogov. Sledovateli Dobivayutsya Vozbuzhdeniya Ugolovnogo Dela." September 9.

Vasil'eva, Liudmila. 2016. "Edinoi Rossi V Primor'e Ishchut Novogo Lidera." *Nezavisimaia Gazeta*, November 2.

Vinogradov, Nikoai. 2009. "Khoroshii Zanos Prevreshaetsya v Deputatskiy Zapros." *Russian Newsweek*, June 2.

Vygon, Solomon. 2006. "Aleksandr Shpeter: Svetyashhiesja Okna Novogo Doma? Bal'zam Na Dushu." *Argumenty i Fakty*, October 18–24.

Walker, Edward T. 2014. *Grassroots for Hire: Public Affairs Consultants in American Democracy*. Cambridge: Cambridge University Press.

Walker, Edward T., and Christopher M. Rea. 2014. "The Political Mobilization of Firms and Industries." *Annual Review of Sociology* 40: 281–304.

Wang, Cecilia. 2016. "Stop That Revolving Door: Analysis of the Appropriate Application of the Cooling-off Period beyond Senior Government Employees." *Cardozo Public Law, Policy and Ethics Journal* 15: 297.

Weeks, Jessica L.P. 2014. *Dictators at War and Peace*. Ithaca: Cornell University Press.

Williamson, Oliver E. 1981. "The Economics of Organization: The Transaction Cost Approach." *American Journal of Sociology* 87 (3): 548–577.

Wilson, Carole J. 2008. "Consideration Sets and Political Choices: A Heterogeneous Model of Vote Choice and Sub-National Party Strength." *Political Behavior* 30 (2): 161–183.

Witko, Christopher, and Sally Friedman. 2008. "Business Backgrounds and Congressional Behavior." *Congress and the Presidency: A Journal of Capital Studies* 35 (1): 71–86.

Wittman, Donald. 1989. "Why Democracies Produce Efficient Results." *Journal of Political economy* 97 (6): 1395–1424.

World Bank. 2013. *Income and Asset Disclosure: Case Study Illustrations*. Washington DC: World Bank Publications.

Xia, Jun, Justin Tan, and David Tan. 2008. "Mimetic Entry and Bandwagon Effect: the Rise and Decline of International Equity Joint Venture in China." *Strategic Management Journal* 29 (2): 195–217.

Yadav, Vineeta. 2011. *Political Parties, Business Groups, and Corruption in Developing Countries*. Oxford: Oxford University Press.

Yadav, Vineeta, and Bumba Mukherjee. 2015. *The Politics of Corruption in Dictatorships*. Cambridge: Cambridge University Press.

Yakovlev, Andrei, Anton Sobolev, and Anton Kazun. 2014. "Means of Production versus Means of Coercion: Can Russian Business Limit the Violence of a Predatory State?" *Post-Soviet Affairs* 30 (2–3): 171–194.

Yakovlev, Andrei, Lev Freinkman, Sergey Makarov, Victor Pogodaev et al. 2017. In Response to External Shocks: How Advanced Russian Regions React to Changes in Federal Policies: Experience of Tatarstan. Technical Report 10 BOFIT Policy Brief.

Yakovlev, Andrei, Oleg Vyglovsky, Olga Demidova, and Alexander Bashlyk. 2016. "Incentives for Repeated Contracts in Public Sector: Empirical Study of Gasoline Procurement in Russia." *International Journal of Procurement Management* 9 (3): 272–289.

Yakovlev, Evgeny, and Ekaterina Zhuravskaya. 2009. "State Capture: from Yeltsin to Putin." In *Corruption, Development and Institutional Design*, ed. Janos Kornai, Laszlo Matyas, and Gérard Roland. London: Springer pp. 24–36.

Yekaterinaburg Online. 2005. "Deputaty Gosdumi Nashli Zakonniy Sposob Brat Vzyatki - Deputatsky Zaprosy." September 16.

Yu, Hsin-Yi, and Brian G.M. Main. 2012. "Political Intervention, Corporate Governance and Firm Performance: An Empirical Investigation in Japan and Taiwan." *Accounting and Finance Research* 1 (1): 134.

Zaitseva, Elena. 2014. "Meru Iaroslavlia Prediavili Novoe Obvinenie." *Komsolmoskaya Pravda*, June 3.

Zavadskaya, Margarita, Andrey Semenov, Aleksei Gilev, and Vsevolod Bederson. 2015. "PEI-Russia: Regional Elections, September 13 2015." *Electoral Integrity Project.*

Zaytsev, Petr. 2011. "Parlamenta Biznes Klassa." *Agency for Business Monitoring*, March 3.

Zercalo.org. 2018. "Koshelev I Panov Proshli Na Vybory Mjera Nizhnego Novgoroda." *Zercalo.org*, January 12.

Zhmirikov, Aleksander. 2005. "Vesyny Zvonok." *Independent Analytic Observer*, November 11.

Zimin, Dmitry. 2010. "Promoting Investment in Russia's Regions." *Eurasian Geography and Economics* 51 (5): 653–668.

Zinnbauer, Dieter. 2015. The Vexing Issue of the Revolving Door. Working paper Edmond J. Safra Research Lab.

Index

Other Books in the Series (*continued from page ii*)

Laia Balcells, *Rivalry and Revenge: The Politics of Violence during Civil War*
Lisa Baldez, *Why Women Protest? Women's Movements in Chile*
Kate Baldwin, *The Paradox of Traditional Chiefs in Democratic Africa*
Stefano Bartolini, *The Political Mobilization of the European Left, 1860–1980: The Class Cleavage*
Robert Bates, *When Things Fell Apart: State Failure in Late-Century Africa*
Mark Beissinger, *Nationalist Mobilization and the Collapse of the Soviet State*
Pablo Beramendi, *The Political Geography of Inequality: Regions and Redistribution*
Nancy Bermeo, ed., *Unemployment in the New Europe*
Carles Boix, *Democracy and Redistribution*
Carles Boix, *Political Order and Inequality: Their Foundations and their Consequences for Human Welfare*
Carles Boix, *Political Parties, Growth, and Equality: Conservative and Social Democratic Economic Strategies in the World Economy*
Catherine Boone, *Merchant Capital and the Roots of State Power in Senegal, 1930–1985*
Catherine Boone, *Political Topographies of the African State: Territorial Authority and Institutional Change*
Catherine Boone, *Property and Political Order in Africa: Land Rights and the Structure of Politics*
Michael Bratton and Nicolas van de Walle, *Democratic Experiments in Africa: Regime Transitions in Comparative Perspective*
Michael Bratton, Robert Mattes, and E. Gyimah-Boadi, *Public Opinion, Democracy, and Market Reform in Africa*
Valerie Bunce, *Leaving Socialism and Leaving the State: The End of Yugoslavia, the Soviet Union, and Czechoslovakia*
Daniele Caramani, *The Nationalization of Politics: The Formation of National Electorates and Party Systems in Europe*
John M. Carey, *Legislative Voting and Accountability*
Kanchan Chandra, *Why Ethnic Parties Succeed: Patronage and Ethnic Headcounts in India*
Eric C. C. Chang, Mark Andreas Kayser, Drew A. Linzer, and Ronald Rogowski, *Electoral Systems and the Balance of Consumer-Producer Power*
José Antonio Cheibub, *Presidentialism, Parliamentarism, and Democracy*
Ruth Berins Collier, *Paths toward Democracy: The Working Class and Elites in Western Europe and South America*
Daniel Corstange, *The Price of a Vote in the Middle East: Clientelism and Communal Politics in Lebanon and Yemen*
Pepper D. Culpepper, *Quiet Politics and Business Power: Corporate Control in Europe and Japan*
Sarah Zukerman Daly, *Organized Violence after Civil War: The Geography of Recruitment in Latin America*
Christian Davenport, *State Repression and the Domestic Democratic Peace*
Donatella della Porta, *Social Movements, Political Violence, and the State*

Alberto Diaz-Cayeros, *Federalism, Fiscal Authority, and Centralization in Latin America*
Alberto Diaz-Cayeros, Federico Estévez, Beatriz Magaloni, *The Political Logic of Poverty Relief: Electoral Strategies and Social Policy in Mexico*
Jesse Driscoll, *Warlords and Coalition Politics in Post-Soviet States*
Thad Dunning, *Crude Democracy: Natural Resource Wealth and Political Regimes*
Thad Dunning et al., *Information, Accountability, and Cumulative Learning: Lessons from Metaketa I*
Gerald Easter, *Reconstructing the State: Personal Networks and Elite Identity*
Margarita Estevez-Abe, *Welfare and Capitalism in Postwar Japan: Party, Bureaucracy, and Business*
Henry Farrell, *The Political Economy of Trust: Institutions, Interests, and Inter-Firm Cooperation in Italy and Germany*
Karen E. Ferree, *Framing the Race in South Africa: The Political Origins of Racial Census Elections*
M. Steven Fish, *Democracy Derailed in Russia: The Failure of Open Politics*
Robert F. Franzese, *Macroeconomic Policies of Developed Democracies*
Roberto Franzosi, *The Puzzle of Strikes: Class and State Strategies in Postwar Italy*
Timothy Frye, *Building States and Markets After Communism: The Perils of Polarized Democracy*
Mary E. Gallagher, *Authoritarian Legality in China: Law, Workers, and the State*
Geoffrey Garrett, *Partisan Politics in the Global Economy*
Scott Gehlbach, *Representation through Taxation: Revenue, Politics, and Development in Postcommunist States*
Edward L. Gibson, *Boundary Control: Subnational Authoritarianism in Federal Democracies*
Jane R. Gingrich, *Making Markets in the Welfare State: The Politics of Varying Market Reforms*
Miriam Golden, *Heroic Defeats: The Politics of Job Loss*
Jeff Goodwin, *No Other Way Out: States and Revolutionary Movements*
Merilee Serrill Grindle, *Changing the State*
Anna Grzymala-Busse, *Rebuilding Leviathan: Party Competition and State Exploitation in Post-Communist Democracies*
Anna Grzymala-Busse, *Redeeming the Communist Past: The Regeneration of Communist Parties in East Central Europe*
Frances Hagopian, *Traditional Politics and Regime Change in Brazil*
Mark Hallerberg, Rolf Ranier Strauch, Jürgen von Hagen, *Fiscal Governance in Europe*
Henry E. Hale, *The Foundations of Ethnic Politics: Separatism of States and Nations in Eurasia and the World*
Stephen E. Hanson, *Post-Imperial Democracies: Ideology and Party Formation in Third Republic France, Weimar Germany, and Post-Soviet Russia*
Mai Hassan, *Regime Threats and State Solutions: Bureaucratic Loyalty and Embeddedness in Kenya*

Michael Hechter, *Alien Rule*
Timothy Hellwig, *Globalization and Mass Politics: Retaining the Room to Maneuver*
Gretchen Helmke, *Institutions on the Edge: The Origins and Consequences of Inter-Branch Crises in Latin America*
Gretchen Helmke, *Courts Under Constraints: Judges, Generals, and Presidents in Argentina*
Yoshiko Herrera, *Imagined Economies: The Sources of Russian Regionalism*
Alisha C. Holland, *Forbearance as Redistribution: The Politics of Informal Welfare in Latin America*
J. Rogers Hollingsworth and Robert Boyer, eds., *Contemporary Capitalism: The Embeddedness of Institutions*
Yue Hou, *The Private Sector in Public Office: Selective Property Rights in China*
John D. Huber, *Exclusion by Elections: Inequality, Ethnic Identity, and Democracy*
John D. Huber and Charles R. Shipan, *Deliberate Discretion? The Institutional Foundations of Bureaucratic Autonomy*
Ellen Immergut, *Health Politics: Interests and Institutions in Western Europe*
Torben Iversen, *Capitalism, Democracy, and Welfare*
Torben Iversen, *Contested Economic Institutions*
Torben Iversen, Jonas Pontussen, and David Soskice, eds., *Unions, Employers, and Central Banks: Macroeconomic Coordination and Institutional Change in Social Market Economics*
Thomas Janoski and Alexander M. Hicks, eds., *The Comparative Political Economy of the Welfare State*
Joseph Jupille, *Procedural Politics: Issues, Influence, and Institutional Choice in the European Union*
Karen Jusko, *Who Speaks for the Poor? Electoral Geography, Party Entry, and Representation*
Stathis Kalyvas, *The Logic of Violence in Civil War*
Stephen B. Kaplan, *Globalization and Austerity Politics in Latin America*
David C. Kang, *Crony Capitalism: Corruption and Capitalism in South Korea and the Philippines*
Junko Kato, *Regressive Taxation and the Welfare State*
Orit Kedar, *Voting for Policy, Not Parties: How Voters Compensate for Power Sharing*
Robert O. Keohane and Helen B. Milner, eds., *Internationalization and Domestic Politics*
Herbert Kitschelt, *The Transformation of European Social Democracy*
Herbert Kitschelt, Kirk A. Hawkins, Juan Pablo Luna, Guillermo Rosas, and Elizabeth J. Zechmeister, *Latin American Party Systems*
Herbert Kitschelt, Peter Lange, Gary Marks, and John D. Stephens, eds., *Continuity and Change in Contemporary Capitalism*
Herbert Kitschelt, Zdenka Mansfeldova, Radek Markowski, and Gabor Toka, *Post-Communist Party Systems*
David Knoke, Franz Urban Pappi, Jeffrey Broadbent, and Yutaka Tsujinaka, eds., *Comparing Policy Networks*

Ken Kollman, *Perils of Centralization: Lessons from Church, State, and Corporation*

Allan Kornberg and Harold D. Clarke, *Citizens and Community: Political Support in a Representative Democracy*

Amie Kreppel, *The European Parliament and the Supranational Party System*

David D. Laitin, *Language Repertoires and State Construction in Africa*

Fabrice E. Lehoucq and Ivan Molina, *Stuffing the Ballot Box: Fraud, Electoral Reform, and Democratization in Costa Rica*

Benjamin Lessing, *Making Peace in Drug Wars: Crackdowns and Cartels in Latin America*

Mark Irving Lichbach and Alan S. Zuckerman, eds., *Comparative Politics: Rationality, Culture, and Structure, 2nd edition*

Evan Lieberman, *Race and Regionalism in the Politics of Taxation in Brazil and South Africa*

Richard M. Locke, *The Promise and Limits of Private Power: Promoting Labor Standards in a Global Economy*

Julia Lynch, *Age in the Welfare State: The Origins of Social Spending on Pensioners, Workers, and Children*

Pauline Jones Luong, *Institutional Change and Political Continuity in Post-Soviet Central Asia*

Pauline Jones Luong and Erika Weinthal, *Oil is Not a Curse: Ownership Structure and Institutions in Soviet Successor States*

Doug McAdam, John McCarthy, and Mayer Zald, eds., *Comparative Perspectives on Social Movements*

Gwyneth H. McClendon and Rachel Beatty Riedl, *From Pews to Politics in Africa: Religious Sermons and Political Behavior*

Lauren M. MacLean, *Informal Institutions and Citizenship in Rural Africa: Risk and Reciprocity in Ghana and Côte d'Ivoire*

Beatriz Magaloni, *Voting for Autocracy: Hegemonic Party Survival and its Demise in Mexico*

James Mahoney, *Colonialism and Postcolonial Development: Spanish America in Comparative Perspective*

James Mahoney and Dietrich Rueschemeyer, eds., *Historical Analysis and the Social Sciences*

Scott Mainwaring and Matthew Soberg Shugart, eds., *Presidentialism and Democracy in Latin America*

Melanie Manion, *Information for Autocrats: Representation in Chinese Local Congresses*

Isabela Mares, *From Open Secrets to Secret Voting: Democratic Electoral Reforms and Voter Autonomy*

Isabela Mares, *The Politics of Social Risk: Business and Welfare State Development*

Isabela Mares, *Taxation, Wage Bargaining, and Unemployment*

Cathie Jo Martin and Duane Swank, *The Political Construction of Business Interests: Coordination, Growth, and Equality*

Anthony W. Marx, *Making Race, Making Nations: A Comparison of South Africa, the United States, and Brazil*

Daniel C. Mattingly, *The Art of Political Control in China*
Bonnie M. Meguid, *Party Competition between Unequals: Strategies and Electoral Fortunes in Western Europe*
Joel S. Migdal, *State in Society: Studying How States and Societies Constitute One Another*
Joel S. Migdal, Atul Kohli, and Vivienne Shue, eds., *State Power and Social Forces: Domination and Transformation in the Third World*
Scott Morgenstern and Benito Nacif, eds., *Legislative Politics in Latin America*
Kevin M. Morrison, *Nontaxation and Representation: The Fiscal Foundations of Political Stability*
Layna Mosley, *Global Capital and National Governments*
Layna Mosley, *Labor Rights and Multinational Production*
Wolfgang C. Müller and Kaare Strøm, *Policy, Office, or Votes?*
Maria Victoria Murillo, *Political Competition, Partisanship, and Policy Making in Latin American Public Utilities*
Maria Victoria Murillo, *Labor Unions, Partisan Coalitions, and Market Reforms in Latin America*
Monika Nalepa, *Skeletons in the Closet: Transitional Justice in Post-Communist Europe*
Noah L. Nathan, *Electoral Politics and Africa's Urban Transition: Class and Ethnicity in Ghana*
Ton Notermans, *Money, Markets, and the State: Social Democratic Economic Policies since 1918*
Simeon Nichter, *Votes for Survival: Relational Clientelism in Latin America*
Richard A. Nielsen, *Deadly Clerics: Blocked Ambition and the Paths to Jihad*
Aníbal Pérez-Liñán, *Presidential Impeachment and the New Political Instability in Latin America*
Roger D. Petersen, *Understanding Ethnic Violence: Fear, Hatred, and Resentment in 20th Century Eastern Europe*
Roger D. Petersen, *Western Intervention in the Balkans: The Strategic Use of Emotion in Conflict*
Simona Piattoni, ed., *Clientelism, Interests, and Democratic Representation*
Paul Pierson, *Dismantling the Welfare State? Reagan, Thatcher, and the Politics of Retrenchment*
Marino Regini, *Uncertain Boundaries: The Social and Political Construction of European Economies*
Kenneth M. Roberts, *Changing Course in Latin America: Party Systems in the Neoliberal Era*
Marc Howard Ross, *Cultural Contestation in Ethnic Conflict*
David Rueda and Daniel Stegmueller, *Who Wants What? Redistribution Preferences in Comparative Perspective*
Ignacio Sánchez-Cuenca, *The Historical Roots of Political Violence: Revolutionary Terrorism in Affluent Countries*
Ben Ross Schneider, *Hierarchical Capitalism in Latin America: Business, Labor, and the Challenges of Equitable Development*
Roger Schoenman, *Networks and Institutions in Europe's Emerging Markets*

Lyle Scruggs, *Sustaining Abundance: Environmental Performance in Industrial Democracies*
Jefferey M. Sellers, *Governing from Below: Urban Regions and the Global Economy*
Yossi Shain and Juan Linz, eds., *Interim Governments and Democratic Transitions*
Beverly Silver, *Forces of Labor: Workers' Movements and Globalization since 1870*
Prerna Singh, *How Solidarity Works for Welfare: Subnationalism and Social Development in India*
Theda Skocpol, *Social Revolutions in the Modern World*
Austin Smith et al., *Selected Works of Michael Wallerstein*
Regina Smyth, *Candidate Strategies and Electoral Competition in the Russian Federation: Democracy Without Foundation*
Richard Snyder, *Politics after Neoliberalism: Reregulation in Mexico*
David Stark and László Bruszt, *Postsocialist Pathways: Transforming Politics and Property in East Central Europe*
Sven Steinmo, *The Evolution of Modern States: Sweden, Japan, and the United States*
Sven Steinmo, Kathleen Thelen, and Frank Longstreth, eds., *Structuring Politics: Historical Institutionalism in Comparative Analysis*
Susan C. Stokes, *Mandates and Democracy: Neoliberalism by Surprise in Latin America*
Susan C. Stokes, ed., *Public Support for Market Reforms in New Democracies*
Susan C. Stokes, Thad Dunning, Marcelo Nazareno, and Valeria Brusco, *Brokers, Voters, and Clientelism: The Puzzle of Distributive Politics*
Milan W. Svolik, *The Politics of Authoritarian Rule*
Duane Swank, *Global Capital, Political Institutions, and Policy Change in Developed Welfare States*
Sidney Tarrow, *Power in Movement: Social Movements and Contentious Politics*
Sidney Tarrow, *Power in Movement: Social Movements and Contentious Politics, Revised and Updated Third Edition*
Tariq Thachil, *Elite Parties, Poor Voters: How Social Services Win Votes in India*
Kathleen Thelen, *How Institutions Evolve: The Political Economy of Skills in Germany, Britain, the United States, and Japan*
Kathleen Thelen, *Varieties of Liberalization and the New Politics of Social Solidarity*
Charles Tilly, *Trust and Rule*
Daniel Treisman, *The Architecture of Government: Rethinking Political Decentralization*
Guillermo Trejo, *Popular Movements in Autocracies: Religion, Repression, and Indigenous Collective Action in Mexico*
Rory Truex, *Making Autocracy Work: Representation and Responsiveness in Modern China*
Lily Lee Tsai, *Accountability without Democracy: How Solidary Groups Provide Public Goods in Rural China*

Joshua Tucker, *Regional Economic Voting: Russia, Poland, Hungary, Slovakia and the Czech Republic, 1990–1999*
Ashutosh Varshney, *Democracy, Development, and the Countryside*
Yuhua Wang, *Tying the Autocrat's Hand: The Rise of The Rule of Law in China*
Jeremy M. Weinstein, *Inside Rebellion: The Politics of Insurgent Violence*
Stephen I. Wilkinson, *Votes and Violence: Electoral Competition and Ethnic Riots in India*
Andreas Wimmer, *Waves of War: Nationalism, State Formation, and Ethnic Exclusion in the Modern World*
Jason Wittenberg, *Crucibles of Political Loyalty: Church Institutions and Electoral Continuity in Hungary*
Elisabeth J. Wood, *Forging Democracy from Below: Insurgent Transitions in South Africa and El Salvador*
Elisabeth J. Wood, *Insurgent Collective Action and Civil War in El Salvador*
Deborah J. Yashar, *Homicidal Ecologies: Illicit Economies and Complicit States in Latin America*
Daniel Ziblatt, *Conservative Parties and the Birth of Democracy*